ECUMENISM AND PEACE

FROM THEORY AND PRACTICE TO PILGRIMAGE AND COMPANIONSHIP

FERNANDO ENNS

Translated by
JONATHAN SEILING

Gelassenheit Publications
St Catharines, Ohni:kara, Ontario, Canada
and
World Council of Churches Press, Geneva, Switzerland

Cataloguing in Publication Data
Enns, Fernando, 1964-
Ecumenism and peace: from theory and practice to pilgrimage and companionship / by
Fernando Enns.

ISBN (pbk): 978-1-990827-04-4

Subject Headings:
1. Christian union
2. Ecumenical movement
3. World Council of Churches
4. International peace movements

BT736.4 .E2964 2022

Where indicated, Scripture is cited from the New Revised Standard Version Bible,
copyright 1989, Division of Christian Education of the National Council of the
Churches of Christ in the United States of America.
Used by permission. All rights reserved.

CONTENTS

PREFACE

The nine chapters included in this volume make available to English readers over two decades of published articles (1998-2021), previously available in German, which chart both the theoretical challenges and also practical examples of global ecumenism. In its various regional-global, grassroots-institutional dimensions, commitments to seek peace with justice -- for the Church and as the churches -- have continued to grow and evolve in bold and creative ways. We see both despair and hope around every corner and constantly recall and "re-member" our separated identities as those who are reconciled in Christ, as "companions" of Christ.

The English translation and editing of much of this book was completed by Dr. Jonathan Seiling in 2014-16, while working with us at the Center for Peace Church Theology at the University of Hamburg in Germany. Those were years when Europe and the world was re-awakened to the urgency of seeking realistic proposals to ensure regional security for governments, when we were called to action in our local communities to assist the most vulnerable people fleeing the devastation of war and economic oppression. Debates about the immediate role of churches in welcoming refugees circulated as we continued the long-term task of discerning how the Church is called to act in situations of direct, systemic, and structural violence.

I am most grateful for Dr. Seiling's diligence in pursuing the completion of this book project, which continued to expand and develop since 2016, with the addition of the last chapters on that spiritual ecumenical journey called "Pilgrimage of Justice and Peace," the last of which was written at the height of the COVID-19 pandemic. Currently the ongoing war in the Ukraine reminds us (in Europe) again of our own vulnerability and also the senselessness of global violence, which once again challenge us as a global ecumenical community to seek the way of Christ.

As the 11th Assembly of The World Council of Churches is underway at Karlsruhe, Germany, we offer this volume of ecumenical studies in thanks for God's wisdom, Christ's love, and the power of the Spirit.

Hamburg, August 26, 2022

Fernando Enns

INTRODUCTION

Experience, Theory and Reflective Action: Ecumenism "in the making"

The first World Missionary Conference in Edinburgh (1910) is generally considered the birth of the modern ecumenical movement; therefore we may now look back on at least a century of the institutionalized development of relationship formation in international ecumenism.[1] This process of relationship formation is not possible without the ongoing analytical and constructive function of theological reflection at all levels and in all denominations of the global Church. Conversely, it can also be noted that the growing process of ecumenical relationship formation among the historically mature denominations and the various cultural manifestations of the Church – through a steady process of inculturation – has influenced the respective theological movements within individual denominations. This can be illustrated by such radical milestones in ecumenical history as the rebirth of the pan-Orthodox conferences (1961),[2] the Second Vatican Council (1962-1965),[3] the Lambeth Conference of the Anglican Communion,[4] which launched in 1867, and over time developed the so-called "Lambeth Quadrilateral," as well as the "Community of Protestant Churches in Europe" (starting in 1973 as the "Leuenberg Church Fellowship").[5] Also the emergence of "World Alliances" or "World Federations" of denominational bodies[6] is ultimately an expression of this current, growing willingness to facilitate the Church's global, ecumenical reality and for such alliances or federations also to theologically reflect this reality.[7] The dialectical relationship between the ecumenical movement and theological reflection must surely be counted among the most influential and creative impulses within theology and church history.

The growing recognition of the necessity for reflection and the institutionalization of the ecumenical reality of the Church ultimately becomes manifested in numerous interdenominational institutions at all levels: the *international* – in the founding of the World Council of Churches (WCC, 1948), the *regional* – in the multiple ecumenical mergers in all parts of the world (such as the Christian Conference of Asia, 1959), the *national* (such as the National Council of Churches USA, 1950, emerging from the Federal Council of Churches, 1908) and the *local* (such as the many local associations of Christian churches in Germany).[8] Structures like these can facilitate the mutual commitment of churches as they move toward a growing, visible unity and for the greater credibility of their common witness. As much as these institutional forms attempt to support the ecumenical movement and provide a sort of permanence, they do not exclusively represent the vitality of the movement over the past century. In many cases, there were initially – and there still are – notable lay movements (the oldest being the Women's World Day of Prayer, beginning in 1884)[9] or movements among theologians.[10] Facing the disintegration of their churches, these movements were the first to call for the facilitation and ultimately the establishment of ecumenical institutions.

Of course, the notion of ecumenism itself is much older than the modern movement. The Ecumenical Councils of the early Church[11] ultimately go back to the idea of the apostles meeting in Jerusalem, found in the book of Acts (Acts 15, cf. Gal 2), which probably took place in the year 49 or 50 C.E. These councils facilitated repeated attempts to express an ecclesiological understanding of the one

Church, as based on the deep-seated theological conviction of the oneness of God the Creator, Christ the Son as Redeemer and the Holy Spirit as the Perfecter (cf. Jn 17, Eph 4). All ecumenical efforts, from their beginnings to the present day, can originally be traced back to this understanding. And at all times there have been people in the Church who deliberately put these ecumenical notions front and center in order to overcome the schisms – whether actual or potential – without thereby allowing "heresies" to attenuate.[12] But at no time has this idea of unity through the process of relationship formation become as dominant in the structure of the Church and theological reflection in general as it has in the twentieth century.

Currently we face a highly differentiated theory of ecumenism and an equally complex configuration of ecumenical relationships based on a plurality of theological approaches, methodologies and objectives.[13] This complex reality of lived ecumenism need not be artificially downsized or truncated, simply to make it more manageable. Such an approach would surely mean the many "gifts" of the one universal Church would too easily fade from view.[14] Even more so, the very diverse and occasionally conflicting theories of ecumenism, theological reflection, methodology and objectives need to be exposed to different *testing grounds* in order to arrive at a balanced judgment. Such testing will ultimately serve the goal of a deepened and visible representation of the – commonly believed and acknowledged – unity of the Church which is always on the horizon, and which will promote the credibility of the gospel-inspired witness of this unity.

As such, *testing grounds* for ecumenism are presented and analyzed in the present study. First, it is important to get an overview of the central *theologoumena* and methodological issues in the theory of ecumenism, in order to stay focused on the specific avenues for approaching various challenges. This section will demonstrate how basic the question of ecclesiology is for the theory of ecumenism, as is the need to discard an ecumenical theology that was previously undergirded by Christocentrism. In lieu of this, a Trinitarian-oriented theological foundation is now preferred for all ecumenical issues.[15] The question of what determines the relation of *Scripture, Tradition, Doctrine* and *Truth* will be continually kept in mind because all ecumenical meetings are held accountable to the degree these factors have determined the development of doctrines and of hermeneutics. A dialogue between different traditions, religions or cultures should not remain on the surface but should actually dive deep into the possibility of a common, substantive, learning experience. Thus ecumenism is not to be seen simply as a *superadditum,* something exotic tacked onto denominational doctrine and ecclesial existence; rather it is the necessary condition for deepening the entire contents of Christian belief, through moving ecclesiology beyond the inherent limitations set by denominational traditions and particular cultures. The universality of the Church in all its particularities will only be conceived through ecumenism. It is implied that the present theological reflection is not aimed at a fixed endpoint, a putative final achievement of a certain type of institutionalized unity. Instead it is an ever-advancing process that will constructively and artfully envelop the greatest potential for all members of the one Church: this is ecumenism "in the making."

Dialogical Ecumenism

The *first testing ground* in this ecumenical study are the classic, interdenominational doctrinal dialogues between two separated or distinct traditions.[16] As a point of departure, the respective denominational specifics are considered here, which may constitute or determine the methodology, the function, possible goals and, last but not least, the specific content of such dialogue. There is no uniform pattern for interdenominational dialogues, although over the decades certain logical steps or protocols have emerged for processes both prior to and during a dialogue. In a few cases, protocols have been developed that would allow the dialogue's outcome to be received by the wider denominational constituency.

This study examines the bilateral dialogue between the Roman Catholic Church and the oldest Protestant Free Church, the Mennonites as one exemplary *testing ground.*[17] The challenges for the dialogue partners are evident. Due to the previous mutual condemnations resulting from their radical theological differences, the task of reappraisal requires that we first enter into a "healing of memories." Interdenominational dialogue is always about more than the clarification of theological doctrinal differences. Such differences invariably originate from within certain historical, cultural and political constellations, which were experienced and passed on in quite different ways. Without the process of reappraisal one can hardly even hope to arrive at an understanding that would undergird a development of doctrine. Of course this historical challenge determines nothing as far as potential convergences are concerned or even those similarities that may exist in the present. Initially there is the question of whether a common historical hermeneutic can be developed before the apparent differences in the statements of faith are considered. The complex process of such a dialogue clarifies the pertinent hermeneutics, goals, and protocols.

Theme-Centred Ecumenism

In a *second testing ground* we see how the process becomes narrower on the one hand by focusing on certain themes, and on the other hand, it becomes expanded by the participation of multiple denominational families. Certainly the best known example of such an ecumenical process is the development of "declarations of convergence" at the meeting in Lima (Baptism, Eucharist and Ministry, 1982).[18] In several rounds of discussions a central theme, or sometimes several themes, are discussed by the participants of various denominations to determine which statements could be jointly formulated and which divergences, or actual differences, still remain. The process of mutually determining relationships is critical in this type of dialogue, such as also pertains to bilateral dialogues, as to whether the enduring differences actually amount to church-dividing issues. Concentrating on one object of theological doctrine can result in such a far-reaching agreement that the belief or practice of a denomination is accepted by the other as fully valid. The mutual recognition of baptism by several churches in Germany in Magdeburg (2007) is one key example. However, further questions result concerning other differences, which, due to the interdependent nature of doctrines, are rarely overlooked or ignored. The section below concerning the mutual recognition of baptism makes an attempt at such an analysis, using the example of the enduring difference between churches who practice both infant and adult baptism and those churches in the Anabaptist tradition that exclusively accept "believers' baptism." Here it is more accurate to observe how the mutual recognition of a practice in the other denomination can be offered without relativizing one's own teaching (and thus their identity) for the sake of "cheap ecumenism." It is clear that the combined growth in the ecumenical community of churches will not have to be at the expense of individual identities. Only through respecting the various traditions and through fidelity to the biblical witnesses, will there be joint development of theological recognition.

Ecumenism is not an end in itself. All efforts are aimed ultimately toward the credibility of Christian witness to the evangelical truth in Jesus Christ. It was the experience of the modern missionary movement that the actual state of the Church – as separated and mutually delimiting churches with differing denominations – in fact has inhibited the credibility of its witness. In response to this realization arose the first crucial impetus for the modern ecumenical movement.[19] In the 1800s the mission contexts of western European churches around the world became more aware of the need for mutual understanding.[20] The early establishment of the International Missionary Council (1921) and its subsequent inclusion in the WCC (1961) are illustrations of the close interweaving of international mission and ecumenism. But in order to theologically clarify how they are relatively or mutually determinative – and ultimately in order to measure whether and to what degree the mission of the church is an appropriate, crucial *testing ground* of ecumenism – it is necessary to give an account of what is meant by mission in the horizon of the global Church.

Missionary Ecumenism

Thus we attempt to investigate a third *testing ground*, first by clarifying the history of the often misunderstood and abused term "mission," and second, by examining recent examples. The Ecumenical Church is presumed here simply to be the global Church, as is believed and formulated in the confession "one, holy, catholic and apostolic Church."[21] The thesis is that mission is the Church's actualization. Said differently: *Mission is the Church as event.* Mission is not simply to be understood as one field of ecclesial activity among others, but as the total actualization of ecumenism through being the Church. If mission is seen as a dynamic force that directs the Church steadily (back) toward its renewal and thus to its actual center – the Gospel – then the Church becomes actualized in mission. Of course, as with all ecclesiological statements, it is crucial to keep in mind the distinction between the "believed" and "experienced" Church.[22] This distinction is only comprehensible when our concerns correspond with the *missio Dei*, in which the ecumenical Church is participating, and when we are considering the missionary efforts of the experienced Church as *opus hominum*. This distinction preserves the Church in mission against overconfidence on the one hand and on the other hand, against inferiority complexes, thus effectively relieving it of "missionary ecumenism."[23]

Missions-based ecumenism always encourages activity *as* the ecumenical Church, because it participates actively in the *missio Dei*; and the credibility of the witness depends on the merit of the Church's *collaborative action*. It is precisely the so-called "young churches" who stressed that the actual testing ground for ecumenism is found in the opportunities for collaborative action. And it is these churches who are becoming more prevalent in the ecumenical movement, since they have stepped forward with their own highly contextualized approaches to theology and they are beginning to outnumber the historic (state-) churches in Europe. Basically they became strengthened by discovering right from the start, what worked as means of motivation. This was clearly visible in the early "Life and

Work Movement," one of the active, ecumenically reflective move-ments prior to the founding of the WCC.[24] What resulted was the awareness of the contextual nature of theology *par excellence*, and consequently, the need for an understanding of intercultural dialogue. Likewise, there was the recognition of the concept of *oikoumene* as "the whole inhabited earth"[25] and as "God's one household" and further, the open opportunity for dialogue between religions. Ultimately, these extensions, as can be shown, do not spring from *one* academic school of thought, but rather from the experienced ecclesial reality, which demands an adequate, Gospel-worthy ecclesial existence and function of the Church as *oikoumene*. By recognizing the sometimes life-threat-ening challenges in different parts of the world as the shared grounds of the Holy Spirit's activity, and thus of the global Church, we can name this concrete reality as *oikoumene*. The growing understanding of life's interdependence also raises awareness of the urgency for joint action to be seen as the testing grounds of ecumenism. This will be shown and discussed in detail concerning the following *testing grounds*.

Action-Oriented Ecumenism

The worldwide community of churches was put to the test with the emergence of ecumenical peace theology and ethics. The complexity of this process is shown below. It starts with a historical overview to highlight the centrality, both today and in the recent past, of the struggle to identify concrete, collaborative courses of action for the modern ecumenical movement. From the early beginnings of the growing international awareness of the churches' failure in two devas-tating world wars which led up to the regional confrontation during the "Cold War," the churches had different perspectives in various global contexts. Subsequently there has been an ever-present and urgent challenge for a theological-ethical questioning of the use of force in general, and in particular the legitimacy of war as "revolu-tionary violence," which has remained controversial among the churches. Notably the positions that churches and representatives have taken have not necessarily always been aligned with the historically-developed religious convictions of former state churches on the one hand and historical peace churches on the other. The process of dialogue has led to some surprising and creative twists at various stages, which will be detailed below.

It is noteworthy that on the one hand the "collapse" of the former Soviet bloc was facilitated by the ecumenical world through nonviolent revolutions arising from the growing ecumenical relations of support as a counter to the "Cold War."[26] Subsequently this new political reality opened possibilities for the development of a common peace witness of the ecumenical Church. Yet on the other hand, very soon there were new, life-threatening situations of violence, which in turn created a difficult *testing ground* for the churches. The initiation of the ecumenical "Decade to Overcome Violence, 2001-2010: Churches Seeking Reconciliation and Peace" was a triumph in providing a common goal towards which differing positions could strive, namely, the theological de-legitimation of the "spirit, logic and practice of violence." This global ecumenical enterprise launched by the WCC, is presented here for the first time from its beginnings to the end of that "Decade." The various topics are analyzed as they crystallized in theological discussions, alongside the attenuating theological and social impulses. The origins of ongoing differences in peace ethics positions are also shown, primarily on the basis of the ever-challenging question of the responsibility to protect endangered populations. Even if the churches do not speak on this vital issue with one voice, the analysis presented here shows a convergence of doctrinal positions that had previously been absolutely divergent, and their task to find convergences was something which had been widely seen as a central ethical challenge for the ecumenical movement.

If peace theology reflects the anticipation and celebration of God's peace (*leiturgia*), as well as the witness (*martyria*) and the commitment to a just peace (*diakonia*) of the entire ecclesial community (*koinonia*), then ecumenism has at its core the ministry of reconciliation (2 Cor 5). This leads to the realization that in this particular *testing ground* or realm we desire not only the formulation of joint peace ethical positions or courses of action – which of course should always be developed multivalently, simultaneously in multiple directions[27] – but also, of necessity, it concerns the nature of the Church itself. When ecumenism aspires to fulfill what it is called to be, namely the "messenger of reconciliation," then an adequate, ecumenically-oriented peace theology will have to constantly bear in mind that the social form of the Church itself is relationally integral.[28] Just as it was first brought into existence in Christ, only insofar as the community is already reconciled in Christ can it seriously claim to participate in the *missio Dei* in the world. Thus the emergence of an ecumenical peace theology and ethics is not only an ethical question on the level of applied ethics, but it also concerns fundamental theology.[29]

From this fundamental conviction concerning the self-reflection of the Church, an *ecumenical peace-church ecclesiology* is developed here, not in the narrowly denominational sense of the historic peace churches, rather, according to a more basic or general definition. According to the Trinitarian affirmation that is shared by the ecumenical Church, the doctrine of the Trinity will serve as a theoretical framework.[30] In this way, the ecclesial community can be conceived as a Eucharistic community, which is always developing its social forms in anticipation of the consummation of the whole creation. Accordingly, out of the ethical community emerge relational positions of peace ethics, as well as common actions.

Thus it is clear that inter-denominational meetings, thematic dialogues, missionary and action-oriented forms of ecumenism are not mutually exclusive. Rather they may be seen as mutually complementary *testing grounds* for the *one* ecumenical Church, which, through a singular commitment is facing the triune God, developing this self-image as *una, sancta, catholica et apostolica ecclesia* even in the face of all enduring differences.

Next to these we might add as a *further testing ground* the task of clarifying what is meant by "Ecumenical Formation," which is already an issue in all other fields and is therefore not developed here specifically.[31] Moreover, the question of "ecumenical spirituality" is only analyzed here insofar it relates to the new and evolving "image of Justice and Peace," which was initiated by the X. Assembly of the

WCC in Busan, South Korea in 2013. However, spirituality might be considered less as a *testing ground* of ecumenism, since it is distinguished categorically from the development of theological doctrines, missiology, or "ecumenical social ethics."[32] Therefore, the analysis and reflection on spirituality, as it is ecumenically experienced and celebrated, warrants an entirely separate study. That such a study of spirituality is not undertaken here, should in no way be interpreted as devaluation of the central doxological dimension of church and its importance for ecumenism. To the contrary! Within the framework of the evolving "Pilgrimage of Justice and Peace," this dimension of a *transformative* spirituality is an invitation to re-visit doctrinal insights, ethical convictions and social actions from yet another perspective: to discover and experience together the power of being set in motion once again by "walking gently with our God" – and in moving together, allowing the Church to become what it is called to be: a community of justice and peace.

Oikoumene *in via — positiva, negativa, transformativa*

In the twenty-first century every denomination which is not self-sufficient and closed to what is outside, will want their theological doctrine (in the majority of their proposals) to account for the "horizon" of ecumenism as a reality of the Church, even if only for their own sake. For any theology that claims to reflect the universality of reconciliation in Christ cannot avoid being accountable for how its own position is related to that of other denominations. Yet that conviction does not itself necessarily lead to convergences. There is always the possibility, indeed the necessity, of naming any permanent or emerging differences with clarity, preferably in a way that these can be understood in other theological discussions or contexts, at least insofar as others can grasp the structure of their argument and also the substance of their statements, even if they are not shared by other denominations. Otherwise theology would need to relinquish any claim to being rational, or taking part in academic discourse in the humanities.

In ecumenism it is not simply a matter of one denomination abandoning its duly considered statements which it regards as being "adequate to the gospel" for the sake of greater Christian unity. That would not be the desired unity of the Church, because the fellowship of the Church does not increase in this way. On the contrary, community and identity mutually condition each other. Of course, this presumes an understanding of unity that does not merely consider plurality acceptable but seeks to shape this plurality into something meaningful, while at the same time not accommodating what is merely arbitrary.

All theological proposals that clearly exhibit the approaches of a single tradition are always denominationally and contextually shaped, even when they take a self-critical approach to their own tradition. The fact that they can consider self-critique to be legitimate, without needing to renounce their own tradition, may be considered proof that a degree of pluralism within the ecumenical movement can be assumed, to the degree that it exists within the respective denominations themselves. In this way it will be possible without prejudice to receive denominational teaching systems not simply as hermetically sealed, but to inquire constantly as to the possibility of alternative expressions of such understandings that had long been solidified in a denomination. In the ecumenical movement, it can therefore also be possible that through new formulations of what is commonly believed and recognized, we can speak jointly, without leaving the secure identity of our respective traditions.

Thus, ecumenism will not produce its own "ecumenical theology" in the sense that this would be in addition to or outside of denominational traditions. Rather, an ecumenically oriented theology will evermore want to rely on these very traditions to elicit of themselves, and for their part, such theological proposals that make their respective denominational and contextual roots as transparent as possible for others, in order that they may be taken into account and considered within the reality of the ecumenical Church. The ecumenical theory presented here aims to provide the necessary methodological considerations and general framework for this task.

Part II, 'From Overcoming Violence to Pilgrimage and Companion-ship' comprises chapters 6-9, which analyze and theologically reflect on the WCC's programs of the 'Decade to Overcome Violence' (2001-2010), The Ecumenical Pilgrimage of Justice and Peace, ending with a theological proposal for *Companionship* as the motif of the ongoing journey of action-oriented ecumenism, on the path toward a realiza-tion of just peace through the Church's faithfulness to its calling.

PART I

OIKOUMENE IN VIA: ECUMENISM "IN THE MAKING"

CHAPTER 1
ECUMENICAL THEORY
MODELS OF UNITY, NEW PARADIGMS

una, sancta, catholica et apostolica ecclesia

a. Doctrine Divides, Action Unites – or vice versa?

"DOCTRINE DIVIDES, ACTION UNITES" – that is, according to the dictum of the first "World Conference on Practical Christianity" in Stockholm, 1925.[1] If one accepts this statement, then wouldn't ecumenical theory imply a contradiction in terms? Can we speak meaningfully about theories, when praxis is actually what offers the possibility for unity? However, the opposite of this dictum has been presented with equal conviction since the beginnings of the modern ecumenical movement, namely, "theology unites, praxis divides."[2] From the outset this contrast appeared to be reflected institutionally on the one hand in the Faith and Order Commission[3] and on the other in Life and Work.[4] One was more oriented toward the doctrinal questions (ecumenical dialogue),[5] the other being more action-oriented (social ethics ecumenism). It was their institutional merger in 1948 that led to the founding of the World Council of Churches (WCC). Yet even today the traditions and understandings of the impacts of both streams can be perceived in this way, although it may already be evident that they are overcoming such opposing orientations, and perhaps are even deemed necessary. Thus both streams are specifically pursued in the different programmatic approaches of the WCC.[6] Therefore one cannot decide which of the two orientations is correct since both have their place, and the particularity of each only becomes apparent in isolation, acting as a necessary counter-movement to the other.

In this way it immediately becomes clear that the analytical-critical function of theories can be usefully applied "in research concerning the reasons for the emergence of particular and divergent traditions and in the effort to translate the language of one tradition into the other."[7] Added to this in equal measure is the constructive-visionary function, namely, "to provide new concepts, definitions of tasks and understandings that go beyond what is merely a new selection, rebalancing or combination of known positions."[8] This is how the task of ecumenical theory is roughly described. The specific challenge is the attempt to identify and to keep in mind the uniqueness or differentness of the other denominations in all matters (theological doctrine or the practical implications for church action), while always critically perceiving how one is already influenced by one's own denomination and how this predisposes one's theological reflection. Ecumenical theory reflects the diversity of denominations and contexts. It develops understandings of unity, models of agreement and also methods of ecumenical encounter in the areas of teaching, worship, and ethics. It also inquires as to the common situation of the churches as well as the potential for their common confession and action in the world.[9]

In the following chapter such theories are presented in an introductory fashion using examples, organized by subject areas. This approach will clarify challenges and schematize various directions and trends. It is perfectly legitimate to ask in each case whether it is appropriate to speak of "theories." Theories are formed through differentiation. Therefore in ecumenical theology one asks: Which differentiations are useful to develop theories?

Ideally, this theory will take place in dialogue between partners who come from different denominational traditions and cultural contexts and yet presuppose the unity of the Church. Both the theological reflection and construction of an individual serve as clarification and these are legitimate if conceived and reflected within that person's own context. Ecumenicists do not want to repudiate their own context in ecumenical theory construction, but on the contrary, to explicitly take account wherever possible of the extent to which their own theory is possibly shaped, influenced or predetermined by their denomination. It is simply not tenable to have a perspective that floats above all denominations, because participants always belong to a denomination and/or tradition and they argue from this position – either in dissenting or consenting ways. Thus individual proposals are developed in which their proximity to their own tradition and even their critical distance from their own is quite blatant. In ecumenical theory this happens with a specific goal, namely, *to participate in the search for how the already existing unity of the Church will become visibly manifest in Christ* (cf. Jn 17) and the discussion and schematization of the enduring divisions. Each ecumenical theory is ultimately motivated toward this end.

b. Beginning and Ending: Ecclesiology on the Horizon of Ecumenism

Naturally one asks the ecclesiological question at the very start: Which understanding of the Church is ecumenical theory actually based upon? Immediately the conflicts concerning divergent ecclesiologies break out because the ecclesiological question is not only the central topic of ecumenism; it also constitutes its most formidable challenge and *testing ground.*[10]

The different ecclesiologies are on one hand the decisive issues of contention between the different denominations, because ultimately the controversial ecclesiological conceptions of these denominations had been the very reasons for their breaking into different denominations. At the very least one can say that different opinions in theology have crafted differently-shaped church communities (in addition, there are always some non-theological factors, of course).[11] In their "analytical function," first of all, each ecumenical theory offers an account of which respective ecclesiology is represented by which theological arguments, noting whether divergent doctrines are indicated and if possibilities of convergence can be explored. On the other hand, ecumenical theory in its "constructive function" – explicitly or implicitly – allows one to propose a conception of the visibility of the *una, sancta, catholica et apostolica ecclesia*. What visionary proposals of visible unity will be ventured in the future, and associated with which corresponding theological foundations?[12]

Within ecclesiology a second level of differentiation is fundamental. Even if these issues among the denominations are uncontroversial, there are distinctions made here between *ecclesia visibilis* and *ecclesia invisibilis*,[13] the "legal-Church and love-Church,"[14] between the phenomenality of the Church and its actual constitution,[15] between the experienced and the believed Church,[16] or between the "essence and appearance" of the Church.[17] Primarily they have an "ordering function" in relation to the theory. It is of fundamental importance whether each statement concerning the ideal Church can be formulated as in the confessions of those denominations, or whether these are based upon the actual, existing ecclesial identity as seen, for example, in the Roman Catholic Church in Brazil, the Georgian Orthodox Church and the Mennonite Church in North America. Ecclesiological statements are therefore first of all to be clarified to determine whether they are addressing the experienced "divided body," or the existing and the believed *una, sancta, catholica et apostolica ecclesia*.

c. Scripture and Tradition(s): The Question of Hermeneutics

If one inquires as to the basis of denominational ecclesiologies, one can easily see that the divergences already have their roots in the writings of the biblical canon. Each tradition represented in the ecumenical movement sees, in the final analysis, how its own ecclesiology is based in the witnesses of the Old and New Testaments. In most cases confessional documents (whether of patristic origin or subsequently formulated) are eventually added as additional sources that are understood as adequate interpretations of the biblical witness.[18]

Passages in Romans 12, 1 Corinthians 12 and Ephesians 4 among others, suggest how the relationship develops between unity and diversity, with the metaphor of one body with many members. Again different emphases can be discovered in this metaphor. According to Rom 12, the many become one body in Christ, but also each member has different charisms; 1 Cor 12 begins with the existing body in which all members are committed in the same Spirit without distinction, confessing the same Lord and God; in Eph 4, there is the confession of the one Lord, as well as becoming one in baptism as that which binds us together, with Christ as the head (of the whole cosmos). Matt 16 names a "rock" upon which the Church is to be built. Can a singular "Petrine Office" be derived from this biblical passage or is it meant as a commitment to all people who have confessed Christ? Ignatius of Antioch already developed his concept of *henosis* based on John 17 (in which the Father and the Son are one, therefore the Son and the bishop are also one, as are the bishop and the Church). In Matt 18, the reconciling action of the community is emphasized. A variety of other images, metaphors, descriptions of the *ecclesia* can be drawn from the biblical witnesses.[19]

Based on these observations, one might conclude that such differentiation is to be considered as legitimate if such diversity has already been created in part by the biblical canon itself.[20] Only with an undifferentiated biblicistic approach might one attempt to artificially harmonize the different conceptions. The question is rather one of hermeneutics, the respective determining criteria for the selection and evaluation of the individual writings by the various traditions. The explicit doctrines formed by agreements in councils or synods clarify this issue. But also the implicit doctrinal ideas that clarify what is meant by the traditional formulations should be identified and taken into account. Furthermore, we may inquire as to the meaning inherent in the biblical text itself. Was it suggesting something of primarily descriptive nature, which only later became normative?[21] And finally, to whom is the teaching authority in the respective traditions ascribed and how is this established?

Such factors are to be taken into account also in the visionary proposals of a common ecclesiology on the horizon of ecumenism. In order to find out what innovative power the biblical texts hold for ecumenism, a common exegesis of the biblical witness is required. "Only Scripture is able to bring all Christian denominations into a conversation with each other."[22] In this way they can also determine whether they have been broadly interpreted in light of the historical application of these formulations. As such and in what ways might they also have been "hijacked" and/or whether the ecumenical community can again be challenged by these texts?[23] Such a critical-reflective approach thus renounces the usual recourse to citing Scripture merely to legitimize the status quo.

d. Understandings and Models of Unity – Which Goal?

The ecumenical movement must be directed toward a definite goal, otherwise it becomes inconsistent.[24] Harding Meyer expressed this thesis illustrating that an initial consideration should be: how uniformly this goal can actually be formulated and whether the ecumenical process is not pre-empted by it. Meyer differentiates on the one hand between the understandings of unity (which can be diverse), and models of unification on the other. We might add to these also considerations of the methodology of ecumenical dialogues, which can likewise differ. In any case such methodology is not determined by a preconceived model. It can be observed that the member denominations constantly redefine the methodology of their ecumenical doctrinal discussions.[25]

. . .

Understandings of Unity

Granted that there are different ways to understand unity, according to Harding Meyer they are ultimately based on three core beliefs concerning ecumenical consensus, namely: the *essential, indicative and imperative*:

(1) Unity is part of the Church's essence. It is one of *notae ecclesiae*, as expressed in the Nicene-Constantinopolitan Creed (381).[26]

(2) Despite efforts for unity, the essential unity of the Church has always preceded efforts to bring it about ("the ecumenical indicative"). Unity is therefore first and foremost not anything to be manufactured, but a gift that is part of the constitution of the Church.

(3) The essential unity of the Church must be lived and made visible ("the ecumenical imperative"). All ecumenical effort aims to bring the gift of unity in it is expressed in phenomena, as seen in the "experienced Church" through doctrine, worship and practice.

To these three – the *essence*, the *indicative* and the *imperative* – we may add a fourth: *ecumenical vision*. If one takes the constructive function of ecumenical theory seriously, then the eschatological dimension comes into view. The anticipated, perfect realization of unity in the eschaton is accompanied at the same time by the church's motivation and release of burden. Complete unity, of whatever sort, is one of the measures that lies before us. This unity orients us in the present because it is now already being anticipated. Most notably the dialogues between representatives from the Orthodox Churches and the Roman Catholic Church refer time and again to this central theological notion. And it is precisely in the eschatological dimension that unity is not dependent on the efforts of the experienced Church. Thus, the seemingly unattainable resolution of the tension between the believed unity of the Church and experienced separation of the churches is tolerable due to the eschatological dimension. This encourages further steps toward unity, because the productive dynamics released through this dimension allow for what is historically given to appear tentative and ultimately surmountable. In my view this is what is meant by the actual "ecumenical vision."

The institutionalized fellowship of churches in the WCC is ultimately legitimized by this vision:

> The World Council of Churches is a fellowship of churches which confess the Lord Jesus Christ as God and Saviour according to the scriptures and therefore seek to fulfil together their common calling to the glory of the one God, Father, Son and Holy Spirit.[27]

Distinct from this is the utopia that had been pursued in the *Una Sancta* movement,[28] namely their desire to simply leave behind whatever was perceived as a deficient reality. Yet there is no describable place given, where this unity could then be made visible.

That understanding of unity is reflected in different models of unity, each expressing various versions of this understanding. If the ecumenical movement is understood as a tree that has a common root (Jewish tradition), a trunk (primitive Christian community and origins in the early Church), with various branches (forming the different, separated traditions, emerging from divisions of the Church), then this can illustrate fundamentally important aspects of unity. The eschatological dimension is, however, only recognized in another metaphor: the "river delta" model represents the very different streams and rivers that ultimately flow out into the open sea.

Over the past two decades, in particular the reversion to a concept of unity as *koinonia* has had a strong impact upon all discussions concerning integrative concepts of unity. It is based on the rediscovery and acceptance of a Trinitarian-based understanding of the Church, rooted in a Trinitarian understanding of God himself. The effectiveness of the joint perspectives of theological, Christological and pneumatological aspects that are grounded in the *koinonia* concept is demonstrated in the possibility of holding perspectives together that are "from above" (ecclesiological in nature) and "from below" (ecclesiologically-implied ethics), which cannot be separated from each other.[29] *Koinonia* is given and expressed,

in the common confession of the apostolic faith; a common sacramental life entered by the one baptism and celebrated together in one
eucharistic fellowship; a common life in which members and
ministries are mutually recognized and reconciled; and a common
mission witnessing to the gospel of God's grace to all people and
serving the whole of creation.[30]

The different levels of community, which are not independent of
each other, are expressed as follows:

(1) *koinonia* with God, as participation in the immanent Trinity,

(2) *koinonia* within the Church (as a synonym for the Church),

(3) *koinonia* as a community among the churches,

(4) *koinonia* with people of other faiths or no faith, and

(5) *koinonia* with creation.

In this diversity of interpretation one finds the potential for ecclesiological convergence on the idea of *koinonia*, because the Eastern
Orthodox idea of the Church as "mystery" is also included in it,
similar to the western Protestant idea of the Church as *creatura verbi*.
The extensive use of the term itself also poses a danger because the
specific ecclesiological traditions may interpret it according to their
own understanding and do not have to reach a common understanding of the concept. In this way a new metaphor could simply be
(re)introduced that is not yet contributing to its collective clarification.[31] For reasons of sustainability a unified development of the
concept is therefore necessary.

Models of Unification

Due to the diverse models of unification it was agreed in the 1970s
that four requirements for unification models are to be taken into
account:[32]

(1) the termination of prejudice and hostility,

(2) joint participation in the one faith,

(3) the mutual recognition of baptism, Eucharist and ministry,

(4) unifying methods of joint decision and joint action.

On this basis ecumenical theory can develop models, but not without continually reflecting anew upon these, and further developing the list of requirements. Since an understanding of unity does not yet necessarily predetermine any model in particular, different models will each correspond to the same basic understanding of unity. Depending on the starting point, the anticipated goal and the *testing grounds*, entirely different models emerge. Ecumenical theory analyzes these models against the background of their compatibility with the different confessional traditions and inquires as to the rationalization, limits and constructive functions that would enable the unity of the churches to be made visible.

The model of organic union was only pursued in the early ecumenical movement.[33] As an alternative, the "Rahner-Fries Plan"[34] was introduced in 1983 and was programmatically aligned with the Church's structure. It suggested that the self-sufficiency of the particular churches shall be respected and they shall be recognized in turn by each other as fully valid churches, and also that they would jointly place themselves under the specific Petrine office of the Bishop of Rome as an office of unity. The basic truths of the Christian faith as expressed in Scripture and the early Church creeds serve as common grounds. This model has been criticized heavily by some on the Protestant side.[35]

Oscar Cullmann offered New Testament exegesis as a starting point and basis for legitimizing a model of "unity through diversity."[36] Through the analysis of group sociological processes Peter Lengsfeld arrived at a "theory of collusion." He opined it was out of the principle of opposition among individual churches that a denominationally specific consciousness of truth arose, having a specific social form and a homogeneous internal space and a strict separation from what lay outside of it. If these particulars can be liberated from the principle of antagonism through dialogues, wherever possible they can be jointly accountable for all the churches and lead to a "conciliar community." In this process a common Christian identity would receive priority over divisive particularities.[37]

All models that are earnestly discussed in the present, start from one type of unity in ongoing diversity.[38] There are pulpit and Eucharistic communities,[39] unity in reconciled diversity,[40] the Church as a conciliar fellowship, ecumenism consisting of opposites[41] and other models of differentiation.[42] The fact that differences exist is no longer a decisive issue, rather it is the question of whether these differences are of a church-dividing nature.

e. Methodology of Doctrinal Discussions

In all previous models of unification, bilateral and multilateral dialogues have played a decisive role, although their result and their potential to achieve actual unification are increasingly being questioned.[43] In Germany, this criticism arose especially in the wake of the "Joint Declaration on the Doctrine of Justification by the Lutheran World Federation and the Roman Catholic Church."[44] The first indisputable success of the dialogues lies in the mutual recognition and rapprochement of alienated positions, the healing of painful memories of the previous condemnations each side made against the other, as well as the attempt to *jointly* identify convergences and divergences. This also serves to build mutual confidence (at least between the actual parties in the conversation). New aporias do arise. These conversations always yield the effect of self-assurance and the reinforcement of denominational identity, given that the enduring separation is starkly highlighted in relation to that identity. The concept of faith is reduced to doctrine, while worship and contemporary church life are only marginally in view, such that the actually existing, "experienced" institutional churches are barely taken into account. This leads to a poor process of reception, especially among the laity, so that ecumenical dialogue remains a mere discussion among experts. Yet in addition to this, there is also the experience that after many decades of dialogues, despite multiple, fully-formulated and different consensuses, convergences and divergences, there has been no significant institutional change in the relations of the churches to each other.

Thus scrutinizing the methods of these bilateral and multilateral discussions is essential. In each case there is the conviction of a common Christian heritage and of hope, as read in the Reformed-Roman Catholic document on ecclesiology: "What unites us as Christians is more important, more essential than that which separates us..."[45] The long standing project called, "Are mutual doctrinal condemnations still dividing the Churches?" originally directed by Wolfhart Pannenberg and Karl Lehmann,[46] highlights the denominationally-specific doctrines together in the historical context of their origin. This does not lead to a reformulation of historical (confessional or denominational) texts, but to the mitigating awareness and assertion that previous condemnations since the Reformation period no longer pertain to the present partners in the ecumenical movement. The question remains whether this procedure can yield a new, joint discovery of the "basic truths" of Christian faith, and whether these can be advanced mutually. Thus there arises the general question of the truth content of doctrine.

What is (Ecumenical) Truth?

There are at least three different methods of inquiry or rapprochement, namely, *compromise, convergence* and *consensus*:[47]

(1) *Compromise* involves a yielding of all sides for the sake of a generally satisfactory solution. Here one can distinguish between a substantive compromise, which finds the lowest common denominator, and a dilatory compromise, the postponement of a decision. Depending on the truth claim in a doctrine, compromise may be impossible.

(2) *Convergence* is the rapprochement of different positions by all partners toward a position that is yet to be formulated. Together they approach the question of truth.

(3) *Consensus* is the interconnecting, overarching agreement of different positions towards uniformity. The willingness to do this includes the possible admission of mistakes or even the recognition of partial truths.

These three achievable forms of rapprochement can be further subdivided. The power of dialogue lies in the potential for joint confession. The results of such dialogues depend critically upon the methodology used in each case and whether it is actually possible to recognize the otherness of the other as a prerequisite and not only as an obstacle to fellowship. Of course, that can only succeed when it is not necessary to relinquish one's own identity, or the truth one has recognized. That would harken the end of the dialogue. The quality of the dialogues thus depends on the requirement to accept that truth still lies ahead, beyond all church teachings and that verbalized expressions of this truth are not necessarily something to be formulated all at once.

This insight was formulated in an impressive way by the Joint Working Group between the WCC and the Roman Catholic Church:

> Dialogue is appropriate to a situation where differences (or even opposition) exist between men who have nevertheless certain common ground, and who aim at greater fellowship in thought and action. At the outset it assumes the existence of some common points of reference and a common orientation. Our common reference is Revelation as expressed in the witness of the Holy Scriptures. These are something more than a mere book or set of regulations. Through them we hear the Word of God. Their witness is centred in Jesus Christ and has meaning through relation to him; it is lived and understood through the action of the Holy Spirit in the tradition of the Church and through the faithfulness of God's People. All the Christian communions are bound by this faithfulness; each gives it a concrete form in its Confession or Confessions of faith and through its spirituality.[48]

Thus we see how the search for ecumenical truth has laid groundwork for ongoing efforts toward unity.

f. Ecumenical Theology: The Question of the Relationship between Doctrine and Truth

Ecumenical theory deals with the phenomenon of church doctrine. But how does it develop and which truth claims are made concerning particular doctrines? The answer to this question depends precisely upon the relationship of the different doctrinal traditions to each other, which models of unification are realistic and finally, which understanding of unity can be presupposed?

Naturally, opinions diverge strongly here, not only between denominations and cultural contexts, but also within them. This cannot be otherwise, for theology as the critical reflection upon how to speak about God should be seen as something perpetually ongoing, in which the wide variety of schools of thought, results of research projects, and experiences of encounter continually exert an influence. In this way it seems impossible on the one hand for individual confessions to be clearly associated with a singular theological tradition. At best this can appear legitimate in a preliminary way with regard to church dogma, seeking to be bound by the official teaching authority of a denomination. On the other hand there is the legitimate question of whether and to what extent one can properly speak of an ecumenical theology.

Yet ecumenical theology is not itself a single school of thought; it describes a *horizon* of theological expansiveness. The focus should always be foremost upon the totality of global theological traditions, and secondarily, upon a particular, central subject matter. That is because theological reflection occurs on such a broad horizon, always with special reference to the already presupposed unity of the Church in Christ, seeking its visibility and the eschatologically formulated certainty of its realization. Likewise in ecumenical theology various approaches arise that should be brought into dialogue with each other. Since this variety is almost unmanageable, in what follows only one approach will be noted as exemplary of an "ecumenical theology," supplemented by a condensed version of the ongoing discussion.

Dietrich Ritschl, longtime director of the Ecumenical Institute of the Ruprecht-Karls-University of Heidelberg and member of many national and international ecumenical bodies,[49] differentiates between doctrine and doxology using linguistic analysis.[50] There is a difference whether a statement is to function as church doctrine or whether it only relates to worship. Doctrine uses *descriptive* language, while doxology is *ascriptive*. Doxology must let itself be questioned by doctrine, being responsible to it. But its very character is lost if cast in explicit formulas or propositions, according to Ritschl. Doctrine, however, has the function of clarification, delineation and precise definition. In the Bible, both could be found side by side, often in mixed forms (cf. Rom 9-11). There are also many stories one can find (e.g., Exodus, Ruth, Acts), which together would result in a "meta-narrative," which in turn could only be mediated by retelling the individual stories. The stories are summarized – to a degree already in the Bible itself, such as in Paul's writings – and a "doctrine" is drawn from them. From these summaries then, derivations and derivatives of derivations arise, according to Ritschl.[51]

Yet a problem also arises when such summaries — and then also the derivations of the same — come into tension with each other. For example there were already early differences between Peter and Paul, or the fact that Paul addressed Jews differently than Gentiles concerning the resurrection of Jesus. In this way rather different doctrines can be derived from the same story. A consequence of this is seen in the pluraform confessional development that can be plausibly explained in this manner.

But then again, by what means is a truth claim justified? These doctrinal summaries can ultimately only be assessed based on the implicit assumptions ("directives") which have controlled the formation of the stories, says Ritschl. If one follows this realization, then it assumes the readiness not only to bring into question the distinctive ecclesial doctrine of the "story," but also the underlying "directive." Of course, there is nothing said here about a substantive determination as Michael Welker rightly points out.

> Even the logical nature of theology can only be considered to the extent that theology can be compared with other cognitively and normatively verbalized forms of interaction.[52]

But on the other hand if orthodoxy were measured primarily on the basis of loyalty to one's own denominational beliefs, then the problem becomes most poignant. For as such, doctrines themselves can easily be made absolute so that they overtake the function of distinguishing between orthodoxy and heresy, and become apologetic and identity-defining. Ritschl speaks of such cases being "coagulations." Here the question of the function of denominational confessions also seems relevant and perhaps with Ritschl this issue receives too little consideration. If confessions are (only) valid as objective interpretations of the biblical witness then either the task of accounting for the formation of the confessions must be put aside, or they themselves are elevated to become the substance of faith. Then there must be an account of how such a position relates to the uniqueness of the biblical witness as a bearer of the "believed" revelation.

In the search for visible unity, one first asks modestly: Are there "basic truths" in or behind the respective doctrines which could be equally valid for all denominations? If that is the case, then one may ask which, albeit rather different, "derivations" appear to all participants as legitimate, without needing to be accepted by all as mandatory. In this case at least mutual condemnation could be abandoned and the church-dividing nature of the differences would be examined anew. However, not only the origin and content of the doctrine are to be considered, but also the respective function that a doctrine assumes in a particular tradition. Is it simply a varying derivation of the doctrinal "summaries" or a central determining feature within the understanding, articulation and communication of Christian faith?

A problem arises in the ecumenical movement when two seemingly contradictory doctrines collide; meanwhile the participating dialogue partners insist that they concur concerning the "basic truths." This then appears paradoxical, since doctrinal statements, when understood as a set of truths, allow for only one conclusion: A doctrine that was true must forever be true.[53] In this case there would be no cause for a denomination to reformulate its own doctrine. Also, if no institutional changes in the mutual relationship of the participating denominations arise from the accepted agreement, then it is critical to inquire as to the relevance of such an agreement upon basic truths regarding the Church's visible unity.

A different position views doctrinal statements as experientially and expressively oriented symbols of existential orientations and attitudes. This results in a completely different way of dealing with doctrine. Its meaning may change without doctrine itself being changed. However, it can also be reformulated, so that its significance need not be changed. Here again new issues arise such as the consistency and continuity (apostolicity) of doctrines.

George A. Lindbeck has observed this and offers as a third alternative, a combination of the two positions described above, namely, a "cultural-linguistic approach."[54] Doctrines should be used neither as expressive symbols, nor even as truth claims, but as authoritative rules valid for a community, concerning their attitudes and actions as well as their discourse. Consequently, church doctrine is to be considered as a "regulative" theory or "control theory."[55] Church doctrines act as "regulative principles," according to Lindbeck, such that they are equally both variable and invariable. Lindbeck's approach is

> equally fruitful for fundamental theology and hermeneutics, dedicating itself to the tacitly assumed rules of understanding[56] of theological doctrinal development.[57]

However, the question remains here as with the approaches described above, to what degree does such an approach remain bound to its own specific confessional, contextual and temporal – in this case post-liberal – context? Furthermore, how do others, for understandable reasons, not seem plausible or legitimate? Given these issues, each approach must be accounted for in the development of ecumenical theology.

g. New Orientations–Paradigm Shift?

The oft-repeated phrase, "crisis in the ecumenical movement" contains at its core the same features found within the development of the theory itself. That is, it implies the status quo is to be rigorously analyzed, as to expose the potential for constructive new breakthroughs. But one might ask, which criteria are to be considered, at what time, and in what constellation of relationships is this phrase about the crisis of ecumenism seemingly appropriate?

Can language about a paradigm shift express something meaningful here? This explanatory model of Thomas S. Kuhn[58] comes from the field of natural sciences, and demonstrates that advances in science are usually made in individual steps, but sometimes in major leaps. A new idea or hypothesis replaces an old one and gradually all follow this new guiding principle. A new paradigm emerges and now all previously valid concepts are checked and aligned with this standard. The applicability of this model of explanation to ecumenical theory was discussed in the 1980s and 1990s, especially by David Tracy and Hans Küng.[59] Konrad Raiser and others expounded this theory as applied to the theological discussions within the ecumenical movement.[60] It should be remembered here, however, that in the humanities there are always several paradigms simultaneously alongside one other that are considered legitimate and will continue to be pursued further. But generally the main currents can be identified.

Universalism and Particularism–Christocentrism and Trinitarian Approaches

The themes and messages of the WCC assemblies illustrate poignantly such basic currents, and they even designate the respective theological challenges and, as such, each can be counted as snapshots in time of the worldwide ecumenical movement, for example:

Evanston in 1954: "Christ–the Hope of the World";[61]

New Delhi in 1961: "Jesus Christ, the Light of the World";[62]

Uppsala in 1968: "Behold, I make all things new";[63]

Nairobi in 1975: "Jesus Christ frees and unites";[64]

Vancouver in 1983: "Jesus Christ, the life of the world."[65]

In retrospect, they are important documents of their respective eras. Various tendencies can also be observed. Following the first World Missionary Conference in Edinburgh in 1910, which is considered the birth of the modern ecumenical movement, missiology became more marginal after the integration of the International Missionary Council into the WCC in 1961. Moreover contextual theologies, intercultural approaches and issues of social ethics since the 1970s in the international ecumenical arena became increasingly prominent. Until Vancouver in 1983, the prevailing motif remained strictly Christological.

Since the beginning of the modern ecumenical movement, the Christocentric postulate was considered the basis for unity efforts. The one Christ, Lord of the Church and the world, is the giver of unity and its perfecter. This confession of Christ that is common to all churches, led them into fellowship with one another. Above all, dialectical theology was leading the way in this respect during the first half of the twentieth century, especially the theology of Karl Barth. Edmund Schlink, the founding director of the Ecumenical Institute at the University of Heidelberg, can be noted as an influential ecumenical representative of this "paradigm": the churches circle like planets around the one Christ as (solar-)center.[66]

Different studies on the theological adequacy of Christocentrism appeared since the 1960s, first of all through the so-called "young churches," but also through feminist theology and other so-called "genitive theologies." Their quest for independence, the discovery of their own cultural and religious roots, and contextual theological reflection led them to interpret any theology ultimately as a contextual theology. In addition, sociological analyses of power relations and structures and political systems are supported or challenged by theological concepts. Psychological insights are increasingly taken into account in the analysis. Questions continually arise concerning whose interests and by whom theology is driven, and which goals does it pursue?

If one re-examines the relationship between universality and particularity in this way, then church doctrine cannot remain unaffected. This can be shown for example in an exchange of letters between M.M. Thomas and Wolfhart Pannenberg.[67] Thomas, a Christian and sociologist from India, played a leading role in the South Indian Church Union and the WCC. He inquires as to the significance

of the life and the actions of Jesus for a new social order in his country. Pannenberg, a German professor who criticizes radical contextualization, warns against capturing and using God for one's own political
goals. The extent of these differences can be shown in the example of
their different understandings of sin and redemption. In the first case
sin is seen especially in the oppression of a collective group. Sin is
then used mainly in its political dimension as a structural concept and
the term "redemption" primarily implies political liberation. In the
other case there is an individual concept of sin. It is a personal trans-
gression against God and salvation is thus first understood as forgiveness of personal guilt and renewal of the individual's relationship
with God.

In this way, the different emphases of doctrine and practice are
made visible. Questions of ortho*praxy* and the so-called "ethical
heresy" (Visser 't Hooft) become urgent in the face of the precarious
political and economic conditions in the various contexts of the
ecumenical world, because there is greater awareness of global interdependence. Following the Conciliar Process for Justice, Peace and the
Integrity of Creation, which was initiated during the sixth WCC
Assembly in Vancouver in 1983, there came the Decade to Overcome
Violence, 2001-2010, and the AGAPE Process (Alternative Globalization Addressing *People and Earth*). Both were adopted by the Eighth
Assembly[68] of the WCC in Harare 1998 and the Ninth Assembly in
Porto Alegre in 2006.[69] For a large part of the Christian world, the
search for unity in the struggle for justice, peace and the integrity of
creation is the leitmotif of the aspirations for unity. The Christocentrism of earlier years is no longer seen in these circumstances of divergent and pluralized currents as being the only orientation.

Accordingly, the concept of ecumenism becomes even further
nuanced. At the Seventh Assembly in Canberra in 1991, pneumatology already came to the foreground, which again, is illustrated by
the theme of the General Assembly: "Come Holy Spirit, Renew the
Whole Creation."[70] This prayer expresses the hope that the Holy
Spirit would move even in those cultures (those not solely shaped by
Christianity) as the power of renewal and the life-giver, going beyond

the limits of the ecclesial community to include the whole of creation. Thus the relationship between culture and the gospel is reflected in new ways.

This is precisely what Konrad Raiser described as the paradigm shift.[71] Based upon the understanding of the interdependence of all life in all places, new analyses and assessments of economic, environmental and social issues arise. Ecumenism is described with the metaphor *oikos* ("the one household of life"), which seeks meaningful life for all creation. Hence the search for a mutually-committed ecumenical community is a guiding concept for ecumenical ecclesiology. Since these considerations are now based on pneumatological, or even Trinitarian arguments, the thesis can be argued that the paradigm of universalistic Christocentrism has been replaced. Finally, the increased acceptance of theological influences from the Orthodox Churches by western theologies has resulted in a renaissance of the doctrine of the Trinity.[72] Ever since this shift, Trinitarian-based concepts of unity have predominated in ecumenical theology, particularly in the studies of the Commission on Faith and Order concerning ecclesiology.[73]

Israel and the Church

A second issue arises from the rediscovered – and still to be further unpacked – reality of the Judeo-Christian relationship. For some this issue is the overarching ecumenical challenge.[74] Karl Barth considered the relationship of the Christian Church to Judaism to be the single greatest ecumenical issue.[75] The continued election and existence of the people of Israel, God's people, who live in the ongoing covenant, remains a challenge for an ecclesiology on the horizon of ecumenism. The Church can only be conceived as being with and for Israel. Supersessionist positions are not tenable, nor is it assumed that there are two different covenants. Rather, according to Christian belief, the "Gentiles" are taken into the existing covenant through Christ (cf. Eph 2). If this theological acknowledgement is taken seriously and if Christian theology is to be freed of all anti-Judaism, then an entirely new self-understanding will begin to develop, one which will impact all areas of theology.[76] The ever-developing ecumenical theory proposes different models[77] to constructively deal with this tension and openly examine any remaining differences.

Inter-Religious Dialogue

A third inquiry concerning the paradigm of universalistic Christo-centrism establishes a framework acknowledging the permanent and vibrant existence of the other world religions alongside Christianity and Judaism. The hope at the beginning of the ecumenical movement in the twentieth century to win all people for the gospel now seems far removed from reality; the outreach motto of the first World Missionary Conference in Edinburgh in 1910 was "the evangelization of the world in this generation."[78] The nuanced reflections on the relationship with non-Christian religions were ultimately applied to the Christian faith itself. Here theological considerations focused mainly on the possibilities of the knowledge of God in other religions and soteriology as a question of "salvation." In order to determine the relationship of these diverse conceptions there are systematic typologies (exclusivism, inclusivism, pluralism and relativism) and they provide different models.[79] In addition, there are orientating concepts toward practical, experiential encounter are necessary, such as Theo Sundermeier's early "convivence" model,[80] and later the models of inter-religious education.[81] The "global ethic" project by Hans Küng focused on the field of ethics. His thesis on the possibility of world peace solely concerning the path of peace between religions enjoys broad agreement, but also has undergone critical questioning.[82] The reality of the coexistence of different religions will ultimately be reflected in all theological disciplines in order to develop appropriate and theologically defensible means to define their mutual relationship.[83]

As much as the current ecumenical reality – in the sense of God's household – is shaped by the reality of the coexistence of different religions in a globalized world, it is still not clear how inter-religious dialogue is expected to become the actual subject of ecumenical theory. Undeniably there is the qualitative difference that remains with inter-Christian denominational relations, as they share a confession in the one Christ. From this perspective, the explanatory power of the paradigm shift thesis appears to be limited.

h. Evaluating Ecumenical Processes with Four Criteria – Ecumenism in the Making

The German Ecumenical Study Committee[84] has developed a helpful "constructive-critical grid" for the assessment of ecumenical processes:[85]

(1) Do they allow for the itinerant nature of the ecumenical movement to be apparent?

(2) Do they maintain the three dimensions of faith (spirituality, doctrine and way of life)?

(3) Is unity conceived so as to guide and preserve a wide variety of churches in the *koinonia*?

(4) Is the ecumenical movement understood as an instrument for the compelling message of Jesus Christ?

As an encounter of the various theological traditions and denominations, ecumenism endures ultimately through building relationships: through God's being placed in relationship to creation, through Christ's reconciliation and through the Holy Spirit's abiding presence for its perfection, as the capacity for relationship formation among people results, both in spite of and due to all differences and distinctions. This acknowledgement is particularly true for churches who are called to confess this reality. Ecumenism is experienced in worship as a place of the spiritual practice of the gathered community, being accountable for each other and for all creation, in diaconal and charitable activity, as well as in common ecumenical learning.

Ecumenists have always been part of this movement toward the formation of relationships and they participate in the ongoing process

of theory formation through their analytical and constructive functions. In this way they make their particular contribution to theology
as a whole, which will remain a "thorn in the flesh" for any ecclesial
and theological orientation which chooses to be self-enclosed or isola-
tionist.

CHAPTER 2
DIALOGICAL ECUMENISM
BILATERAL METHODS AND PRACTICES

Speaking the truth in love

— EPHESIANS 4:15

(NRSV)

INTERDENOMINATIONAL DOCTRINAL DIALOGUES are presented here as the primary *testing ground* of ecumenism. First, we focus on the respective denominational particulars of the participating churches, which are decisive for the methodology, function, potential objectives and the specific content of each dialogue. This is done using the example of Mennonites and Catholics, as clarified and critically analyzed below in the bilateral dialogue between the Pontifical Council for Promoting Christian Unity and the Mennonite World Conference (1998-2003).

a. Denominational Particulars in Ecumenical Dialogue – The Example of Mennonites

In dialogical ecumenism one begins by identifying specific, substantive and methodological challenges. For Mennonites,[1] who are the oldest

Evangelical Free Church in Europe[2] and a "historic peace church,"[3] doctrinal dialogues are not the primary expression of their ecumenical profile. The documents arising from bilateral dialogues give evidence that theological convictions of this tradition are expressed first and foremost as living witnesses of faith in a concrete context.[4] The congregation gathered in worship and service to others is considered by Mennonites as the primary reality of the Church; the right religious practice (orthopraxy) was always at least as important to them as right doctrine (orthodoxy). This leads to challenges in interdenominational doctrinal conversations, and these can be significant for current ecumenical methodology. This is especially the case when official representatives of denominations produce statements, which are based primarily on their denomination's confessional texts and contain their own interpretation of the doctrines and then seek (canonically) binding formulations in dialogue with representatives of the Mennonite tradition.

The first challenge arises from the congregationalist constitution among some Mennonites. For them, the local church is largely autonomous in all aspects of doctrine and administration, although not completely isolated from larger, institutionalized, denominational forums. Thus, within the Mennonite community of churches a considerable diversity has developed, but they nevertheless see themselves as a unity. The absence of church hierarchies or doctrinal offices equipped with authority provides an additional challenge. Dialogue partners usually ask for binding doctrinal statements which potential interdenominational agreements could support. Given Mennonites' skepticism toward written confessions, plus the fact that they interpret common confessional texts within the limits of their geographic and temporal context, such texts cannot serve as a basis for dialogues in the sense of being ultimate written statements of "Mennonite doctrine."[5]

This alternative church structure constantly creates challenges for both sides of a dialogue. It is problematic for the dialogue partner, because they legitimately inquire as to the binding nature of statements they provide. Meanwhile Mennonites are required by them to follow a methodology which does not directly correspond to the reality of their tradition and their community's mentality.[6] However, this mutual challenge presents an opportunity for successfully establishing a dialogue in alternative ways. The starting points for dialogues with Mennonites in fact are not usually historically-entrenched doctrinal differences, but the description of the present community's realities. This approach initially presents the possibility of a mutual understanding, which does not begin with the doctrinal differences of the past, nor does it expend all the available energy on resolving inherited differences. Rather, it begins with the situation of believers themselves and their questions about how their faith is being tested in current contexts and in considering the future challenges.

The task of distinct, self-conscious positioning within the corresponding tradition begs one to ask in return, how and why have certain beliefs and theological doctrines emerged? How have they been updated during the formation of that tradition and which arguments and justifications have stood the test? Thus, the possibility of a common study process was created through the encounter with the other, because as such dialogue will never remain bound or confined to the repetition of fixed doctrinal systems. Rather it becomes a joint exploration into history and it is this approach that can lead to a joint revision of theological understandings, one which is based on the different perspectives of the respective traditions. Quite often in this process it is also recognized that assumed differences are not necessarily always perceived to follow denominational boundaries, but they often run crosswise in relation to it. An enquiry into, or even correction of, previous elements of tradition is not excluded; the ecclesiological self-understanding of Mennonites as *ecclesia semper reformanda* in this sense provides a noteworthy illustration.

The Functions of Dialogue: Sharpening of Identity, Translation Aids and Renewed Definition of Relationships

Dialogues must not lead to relativizing one's identity or to arbitrariness, but should serve in their own way to enhance precision, to a sharpening of identities. Through the direct and also personal experience of the encounter with the other, this sharpening no longer depends, as often happened in history, upon the polemical devaluation of another tradition. Instead it gains its dynamism by describing its own experiences and the positively grounded justification of its particular insights in contrast to the other denomination. These insights are experienced in new ways due to the listening presence of the "sister church" in the dialogue. Such an atmosphere of mutual respect can enable the assessment of a different position without their needing to be shared or appropriated. On the contrary, only through the clearest possible verbalization of differences can decisive examinations be undertaken to determine which of the divergences still remain. Only in this way can one determine if differences actually amount to church-dividing issues, or whether they should be valued as expressions of a legitimate pluralism and freedom of interpretation within the one Church. In this respect, identity is not relativized in the dialogue, but updated.

This approach of dialoguing with Mennonites, given the present realities of the faith community, allows for one to make conclusions about the motivation for bilateral meetings. In no way are institutional church unifications by definition the goal of dialogue, rather there is first of all the understanding and explanation of the denominationally-shaped theological positions in the face of jointly-acknowledged, contemporary challenges. Ecumenical dialogue can therefore also be described as a "translation aid" which enables the acquisition of the "foreign language" of another denomination in rudimentary form and thus it offers the chance to explain in one's own "mother tongue" those aspects which are of fundamental importance and those understandings which have generally prevailed historically. Sometimes it may be possible that the particularity of the "language" of the other also finds an appropriate expression. There is no need for it to result in consensus, but in many cases convergences can be distinguished where differences were simply assumed previously. Sometimes the recognition of the complementarity of theological statements also becomes apparent.

Another function of the dialogues can be seen in the basic definition of the relationship of faith traditions through working toward a recognition of a common history. Except for their experience of dialogues with Baptists and Seventh-Day Adventists, Mennonites consider themselves to have been met historically with harsh judgement by all other denominations with whom they have held dialogues thus far. This historical experience has also been reflected in the form of "condemnations" of Anabaptists (the forebears of Mennonites) in certain confessional texts from the sixteenth century. Since these confessional texts – including their condemnations – are still valid in present-day churches, the memories of condemnation remain present at contemporary encounters. The many martyrdoms that Anabaptists and Mennonites suffered because of their interpretations of Scripture and the way they expressed the Christian faith have been deeply etched in that denomination's memory. In this respect, the present-day official encounters are also marked by first-time recognitions of guilt towards Anabaptists and Mennonites and a search for ways to overcome these (sometimes mutual) condemnations, leading toward a "healing of memories."

In order for these features of the dialogue to actually be able to bear fruit, Mennonites always inquire as to the practical consequences of the results of such dialogues. The reception process of an ecumenical dialogue must be considered and structured as an integral part of the dialogue. It can be observed that in all cases, newly-perceived identities can be introduced and major steps are taken toward mutual awareness and respect as a result of the dialogue. The long-term effect of the dialogues then shows up in other points of contact and meetings at different levels, in which the dialogue texts always take on a function as "translation aids." They find practical application in marriages between members of different denominations, in the shaping of religious instruction, with questions about gaining or transferring church membership, in Christian social service agencies, in socio-political involvement, and in mission.

However, the fact cannot be overlooked that this very structure of reception processes in the ecumenical movement has enjoyed only limited success. Previously there had been too little reflection on the need for this, despite the constant calls for attention to the reception of the results of a dialogue. Too rarely has an appropriate ecumenical hermeneutic been developed, and the considerations for determining the relation of individual dialogues to each other have been quite marginal. Here there is a wide range of tasks for ongoing ecumenical research.[7]

The Interdependence of Catholicity and Peace Witness

Ecumenical dialogue is not an end in itself. The intrinsic motivation arises from the serious effort to ensure the credibility of Christian witness. A Church that is divided into separate, mutually-condemning "institutional churches" can hardly be convincing in its proclamation – in either its words or actions. If one conceives of the Church in its true catholicity, in its actual and all-encompassing unity in the Christian confession of God understood as Trinity, and not in a manner that is artificially limited to one's own denominational peculiarity, then the effort for the visible unity of the Church occupies a central location in the life and confession of the individual believer and the denominational families. Without such an "ecumenical profile" the claim of the catholicity of one's own denomination is empty.

According to the Mennonite understanding, the eventual abolition of all doctrinal differences is not a necessary condition for such a visible unity, as this denomination is able to demonstrate in its congregationalist approach to constituting plurality.[8] But this diversity needs to be aimed at a *reconciled* diversity[9] in the community of churches, because the peace witness of the Church is also put to the test and made credible as a result.

As a peace church Mennonites need their structure to be dialogical, just as their thinking is. It was rarely possible in the past for this peace church to achieve reconciliation in relation to the other denominations, due to the condemnations and persecutions it experienced.

The path of separation and separateness was their only option. Thus with the beginnings of the modern ecumenical movement and the willingness of denominations for ecumenical dialogues they were not only presented with an opportunity – rather, there was virtually an obligation to also suspend its separatist peace theology in order to engage in inter-denominational relations. Then this context began to give expression to its ethic of nonviolence, so that the believed possibility of reconciliation in Christ could become a reality. Peace convictions and the willingness for dialogue are not mutually exclusive, but one is a fundamental expression of the other.

Multilateral Conversations

Besides the numerous bilateral dialogues undertaken by Mennonites (with Catholics, Lutherans, Reformed, Baptists, etc.) there are official statements on broader, national or international ecumenical study processes. In terms of their significance for the ecumenical movement, they are no less important, but in their multilateral orientation they are concentrated more on the clarification of specific topics and issues of the ecumenical community as a whole and therefore these also require a separate, more detailed investigation. Among the most important multilateral meetings, from a Mennonite perspective – in addition to encounters with other peace churches – include the convergence statements by the Commission on Faith and Order of the World Council of Churches (*Baptism, Eucharist and Ministry,* "BEM") in 1982,[10] the consultations for the Commission on Faith and Order and of the National Council of Churches in the United States on apostolic faith and the peace witness of the Church (1990-1991),[11] or even the more recent study of the German Ecumenical Committee on the doctrine of justification.[12]

A noteworthy, but seldom acknowledged, multilateral encounter was the international dialogue process between the various churches of the Reformation. The multilateral dialogues on the common heritage of the Reformation(s) first brought together a group of churches that were often placed in a common tradition throughout church history, but until then, had not held any such direct, joint dialogues. These included the Church of the Waldensians, the Hussite Church, the Evangelical Church of Czech Brethren, the Moravian Church, Hutterites, Mennonites, the Society of Friends (Quakers), and the Church of the Brethren.[13]

The series of multilateral meetings that began in the mid-1980s was motivated by the question of whether there would be a joint contribution to the recent ecumenical movement from the perspective of these churches. Situations of violence and injustice were named as current ecumenical challenges, particularly in view of the economic issues concerned. These particular traditions bore a pronounced hope for the transformative and renewing powers of the Gospel itself: the "first Reformation," which starts with the Waldensian (12th-13th century) and the Hussite movements (15th century) unleashed faith perspectives that inspired the later Reformation impulses. Yet it would be wrong to reduce these early movements to that of a precursor role for the sixteenth-century Reformation. They were carried forward "by the faith that Jesus Christ is the Lord of the world and that the social order should be shaped by his Lordship."[14] The modern-day heirs of these traditions are quite self-critical and in the present are seeking to translate the leading theological axioms in dialogue with others. This also characterizes the heirs of the "radical Reformation."[15] Through the confession of the lordship of Christ, representatives of the Anabaptist movement of the sixteenth century saw themselves as immediately called to concrete discipleship. They accepted Scripture not only as the sole basis for doctrine, but also for ethics and they pursued the goal of a restitution of an early Christian communal ideal.

After three meetings of representatives of these traditions (Prague I-III), they decided to include representatives of the "Second Reformation" (magisterial Reformation), namely, Lutheran, Calvinist and Zwinglian traditions in the circles of dialogue participants, as it became increasingly apparent that these insights needed to be added as a fundamental supplement to their own tradition. The *magisterial Reformation* in some ways also drew on earlier reform efforts, but more heavily stressed justification by grace alone through faith and freedom through the Gospel. This consultation in Geneva ("Prague IV") was organized by the World Alliance of Reformed Churches in cooperation with the Lutheran World Federation and the Mennonite World Conference. Representatives of the Methodist, Baptist and also the Roman Catholic Church were present. By developing a common understanding and a common interpretation of their heritage from the Reformation(s), could the churches today make a joint contribution to ecumenical social ethics? The subsequent dialogues were concerned with questions about the relationship between justification and sanctification (Prague V, 1998),[16] "Life in Christ" (Prague VI, 2000) and the importance of reformist and prophetic movements for Church and society (Prague VII, 2003).[17]

The Mennonite contributions to peace and justice merit special attention, as discussed at the influential and groundbreaking international dialogue process of the World Council of Churches called the "Puidoux Conferences" (1955 to 1973),[18] and more recently in the ecumenical "Decade to Overcome Violence, 2001-2010."[19](see below, Ch.6)

b. Bilateral Dialogue between Catholics and Mennonites: Analysis, Critical Evaluation and Enduring Questions

The *Mennonite Encyclopedia* states: "There are unbridgeable differences between Catholicism and Anabaptism."[20] Catholics had seen the churches of Anabaptist origin primarily as schismatic and heretical sects who followed a Pelagian-oriented theology of free will and rejected a sacramentally-mediated grace.[21] Only by the Second Vatican Council was there a fundamental reorientation of relationships with other denominations, which also led to a modified view of the churches of the Anabaptist tradition.[22] On the other hand, Anabaptists and Mennonites had always exhibited a latent anti-clericalism within their own identity,[23] which was explicitly expressed more or less generally as anti-Catholicism.

An international dialogue between the Pontifical Council for Promoting Christian Unity and the Mennonite World Conference has now been held "in the spirit of friendship and reconciliation." The document of these international dialogues, which ran from 1998 to 2003 is: "Called Together to be Peacemakers."[24] Thus this ecumenical dialogue joins the series of many bilateral doctrinal dialogues, which separated churches have held together since the twentieth century.[25]

The special feature of the dialogue that will be analyzed here is that the churches in the encounter could hardly be more different. On one side is the centrally-structured global church, with its hundreds of millions of members, and on the other, the radically congregationally-constructed minority church; next to the hierarchical High Church offices with a distinctive doctrine of the sacraments, is the bottom-up, congregationalist church that is ever carried by the laity, a tradition which always saw the practical way of life in the imitation of Christ as taking precedence over doctrinal uniformity. On the one hand there are the tradition-conscious offices of succession and structure, carefully respecting apostolicity, while the other is engaged with the current challenges of the faithful in specific places; with one there is even a separate "state apparatus" with diplomatic relations, while the other, since the Reformation, maintained a radical separation from the state as "historic peace churches," as in the teaching of the anti-clerical and pacifist-minded Anabaptists.[26] The list of apparent differences could go much further. Thus this encounter already contained in its initial circumstances quite a bit of tension. What motivation drove the dialogue partners toward these encounters? What aspects of the totality of theological and historical references are identified as worthy of dialogue? And what results might one realistically expect?

These questions will be investigated here by way of presenting and critically analyzing the results of the dialogue. It should be noted that the author himself belongs to one of the denominations (Mennonite) and is rooted in the German context, in which a longstanding relationship between the participating denominations has been maintained. In the Council of Christian Churches in Germany,[27] there are many ecumenical initiatives for peace and justice and on special occasions such as church conferences, but especially in some local communities. The experiences of being together are not unexceptionally positive. In direct encounters the experience of being from estranged traditions can still be nettlesome. During the presentation of the results of the dialogue at the General Assembly of the Mennonite World Conference in Bulawayo, Zimbabwe (2003), the disparity of the relations in various parts of the world clearly became apparent: mutual trust has not developed everywhere as widely as it has in Germany.[28]

In terms of methodology, the dialogue primarily followed the well-recognized pattern of bilateral conversations. First there is a mutual presentation of specific theological, doctrinal items after agreement has been reached on major issues. Then the actual call for a common formulation of convergences and divergences is advanced. The dialogue was conducted without the expectation of a specific result, as no concrete institutional or doctrinal objectives were anticipated or stated, but the title of the final document in this case already indicates that above all there was *one* item that is especially interesting and motivating: the common vocation of supporting peace and being peacemakers. In addition to the motivations of efforts for the unity of Christianity that are known from the ecumenical movement, there is first of all the common belief that "peace is at the heart of the Gospel" which was seen as a particularly compelling reason for the dialogue (§14). In an era of weapons of mass destruction, the challenge of peacemaking is presented anew to all the churches and viewed differently than in previous centuries (§9). Already the preface mentions the self-understanding of Mennonites as a historic peace church whose commitment to peace "is essential" to their self-understanding (§5).[29] The Roman Catholic Church also considers the promotion of unity, with peace being directly inferred from this, as "belonging to the innermost nature of the Church" (§147).[30]

On the other hand, contemporary historical studies of medieval sources point to a spirituality that Catholics and Mennonites hold in common. In addition to the discussion of relevant theologoumena, both those that separate and those that bind, the interpretation of the common history of the Church is a significant and very promising step on the road to reconciliation. In the background there is the fundamental recognition that many painful separations have not only grown out of different theological insights, but different interpretations of history prevent an adequate understanding of the theological statements of the other. "This was a new process of reconciliation," and a new start is marked in a relationship, with the declared goal of overcoming "the consequences of almost five centuries of mutual isolation and hostility" (§2).

Based on this goal, the structure of the individual paths for dialogue is determined: parallel, corresponding interpretations of historical events or epochs that caused the separations or made them visible, were discussed for each of the chosen theological themes (ecclesiology, baptism and the Eucharist/Communion, peace theology and ethics).

The key epochs are the "Constantinian era" in the Middle Ages and the Reformation of the sixteenth century. The structure of the dialogue will also be followed below: (I) Common View of History, (II) Joint Consideration of Theology, and (III) the "Healing of Memories."

(1) Common View of History

Denominations develop their own interpretation of an overall history, naturally elevating periods that were especially formative for them and particularly highlighting their points of divergence from other denominations, using their own version of the events that make the theological insights obtained in these situations of conflict plausible.[31] In this way interpretations of history are provided, often in ways that are contrary to understandings that are solidified in other denominations' confessional texts, which can often lead to mutual biases, especially in the description of the historical developments.

In this way negative views become self-justifying and form constricting stereotypes that were minted in "times of the great theological polemics" and are further passed on. Ultimately, to the present day these historical views obstruct one's ability to envision the unity of the Church.

Common Hermeneutics – Reading Church History Together Anew

A potential correction of a biased approach to presenting history involves a historical-critical investigation, but due to the complexity of the cultural, political, social, economic and religious contexts, such a process alone cannot completely erase the reproach of the interests that had led to such a depiction of history. The writing of church history is precisely the assessment of the results of historical research, which too often prejudices a particular ecclesiological preconception. On the other hand ecumenical dialogues offer an opportunity – one that can hardly be underestimated – for overcoming a selective perception and unilateral interpretation through joint historical study. This is one of the appreciable findings of the Catholic-Mennonite dialogue: "By studying history together, we discovered that our interpretations of the past were often incomplete and limited." (§23) Catholics and Mennonites had, after all, shared fifteen centuries of common church history, prior to the division experienced during the Reformation. Regardless of the tenability of this perspective, in my opinion the dialogue failed to adequately schematize this issue and therefore it still begs further investigation due to the fact that the Roman Catholic Church did separate itself from dissenting groups (such as Waldensians or Hussites), which signifies that the western Church had already experienced division prior to the Reformation.

A continuation of joint research is needed, as the dialogue report repeatedly identifies. The partners foster the hope that a common memory of history could finally "free us from the prison of the past." (§27) This, however, requires a willingness to repent, as the Mennonite theologian John Howard Yoder pointed out years ago.[32]

The Constantinian Era – Becoming *ecclesia vincens*

In the era in which Christian faith was declared the official religion of the Roman Empire and when the Nicene Creed became imperial law, the church of the persecuted (*ecclesia pressa*) changed to being tolerated (*ecclesia tolerata*) and finally to the established church (*ecclesia vincens*).[33] Mennonites interpret this fundamental transformation as the "Constantinian fall" of the Church.[34] Catholics also do not view this development uncritically:

> Together we repudiate those aspects of the Constantinian era that were departures from some characteristic Christian practices and deviations from the Gospel ethic. We acknowledge the Church's failure when she justified the use of force in evangelism, sought to create and to maintain a unitary Christian society by coercive means, and persecuted religious minorities. (§55)

That such far-reaching, shared assessments now became possible is primarily the result of the completely changed reality of the churches in the present. Mennonites increasingly recognize that they need to accept social responsibility in liberal, democratic, constitutional forms of government and to help shape political life if they want their witness to be credible. And since the Second Vatican Council, Catholics have been calling for freedom of religion and conscience for all people and they repudiate any use of force in religious matters.[35] These were key demands of the Anabaptists in the sixteenth century.[36] Here the common rejections of the state church can be seen clearly and unambiguously, whose beginnings date back to the Constantinian era.

The joint assessment finally opens up the possibility to evaluate such developments which are in continuity with the early history of the Church. The degree to which the respective theologies have been shaped through these centuries by different influences and emphases, is not ignored or underestimated:

> Catholics would see matters such as the generalization of infant baptism, the evolution of the meaning of conversion, as well as Christian attitudes toward military service and oath taking as examples of legitimate theological developments. Mennonites consider the same phenomena as unfortunate changes of earlier Christian practice and as unfaithfulness to the way of Jesus. (§59)

While creating a Christian society today still appears as a "worthy goal" for Catholics, Mennonites recognize the continuity of the early Christian witness throughout, also in movements that have been classified by the Roman Catholic Church as heretical. On the Catholic side, there were regrettable actions that were "hardly in accord with the spirit of the Gospel, or even opposed to it. Nevertheless, the doctrine of the Church that no one is to be coerced into faith has always stood firm." (§61) Mennonite historiography tends to "doubt such a claim," since theologians, popes and Ecumenical Councils theologically justified the admonition for the state to convert and punish heretics.[37]

Western Europe on the Eve of the Reformation – Piety and Spirituality

Catholics and Mennonites agreed that in the transition from medieval to modern times the central power and authority of the Church had been brought into question by the first "modern states."[38] This led to a deterioration of the unity of consciousness of *christianitas*, which experienced its peak in the Crusades. Massive social and economic changes led to unrest and riots, which also became a breeding ground for the "radical Reformation." Among the cultural elite a spiritual renewal arose (in the Renaissance and humanism), which led to the increased study of sources and classical texts in the original languages in the life of the Church. What is often described as a crisis and decline of the Church actually reveals the opposite: "On the eve of the Reformation, church life and piety were flourishing," (§34) so that both the Reformation and "Catholic Reform" can basically be evaluated as a result of this "religious vitality."[39] Again, it is conceded that there were certainly "abuses among the clergy, among the hierarchy and the papacy, and among the friars" (§34) in the ecclesiastical taxation system, in pastoral ministry, and superstitions within popular piety, such as the veneration of relics. But it also evidences the zeal and the desire for religious experience. Basically, religious life was "characterized by a renewed emphasis on good preaching and on religious education..." (§35) Lay movements (*Devotio moderna*),[40] preachers and writers spread a spirituality of discipleship (*imitatio Christi*) and "envisioned ideals that a century or two later would become common in the Protestant Reformation, the Radical Reformation, and the Catholic Reform as well." (§36)

It was precisely the spirituality of the Anabaptists with an emphasis on nonresistance, discipleship, repentance and conversion, which paralleled Benedictine and Franciscan tradition as well as German mysticism in the emphasis upon "holy living in word and deed." (§66) Reform movements, such as those at Cluny or the Gregorian reform marked attempts to free the Church from the influence of political power, albeit with limited success.[41] But while Mennonites evaluate such movements as positive exceptions within the medieval Church, Catholics tend to see them as evidence of a widespread medieval piety. Conjectures are initially formulated cautiously. Is Anabaptist piety, as some scholars have suggested, somehow a nonsacramental and communitarian transformation of medieval spirituality and asceticism?[42] Such historical insights as these assist the dialogue processes, which are borne of an investment in jointly developing historical hermeneutics.

These interpretations of church history beg for further joint studies to be carried out. Is it already appropriate to discuss movements arising from the Reformation, about connections between radical political reforms with the first "modern nation states" or did such terminology only become pertinent during the course of the French Revolution? Weren't the abuses in the medieval church at least one cause of the breakup of the assumed unity prior to the Reformation?[43] If the majority of demands for reform were basically common knowledge, why then were they not enforceable within the existing church? Finally, are the parallel conceptions of the Protestant Reformation, radical Reformation and "Catholic Reform" acceptable, or should the latter not be used to describe the response to the first two movements?

The dialogue report does not pose these questions, but it raises the challenge as to whether common historical hermeneutics should deal from the beginning with the issue of wanting to represent the fore-bears of the dialogue partner as positively as possible. A common hermeneutics will precisely have to stand the test of the criteria of historical-critical research if it is to offer an effective explanation for the redefinition of the mutual relationship in the present. It should be recognized that now the dialogue partners all agree that the Middle Ages were probably not so profoundly Christianized to the extent that Catholics had still been describing that era in the nineteenth century, but it was also not so "not as barbaric and decayed as their [Mennonite] restitutionist view depicted."(§63) In this way there are at least potential corrections hinted at in each historical tradition.

The Sixteenth Century – The Rupture between Catholics and Mennonites

"Anabaptists shared many of the common Reformation images of the Catholic Church" (§42) and consequently, also the allegations against the Catholic Church: works-righteousness, idolatry in the distribution of the sacraments, incompetence of the priests and the abuse of the pope as "the Antichrist." In addition, however, they also criticized the other reformers for their proximity to political power.[44] The unity of Church and State was quite simply the "fall" of the Church, with infant baptism being the most obvious manifestation of this unholy alliance.[45] For the Anabaptists the only goal could be the restoration (restitution) of the "apostolic church,"[46] which is not secured by passing on the episcopal consecration in an uninterrupted manner, but should be measured by the "compliance with the ethical and doctrinal content of the New Testament."[47]

Recent Anabaptist research, dating from the mid-1970s, has expounded the diversity and heterogeneity of the so-called "Anabaptist movement."[48] The rejection of infant baptism that was common to all Anabaptists moved them away from the Lutheran[49] and Zwinglian[50] side of the Reformation, and from the Roman Catholic Church, who shared with the Protestants their rejection and condemnation as heretics.[51] Since 529 C.E. (Emperor Justinian I) rebaptism was punishable by death. This sentence was renewed at the Diet of Speyer in 1529, which subsequently led to mass martyrdoms.

Hans-Jürgen Goertz reminds us that the Diet of Speyer has been called "the birthplace of Protestantism. However, it should not be forgotten that it also sounded the death knell of Anabaptism."[52]

The "Constitution" of this Anabaptist Mandate stated:

1. Anyone who performs or undergoes rebaptism, whether man or woman, is to be punished by death, without the need for a prior trial before an ecclesiastical inquisitorial court.

2. Those who recant their Anabaptism and are prepared to atone for their error shall be pardoned. However, they must not be given the opportunity, by banishment into another territory, to escape from constant surveillance and thereby perhaps relapse. Those who stubbornly persist in their Anabaptist faith are to be punished by death.

3. Those leading or promoting Anabaptism (preachers, main leaders, missionaries or rabble-rousers) should 'in no way' be pardoned, even if they recant.

4. Anyone who, following a first recantation, relapses and then recants again should not be pardoned again, but should receive the full punishment.

5. Those refusing to have their newborn children baptised are likewise subject to the punishment for rebaptism.

6. Any Anabaptist escaping into another territory should be arrested there and punished.

7. Any official who is not prepared to proceed forcefully, according to these orders, will incur imperial displeasure and severe punishment.[53]

Increasingly the Anabaptists perceived the representatives of the Roman Church as torturers and executioners, which is vividly reflected in documents such as the *Martyrs Mirror*,[54] and it was handed down in the following centuries as an image of the Catholics. On the other hand, the Anabaptists were for Catholics the "logical outcome of Protestant heresy and schism." (§43)

All this was complicated by the fact that during the sixteenth century, Catholic theologians were writing against people whom the state, at the request of both Catholic and Protestant princes, had already condemned to death at the Diet of Speyer (see para. 40 above), and who therefore lived outside the protection of the law. (§43)

The Religious Peace of Augsburg of 1555 (*cuius regio, eius religio*) is considered as an additional source of intolerance, which, through martyrdom, became a "common experience for Christians of all confessions." (§45)

The Report of the dialogue demonstrates a lot of understanding for those who did not know a better way to assess the "chaotic movement" of the Anabaptists. Ultimately Martin Luther made a sweeping charge that the "fanatics and Anabaptists" were responsible[55] for the Peasants' War and the Melchiorite-influenced Anabaptist "Kingdom of Münster" 1534-35, allowing "the rulers" to assume that all Anabaptists were basically prepared to be violent.[56]

The rejection of all forms of violence by the South German Anabaptists as seen already in the 1527 Schleitheim Articles,[57] along with other clear witnesses to nonviolence[58] did not lead church historians to make distinctions between violent and nonviolent Anabaptists. Speculations as to the reasons for this failure on the side of "the rulers" as on the part of the Roman Church representatives are not discussed here. After all, it is noted that of the total nearly 5,000 people in Europe who were killed in the sixteenth century because of their faith, half were Anabaptist or Mennonite, and that the majority were killed in Catholic territories.[59] Also, it is emphasized that, inversely, Catholics never had to suffer persecution at the hands of Mennonites. Yet "Mennonites need to rethink how difficult it must have been in the sixteenth century to sort out the differences among those who had rejected both Rome and Luther." (§51) Otherwise in Lutheran areas and in England, Catholics experienced martyrdom and in these regions Catholics also called for religious freedom.[60]

Among the interesting questions for further dialogue is: Why did this experience of martyrdom not result in an early reversal and reflection upon tolerance and persecution by Catholics who lived in Catholic regions? In the deliberations of the dialogue there was no discussion of the important perspective of those who were in power (or close to it), or those who were powerless, nor of those who appear to have played a determining role in the respective positions with the corresponding theological reflections concerning both the relationship of church and state, and of religion and violence. Statements that may apply to the political and social circumstances of the atrocities committed should never give the impression of wanting to serve as subsequent apologies if we are now actually to prepare the ground for a "healing of memories" through the joint study of history. An explicit (perhaps mutual) recognition of forebears' guilt could be more promising than the rather sweeping categorization as "victims" of all those involved.

This could become relevant in the designated "fields for further study," if the aim of developing a common hermeneutics is for a growing integration of the Mennonites into the larger society's political and social relationships, as well as for reflecting the growing experience of Catholics who are becoming a minority. A further, critical analysis could then ultimately also contribute to a correction of those images the denominations have of themselves in relation to others. Consequently such a re-reading of history could free Mennonites from their mentality of being a persecuted minority and lead Catholics to have more courage to actually accept responsibility for the errors of the past.

(2) Joint Consideration of Theology

The real motivation for this dialogue is grounded in the New Testament witnesses themselves, especially the high-priestly prayer. The divisions among Christians will be overcome in order that the world believes that the Father and the Son are one (see Jn 17:20-23), "speaking the truth in love" and "building itself up in love" (Eph 4:15-17). These are classic sources for the ecumenical movement. Furthermore, theological convergences should be identified just as the established differences are also identified. Yet it should be anticipated that both sides are limited in general to carrying forward their inherited positions and that, above all, dialogue will result in convergence formulations where unobstructed, direct reference to the biblical sources is possible for both. The inclusion of peace theology as a separate topic deserves special attention because so far this has been unparalleled in spearheading bilateral ecumenical dialogue.

The identity of a denomination lies not only in its expression of *what* it says and lives, but also in *how* it arrived at such statements and actions. In order to go from a mere description of the particular theological aspects of a tradition in order to arrive at a genuine dialogue, that would be, in my view as a Mennonite, to move necessarily from "considering theology together" to "doing theology together."

The Common Vocation of Witnessing for Peace

> Mennonites and Catholics can agree that God, 'who from one man has created the whole human race and made them live all over the face of the earth' (Acts 17:26) has destined humanity for one and the same goal, namely, communion with God's own self. Likewise, created in the image and likeness of God, human beings are called to unity with one another, through reciprocal self-giving. (§172)

Through the redemptive work of Christ peace is to be restored, which was lost in the fall. In this way "Christians are called to live a new life in peace with one another and with all humankind (cf. 2 Cor 13:11; Rom 12:18)." (§172)

For both dialogue partners Christian peace witness is rooted first in Christology. He, who "is our peace" (Eph 2:14), established reconciliation through the cross, which happened in order to become "signs of God's love for his enemies."[61] In the resurrection the completion of this reconciliation is confirmed. Therefore, the Church is "called to be a peace church," (§175) which seeks to overcome any form of hostility. Through baptism in the triune God, the internal divisions are overcome (Gal 3:28); hatred and violence among peoples and religions "are incompatible with the Gospel." (§175) "The Church has a special role in overcoming ethnic and religious differences and in building international peace."[62] With reference to the diverse meanings of *shalom* in the Old Testament this appeal for peace is extended to the whole of creation and gains its methodological orientation in the formation of what is "right," that is, just relationships (cf. Is 32:27; Ps 85,10 and 13). The Church is distinct from "mere human organizations" due to its shared commitment to religion and freedom of conscience in virtue of the dignity that is rendered to each person by God, in the same way as its comprehensive witness to society by its independence from all governmental influence. This is something the former state churches and the historic peace churches now formulate in common.

> We agree that the Gospel's vision of peace includes active non-violence for the defence of human life and human rights, for the promotion of economic justice for the poor, and in the interest of fostering solidarity among peoples. (§178)

It is clear that the renunciation of violence is broadened to both personal and structural forms of violence. Therefore, the term "freedom from violence" (*Gewaltfreiheit*) should be used in contrast to "non-violence" (*Gewaltlosigkeit*), as in the following formulation: "We hold the conviction in common that reconciliation, nonviolence, and active peacemaking belong to the heart of the Gospel (Matt 5:9; Rom 12:14-21; Eph 6:15)." (§179) Both sides recognize that the establishment of non-violent conflict resolution reduces the temptation to use force as a "last resort" (*ultima ratio*) – one of the known criteria in the doctrine of just war.[63] This active nonviolence belongs essentially to discipleship, in which the Church is appointed as the new community.

"Love of neighbour is the fulfilment of the law, and love of our enemies is the perfection of love (Rom 13:8; Matt 5:43-48)." (§180) This results in a clear obligation "to discern the signs of the times and to respond to developments and events with appropriate peace initiatives based on the life and teaching of Jesus (Lk 19:41-44)." (§181)

Such discipleship then involves the willingness to suffer, as the lives of many martyrs show.

> It is by uniting his own sufferings for the sake of truth and freedom to the sufferings of Christ on the Cross that man is able to accomplish the miracle of peace and is in a position to discern the often narrow path between the cowardice which gives in to evil and the violence which, under the illusion of fighting evil, only makes it worse. (John Paul II)[64]

For this reason it was necessary to cultivate "the peaceable virtues" (§184): forgiveness, love of enemies, respect for life and the dignity of others, moderation, gentleness, compassion and the spirit of self-sacrifice. Worship and prayer consequently belong to the core of Christian peace work, especially "ecumenical prayer services" because in these actions, the community experiences how to overcome its divisions with God and with one another in terms of faith.

With these far-reaching convergences one recognizes an extensive, theologically-reasoned appeal and commitment to peace by the Church, which pertains to the eschatological dimension: in discipleship the Church anticipates the Kingdom of God by incarnating "the new order of the Kingdom of God." It lives according to "messianic time." (§184) At first glance this chapter seems to constitute that part of the dialogue, which makes the changing relationship between Catholics and Mennonites most visible.

Still there remain divergences and differences, first of all, in terms of the relationship between Church and society. Political authority is seen by Catholics as part of the God-given human order in the world, yet this view is out of the question for Mennonites. For Catholics there is traditionally a high appreciation of the active acceptance of government offices, and naturally also respect for military service (§186), but should not detract from the advocacy for nonviolence, which is possible through objecting on the basis of conscience and resisting immoral orders. Mennonites still tend, however, because of their history, to distrust the State. Yet one could certainly judge this formulation as being stated in too general a manner, because since the sixteenth century the acceptance of government offices by Mennonites was always dependent on context as it is to the present, resulting in some cases of Mennonites even having served in the military.[65] This is not mentioned in the dialogue document.

Second, in this dialogue Catholics make it clear that they hold to the doctrine of just war, and consequently they cannot go along with Mennonites in the rejection of all forms of deliberate acts of violence. However, most surprising then, was the common conclusion, which recognized that in conflict situations, "both Catholics and some Mennonites acknowledge that when all recourse to nonviolent means has failed, the state or international authorities may use force in defence of the innocent." (§187) For the Mennonite position, the apparent dilemma can only be resolved as follows: "Christians should not participate in this kind of action." This argument can hardly be convincing, because even if the Church is seen as a separate community within society, what is the basis for the ethical legitimacy that force should be used by others in the society? Here the radical dualism of the Church and the world is represented in the sense of Schleitheim articles of 1527.[66] Accordingly, the "defenselessness" or nonresistance (*Wehrlosigkeit*) of the Mennonite side is advocated in the dialogue, namely, an attitude that has long been problematic for most contemporary Mennonite proposals for peace theology and ethics, which has been replaced by the position of active non-violence as was formulated in the end with the convergences.[67] In this way, the dialogue does not reflect the current state of discussion.[68]

The same is also true of the representation of the Catholic argument. For a long time the limitations and impossibilities of the doctrine of just war have been recognized (even in the era of weapons of mass destruction) and now the main focus has shifted to "just

peace."[69] Notwithstanding this nuance, the dialogue report emphasizes simply how virtuous military service could also be, and that the
position of just war maintains the means, "for the prevention and
limitation of conflict as well as for warranting force by political
authorities." (§187) For example, the war efforts by western nations
in Iraq, which the Pope John Paul II so vehemently opposed, were
legitimized precisely with this interpretation.[70] In this way, even the
violent persecution of Anabaptists in the sixteenth century could be
legitimated, but the issue of how just war theory relates to religious
persecution was not even discussed.

It is not sufficient in this instance to refer in general to a tradition-
ally-represented political ethic. Instead, one must ask the question as
to how basic theological axioms are related to challenges of ethical
duty in providing emergency assistance. Through the historically-
inherited findings presented in the dialogue, many of the consensus
formulations no longer appear to be as convincing.

Yet this dialogue was seen as a first step. Further areas for common
study are mentioned in the dialogue report. These include: the various
peace positions in relation to the apostolic faith, the question of what
place nonviolent peace initiatives hold in a Catholic peace theology,
how do human rights and justice relate to nonviolence in Mennonite
peace theology, the efforts toward a common, inter-contextual peace
theology, the role of the Church in the development of a culture of
peace, the relationship between theology of peace and unity of Christians and of all people, and the question of ethical adjudication.

Always added to these are questions concerning the ecclesiological
requirements of the respective positions, which were so powerful in
the history of theology; moreover, there are the sociological aspects
such as a denomination's minority or majority status, the situation of
persecution or the claim to be a state church. Is the Church called only
to "make peace" (ethics) or "to be a peacemaker" (which concerns the
nature of the Church)? The latter is suggested in the title of the
dialogue document. It is striking in the overall presentation that,
without the issue being further schematized, Catholics rather
narrowly connect the ethics of peace with the idea of unity, whereas

Mennonites consider ethics primarily in the context of testing through discipleship. Yet ethical and ecclesiological issues seem to hold the greatest potential for future considerations of the concept of ecclesial unity.

These remarks should suffice by way of showing how there is still great potential for mutual learning for both denominations in this field. With regard to some of these questions a new dialogue step was completed five years after the end of the dialogue, which enables further discussion. At the international level Catholics and Mennonites jointly wrote an article for the ecumenical "Decade to Overcome Violence, 2001-2010" organized by the World Council of Churches.[71] The biblical-theological, Christological and ecclesiological foundations of peace are again jointly formulated here, and the more current discussion on contemporary issues of peace ethics are even more strongly considered here.[72] Thus this text already presents an important addition to the report on the bilateral dialogue.

The Nature of the Church – Divergent Ways of Determining of the Relationship of Scripture and Tradition(s)

The Church is described in both traditions by using the familiar biblical images of God's people, the Body of Christ and the indwelling of the Holy Spirit, which are developed in reference to the Trinity. The foundation of the apostles and the prophets, as well as Scripture, bore witness to Christ, who is the "head." This belief is likewise expressed in the Apostles' Creed,[73] in which Scripture is valid as the supreme authority for the faith and life of the Church. Through baptism all people are offered membership in the Body of Christ and are enabled to receive the gifts of the Spirit "in a lifelong process of Christlikeness." (§95) The Lord's Supper/Eucharist connects believers and strengthens communion with the triune God. The Church is to be a visible congregation of believers, the community of a new humanity, because it is a presence and promise of redemption and "provides a foretaste of the glory yet to come." (§99) Mission is inherent in the nature of the Church, but its credibility suffers from the divisions among Christians.

"We agree that ministry belongs to the whole Church, and that there are varieties of gifts of ministry given for the good of all." (§100) Mennonites and Catholics jointly strive for a life of "holiness." (§101) "The gift of faith freely received provides the motivation for Christian works offered to the world as thanksgiving for the abundant grace we have been given by God." (§101) Christian education and formation are the preconditions for this. These formulations are a reassurance of a common ecclesiological basis and in this way could certainly be shared by most Christian churches.

Divergences first appear, as might be expected, in an encounter between the Roman Catholic Church and a denomination stemming from the Reformation, with the question of the relationship between Scripture and tradition. For Catholics, Scripture and Tradition form "the one sacred deposit of the Word of God." (§103) The "Holy Tradition" is clearly distinguished from the various human traditions, as being those that come forth from the apostles: "Through the same tradition the Church's full canon of the sacred books is known, and the sacred writings themselves are more profoundly understood ... (§8)."

> [S]acred tradition, Sacred Scripture and the teaching authority of the Church, in accord with God's most wise design, are so linked and joined together that one cannot stand without the others, and that all together and each in its own way under the action of the one Holy Spirit contribute effectively to the salvation of souls.[74]

For this reason "the whole body of the faithful who have an anointing that comes from the holy one (cf. 1 Jn 2:20, 27) cannot err in matters of belief." (§77) Something that has not yet been discussed, but is important for further dialogue, is the question of whether the Catholic view of the inerrancy of tradition might not conflict with the envisioned joint historical-critical research, even if one considers that this assumption of inerrancy is based solely on the "truths of salvation," and not on an interpretation of history.[75] Does this not at least offer the possibility that through recent historical research even earlier theological insights may be reconsidered and reformulated if necessary, and will possibly need to be revised? At the very least there are critical questions that result from this, which come from the perspective of a church of the Reformation concerning the understanding and role of tradition.

For Mennonites, the Church is a "community in discipleship" and therefore is also described as a peace church, because "peace is essential to the meaning and message of the Gospel and thus to the Church's self-understanding." (§90) Its doctrine and practice must be constantly reviewed "in the light of Scripture" and corrected (sic!), because traditions are biblical interpretations of this Christian doctrine and practice. "Tradition is valued, yet it can be altered or even reversed, since it is subject to the critique of Scripture." (§103) All the churches of the Reformation share this ability and necessity of the correction of tradition, which is the prerequisite of being *ecclesia semper reformanda*. The question of who has the authority is no longer part of the agenda at this point. The "means" of knowledge is Christ himself, "whom no one can truly know except insofar as he follow him with his life. And no one can follow him except insofar as he first knows him," according to the formulation of the Anabaptist leader, Hans Denck (ca. 1500-1527).[76]

Here the ecumenically-controversial question of mutual recognition as a church needs to be revisited, because if Mennonites and Catholics are in agreement as to how to interpret the Nicene Creed concerning the constitutive characteristics that define the Church, then they should also be able to recognize one another as a church of Jesus Christ. This of course presupposes the need to be able to express the apostolicity of the Church differently. However, the Roman Catholic Congregation for the Doctrine of the Faith re-established in 2007:

Why do the texts of the Council and those of the Magisterium since the Council not use the title of "Church" with regard to those Christian Communities born out of the Reformation of the sixteenth century? Response: According to Catholic doctrine, these Communities do not enjoy apostolic succession in the sacrament of Orders, and are, therefore, deprived of a constitutive element of the Church. These ecclesial Communities which, specifically because of the absence of the sacramental priesthood, have not preserved the genuine and integral substance of the Eucharistic Mystery cannot, according to Catholic doctrine, be called "Churches" in the proper sense.[77]

Here the sacrament is raised as the criterion *sine qua non* for apostolicity. In the discussions of the Commission on Faith and Order of the WCC,[78] already several years ago the attempt was made to establish the attribute of apostolicity in a more comprehensive context for the life of the Church. It has already been formulated together in the convergence statements of Lima:

> Apostolic tradition in the Church means continuity in the permanent characteristics of the Church of the apostles: witness to the apostolic faith, proclamation and fresh interpretation of the Gospel, celebration of baptism and the eucharist, the transmission of ministerial responsibilities, communion in prayer, love, joy and suffering, service to the sick and the needy, unity among the local churches and sharing the gifts which the Lord has given to each. [...] A distinction should be made, therefore, between the apostolic tradition of the whole Church and the succession of the apostolic ministry. (§B.35)[79]

Whether the Catholic Church actually institutes this distinction is questionable, yet this distinction is nothing less than the determinant of the churches' mutual recognition. Mennonites otherwise faced the question of whether they can recognize the apostolicity of the Catholic Church, if this in turn is seen as being determined *solely* upon the "sacrament of consecration" of apostolicity. Finally, the interpretation of apostolicity in ecumenical discussion processes for the Nicene-Constantinopolitan Creed in the U.S. (1990-1995) points out that the common peace witness of the churches is a station along the road toward unity in the present-day, joint confession of the apostolic faith: "Peacemaking is now acknowledged by all as an essential element of the apostolic faith."[80]

Catholics "hold to a ministerial, hierarchical priesthood" (§106), that differs from the laity "in essence and not only in degree," [81] given precisely by the sacrament of consecration. The authority of the priesthood is rooted in the priesthood of Christ. Mennonites as well as Catholics teach the "priesthood of all believers," which, however, takes on such a form that men and women are elected by the congregation or a regional community for service. In this way the "patterns of leadership vary from place to place and from time to time as they already did in the apostolic Church." (§91) Such ordinations are sometimes valid for a certain time, sometimes lifelong, but do not amount to a hierarchy. There does not need to be any special mention that Mennonites therefore, will never be able to agree with the absolute teaching authority of the Pope, or to make "religious submission of mind and will" as in the Catholic understanding, as is stated in *Lumen Gentium* (§25). For Mennonites the act of free will and the freedom of conscience are essential gifts of the Spirit (2 Cor 3:17), which originate solely from being directly bound to Christ.

The question for Catholics should be: what value does the gathered local church have in itself? In its presentation it is clear how much ecclesiality depends upon the office; unity has to take precedence over the diversity of the particular churches, "over all particular interests." (§81) The particular churches are organized around the bishops who in turn are bound in a fellowship with one another, especially with the Bishop of Rome.

The structure of the churches in both traditions diverges significantly. For the congregationalist understanding of the Mennonites, the Church is foremost the local congregation, the visible gathering of believers in one location, which in turn forms regional bodies. The Holy Spirit grants unity as a gift. Given the fact that this broader fellowship of local churches is barely reflected upon theologically, unity appears as a real desideratum for the Anabaptist-Mennonite tradition, which again becomes significant through this dialogue, yet this issue is not mentioned in the Report.

Which directions might be explored in further joint studies, given the extent of divergence between common principles in ecclesiology? Mennonites confess that although they "may have an implicit understanding of the role of tradition, little attention has been given to the role of tradition relative to Scripture and to the development of doctrine and ethics." (§107) Here the representation of the opinion of the congregation as a "hermeneutical community"[82] by Mennonites can still certainly contribute something toward a clarification, especially in contrast to a Catholic understanding of ministry. It would be an occasion to examine such far-reaching divergences and even differences concerning the question of the ordination of women. A further item is succinctly stated: "A comparative study of ministry, ordination, authority, and leadership in our two traditions is needed." (§110) The dialogue partners also note the question of the catholicity of the Church as another worthwhile field of study, along with the task of clarifying what each implies for the discussion concerning the invisibility and visibility of the Church. This is precisely what, in my opinion, must also be developed concerning its relevance for peace ethics.

Sacraments and Ordinances – Real Presence, Recognition of Baptism and Inter-Communion?

The Roman Catholic tradition's distinctive sacramental doctrine is easily contrasted with the explicitly non-sacramental understanding among Mennonites and one can hardly expect convergences at the start. The value of this section of the dialogue can be seen in the future potential for a common wording on baptism and the Lord's Supper/Eucharist, using a language that allows room for ongoing difference of interpretations between both churches. For both churches, baptism and the Lord's Supper are "extraordinary occasions of encounter with God's offer of grace revealed in Jesus Christ. They are important moments in the believers' commitment to the body of Christ and to the Christian way of life." (§128) Baptism in the name

of the triune God means a dying and rising with Christ, which signifies the outpouring and presence of the Holy Spirit in the lives of
believers and the Church. It is a public witness to the faith *of the
Church*, the incorporation into the Body of Christ and thus an unrepeatable act.[83]

Catholics interpret baptism as an initiation into the community of
the Church, the "sacramental bond of unity existing among all who
through it are reborn." (§104) Infant baptism, which is granted
because of the faith of the Church, is the beginning. However, the
"fullness" occurs only in confirmation and finally with receiving
Eucharist, which is the "summit of initiation" by which participation
in the Eucharistic Body of Christ also ensues. For Mennonites, infants
and children remain in "the care of God and the grace of Christ until
such a time as they freely request" (believer's) baptism. (§104)
Baptism cannot be based upon the faith of another person or the
congregation. Also it always presupposes a personal, accountable
confession.

The Eucharist is the remembrance of the suffering, death and
resurrection of Christ. It offers an opportunity to recognize one's own
sinfulness and to receive forgiveness. The congregation experiences
strength for its mission and service to justice, peace and reconciliation. The Lord's Supper expresses hope as the foretaste of the heav-
enly banquet. In the gathered congregation and in the proclamation of
the Word of God, the risen Christ is present, and he himself invites
others to the banquet.

The divergences appear all the more strongly as actual differences
when the detailed monographs are consulted. Here some of the implications might be noted as follows: For Mennonites, baptism and the
Lord's Supper "recall" the redemptive work of Christ (§139), yet for
Catholics they also "confer" grace. Catholics recognize the baptism
done by Mennonites, yet Mennonites do not baptize infants or children. The question of whether Mennonites recognize the baptism of
the Catholic Church or in some cases even request that baptism be
repeated, surprisingly is not addressed, even though the experience of
ecumenism consists precisely of the need for such clarification. One

clarification that may be recommended for further studies is the role of the faith of the Church, including the doctrine of sin and soteriology, and the study of the origin and development of the practice of baptism. In my opinion the fact that baptism marks a different point in the whole life process of growing in faith within each tradition, points to one direction for helpful engagement with each other in order to seek mutual understanding and recognition.[84]

Also relevant is the denominations' rather disparate understandings of the nature of Christ's presence in the Lord's Supper, because what for one is primarily a sign and symbol, is for the other the sacrament in which "sacrifice, made once and for all on the cross, is made really present under the species of the consecrated bread and wine, and presented to the Father ...." (§138) While Mennonites reject the idea of real presence in the elements, according to the Catholic understanding it contains all of Christ "truly, really and substantially."[85] For Mennonites, the invitation to the celebration of the Lord's Supper is valid for everyone, precisely because it is Christ and not the congregation who invites.[86] For Catholics, on the other hand, "full ecclesial communion" is a prerequisite for shared Eucharist, without distinguishing which form of community would be sufficient for Eucharist.[87] The question of joint communion does not appear in the list of fields for further study.

(3) Towards the Healing of Memories

For the "healing of memories" first a "cleansing" is required. This calls for a "spirit of repentance — a penitential spirit — on both sides for the harm that the conflicts have done to the body of Christ, to the proclamation of the Gospel, and to one another." (§191) The "penitential spirit" describes the reality of Vatican II, on the Catholic side.[88] Separations did not occur in absence of the guilt born by people on both sides, or to put it differently: neither side of the Church's division can claim innocence.[89]

The document ends with observations by the delegates from both sides. The prayer of John Paul II on the "Day of Pardon" at the turn of the millennium contains a confession of sins, "committed by members of the Church during the past millennium, and a plea to God for forgiveness." (§199) Thus, the sins were addressed which, "have harmed the unity of the Church" (§199) and those which were "sullying in this way the face of the Church." (§201) And even while acknowledging complete changes in the political and cultural circumstances, the Church is not relieved of its duty to "express profound regret for the weaknesses of so many of her sons and daughters."[90] In this way,

> Catholics in this dialogue can apply this spirit of repentance to the conflicts between Catholics and Mennonites in the sixteenth century, and can express a penitential spirit, asking forgiveness for any sins which were committed against Mennonites, asking God's mercy for that, and God's blessing for a new relationship with Mennonites today. (§202)

According to the Catholic understanding, of course the Church *in itself* cannot sin, because, being a mystery, it is a sacrament.

From the Mennonite side, also quoting from a previously existing document on Christian unity: "We confess that we have not done all we could to follow God's call to relate in love and mutual counsel to other brothers and sisters who confess the name of Jesus Christ as Lord and seek to follow him."[91] Despite consciously being a peace church, maximal efforts have not always been taken for the prevention of separations. "We regret Anabaptist words and deeds that contributed to fracturing the body of Christ." (§203) But also concerning the recent failures to encounter Catholics with love, they express regret and ask for forgiveness. Mennonites are committed to self-examination, to dialogue and common action, so "that the reconciling love of Christ is made visible," and they encourage any Mennonite brothers and sisters to join in this commitment.

Despite the significant theological differences that prevent full communion, the report recognizes that the "substantial amount of the Apostolic faith which we realize today that we share, allows us as members of the Catholic and Mennonite delegations to see one another as brothers and sisters in Christ" (§210), namely, without pronouncing a mutual recognition as "church" (see above).[92] The document concludes with a prayer and a request for a blessing, expressing a new quality of community that corresponds to the spirit of this dialogue.

We see here the first attempt to understand the mindset or "mentality" as the "living dynamics" of the historical events that led to divisions between Catholics and Mennonites. This requires effort to purge "from personal and collective conscience all forms of resentment or violence left by the inheritance of the past on the basis of a new and rigorous historical-theological judgment, which becomes the foundation for a renewed moral way of acting." (§192) The goal is "to reconcile" divergent memories together. In my opinion, it would be expedient for a reconciliation process to hope for mutual supplementations or corrections, while not succumbing to the danger of creating a sanitized view of history, merely for the sake of convergence. Finally, such a reconciliation process should facilitate finding a new means of cooperation in the spread of the gospel of peace. This could constitute the actual progress that was begun by the dialogue. It is a first step towards both the reconciled and reconciling action of the Church that is being carried out here: no more, but certainly not less! Further steps remain to be taken.

CHAPTER 3
THEME-CENTRED ECUMENISM
MULTILATERAL APPROACHES TO DOCTRINE FORMATION

> *to lead a life worthy of the calling to which you have been called*
> *... making every effort to maintain the unity of the Spirit in*
> *the bond of peace.*
>
> — EPHESIANS 4:1,3 (NRSV)

THE SECOND TESTING ground of ecumenism which is presented here takes the approach of focussing on a single theme. It will be shown how ecumenism is tested through concentrating on a subject which, although of central importance for all denominations, is one that has led to separations due to differences in doctrine. Such ecumenical opportunities for dialogue occur mostly multilaterally, involving several different denominations. Building on the successes of bilateral talks can be fruitful in most cases. In this way, the bilateral talks themselves encounter an issue and must face the larger context of different statements in different dialogues. The result is a complex set of doctrinal statements, which now requires a particular hermeneutical approach.[1]

In the multilateral dialogues, it is worthwhile to articulate the convergences that can be formulated, while noting the existing divergences that remain, especially those remaining differences which are actually of a church-dividing nature. Therefore, the question of ecclesiology always plays a role here and needs to be reflected upon in parallel with the central theme itself.

The mutual recognition of baptism by several churches in Germany in Magdeburg in 2007 offers a very good example of theme-centred ecumenism: it simultaneously allows for the recognition of this issue, one which has been a key, enduring, and previously church-dividing difference for the churches of the Anabaptist tradition, to be regarded as an additional task within this theme of ecclesiology. The following section, therefore, seeks to identify this difference in particular. Can there also be a mutual recognition between these traditions and those, who are already able to recognize each other's baptism in Magdeburg, so that this "issue" no longer has to be considered as church-dividing? Under what circumstances is it possible to achieve such a result despite the enduring doctrinal differences?

The Ecumenical Challenge of Mutual Recognition of Baptism – Infant Baptism and/or Adult Baptism?

a. The Ecumenical Horizon: A "Hermeneutic of Trust"

"Consensus is not the ultimate goal" – this is a pioneering notion by Dietrich Ritschl, which should be seen as an implied headline concerning the particular issue of defining the relationship between different denominations in the ecumenical movement.[2] Ritschl argues for a "hermeneutics of trust" in the ecumenical movement, which was supposed to bring about a "recasting of the concept of theological doctrine and of the understanding of consensus and dissent, as it is used in the ecumenical movement in bilateral talks today."[3] Ritschl sees this new orientation as urgently needed for ecumenism in the twenty-first century. It is a call to an

analytically proceeding, fundamentally theological and linguistic-philo-
sophical reflection upon the limits of the enormous claim that we have
made on the truth of our respective traditions' doctrines and the
immutability of their detailed formulations.[4]

This comprehensive task cannot be fulfilled here, of course. But
Ritschl's call represents the frame of reference for the following reflections on a very limited, but not insignificant problem between
churches of the Anabaptist tradition, who are committed to practicing
believer's or adult baptism, and those who also practice infant
baptism; such is the challenge of the mutual recognition of baptism.
For many in these denominations the difference between their
baptismal practices is the most visible and decisive characteristic of
distinction, because in each case it is a central axiom of the entire
theological (and especially ecclesiological) doctrinal system, directly
corresponding with other genuine doctrinal statements. Likewise the
lack, thus far, of the mutual recognition of baptism remains the
impediment to "pulpit and table fellowship" between Lutherans and
Mennonites. Yet after all that, it was possible to clarify a mutual
Eucharistic hospitality following the dialogue between the United
Evangelical Lutheran Church of Germany[5] (VELKD) and the Association of Mennonite Congregations in Germany[6] (AMG).[7]

Dialogue partners in the ecumenical movement are primarily
guided by the Pauline "exhortation"[8] in Ephesians 4:1-6, when ascertaining whether and how the different denominations can recognize
each other's baptisms. As a rule the call for "unity in the Spirit" is
taken up in a very direct and immediate way. This unity should be
preserved by a "bond of peace" because oneness is made by the one
body (the one universal Church), the one God understood as Trinity
("One God and Father of all," "one Lord" and "one Spirit"), the one
faith, and finally, the one baptism.

On all these issues of unity there have been considerable debates
throughout ecclesiastical and theological history, but also there have
been unifications. The confessional developments of the Church and
the denominations illustrate this strikingly. The "ecumenical creed" of

Nicaea (325) and Constantinople (381) engages at an early stage all these aspects, through to the one baptism. "We acknowledge *one* baptism for the forgiveness of sins."[9] Obviously, such clarifications were necessary since the beginning of the Church. And it is precisely these aspects of unity that have remained the "dividing points" between the denominations, as evidenced by the many different denominational developments and confession traditions. So what can be hoped for, if the denominations of the ecumenical movement are prepared at the beginning of the twenty-first century to heed this call in Ephesians once again, by turning in particular the issue of the *one* baptism?

A rough perusal of the situation of ecumenical dialogue on mutual recognition of baptism among those churches which are still separated will soon identify that, on the one hand, theological clarifications have already made it possible for actual movements to come together.[10] On the other hand, more such clarifications are pending. Since the lines of separation are apparently drawn most sharply between those churches which practice infant baptism as the norm, and those churches of the "Anabaptist tradition," the continuation of an ecumenical dialogue between these traditions appears to be particularly necessary and challenging.[11] However, one should remain aware that the boundaries of the understandings of baptism no longer run strictly along religious lines today, as Karl Barth clearly demonstrated by his commitment to believer's baptism in the distinction he drew between water and Spirit baptism.[12] Dietrich Bonhoeffer also took a critical look at infant baptism. Although baptism is not "a human invitation, but an invitation by Jesus Christ" and only based "in the gracious calling of the will of Jesus Christ," infant baptism could be granted only where the actual memorialization of baptism is guaranteed.[13]

To practice "hermeneutics of trust" here implies that at all times one may expect unequivocal differences from the other side, as well as being able to pursue the critical examination of one's *own* tradition with total intellectual honesty. Of course, an understanding of theological teaching is presumed, as formulated by Dietrich Ritschl:

We should always regard doctrines as offerings to the sister churches
(and to our own members) rather than as containers of truth, for
which there is no other *modus loquendi*. ... We would then not only
tolerate and allow the neighboring-doctrines to remain for our own
conception, but we reflect upon and test them much more curiously,
and at the same time, critically. A real competition for their articulation could begin and challenge the theological intelligence and imagination of the ecumenicist ...."[14]

This is the sense by which the following considerations are to be
understood.

b. The Dimension of the Question: Mutual Recognition as Church

The importance of mutual recognition of baptism in the ecumenical
movement in the twenty-first century can hardly be overestimated,
according to the bold thesis of the major German ecumenist of the last
century, Edmund Schlink:

> The most profound difference runs its course not between the Eastern
> Church and Augustine, nor between Thomas and Luther, nor even
> between Luther and Calvin, but between all of these on one side and
> Zwingli and the Baptists on the other. The most profound difference is
> not the acknowledgement or non-acknowledgment of infant baptism,
> but the understanding of baptism either as God's deed or as the deed
> of human obedience.[15]

Thus the classical formulation of the distinction in the theology of
baptism is made apparent.

In the reception of the convergence texts of Lima (*Baptism,
Eucharist, Ministry*, 1982)[16] the Fifth World Conference on Faith and
Order of the World Council of Churches in Santiago de Compostela
(1993) formulated with clear conviction:

If the baptism celebrated by a community is recognized, then what else in the life of that community may already be recognized as ecclesial? Insofar as they recognize each other's baptism, the churches may be at the start of developing a baptismal ecclesiology in which to locate other elements of shared belief and life.[17]

Of further interest, however, is not the presentation and consideration of theological arguments for each differently shaped doctrine and tradition. This is done in detail in an overwhelming number of excellent exegetical, historical and systematic-theological studies, and there is probably no aspect of this debate, which has not been processed.[18] Rather, the upcoming challenge for the whole of the ecumenical movement is to ask, what could actually be meant by the "mutual recognition of baptism"? On one hand, the answer to this question would seem to be a prerequisite for determining which convergence or even consensus would be necessary at all for such an advancement to take place, or which remaining divergences or even differences would have to be endured; on the other hand, one should be able to measure the consequences of the potential recognition for the mutual relationship. Therefore, if the mutual recognition of baptism in the twenty-first century is actually supposed to help deepen ecumenical community, then these questions must be answered.[19]

This problem is illustrated here first of all with the current example of the mutual recognition of baptism declared in Magdeburg (2007) concerning at least eleven churches in Germany. The focus will be on the bilateral Lutheran-Mennonite dialogue whereby we will inquire, by way of this example, as to which remaining issues need to be clarified. The situation of the broader, ongoing ecumenical dialogue is included to demonstrate the potential opportunities for convergence that were already formulated in part. The ultimate aim is to formulate the challenge in a nuanced way, namely, the mutual recognition of the *one* baptism for the particular denominations as well as for upcoming ecumenical dialogues. That is probably the way to proceed, ultimately, if one is to follow the dictum of Paul's exhortation.

c. Consensus, Differences and Divergences–The Example of Mutual Recognition of Baptism at Magdeburg in 2007

On 29 April 2007 eleven churches[20] in Germany celebrated the mutual recognition of baptism in the Magdeburg Cathedral.[21] Baptism is a "moving ecumenical sign," as declared in the latest position paper on baptism by the Evangelical Church in Germany (EKD).[22] And this mutual recognition of baptism "is an important fruit of ecumenical efforts and dialogues in the past twenty-five years since the publication of the convergence texts on Baptism, Eucharist and Ministry in 1982," as Konrad Raiser has rightly concluded.[23] Despite the limitation of its range, the statement represents an important step towards the full, visible communion of Christian churches in Germany and offers a more solid spiritual and theological foundation for the cooperation of the churches, as Raiser says. The latter must, however, still be tested, for after all, not all the member churches of the Council of Christian Churches in Germany (ACK) were able to take part: neither the two Eastern Orthodox churches, nor the churches of the Anabaptist tradition (Baptists and Mennonites).[24]

Starting from a common Christological confession, the declaration returned to the basic agreement on baptism that exists despite differences in ecclesiology. In what follows below, the elements are mentioned by which the Magdeburg Declaration expresses its understanding of baptism. In addition, the corresponding New Testament sources are indicated (in parentheses).

Furthermore, formulations of already-existing ecumenical texts are provided, which are not mentioned in the Magdeburg Declaration:

(a) Baptism is participation in the mystery of Christ's death and resurrection (Matt 3:13-17, Rom 6:3-5, Col 2:12; baptism is "rooted in the ministry of Jesus of Nazareth, in his death and in his resurrection");[25]
(b) Baptism "means new birth in Jesus Christ" (John 3:5; "the sign of new life through Jesus Christ"; Gal 3:27; the "action" of Christ, the "change of heart");[26]
(c) Baptism is receiving the "sacrament";

(d) Baptism is affirmation of God's love in faith;

(e) Through baptism, the baptized "are united with Christ and with his people at the same time in all times and places" (1 Cor 12:13; incorporation into the Body of Christ,[27] 1 Pet 2:9; viz. a "chosen people, a royal priesthood, a holy nation");

(f) Baptism is a "sign" of the unity of all Christians, whose foundation is Christ (Gal 3:27-28, 1 Cor 12:13; "Liberation into a new humanity in which the dividing walls of gender or race or social status are to be overcome").[28]

With regard to ritual practice, it is determined that any baptism will be recognized if performed:

(r1) according to the command of Jesus;

(r2) in the name of the Father and of the Son and of the Holy Spirit;

(r3) with the symbolic act of immersion in water or pouring of water.

(r4) The baptism that is accomplished in this manner is to be "unique and unrepeatable."

The statement suggests that these aspects are both necessary and sufficient for the mutual recognition of baptism. The question of why there is not a common understanding expressly provided by the Church, is subsequently addressed below.

Why could Mennonites (here as representatives of the churches of the Anabaptist tradition) not concur with this "basic agreement on baptism"?[29] In a preliminary, cursory dialogue session consisting of a multi-faith working group, a representative from the Anabaptist tradition (Baptists) had still been involved, although it was already assumed that the differences with the churches of the Anabaptist tradition would not be so quickly overcome. Then the Protestant Church in Germany (EKD) and the German Bishops' Conference (Roman Catholic), decided first to bilaterally develop a common text, which was then sent to all member churches of the ACK, coupled with the invitation, on the basis of this common text, to mutually recognize baptism. The condition was, however, not to make any more changes to the text: "So you have to decide on a yes or no."[30]

The Association of Mennonite Congregations in Germany (AMG) at first expressed its surprise and regret regarding such practices in the ecumenical movement, because they consider "baptism to be a unifying element that will eliminate confessional boundaries for us."[31] In the subsequent statement in which they qualified the text that had been presented for approval, they signaled agreement with those statements that are based directly on the witness of the New Testament. However, there were three issues in the formulations on which they could not agree because of the particular understanding of baptism and the baptismal practice in Mennonite congregations.

First, baptism is to be designated as a "sacrament," whereby all traditions not representing a sacramental understanding of baptism are excluded. In ecumenical dialogues one ought to clarify what is being expressed in this terminology and how the corresponding interpretation would potentially be verbalized differently in other traditions.

Second, the statement that "baptism thus accomplished is unique and unrepeatable" (r4) adequately described both the conviction and the common practice of Mennonite congregations, since "in principle" every baptism is recognized which is performed according to the described ritual (r1-r3). However, this is true for Mennonites only insofar as such a baptism would even be recognized as valid by the believers themselves. In addition, it is regrettable that there is so little attention paid to what is the key for the Anabaptist-Mennonite traditions' confession of faith. The Mennonite response also signalled willingness for further dialogue.

Among Mennonites, the invitation to the churches of the Anabaptist tradition to be merely present at the solemn recognition of baptism in Magdeburg – although it included the opportunity to offer a greeting – was taken as a clear sign that the changes taking place here should not lead toward "two-tier ecumenism." In the word of greeting itself, the Mennonites then expressed that the churches stemming from Anabaptist tradition of the sixteenth century cannot agree with this Declaration "due to biblical-theological reasons."[32] However, there was a sense that what was accomplished here in the mutual recognition of baptism was a significant step by the participating churches toward each other, including a wish for God's blessing "for the practical steps resulting from this agreement." Even though currently there is no unity on the question of baptism, it is acknowledged that we are nevertheless bound as "a fellowship of churches which confess the Lord Jesus Christ as God" and seek "to fulfil together their common calling to the glory of the one God, Father, Son and Holy Spirit. ('Basis statement of the Constitution of WCC and ACK')"[33]

For this process one may already derive what is a *consensus* in the interpretation of the contents of baptism:

1. Participation in Christ's death and resurrection (a);
2. New birth in Jesus Christ (b);
3. Affirmation of God's love in faith (d);
4. Union with Christ and at the same time with his people in all times and places (e);
5. All elements of the ritual (r1- r3, even the uniqueness and unrepeatability of baptism, r4).

The following *divergence* remains: The form of speech and the semantic content of a "sacrament" (c);

As *differences* the report notes: Adult baptism by those who have been baptized as infants, but now desire "believer's baptism."

What remains is to be noted as a *desideratum*: The emphasis on the active, individual confession in baptism.

As already mentioned above, the question of the ecclesiological implications of the mutual recognition of baptism comes to mind. Following from the declaration of belonging to the "community of believers" it must be concluded that the other denominations will be recognized by Mennonites as actually being part of the Church. Obviously, the mutual recognition of baptism is not considered as a precondition. But how can that be if baptism is precisely what represents the individual union "with Christ and together with his people in all times and places" (e)? This question will be further considered in parallel in order to assess the coherence of theological doctrines and ecumenical statements.

In essence, the persistence of dissent especially from the Anabaptist tradition (and those Orthodox churches who have not signed the declaration) needs to be *jointly* processed, if justice is also to be served toward the *joint* responsibility for the ecclesiological implications of the one baptism. This overall assessment by Konrad Raiser of the status of ecumenical dialogue after Magdeburg is as follows: "For the churches who have adopted the declaration, it is time for a critical review of their own practice of baptism."[34] The current situation of dialogue would not be adequately evaluated now if only those which were not able to agree with the previously formulated consensus needed to critically investigate their own tradition in order to reach a potential agreement later on. In fact those churches who already expressed this mutual recognition among themselves are facing this very challenge. Indeed the significance of theological doctrines may not be judged on the basis of the numerical value of their followers (especially as it is already clear that these figures are shifting in the context of global ecumenism). Rather, they must be discussed by the mutual and self-reflexive consideration of the justifications for their reasoning. For this purpose, continued ecumenical dialogue is inevitable if the issue of the unity of the one baptism is to be taken seriously.

d. A *Desideratum*: Individual Confession in Baptism

In the following, the focus on practical examples will be restricted to the relationship between Lutherans and Mennonites, as to concentrate upon and properly assess what is meant by the divergences, differences and *desiderati* in ecumenical dialogue.[35]

The preamble of the report on the Lutheran-Mennonite dialogue from France cites the Leuenberger Agreement[36] (the churches of the Anabaptist tradition are not recognized as belonging to the Community of Protestant Churches in Europe). This reference was made in order to place emphasis on the common basis of all the churches of the Reformation, including Mennonites, so that at the outset it was not necessary to address the mutual prejudices handed down historically. The Reformers

> were at one therefore in confessing that the life and doctrine of the church are to be measured by the original and pure testimony of the Gospel in Scripture. They were at one in testifying to the free and unconditional grace of God in the life, death and resurrection of Jesus Christ for all those who believe this promise. (Leuenberger Agreement, 1973, §4).[37]

There is no dispute then between Lutherans and Mennonites, on whether life *and* doctrine are to be aligned solely on the principles of Scripture. In this way, "in order that the biblical message can be the gospel for us, the Holy Spirit is needed."[38] The free and unconditional grace of God (*sola gratia*) comes to each one in the life, death and resurrection of Jesus Christ (*solus Christus*), by faith alone (*sola fide*). Thus, the Reformation elements of exclusivity form a common basis for further doctrinal consensuses.[39] "Justification as the process of God's acquitting and adopting the sinner is very closely connected with the sanctification and renewal of a human, thus becoming enabled to follow Jesus Christ."[40] Certainly it is also seen that this common heritage in the Lutheran and Anabaptist/Mennonite churches/congregations was to some degree represented with different emphases.

Surprisingly the similarities in the understandings of baptism between Mennonites and Lutherans are far reaching.[41] In addition to the above-mentioned aspects of this consensus (a, d, e, f) it can be further determined (again, the corresponding New Testament quotations and formulations from multilateral ecumenical dialogues are supplied to demonstrate how apparently grounded and ecumenically far-reaching this consensus is):

(g) baptism is instituted by Christ (Matt 28:19, Mark 16:15-16);
(h) baptism results from the work of the Holy Spirit (it is a gift of the Holy Spirit,[42] Titus 3:5, renewal by the Spirit; Rom 8:15f, receiving the Holy Spirit, Eph 5:14, illumination through Christ);
(i) the belief in baptism is necessary for salvation (1 Cor 6:11, confession, cleansing, forgiveness, sanctification,[43] 1 Pet 3:20f, the experience of salvation out of the water, 1 Cor 10:1f, exodus from bondage).

Consistent with the Mennonite tradition, the baptismal aspects of confession and discipleship become more prominent in the dialogue with the Lutherans:

(j) baptism is the beginning of a new life with Christ and, therefore, the call to discipleship.[44] ("In the present, the solidarity of Christians with the joys and sorrows of their neighbours, and their engagement in the struggle for the dignity of all who suffer, for the excluded and the poor, belongs to their baptismal vocation.");[45]
(k) baptism also occurs in the consciousness of the congregation's commitment to the member who is baptized, accompanying and strengthening each individual;
(l) baptism is a sign that gives the believer assurance.

The *desideratum* of the active confession in baptism is explained here in a way that can be referred to in any future multilateral ecumenical encounters (see the similar statements in the Catholic-Mennonite dialogue).[46]

The eschatological dimension of baptism should still be added which is found in the reports from multilateral ecumenical dialogues:

(m) baptism is a sign of the Kingdom of God[47] (cf. Eph 2:6); and participation in the Kingdom of God and the life of the world to come.

With regard to the ritual it may be added that in the act of baptism,

(r5) the assurance of the grace of God goes forth "in prayer and laying on of hands (blessing)."[48]

In the context of these consensus formulations, we see how divergences and differences, which previously prevented the mutual recognition of baptism, can now be more effectively explored.

e. Differences between the Exclusivity of Adult Baptism and the Inclusivity of Infant Baptism – Doctrinal Complementarity?

In order to perceive differences, it is first important to note the particular denominational perspectives as to not sidestep the poignancy of the differences. Secondly, the decisive gain from ecumenical encounters lies in the subsequent *joint* consideration of an issue's various theological and practical aspects. Here ecumenism is constantly faced with the creative task of presenting theological content in a common form of verbal expression, without abandoning the mature perceptions of the participating church traditions, namely, the very things they consider important. This cannot happen simply through attrition. This conciliar and reflective process already holds the potential to establish new emphases and to make new discoveries. Sometimes corrections even arise in the conception of their own doctrines, insofar as the denominations can accommodate this within their own doctrinal development, something which may be assumed at least in the churches of the Reformation.

The challenge of the mutual recognition of baptism is manifested in different ways. For some it lies concretely in the accusation of "rebaptism," that is, an adult baptism of those who were already baptized as infants. However, this accusation already assumes that infant baptism is also recognized by Mennonites as a form of legitimate baptism, which is why Mennonites, in turn, reject the accusation of being "rebaptizers." For Mennonites, the difference manifests itself in the so-called "indiscriminate baptism" of infants, as they were not in a position to formulate a personal confession of faith. This charge, in turn, assumes that the faith and the action of the congregation's confession and accompaniment are not considered sufficient for baptism; moreover, they charge that infant baptism is not a sufficient basis for an affirmation of personal faith that is possible later on (in confirmation), a claim that the Lutheran churches reject. It is immediately clear that there exists a further need for clarification here and this appears to be possible if there is a basic willingness to critically scrutinize the common accusations, charges and claims jointly, *with* the dialogue partners, i.e. to mutually accommodate those different perspectives in their own deliberations.

Lutherans already recognize in their self-critical assessment of the condemnations in the Augsburg Confession (1530) the following:[49]

The present-day Mennonites consider their view to be confirmed by recent exegetical studies, namely, that in the New Testament writings, baptism upon personal profession of faith is the most clearly documented practice. Therefore, they are retaining their understanding of baptism. They also expect from Christians who transfer that they accept and share this understanding of baptism. But they do not deny in principle the validity of infant baptism, because this baptism can get them involved in the argument about the gracious action of God.[50]

The remaining differences in the understanding of baptism do not seem to amount to a situation of absolute division, because one denomination now begins to understand the other in their respective interpretations of New Testament statements as defined in the corresponding theological reasoning.

But how can the legitimacy of each other's doctrine be measured? "For Lutherans it is acceptable that baptism be represented as God's gift and then confession can come at a separate time as the response of the baptizand (infant baptism and confirmation)."[51] They emphasize that "God's action in baptism is valid in every case. Doubts as to the timeliness and appropriateness of each and every confession on the human side, in the Lutheran understanding, do not override this validity that might lead to a repudiation of infant baptism or to its 'repetition.'"[52] But "in the practice of baptism upon confession of faith, with the gift of God on the one hand and the response of the candidate on the other, [Mennonites] see a substantively and chronologically necessary connectedness."[53]

Mennonites in France stated in a regional dialogue with Lutherans: "The Mennonite Church only practices the baptism of believers and baptizes all persons who come and request it, regardless of whether one has already been baptized as a child in another church."[54] In a much more cautious and nuanced way, the Mennonites in Germany formulated a statement a few years later: "As a rule Mennonite congregations of the AMG accept Lutheran Christians as being validly baptized and upon their transfer ask them to offer a personal commitment to Jesus Christ before the congregation in a worship service."[55]

As such there is a certain recognition of what is already formulated as a "completed baptism" according to the Lutheran tradition. Otherwise how could someone who is transferring be recognized as "validly baptized," with a mere personal commitment to Christ before the congregation being seen as "sufficient," and if adult baptism is not considered a condition for admission as a member? Obviously the baptismal status of individuals *can* already be recognized as valid. In this way, at least this clarifies what is considered "valid" for those individuals as a complete baptism, although a personal confession must still be given.

Furthermore, it becomes apparent that for Mennonites, the individual, free choice of the person concerned is rated higher than "formulas of recognition" between denominations. As such, it certainly can occur that someone who was baptized as an infant is also baptized as an adult, which from the Mennonite side does not contradict the requirement of a baptism's uniqueness or unrepeatability (r4), since in such a case, the infant baptism is not counted. It can be concluded again, that baptism performed by a Lutheran congregation is neither *generally* viewed as "valid" nor *generally* viewed as "invalid." But if Mennonite congregations proceed in this way, valuing the decision of the individual believer more highly than the relations between denominations, then this raises a number of important questions regarding the ecclesiological implications of their baptismal theology – and these will be discussed at greater length below.

The dialogue partners in the U.S. left this question as yet unanswered and have still not provided a document of the results: "It is not clear to what extent these differences [i.e. between the bases for exclusive adult baptism, or the legitimacy of infant baptism] are simply ones of emphasis, and to what extent they might be shaped by different anthropologies and/or ecclesiologies."[56] Consequently the dialogue partners in the United States recommended "that the Evangelical Lutheran Church in America and the Mennonite Church USA authorize continuing conversation on the divergent practices of baptism and confirmation identified in this common statement to determine whether they can be understood to be complementary."[57]

The examination of the complementarity of the different baptismal doctrines is a conceivable alternative to a simple acknowledgement of the differences. The Lutheran-Mennonite dialogue in Germany acknowledged precisely that the one-sided emphases which are sometimes presented on behalf of denominational traditions only give expression to the gospel truth when seen in their complementarity to others.[58] This is expressed in view of the resulting understanding of baptism and in the multilateral talks when this issue was formulated in the convergence statements of Lima:

> Baptism is both God's gift and our human response to that gift. [...]
> The necessity of faith for the reception of the salvation embodied and
> set forth in baptism is acknowledged by all churches. Personal commit-
> ment is necessary for responsible membership in the body of Christ.[59]

But if this complementarity is acknowledged, then the charge against re-baptism is not only understandable, it is justified and thus an examination of this practice on the side of the churches of the Anabaptist tradition is rather urgent.

Another observation is added here: "However, infant baptism is not the only form of baptism that is practiced in Lutheran churches."[60] Do Mennonites generally recognize that *adult* baptism is also practiced in the Lutheran church? According to the consensus that has so far been formulated, that is what Mennonites would require, yet it can be assumed that a full consensus in the doctrine of baptism shall in no way be a precondition for the mutual recognition of baptism. In this respect the question under discussion can further clarify in what sense is the discussion about the "official recognition of baptism among the churches": Under what conditions can *the baptismal status of a person from other denomination* generally be recognized?

f. Convergences in the Interpretation of the Act of Baptism as a Process of Christian Initiation

For the possibility of complementarity, not only regarding doctrine but also in terms of the issue stated above, namely, seemingly mutually-exclusionary practices of baptism, there are further common formulations that point to constructive dialogue: "Lutherans and Mennonites view baptism not only as a one-time event, but also as an ongoing process that plays a crucial role in the Christian life, both corporate and personal."[61] For both denominations the appropriation of the meaning of baptism continues throughout the Christian life. "Mennonites recognize that even those who are baptized remain always in need of forgiveness."[62]

Thus, on the one hand it is held that the joint reflections on the meaning of baptism, both for the individual and for the congregation/church, cannot be reduced to the instance of the act of baptism, but it is to be placed into a broader frame of reference in the life of the congregation/church. Thus, the perspective is now expanding significantly. This way of thinking is not new in the ecumenical movement, but is becoming increasingly important for the potential mutual recognition of baptism. The convergence texts formulated in Lima already led the way to seeing baptism as "life-long growth into Christ."[63] Therefore, the differences are interpreted below more as differences in "baptismal practices" than in doctrine, therefore the mutual recognition of both practices is advocated.

Here it is first necessary to explain the convergence in the evaluation of exegetical findings. At Lima it was noted:

> While the possibility that infant baptism was also practised in the apostolic age cannot be excluded, baptism upon personal profession of faith is the most clearly attested pattern in the New Testament documents.[64]

If Mennonites agree to that, then a general reference to the New Testament evidence for the rejection of infant baptism alone is not sufficient. They could quite easily justify – both despite and in accordance with this observation – their reasons for continuing to not baptize infants in their congregations, even if they now recognize as "valid" the baptismal status of one who was baptized as an infant.

Further investigation of liturgical orders of the Early Church[65] by the WCC's Commission on Faith & Order recognized it was assumed early on that baptism includes instruction, personal confession and the act of immersion in water, leading to integration into congregational life.

> Baptism is not only a one-time liturgical act, but it must be understood as an initiation into the community of believers, as a lifelong process of growing Christian identity and recognition.[66]

This presents an urgent request for the Mennonite practice of the unconditional priority of the individual profession of faith before the congregation/church. For if one's reflections remain within these broader frames of reference, then it seems *uncompelling*, that the different dimensions of baptism should be given more or less priority, if *all* of these dimensions of the *act* of baptism are actually considered essential and constitutive. From this perspective at least we can then reconstruct why it is *possible* for another denomination to locate the water ritual at the beginning of the whole process. In baptism faith pertains to the individual just as it does to the Church as a community of believers.

The Eighth Report of the Joint Working Group between the Roman Catholic Church and the WCC[67] speaks consistently of "Christian initiation,"[68] and a "pattern of baptismal initiation"[69] as a process. The report therefore proposes "that each church, even as it retains its own baptismal tradition, recognizes in others the one baptism into Jesus Christ by affirming the similarity of wider patterns of initiation and formation in Christ present in every community."[70] Moreover, "children were baptized because God's call to salvation seemed to bear on them no less than on adults."[71] However, the working group also says that the convergences thus described are based on the fact that the churches

> recognize a paradigmatic and normative quality of baptism performed upon personal profession of faith, illustrated in the New Testament and practised by all churches, as the most explicit sign of the character of baptism.[72]

Yet this gives rise to a genuine question to be posed of Lutheran baptismal practice if they cite as the main argument for infant baptism, that the prevenient grace of God and the unconditionality of baptism is more clearly indicated in infant baptism than in adult baptism. Otherwise one might conclude that it is more important for Lutherans to emphasize the grace of God in the baptismal rite, than to represent the whole of the substance of baptism. Such reasoning must in turn appear unconvincing to Mennonites, if they are to affirm the argument of baptism as a lifelong process.

In those churches which *also* practice infant baptism, it appears now that some shift in the accentuation of their own doctrine has become possible, which is to be noted and taken seriously by the churches of the Anabaptist tradition: it will be noted critically that infant baptism in the Latin tradition primarily depended upon the theology of Augustine, which, in a dispute with the Pelagians, took the view that one can expose unbaptized children in case of their death to the risk of not being freed from original sin.[73] What is now being established is:

> A restored theology of baptism and a critical re-evaluation of certain explanations of the consequences of original sin for children would give increased weight to the Christological and ecclesiological reality of baptism.[74]

Three elements are proposed as a framework for considering the baptismal initiation:

1. Instruction / edification in faith
2. Baptism with water
3. Participation in congregational life

All three elements are present in the ritual for all baptizing churches, whether or not they are present in the same way and in the lifelong process of Christian discipleship. This process was marked by its

> continual formation in faith, recollection of baptismal grace and promise, and deepening participation in the life of the church. [...] It is a convergence that is compatible with and even enriched by the fact that different traditions emphasize one or other element of the pattern and put them together in different ways.[75]

This is expressed, for example, in the blessing of newborn infants in some churches of the Anabaptist tradition. The convergence statements of Lima had already rightly pointed out that in some of the churches of the Anabaptist tradition they,

> encourage infants or children to be presented and blessed in a service which usually involves thanksgiving for the gift of the child and also the commitment of the mother and father to Christian parenthood.[76]

The report of the Joint Working Group understands this reference as follows:

> For people so welcomed into the church in childhood, baptism in adult age can be the personal expression of the climax of a journey of conversion and faith, which is one of the principle ways in which the scriptures speak of it.[77]

From these observations and considerations it can now be stated by way of summary that the complete consensus in the doctrine of baptism is by no means a condition for the mutual recognition of baptism or the recognition of *one* baptism. Rather, there are convergences in the common understanding of the biblical witness and the common interpretation of the tradition. Thus, the different teachings are not just tolerated, but can be appreciated as an enrichment of the ecumenical community. In this sense, the Joint Commission of the WCC and the Roman Catholic Church notably formulated:

> Those traditions that practise only this form of baptism [i.e., adult baptism] in their pattern of initiation maintain a living witness to the reality of baptism the churches affirm together, and express powerfully the shared conviction that baptism is inherently oriented to personal conversion. Those traditions that practise infant baptism as part of their pattern of initiation maintain a living witness to the initiating call and grace from God that the churches agree enable human response, and express powerfully the shared convictions that infants and children are nurtured and received within the community of Christ's church prior to any explicit confession.[78]

Thus, the report of the Joint Working Group may suggest that every denomination, even if it retains its own baptismal tradition, would "recognize in others the one baptism into Jesus Christ by affirming the similarity of wider patterns of initiation and formation in Christ present in every community."[79]

One could further pose the question as to whether such

approaches as taken here could function analogously and be of value for further dialogues concerning the joint celebration of the Eucharist. Lutherans and Mennonites have already noted that the celebration of the Eucharist authorizes having a different focus in the experience of reception and in the human response to this divine gift:

> Forgiveness, celebration of Christ's presence, commemorating God's saving acts, communal meal and eschatological hope belong together. One must not be played off against the other as alternatives, even if they are perceived and emphasized differently in the respective tradition.[80]

In this way these dialogue partners already follow a hermeneutic that neither assumes full agreement in doctrine, nor the emphasis upon individual aspects in order to "recognize" each other as participants and invite each other to the Lord's Supper (eucharistic hospitality).

g. 'Conformity to Scripture' as the Sufficient Criterion of for the *Community of Protestant Churches in Europe*

The detailed dialogue series between the Community of Protestant Churches in Europe (CPCE)[81] and the European Baptist Federation (EBF) also illustrate how these convergences were put to the test, namely, as a dialogue between infant-baptizing traditions and one that refuses to baptize infants.[82] The CPCE 2001 had decided in Belfast, with representatives of the Baptist conventions of Europe to engage in theological dialogue on baptism, including "other issues 'which are perceived on either side to stand in the way of mutual church fellowship.'"[83]

For the CPCE churches the unity of the community of churches is affirmed

> when the proclamation of the Word and the administration of the sacraments according to the Gospel are mutually recognized. In this

case church fellowship must be declared and the communities understand one another as true expressions of the One Church of Jesus
Christ.[84]

This Protestant community of churches therefore does not require
the recognition of a different doctrine of baptism, but rather the recognition that each other's doctrines are valid "according to the gospel,"
according to the principle of *sola scriptura*. This criterion is, as we saw
above, relevant for the Mennonites. If the churches of the Anabaptist
tradition followed the methodology of "Leuenberg," then the key
question is therefore whether infant baptism, as it is performed in the
other churches of the Reformation, can *also* claim to be an expression
of the gospel.

Even the dialogue between CPCE and EBF focuses on the
procedural aspect of Christian initiation:

> Baptism is thus the sign and central event of initiation, or the begin-
> ning of the Christian life, but it is not the whole of the beginning.
> Initiation is not complete unless baptism is accompanied by repen-
> tance and initial Christian nurture, until the point is reached where a
> person can make his or her own grateful response of 'yes' to God, is
> commissioned for service in the world, and shares in the Lord's
> Supper for the first time.[85]

The focus of this process, of course, remains on the actual event of
baptism and the participating churches logically ask if it might be
possible to "place different forms of baptism at different places within
a commonly understood process of Christian initiation."[86] In addition
one might ask if such an interpretation can be recognized by all as
being "in accordance with the gospel," but this remains the decisive
testing question, from which a mutual recognition would then logically need to arise.

In this dialogue, however, Baptists maintained that they feel
"obliged by their understanding of the biblical testimony only to prac-
tise the baptism of believing disciples as being according to the

Gospel."[87] However, this does not yet include a statement in principle as to whether infant baptism *can* be "in accordance with the gospel" for others, while still maintaining one's own traditional *practice* of adult baptism, recognizing it as the "clearest" testimony. There could not (yet) be a clarification that one would always abstain from "re-baptism." This is especially the case when infant baptism is not followed by Christian instruction.[88] Basically, the other churches would have to say in such cases that they will consider such baptism, at least as an incomplete process of initiation. But if we can speak together here of infant baptism as an incomplete initiation process, then that should not result in wanting to re-perform the water rite, but rather that the efforts of the community of the faithful should address what aspects remain for completing the initiation process.[89] In this respect, the reasoning of the Baptists is less convincing.

For the CPCE churches, but especially for Lutherans, there is still a general responsibility with regard to the early condemnations against Anabaptists. They say at the end of this series of dialogues that the accusations of the *Augsburg Confession* do not pertain to Baptists today, "with the exception of the one expressed in CA 9. (They condemn the Anabaptists, who reject the baptism of children, and say that children are saved without baptism.)"[90] They are not only saying that they consider the repetition of baptism as not being in accordance with the gospel (which is an ecumenical consensus, as noted above), but that they are *the very people* who teach such and it is not just the teaching that is "condemned" (*damnant anabaptistas*). This is not ethically responsible if one follows the basic Augustinian distinction between the person and action, such that a doctrine can be "condemned," but not a person; nor is ecumenical progress being shut down here as it is already understood that in terms of baptismal practice, Baptists do not believe themselves to be in violation of the prohibition against repetition. This question needs to be clarified by the Lutheran side or the CPCE as a whole.

h. From Divergence to Convergence: Sacraments

Mennonites had raised an issue concerning the mutual recognition of baptism before Magdeburg in 2007, namely, that by using the definition of baptism as a "sacrament," from the outset all the churches with non-sacramental understanding of baptism are excluded. In this way they point to a problem that has been noted in the discussions of the WCC as an enduring difference. Although the convergence statements of Lima had stressed that all churches consider the dimensions of grace and faith as essential to baptism, the "hot potato" of "whether baptism itself 'effects' grace or is only the ethical answer of the baptized" remained open, as André Birmelé noted.[91]

Does the sign also have the effect of what it signifies? The latest ecclesiological study of the WCC asks whether the historical development of the concepts of "ordinance" and "sacrament" are actually so different, as both could be understood as descriptions of that act of people gaining new life in Christ.[92] Here the terms "sign" and "instrument" replace the traditional language of "symbol" and "sacrament."[93]

Therefore one might consider whether the corresponding meanings that are imparted by the word "sacrament" are expressed differently in language by the *non-sacramental*[94] churches of the Anabaptist tradition. This will determine whether this issue is noted as an actual divergence or if there may be potential for converging formulations.[95]

With reference to the Augustinian interpretation *accedat verbum ad elementum et fit sacramentum* ["The word is added to the element, and there results the Sacrament, as if itself also a kind of visible word"],[96] in the Lutheran-Mennonite dialogue the following divergence was established: Lutherans use the term "sacrament" for this sign of divine action, because sacraments are the visible Word of God and desire to support faith and strengthen it. "By contrast, Mennonite Christians avoid this designation because they fear it may be misunderstood as magic."[97] Yet Mennonites, thanks to a greater understanding through communication, the Mennonite side is increasingly prepared to recognize what 'sacrament' means, without including this term in their common speech.[98]

Mennonites will need to more precisely explain what is "particular" about baptism if they want to maintain the different levels of meaning of baptism that they also gather from the witness of the New Testament.

Lutherans and Mennonites confess together that baptism and communion are "signs of God's gracious action," that is, "the assurance of forgiveness and the promise of Christ's being present in the power of the Holy Spirit."[99] Through the preached word and those words that are associated with the acts of baptism and the Lord's Supper, God speaks to the person as a whole and moves one to a life of faith and discipleship. If this adequately describes what a sacrament *means*, then this already would present a potential formulation for convergence, which in the future would not need to impede the mutual recognition of baptism. The remaining difference would then lie only in historically over-burdened terminology, which would always re-import the former disputes and separations that resulted, and would be an unnecessary hindrance to convergence *on the issue* itself.

One example is reminiscent of the Marburg debate of 1529 between Luther and Zwingli.[100] In the *joint* rejection of a "magical" sacramental understanding, and one that would be opposed to that of the medieval church, Luther wanted to be sure to hold that the gift of God in the sacrament does not depend on faith, even if that gift could only be received in faith.[101] Zwingli, however, the original teacher of many Anabaptists in Switzerland,[102] wanted to emphasize with his distinction between "external signs" and "inner (spiritual) gifts," namely, that the elements themselves are not carriers of the gift of salvation, but they are only signs of the salvation that is *already being realized* in Christ. And this salvation could be received through faith alone.[103] If this powerful difference from the sixteenth century can be manifested today in new, converging forms of language, as a new mutual understanding within an entirely different historical context, then the bold thesis of Edmund Schlink (see above) must be revised. Consequently the use of the term "sacrament" alone is not a sufficient justification for further denying the mutual recognition of baptism, especially when it is clear that leading Anabaptists in the sixteenth century themselves deliberately maintained this language, such as Menno Simons[104] and Pilgrim Marpeck who explicitly argued for the retention of the term "sacrament."[105]

However, this issue begs further, in-depth, joint study if real theological differences are not to become lightly veiled by new empty words that carry no benefit of clarification in themselves.[106] Also there clearly remains the issue of the "Mennonite understanding of Christ's institutions" being not simply "identical with what the Lutherans call a sacrament."[107] The proposal of Birmelé that suggests the concept of *promissio* could prove helpful here to bridge the gap between a "causative" and "cognitive" understanding of baptism.[108]

i. The Coherence Argument: Mutual Recognition as the Church

Does the mandatory mutual recognition as the Church then follow from the mutual recognition of baptism? This question now preoccupies the denominations that have expressed the recognition of baptism in Magdeburg. In view of the Anabaptist churches' relations with other churches of the Reformation, the question is different. If different denominations recognize each other as churches, is the mutual recognition of baptism, or the baptismal status of an individual in Christ, not already implied? Formulated negatively, doesn't the rejection of a baptism that is completed in another denomination necessarily also preclude their mutual recognition as churches?

The report of the Joint Working Group formulated precisely that

> the ecclesiological implication which follows is that among the basic issues which need to be resolved in order to overcome the divergence on infant baptism are the questions of the nature and purpose of the church and its role in the economy of salvation.[109]

This question on the ecclesiological implications, as already indicated above and most poignantly in Santiago de Compostela in the context of describing any renewed "baptism ecclesiology," must now be considered separately below, if there is to be any coherence in their own theological views as well as in ecumenical statements.

> The Church seeks to be a community, being faithful as disciples of Christ, living in continuity with the apostolic community established by a baptism inseparable from faith and metanoia, called to a common life in Christ, manifested and sustained by the Lord's Supper under the care of a ministry at the same time personal and communal and having as its mission the proclamation in word and witness of the Gospel.[110]

This is how the community of the churches formulated the issue in Santiago de Compostela (1993). In a bilateral dialogue, Lutherans and Mennonites stated jointly, "baptism is the sole sacrament or ordinance which initiates people into church membership."[111] They of course also say that "personal commitment is necessary to be a member of the Body of Christ."[112] Thus the uniqueness of the unrepeatability of baptism is established and the procedural character of an extensive activity of baptism is indicated. This point precludes anyone becoming a member of the Church in other ways than through baptism. But it follows, however, that the recognition of baptismal status in another denomination is a condition for the opportunity to consider that person as a member of the one, universal Church. If they are seen as members of the Church, then their baptism must be "validly" recognized. Conversely, if the baptismal status of the person is not recognized, then also the ecclesial nature of another denomination is also called into question, because how can it be the Church, if it has no (validly) baptized members? Therefore, mutual recognition as the Church and the recognition of baptism are mutually dependent.

Lutherans and Mennonites see themselves already mutually as the Church. That was not always the case. Numerous Anabaptist churches of the sixteenth century were obviously not able to accept the model of the "state church" and the legitimacy of authoritarian government in the churches because they were not able to reconcile the shape of that church with what they saw in the New Testament.[113] And infant baptism was the strongest illustration of the historically-evolved relationship between the church and state.[114] On the other hand, the Lutheran churches sharply condemned the baptismal and church practice of the Anabaptists, thus condemning the people who represented such (CA 9, see above). These differences of the past are now described as divergences:

> For one side, a confessing church with strict discipline and independence from the state, on the other side an emphasis on a church of the masses for others, often tied to the state, but built up by the Word and the sacraments.[115]

Lutherans and Mennonites today who are finding convergence can formulate that the Church is "the sign of his presence among the people."[116] In its congregational life the Church tries to represent the model of a fraternal society in the world in which love prevails, which could lead to the common ownership of property. The Church is called to promote justice and peace in society. "Thus, it announces the coming kingdom and sets up unequivocal signs. This is its prophetic function."[117] For all "cooperation" is therefore necessary to have a critical attitude towards the state to ensure that the Church can fulfill its prophetic and diaconal ministry. In this way, Lutherans and Mennonites agree "in substance."[118]

> We agree in viewing the Church as a field of the Holy Spirit's action in regard to the sanctification of its members. The Church is not perfect, it remains 'in a state of becoming.' In the Mennonite perspective, the Church watches over its members, helping them to live as disciples of Jesus Christ.[119]

Compared with their stark differences in the sixteenth century, there are now some rather far-reaching convergences formulated in terms of ecclesiology. Accordingly the polemical overburdening of the other understandings of baptism from the sixteenth century need be abandoned. Infant baptism is no longer evidence of the close connection between church and state; likewise, adult baptism by no means represents a demonstrative termination of social unity: it is not a denial of God's mercy or a sign of hubris in faith and discipleship.

If both denominations formulate together, in addition, that "we all consider ourselves as members of the 'communion of saints' of all places and all times,"[120] then the common awareness of the universality of the Church is expressed, which exceeds the particular, denominational, local and temporal limits. The traditional doctrinal differences are expressly not regarded as church-dividing.

> This is also because there is mutual recognition of the exchange of services and offices and because what the respective partners develop as concerns their understanding of baptism will be mutually respected."[121]

Mennonites express in their statement that they see in the persisting differences, "no reason to refuse each other spiritual fellowship and mutual recognition before God as a church of Jesus Christ."[122]

Thus these churches of the Reformation follow the understanding that the unity of the Church cannot be created, but must be *discovered*. The interlocutors of the dialogue between the CPCE and the Baptists also recognized this and clearly formulated: "Despite differences of interpretation we recognize the presence of the true Church of Jesus Christ in one another."[123] But in my opinion this presupposes the full recognition of the baptismal status of members in the other denomination respectively, for one's own theological reasoning to remain coherent. Once their mutual recognition as Church is formulated, it can no longer deal in principle with the question of *whether* baptism can be recognized, but only with the question of *how* this can happen with divergent baptismal doctrines.

j. Potential for the Mutual Recognition of Baptism

Based on these observations one can draw the following conclusions from previous bilateral and multilateral ecumenical dialogues:

Baptism as Comprehensive Act of Initiation

A full agreement in doctrine is not conditional for mutual recognition of baptism. Therefore the question stands for the churches of the Anabaptist tradition, whether *the baptismal status* of a Christian can be recognized according to the ritual of infant baptism. The criterion for responding is conformity to Scripture. If it is recognized that – according to Scripture – the water ritual is regarded as only *one* part of the extensive initiation activity of baptism, and includes the *necessary* personal confession of faith, then the condition for the (mutual) recognition of baptism is granted.

Complementarity in Doctrine

If the denominations can actually detect a complementarity of doctrine in the previously diverging and converging baptismal under-standings, given the identification of various constitutive and evangel-ical aspects of baptism, then the mutual recognition of baptismal status is possible. The essential aspects of baptism may continue to be emphasized and highlighted differently.

In view of S. Mark Heim's study on the convergence texts from Lima a useful distinction has developed between the internal convic-tion of a confession, and what is expected for the recognition of a baptism in other denominations.[124] If this distinction is followed, then different mutual expectations of the dialogue partners become evident, namely, congregations of the Anabaptist tradition would need to recognize the performance of infant baptism as valid, including all the essential elements of a baptismal service. Instead of repeating the water ritual they would point to the need of the subsequent personal confession. Of the churches that practice infant baptism, it would be expected that they not require the recognition of infant baptism from churches of the Anabaptist tradition per se, but the recognition of the "baptismal status" if in each case this is followed by a personal confession of faith.

Convergence in Language

If in the future meetings a form of language can be found, which could bring the interpretation to those levels of expression of what is called a "sacrament" in other traditions. Then even churches of the Anabaptist tradition may agree, without any fear of being "absorbed" into a foreign sacramental understanding, and this would eliminate a profound, historically formidable obstacle in the "recognition of baptism."

Coherence in One's Own Doctrine

If the denominations were to jointly apply the already achieved convergence and consensus concerning ecclesiology to the issue of the recognition of baptism, then that would have to lead to the mutual recognition of baptism so that there would be coherence for the sake of theological doctrine and of the understanding of baptism itself.

No Relativization of One's Own Tradition

It does not necessarily follow from the mutual recognition of baptism that one's own baptismal practices would need to be given up or include a new or "foreign" practice. Churches of the Anabaptist tradition would not need to accept infant baptism "as such," and they need not undermine the emphasis on the confession of faith in baptism, which is such an important element for that tradition, and thus their corresponding ecclesiological understanding does not need to be revamped. Churches with infant baptism are not required to give up the practice of infant baptism and could then count on the abandonment of "re-baptism" by churches of the Anabaptist tradition.

If the other churches of the Anabaptist tradition follow this argument and draw the implied conclusions, then they will have important questions to ask their partners in the upcoming ecumenical dialogues:

What theological arguments can churches who mutually and fully recognize baptism present, as happened in Magdeburg in 2007, for why they do not mutually and fully recognize each other as churches and do not jointly celebrate the Lord's Supper?

How can churches that practice infant baptism pay more attention to the fundamental aspect of a personal faith commitment and participation in the life of the community, when they interpret this as an elementary aspect of the whole initiation process of baptism?

How can it be justified that churches do recognize Mennonites or Baptists as having been legitimately baptized and yet in their confessional texts those same churches regard the Anabaptist tradition as "condemned"?

If the ecumenical climate seems brighter now, given the mutual recognition of baptism, then this indicates a certain degree of relativization. Whether it may finally result in a "mutual recognition of baptism" or of the baptismal status of others, it will depend on far more than a mere clarification of theological doctrine. Dietrich Ritschl has tried to capture exactly this reality with the concept of "trans-intellectual hermeneutics of trust." The requirement is that in the ecumenical community of interpretation there be a sense of solidarity, one which derives from being the common "household."

> Here, doctrine does not have the last word, let alone canon law, nor in the end do lifestyle issues and religious customs. But here is one of the differences between the texts of the marginal realm, which in postmodern philosophy has no writable location and content.[125]

Ritschl argues, whoever can say to other church communities that *Christus praesens* is with them, also stands as an "ecumenical interpreter" for the intellectually responsible analysis and comparison of texts within another framework, a place which one only reaches through verbal consensus.

Thus Ritschl attempts to describe for ecumenism in the twenty-first century the necessary

> horizontal leap of faith [one] which the groups and denominations cannot and do not yet need to take, because they ultimately trust in God that the differences between them, which are intellectually difficult or nearly impossible to bridge, can be graciously embraced.[126]

This result, in my view, is itself also based on the Pauline "exhortation" in Ephesians, which admonishes them to live out their vocation in a way that is worthy of the unity of the Church.

CHAPTER 4
MISSIONARY ECUMENISM
ECCLESIOLOGY AS BELIEVED AND EXPERIENCED GLOBALLY

proclaim the good news, 'The kingdom of heaven has come near.'

— MATTHEW 10:7 (NRSV)

IF THE CHURCH is disintegrated and composed of different denominations, the credibility of its witness is impeded and encumbered – that was the realization in the early phase of the modern ecumenical movement. Thus we turn now to the question of mission as a testing ground for ecumenism. How is this testing ground presented in the context of the global Church? What understanding of mission might it be based upon? These questions are to be examined in the following chapter by using case studies.

Church as Event: Mission in View of the Global Church

If the question of mission is to be explored here in view of the ecumenical community of the global Church, then at least one perspective is always included; it is not primarily the cultural and contextual perspectives that are considered as the default, but those of the denomination. From the perspective of the Roman Catholic tradition, initially the Roman Catholic Church would no doubt see itself as the universal Church, being the primary reference point of experience and reflection.[1] On the other hand if one would ask representatives of the charismatic or Pentecostal traditions, then the primary horizon of experience would be more of a non-institutionalized ecclesial reality.[2] If on the other hand you ask a representative of a historic Protestant church, which is a founding member of the World Council of Churches (WCC), then it is this rather institutionalized shaping of the global ecumenical movement which emerges as its primary connection to the reality of the global Church. This does not necessarily mean that one's reflection must be limited to these terms, but it makes sense to be aware of the question of the various perspectives in order not to posit the terms of reference from one's own experiences as absolute, thereby limiting the global church superficially with a narrow scope. The worldwide church is more than Rome, more than Geneva,[3] certainly more than Lausanne[4] or the world's growing charismatic and Pentecostal movement.

If the question of missions is posed here in terms of the more broadly-conceived reflective framework of the global Church, namely, "mission as an essential characteristic of the Church,"[5] then one may also fundamentally inquire as to its identity, both concerning the identity of the Church in its global reality, and according to what constitutes its mission. In addition, one may inquire as to how one defines the relationship between these two identities. The task is described below as follows: The first part is an attempt to provide a theological reflection on these questions of identity, and then in a second step exemplary case studies are given for purposes of illustration.

a. The Relationship between Mission and Ecumenism

The Worldwide Community of the Church as *una, sancta, catholica et apostolica*

First, then, on the question of identity, what determines the essence of the global Church? Almost all historic churches hold to the ecumenical creed of Nicaea-Constantinople (381), in which the

Church is known as the *una, sancta, catholica et apostolica*.[6] If these essentials are not understood in the normative sense, but descriptively, then the global Church *is* the one, holy, catholic and apostolic Church. On this there is consensus.

These four essentials are referred to as "attributes" of the Church (*notae ecclesiae*) in order to distinguish those denominational characteristics and therefore varying aspects of the Church, which are also considered constitutive by the respective traditions. These distinctives describe the identity of the visible Church, and are therefore called *notae externae*. In the Lutheran tradition, for example, according to the Augsburg Confession, Art. VII: the true Church is where "the gospel is taught purely and the sacraments are admitted rightly."[7] These *notae externae* are denoted here as characteristics of the Church. Moreover, within the *notae externae* one ought to differentiate between those which contain a constitutive characteristic and those that are auxiliary or additional. These non-constitutive aspects will be referred to herein as "features" of the Church. So what is meant when we speak of mission as an essential feature of the Church? What is a necessary attribute, a characteristic of the visible church, or a feature that can be added? The answer to this question depends on whether mission should be attributed to the identity of the global Church as a constitutive and essential character.

External *attributes* and non-constitutive *features* cannot be defined independently of the four attributes that arise precisely from this differentiation. In view of the global Church then the task of identity description can be formulated as follows: each existing in space and time, a specifically denominational and contextual expression of church will have to be measured by the four attributes: *una, sancta, catholica et apostolica*. This is naturally also the case for the global community of churches.

(i) *una ecclesia*

The global Church is "one." That is to say that the Church is indivisible. Its unity is stipulated as an attribute because it is united in a confession of Jesus Christ. There is consequently no theological justification for speaking about the Church in the plural. Yet by no means can it be said that the Church must be structured in a uniform way. It also does not necessarily imply an institutionalized union of all denominations, but simply that they find their oneness in Christ.

(ii) *catholica ecclesia*

Furthermore, there is the catholicity of the Church. The Church is universal/all-encompassing, and it is the universal Church as a communion of particular churches. The theological legitimacy of this term is given in the incarnation event itself. The universal is realized in the particular, thus, the particular is not only undissolved, but it is visible and tangible as a part of the universal. The gospel becomes incarnated and inculturated in different contexts and therefore brings forth also ever new ecclesial forms. This was widely documented by the study process of the WCC on "Gospel and Culture" since the General Assembly in Canberra,[8] which led to the statement at the World Mission Conference in Salvador da Bahia 1996:

> The church must hold on to two realities: its distinctiveness from, and its commitment to, the culture in which it is set. In such a way the gospel neither becomes captive to a culture nor becomes alienated from it, but each challenges and illuminates the other.[9]

This is not a contradiction of the catholicity of the Church, but precisely its justification. How else might it be legitimate to speak of a *community* in terms of the global Church?

(iii) *sancta ecclesia*

The worldwide Church is a *communio sacramentalis*, because the realization of such a community is not primarily a construct of Christian dogma and theology, but an experience (of the "believed" Church), which has its primary place in the doxology of worship and finds its genuine expression in the celebration of the sacraments. Therefore this is where the "believed" and "experienced" church (see below) find their primary point of contact, in striving after one another. In ecumenical discussion, the Eucharist is interpreted as the origin of *communio* or *koinonia*, a community of sharing, because in the Eucharist there is the community with Father, Son and Holy Spirit as an experience for those participating in it.[10] And in baptism the essence of this community is expressed in an exemplary way as a community in which there can be no discrimination based on gender, age, race, culture, social or economic background, if baptism is to be an expression of the "new creature," the gracious acceptance and appreciation of humanity by God in Christ.[11]

(iv) *apostolica ecclesia*

The continuity and integrity of the global Church arise from apostolic faith. The attribute of apostolicity includes permanent hallmarks such as the testimony of faith and the proclamation of the Gospel, the celebration of divine worship, the transfer of ministerial responsibility, the concrete life of the community of believers and ministry in the world. "To be an apostolic community is to be a community contemporary with Jesus, a community that is found where Jesus is."[12] It is thus gathered in his name and knows itself to be guided by his story. From this grows its characteristics of discipleship, witness and service. Christine Lienemann-Perrin sees in the attribute of apostolicity the foundation for unity of mission and dialogue:

> Together mission and dialogue embody the *apostolicity* of the church in
> its dual sense of reconnecting the heritage of faith of the apostles *and*
> encounter with people of other faiths in the performing its mission.[13]

The Church lives out its faith in following Jesus and lends credibility to its witness in service. In this sense we can say that the global Church is the one Church that collectively confesses (*una*), celebrates overcoming boundaries (*sancta*), is ecumenical (*catholica*) and lives out its faith in following Jesus (*apostolica*).

b. Mission in View of the *una, sancta, catholica et apostolica ecclesia*

From here one can now ask, what is mission in view of this global Church which jointly confesses, celebrates the overcoming of boundaries, is ecumenical and faithful in discipleship? For mission was prior to ecumenism in the understanding of the global Church!

Long before thinking about an institutionalized expression of the theological understanding of the unity of the Church, missions recognized this need and provided the decisive impetus for an ecumenical organization of the life of the global Church. The historical development of the ecumenical movement emerged directly out of the missionary movement.[14] A good example of this however, is the historical process of institutionalization, whose motivation can be demonstrated by this theological understanding: the integration of the International Missionary Council and the WCC in 1961 in New Delhi.[15] Dietrich Werner identifies four motives for this step:[16]

i. The principal distinction between young churches and mother churches, between mission-churches and missionizing churches, should be abandoned in favour of a model of equal partnership. The "classic one-sided scheme of the transmitter and receiver role in world mission was thus broken." This step is ultimately based on the understanding of the unity of the Church, the *una ecclesia*. From this arose a structuralist mandate for managing relationships.

ii. The consequence of the theological understanding for the equality of concerns for mission and ecclesial unity within the ecumenical movement,[17] and therefore the inseparability of church and mission (cf. the famous sentence of Johannes Christian Hoekendijk: the Church does not *have* a mission, but is missionary by nature, or it is simply not the Church).[18]

iii. The church-critical mandate: Visser 't Hooft, the former general secretary of the WCC said already, it is not a question of "churchifying" missions, but of mobilizing the Church for mission. Underlying this is the view that "the missionary responsibility cannot be separated from any other aspect of the life and teachings of the Church."[19] Contained herein was the clear hope of renewal of the global Church.

iv. Mandate to be critical of missions: The realization that the credibility of the churches, their confession and witness had been weakened by the separation of the churches. If the community of the global

Church is not visible as the *una catholica*, then its mission can hardly be convincing.

Thus followed an extensive identification of mission and global Church (the fellowship of churches). If we follow this understanding, it can be a preliminary answer to our question and formulated as follows: mission that takes the global Church into perspective jointly confesses, celebrates overcoming boundaries, is ecumenical and faithfully in solidarity through discipleship. However, it should not be said that mission and Church are to be synonymous, but the degree of identification is qualified more precisely: Mission is Church in its fullness, which expresses the attributive definition of the Church. But then mission is not simply an attribute of the Church, but it is the Church *as event*.

Negatively formulated it means that where there is no mission, there is no church. The reversal of the statement, therefore, is also not valid: where there is no church, there is also no mission. For just as mission was prior to ecumenism, mission in terms of *missio Dei*[20] was prior to the Church. Therefore mission is more than an attribute of the Church or the sum of the attributes of the Church.

In view of the way the Church's relationship to other religions is defined, the following notion becomes plausible. At the Fifth Assembly of the WCC in Nairobi in 1975 delegates established the notion whose expressiveness has hardly been surpassed:

> While we cannot agree on whether or how Christ is present in other
> religions, we do believe that God has not left himself without witness
> in any generation or any society. Nor can we exclude the possibility
> that God speaks to Christians from outside the Church.[21]

From these two statements it not only follows that mission has always been ahead of the Church, but they also describe the further horizon of experience of the encounter with God. The global Church therefore finds its identity first within the mission of God, not vice versa.

Thus, statements are made about the nature of the Church, the nature of mission and the way their relationship to each other is determined. But the mission of the global Church itself is not stated, because we have only spoken of both church and mission in terms of *opus Dei*, but not in the sense of *opus hominum;* these are to be categorically distinguished from each other.[22] "Mission is human service, but not human work," says Ferdinand Hahn in his interpretation of Matt 28.[23] Concerning mission in the sense of a human service, the statement below should now be considered as follows, as it concerns the global Church, church is not what we believe it to be in an ideal sense and as we have described so far, but how we experience it. This is so because the global Church is not only a theological confession that can be described in terms of attributive revelation, but it is simultaneously experienced as a global community *with* "spot and wrinkle" (Eph 5:27).

c. The *Experienced* and the *Believed* Global Church

Our confession says that the Church actually is *una, sancta, catholica et apostolica* because it is neither a creation of its members, nor is it dependent on actions taken or not taken in the ecumenical movement. And yet the global Church is often experienced quite differently: as a defective, institutionally fossilized museum piece, in which the communality of its confession is nearly imperceptible. The common worship celebrations can become crucial tests because we are not even in a position to share the Eucharist, the very thing which is capable of really connecting us with each other. Also, we can hardly agree on what elements and forms of expression would be considered legitimate. Are the traditional Orthodox liturgies more appropriate than the vibrant cultural elements that have been inculturated in the liturgies of various younger churches?[24] Rarely enough does the global ecumenical fellowship of churches actually behave ecumenically when some of them still do not recognize other denominations as churches in the full sense of the word. This applies not only in the denominational sense, but also in view of the extensive meaning of the word *oikoumene*, as the "whole inhabited earth." Even in the ethical sphere, where it would be so necessary for the benefit of this "earth" to have a comprehensive solidarity with the poor and disenfranchised, even with nature, the Church as a worldwide communion of churches can rarely be convincing enough because it does not possess an unequivocal identity.

This experience of the global Church is just as real as the truth of confessing the Church as *una, sancta, catholica et apostolica.* Helpful, therefore, is the distinction between the "believed" and "experienced" Church, as suggested many years ago by Wolfgang Huber.[25] The experienced Church is what really exists in its respective historical forms. The believed is that which is known by the four attributes. Again and again the experienced Church remains as something to be questioned by the believed Church, that to which it is called forth. There is a tension expressed here, as the promise to be the Church is given precisely to this defective, experienced Church. Without taking into account this tension one cannot craft adequate ecclesiological statements, because either we would present a merely idealized image of the believed Church that removes us far from the reality of this world (and precisely the hardships and fears of many people), or we prematurely let ourselves reduce the real, existing Church with all its constraints and conditions and thereby lose every perspective on the renewal of the Church, because of its stated promises. The energy of this tension between the experienced and believed Church is the condition of the possibility to speak of the Church as *ecclesia semper reformanda.* If this tension is resolved for one side or the other, then the Church loses that energy, which is necessary for its constant renewal, to be the Church, being that which it is called to be.

d. Mission as *opus hominum* is the *ecclesia semper reformanda*

The question now is what these considerations bring to bear upon the view of mission as *opus hominum*, as "human work." How can the service of the Church be described while taking into account the tension between the believed and experienced Church?

If we were able to say above that mission is not simply an attribute of the Church, but the Church in its fullness to which it is called, meaning the Church as event, then it is appropriate now to examine whether this is especially true in view of the experienced Church. Mission would practically be an expression of this tension of the believed and experienced Church. The mission of the Church is conscious of the greater *missio Dei*, which it wants to witness because it is certain of the promise of the believed Church, of a worldwide community as the Church which collectively confesses, celebrates overcoming boundaries, is ecumenically proved and shows solidarity in discipleship. Mission is the constant effort to make tangible the promise. It always keeps in mind the concrete, historical existence in time and space, not just the experienced Church, but all of creation. With this it wants to achieve the promise to be the Church, that to which it is called and will thus also help the world to be what it already is, namely reconciled with God. To that degree, mission as human service means precisely that energy that allows the Church to grow out of this tension.

The service of the Church to the larger *missio Dei* consists in actually being the Church. This may seem rather modest, yet it is not. Rather, it is the biggest challenge of the Church, namely, to actually be the confessing, celebrating, ecumenical and inclusive Church. That is its real mission. Its credibility depends on that, namely, the enduring tension between the earthly reality and believed truth, on the search and the pursuit for the realization of the Church's true nature. On these also depends its ability to be a witness and its attractiveness. If this tension is no longer perceived as a tension, then the Church can no longer undertake any missional service. Admittedly it is then no longer *semper reformanda*, because then it lacks any power for self-renewal, certainly for the renewal of the "whole inhabited earth."

When we describe mission in view of the global Church in this way, then it is also clear that mission includes all that which helps the Church to actually be the Church in the sense of its calling as, "salt of the earth," and "light of the world" (Matt 5). And in this sense mission as *opus hominum* is again more than just one of the external marks or characteristics of the Church, it is more than a subdivision of the WCC or a world mission conference or a global mission agency. All this will continue to be helpful in making the Church always remain aware of its mission and reflected together, as a global community. But one should not think that this in itself is its mission, or that everything is already in view of mission. If the Church does not have its own mission as the Church *in the making*, this simply reflects once again its inability to create energy from the tension between the believed and experienced Church. Mission as *opus hominum* is the *ecclesia semper reformanda*.

This understanding is itself rooted in the nature of the Christian confession. A look at the beginnings of Christian faith shows that this search for realization of its intrinsic identity was present from the beginning. According to Lienemann-Perrin,

> Christianity did not begin with a ready-made – especially not with a comprehensive – concept of mission, rather, it first needed to search for its identity between the Jewish community of faith and pagan religions, and what it formulated as a result of this search process, was not a glorious beginning, but the result of a difficult birth.[26]

e. Examples in View of the Current Global Challenges

The fact that the WCC Central Committee had decided at its meeting in Potsdam (2001), for the year 2005 to once again convene a World Mission Conference[27] – something which was not to be taken for granted – can be seen as a strong signal that among the global community of churches, there is a consensus on the constitutive role of mission.[28]

In the face of stagnation and financial crises in the churches, with mission simply being a fellow captive, Dietrich Werner asks whether today "there is not a renewed need for greater autonomy of mission and a greater [...] independence of the movement of mission and partnership."[29] It is also said that the vitality of mission has regressed through becoming integrated into the Church. Therefore, the establishment of foundations, associations and societies that are independent of the Church is now again increasingly being considered. This may be necessary, but it puts the theological understanding of integration into question. It proves rather the reverse, how necessary a reassurance of the Church is for its mission. How mission is ultimately organized and managed will certainly always be re-thought and will remain in flux. But the concept of mission can in no way be reduced to mission agencies that are more or less independent, if we say that mission happens where Church is a reality. Neither the mandate that is critical for the church nor that which is critical for mission should be put aside. The global Church cannot afford it, just as there could be a Christian mission independent of the global Church in the sense of it being *una, sancta, catholica et apostolica*. It would lose its bearings. These issues will be illustrated in three examples in view of the global Church (as is seen in the realm of the WCC).

Globalization – "All Nations"

Mission – or 'Church as event' – is not confined to a particular culture or people, but aims toward "globalization," because mission as Church has been oriented toward the whole *oikoumene* since its inception. This global orientation was aimed at creating individual, independent churchdoms, but these were to be structured so as to be in communion with one another – not as something homogenous, but as a plurality – yet always existing in the sense of *una catholica*. Thus, the world-wide Church as the global Church is presented as an alternative form of community, in contrast to other prevailing globalization trends. As an ecumenical community it is precisely contrary to all homogenizing and leveling tendencies of the boundless, globalized market.[30] The North American theologian Robert Schreiter calls this the "new catholicity of the Church."

The former chairman of the Central Committee of the WCC, Aram I, formulated the following during the Eighth Assembly of the WCC in Harare:

In fact, the *Gospel and Culture study* has helped us not only to focus on the symbols and values of our cultures in relation to the gospel, but to examine the structural realities in cultures that suppress and deny the presence of the gospel. We have been powerfully reminded that the forces of racism, social, economic and political marginalization and the destructive repercussions of globalization need to be countered with the churches' resolute witness to the liberating news of God's inclusive and reconciling love for all people and the whole of creation. I believe that *globalization, contextualization* and *pluralism* with all their implications for mission and evangelism must continue to be seriously studied in the coming years.[31]

Due to the propagation of western lifestyle, genuine cultures are being leveled by the domination of economic globalization. The dissolution of borders, allowing capital to flow without political regulation or taxation, plunges entire economies into crisis. The policy here is the scourge of the market, which only a few determine.

The worldwide Church as *una catholica* however, is not aimed toward a united civilization. Already in the WCC's study "A Common Understanding and Vision" it was noted: The emergence over the last decades of transnational and increasingly worldwide structures of communication, finance and economy has created a particular kind of global unity."[32] The price for this is the

growing fragmentation of societies and exclusion for more and more of the human family. ... This therefore constitutes a serious threat to the integrity of the ecumenical movement, whose organizational forms represent a distinctly different model of relationships, based on solidarity and sharing, mutual accountability and empowerment.[33]

As a global community the global Church is invested with unique requirements to meet these tendencies to marginalize on the one hand, and the simultaneous homogenization on the other hand, a global social construct, a community based on alternative values.

The WCC has endorsed the position of the World Alliance of

Reformed Churches on economic globalization, namely, "a committed process of recognition, clarification and confession (*processus confessionis*)."[34] Herein there is a growing realization that through economic globalization, the confession of a church is affected. This is precisely the mission of the Church: to realize that through the exclusion and destruction of life by unjust economic systems, the confession of the Church is challenged and simultaneously needs to make visible what alternatives or additional measures are necessary.

For this reason, the WCC has co-founded an "Ecumenical Advocacy Alliance."[35]

> Ecumenical advocacy represents the prophetic voice of the churches. Advocacy complements the actions of solidarity and accompaniment which are essential elements of Christian ministry. It also seeks to address the causes of poverty, conflict and injustice. By working together on concrete issues, those engaged in ecumenical advocacy seek to strengthen and broaden relationships within the fellowship.[36]

In this respect one sees an expression of recognizing the universal Church in the twentieth century, because the view does not remain constricted to the self-management of mission in the Church, but encourages the Church to look to its mission, its actual service, namely, that of being the Church.[37]

HIV/AIDS – "behold, I am with you"

As we reflect on the question of the mission of the New Testament witness in Matthew's Gospel, we encounter the so-called "Great Commission" (Matthew 28).[38] To learn what it means to "make disciples" we have extended our view to the central Matthean missional discourse in Matthew 10: "As you go, proclaim the good news, 'The kingdom of heaven has come near.' Cure the sick, raise the dead, cleanse the lepers, cast out demons." (Matt 10:7-8a, NRSV). Discipleship means, therefore, first of all to remain in a movement which witnesses to the in-breaking of the Kingdom of God. The Kingdom of

God is the hermeneutical key to all action of the Church. However, the action here is first a charitable act, one of healing.

The second focus in addition to the challenge of globalization, for which the newly founded Ecumenical Advocacy Alliance was established, is to contain the epidemic of HIV/AIDS, the immune deficiency disease which destroys life and community.[39] The extent of this disease will not be presented here in detail. To each and every person who has visited a country in southern Africa or Southeast Asia in recent years, this reality could not remain hidden.[40]

To be the global Church here means this will not be described as an isolated contextual problem, but instead we must perceive that it requires the solidarity of the entire global community. The network of church communities is ideally suited to provide the necessary educational work. For too long churches have been limited to moral persuasion, which completely ignored the reality of basic human needs. Also the Zimbabwean President Mugabe (who received his education in mission schools), called on the churches of the WCC during the Eighth Assembly in Harare to preach to the people, especially concerning morality, in a country where every third person is already infected. Perhaps the churches have for too long only preached the believed Church and lost sight of the experienced Church. Mission confronts this. If the Church is now launching its own education campaigns locally and seeking equal access to medicines around the world, then it can become a beacon of hope again. That is where the Church is being the Church.

Violence – "teaching them to obey everything I have commanded you"

The third example is the ecumenical "Decade to Overcome Violence: Churches Seeking Peace and Reconciliation, 2001-2010." It is mentioned to show how mission as church-in-the-making, is the Church as *semper reformanda*.[41] A view of Matt 28 may also illustrate the rootedness in the Great Commission: "teaching them to obey everything I have commanded you" (v.20). Matthew indicates by the location of the mountain (v.16) that all of the teachings of the Gospel, which comprise a long discourse, have authority in the Sermon on the Mount (Matt 5-7). The content of Christian doctrine is the *act* of improving justice.

To the disciples and the Church it is said that love is not exhausted in the neighbor (in his own denomination and local congregation), but rather overcomes boundaries and extends also to the other, potentially even "enemies," by going the "second mile," such that the prohibition on killing is basically a renunciation of all forms of violence. All of this belongs to their confession of faith.

Today, we see the complexity of the different causes of violence, its global power of destruction and the complicity of the churches in it. Hence, the WCC declared the ecumenical Decade to Overcome Violence, 2001-2010. After the international launch of the Decade in Berlin and Potsdam was celebrated in 2001, regional workshops were held in all parts of the world, citizens' groups were formed, projects were developed or existing ones were strengthened, depending on the contextually influenced forms, which were desired for a global community network. Churches worldwide committed for the next ten years to reminding themselves that overcoming violence belongs to the center of their mission. This is how the Church can exist *in the making* and thus it is reasonable to interpret this as mission. The World Mission Conference in 2005 coincided with the midpoint of the Decade. "In this context, the ministry of reconciliation is a concept which we must deal with in order to renew the practice of mission and evangelism."[42]

These three examples serve to illustrate that:

(1) mission is where Church occurs,
(2) Church occurs where it is a confessing Church,
(3) the confessing Church is the global community of churches in its solidarity, healing and overcoming violence.

These are constitutive elements (*notae externae*) of *una, sancta, catholica et apostolica ecclesia*.

CHAPTER 5

ACTION-ORIENTED ECUMENISM

PEACE THEOLOGY AND PEACE ETHICS AS TESTING GROUNDS

All this is from God, who reconciled us to himself through Christ
and has given us the ministry of reconciliation

— 2 CORINTHIANS 5:18 (NRSV)

ECUMENISM IS PUT to the test in the Church's collective action. Despite many differences in doctrine, ecumenism has found that its greatest challenge since its inception consists in not attending to the collective diaconal and social ethics-oriented activities. The needs of affected people or even of creation in general were and still are too urgent for the option of waiting until all doctrinal divisions are overcome before the churches are able to collectively craft an expression of their common faith and witness for justice and peace. This awareness created a unique movement of thought that considered action-oriented ecumenism as the primary testing ground and always reflected upon the rapprochement of the community of churches in light of this context.

The global community of churches is tested through the formation process of ecumenical peace theology and ethics. The difficulty and complexity of this process is delineated in the following chapter and illustrated in detail. First, a brief historical overview will demonstrate the long-term centrality of this struggle for the modern ecumenical movement – a struggle which was aimed toward concrete, joint courses of action, joint social ethics and fundamental theological convictions.

The common task of the churches is, according to Wolfgang Huber,

> to give voice to the peace message of the gospel, the ability of religions to enable peace, and the need for peace in the modern world, in order to adequately respond to the banal thesis that without religion everything is easier, more peaceful and amiable.[1]

Ulrich Körtner suggests one should note the difference between Christian social doctrine and theological social ethics.[2] Ecumenical social ethics will not operate beyond denominational differences, but can only be "multi-perspectival"; actual historical developments substantiate this thesis.

These multiple perspectives are also evident in the second part of the study presented here, namely, the ecumenical "Decade to Overcome Violence, 2001-2010: Churches Seeking Reconciliation and Peace," as initiated by the World Council of Churches. However, it is clear in this ecumenical initiative that the divergent perspectives can no longer be described consistently as historic-denominational, even if these factors remain visible to some degree. The multiple perspectives arise primarily out of the different contexts and the respective individuals who are directly or indirectly concerned with these issues.

a. Contention amid the Community of Churches: Peace Ethics

The "Ministry of Reconciliation" – Not a superadditum in Ecumenism

The fragmentary and provisional nature of the Kingdom of God does not mean that Christians must simply accommodate whichever realities are present. On the contrary, it encourages them not to accept the seemingly insurmountable conditions of injustice and violence as the final answer to life, because they are anticipating the consummation of the world, of the whole cosmos, and thus they participate in it already. This is the profound and ultimate meaning of the title, "Decade to *Overcome* Violence," a formulation inspired by Paul's admonition: "Do not be overcome by evil, but overcome evil with good" (Rom 12:21). Evil is to be taken seriously and considered as realistically as possible, while at the same time knowing the limitations of its power, because another reality – the reality of God's Kingdom – is believed to be present in the midst of this world. The Church only exhibits a messianic dimension insofar as the Church lives according to messianic ethics – or else it is not (yet) the Church. Walter Dietrich opines:

> Whoever is convinced that God aims for a world with less, and in the end, no violence, will not regard those who resign themselves to accommodating violence as expressing realism and sobriety, but of opportunism and a lack of perspective. And vice versa: To count on God means to bet that violence can be conquered.[3]

Peace theology reflects the anticipation and celebration of this peace of God (*leiturgia*), the witness for peace (*martyria*) and the commitment to peace (*diakonia*). Worship, witness and service for peace are essentially social and effectively bring about community formation (*koinonia*). As formulated by the World Convocation on Justice, Peace and the Integrity of Creation in the years 1988-1989 in East Germany: "Communion with Jesus Christ liberates us for fellowship with one another. Our Lord enables us to look beyond respected borders with dissenting communities, even with non-believers."[4]

As mentioned above, at the beginning of the modern ecumenical movement was the notion that church disunity stands in the way of their witness and mission. Whether in the *Faith and Order Commission*, the *Life and Work Movement*, the *International Missionary Council*, or the *International Fellowship of Reconciliation*, in each case they were concerned for the credibility of Christian witness and thus for the sake of the self-understanding of the churches, in communion with other churches. The churches have needed to clarify their position concerning violence rather urgently in the intervening decades, as a lack of clarity on this central global, humanitarian issue leads precisely to a lack of credibility in modern society.

Therefore the effort to both clarify the Church's position and to overcome violence is not a *superadditum* of ecumenism; for the global ecumenical Church and the World Council of Churches this task is its most fundamental undertaking, namely, as the ministry of reconciliation (2 Cor 5). The act of reconciliation itself includes two dimensions, namely, the grace-given *gift* of reconciliation, which cannot be separated from the *duty* of reconciliation. And in this sense peace theology and ethics in particular may be considered as *the* testing ground of ecumenism, in which the self-understanding of the churches as a reconciled community as the joint actions of the churches always reflects peace.

The Continual Urgency of Ethical and Theological Clarifications

From the perspective of Christian faith all ethical questions are implicitly theological issues, and vice versa: all theological questions bear ever in mind their ethical implications. There is hardly any context of theological reflection and ecclesial praxis, in which this insight pertains so strongly as in the ecumenical movement. The basic theological and ecclesiological challenge for Christian peace ethics is always the complete clarification of the relationship between the promised Kingdom of God and global society, the political and governing bodies, institutions of the Church and those structures of injustice that serve to divide humanity.[5] But, in order to focus the traditional issue of peace ethics in ecumenism, Reinhard Frieling asks, "is the work of peace a contribution toward building the Kingdom of God here on earth, or does it arise simply from God's commandment to make peace and to love?"[6] Since its inception the modern ecumenical movement in the late nineteenth and early twentieth century "considered the question of the Kingdom of God to be of utmost importance," according to Wolfram Weiße.[7]

The extensive and sometimes controversial discussions concerning peace ethics within the modern ecumenical movement have always tried to promptly respond to both the specific contextual challenges,[8] and to make careful and comprehensive assessments, as well as develop joint strategies in terms of local and global challenges.[9] From the start, the ecumenical movement has been motivated and shaped by peace ethics discussions, to the degree that one could trace the entire history of modern ecumenism from that distinct perspective.[10] Even when the question of the unity of the Church in its inseparable connectedness did not always emerge explicitly concerning its peace mandate, it was always implicitly present.[11] It has always been considered, as Frieling argues, that "Christian peace witness ... has to emphasize the multi-dimensionality of peace," namely, "in relationship to God, to oneself, to others and to the political and social order."[12]

"Glory to God and Peace on Earth" was the motto of the International Ecumenical Peace Convocation (IEPC) in 2011, which was implemented as the culmination of the WCC's "Decade to Overcome Violence." Many churches, ecumenical groups, initiatives and networks, including conferences, expert consultations and study processes sought intensively within this Decade to make existing alternatives to violence and injustice visible, and to network and further develop them.[13] In addition to the decision to convene this Peace Convocation, and in order to focus on the different approaches and results such that a more concentrated effort for peace through justice might be brought to fruition, the ninth WCC General Assembly in Porto Alegre, Brazil (2006), decided to initiate an extensive consultation process to develop an "Ecumenical Declaration on Just Peace."[14]

This declaration of peace is meant to enable a clear, compelling, and theologically profound expression of the churches concerning peace education in the context of the global challenges in the twenty-first century, and to serve as one of the pillars of the Peace Convocation and the future work of the Council. This study will take into account more than one hundred years of the long and extensive process of ecumenical decision-making.[15] As such, only the highlights of this process can be traced, but further work is urgently needed if future discussions are not to become exhausted in repetitions of age-old theological arguments or moral appeals.[16]

With the decisions of the ninth WCC Assembly, the fellowship of churches has clearly acknowledged the ongoing urgency for ethical and theological clarifications that result from the multifarious, prevailing injustices and violence, which challenge the churches' ability to be the Church in all regions of the world. Thus the churches of the WCC now jointly face the responsibility for peace-building and to embrace in authentic ways the promotion of justice *in* the world. This cannot happen without fundamental theological reflections concerning the *nature* of the *mandate* and the *mission* of the Church.[17]

b. Internationalism and the Condemnation of War: Definitions

The initiation of the World Council of Churches is deeply rooted in the strong will of the churches to save the world from repeating a disastrous world war, which in the years 1914 to 1918 cost millions of human lives.[18] After the initial contacts by some Christian social initiatives and peace organizations from different churches and countries at the start of the twentieth century, on August 2, 1914, coinciding with the outbreak of the First World War, the "World Alliance for International Friendship through the Churches," was founded, which began organized ecumenical efforts for peace.[19] One of the most influential figures of the World Alliance was the German theologian Friedrich Siegmund-Schultze (1885-1969).[20] The boundaries of nation, religion, social class and ethnicity that were hitherto accepted and theologically legitimated almost as "orders of creation" came to be increasingly ranked as "second-order" issues, beneath the higher goal of the peaceful coexistence of all peoples. These "ecumenical pioneers" realized that the unity of the one body of Christ, the *una sancta*, must transcend those limits. Following the establishment of the World Alliance in 1919, after several previous regional groupings within the growing Christian peace movement the non-denominational "International Fellowship of Reconciliation" was founded, in which Christians joined together who consistently profess nonviolence. [21]

Given what were the already high-tech armaments during the First World War and their extensive, destructive potential, the classic "doctrine of just war" (q.v. Thomas Aquinas[22]) was questioned by some representatives of the mainline churches for the first time. It no longer appeared evident that the criterion of "proportional means" could be met in times of mass destruction and air-based wars. From then on ecumenical discussions have been shaped by different positions.[23] Deeply opposing positions faced off against each other: radical pacifism represented by the Christian peace movement on the one hand, and most notably on the other hand, German Protestant positions in which the use of military force was still considered a legitimate means (for some it was only for the defense of their own country).

In 1925, at the Universal Christian Conference on Life and Work in Stockholm the following joint resolution was adopted in the report on "The Church and International Relations":[24]

1. War, as a means of settling international disputes through physical violence, accompanied by malice and falsehood, is incompatible with the views and the behaviour of Christ, and therefore also with the views and the behaviour of Christ's Church.
2. Construed as such, war is the abuse, rather than the good use of force, because in an instance it entrusts to one party namely, violence, the power of the authoritative adjudication of moral values.
3. An aggressor is that nation which rejects a decision to seek arbitration or refrains otherwise from the steps toward law and order that are being contemplated.
4. It is the duty of the churches to assert the entire weight of their combined influence toward the fraternal organization of nations.
5. None of the above sentences infringe upon the innate right of every nation to defend itself against attacks or oppression.[25]

The theological reasons for rejecting military force in this case are based on the "views and behaviour of Christ," which are relevant for the Church. The fifth article makes clear, admittedly, how much the conviction of an "innate right" to defense and wars of liberation is still maintained.

During the "Congress of Peace and Friendship" convened by the World Alliance in 1928 in Prague, over 500 high-ranking delegates demanded the condemnation of war as well as insisting upon far-reaching disarmament.[26] In the so-called "Disarmament Resolution" that was adopted by a large majority, the assembled Congress called for the Christian churches to advocate disarmament, among other things.

> This conference [...] appeals to the Christian Churches to bring their people the foregoing considerations and to represent to them the solemn obligations that all nations, forming part of the League of Nations, are under to reduce and limit their armed forces as provided by the Covenant, and to accept an universal system whereby disputes shall be settled by peaceful judicial methods in lieu of war [...] The Conference earnestly requests the Churches to throw the weight of their educative influence and of their religious inspiration into supporting the idea that henceforth the peoples, by accepting the bonds of their fraternal unity and the mutual compacts of concerted collaboration, should renounce their claim to unrestricted right of action regardless of international obligations. The Churches of Jesus Christ must accept as their primary obligation the commandment of their common Master: 'Seek ye *first* the Kingdom of God.[27]

This optimistic view of the possibility of a resolution of conflicts through arbitration was, however, already greatly compromised in 1937 at the "World Conference on Church, Community and State" in Oxford. Fascism, nationalism and racism, coupled with military arma-ment and economic instability that was previously unimaginable, once again determined the global political agenda[28] and the (Protestant) churches found themselves on different sides of the political oppo-nents, the church leaders being largely loyal to their own countries.[29]

The World Conference on Church, Community and State at Oxford did introduce, in addition to the Christological, the *ecclesiological* argument that the Church is of such a magnitude that it relativizes all other divisions or boundaries:

> This fact of the ecumenical character of the Church carries with it the important consequence that the Church brings to the task of achieving a better international order an insight that is not to be derived from ordinary political sources. To those who are struggling to realize human brotherhood in a world where disruptive nationalism and aggressive imperialism make such brotherhood seem unreal, the Church offers not an ideal but a fact, man united not by his aspiration but by the love of God.[30]

Despite the degree of unity felt there, this conference was not inclined toward offering the unique "word" (Cf. below, Dietrich Bonhoeffer) to speak against the next world war that was already looming. It had to be satisfied rather, with delineating various positions:

1. The Christian Pacifist Position

"The Church will become a creative, regenerative, and reconciling instrument for the healing of the nations only as it renounces war absolutely."[31] In the face of modern warfare, the effects of war are simply always destructive, ending in futility, ultimately destroying even the "most noble goal" for which it was carried out. Therefore in each case war is considered sinful. As such it could hardly be justified in a fundamental way: War stands in opposition to "the nature of God as love"; it also stands in opposition "of the redemptive way of the Cross, and of the community of the Holy Spirit."[32]

2. The Position of "Just War"

2a **Legitimized by international law**: Christians have almost the "duty" to participate in wars legitimized by human rights law that sought to protect international law and peace. Just as the state in the "sinful world" is committed to law and order and to protect "in obedience to God" it could also use force if these are at risk, and this is also true in the international arena. Such wars are to be compared with police measures.

2b **Morally legitimized**: In the case of an emergency or for the liberation of the oppressed, when all other means have been exhausted then this position is presented as a "Christian duty" to go to war, because then there is "what they believe to be an essential Christian principle."[33] The final decision to participate in such a "just" war is ultimately left to the conscience of the individual.

3. The Christian-Bellicose Position

It is the "duty of Christians" that state power – as an ordinance established by God – as much as humanly possible be obeyed and to always refrain from anything that could weaken it, even if it is acknowledged that political authority is applied "in a selfish and immoral way." The primary task of the state is, however, "to preserve a nation from the detrimental effects of anarchic and criminal tendencies amongst its members, and to maintain its existence against the aggression of its neighbours." Certainly there is also a Christian duty to work for peace and mutual understanding between peoples, but "no such effort can end war in this world."[34]

c. Dietrich Bonhoeffer: The Christological and Ecclesiological Argument

In 1934, about three years before the World Conference on Church, Community and State at Oxford, Dietrich Bonhoeffer had called the churches of the ecumenical movement to a comprehensive "council of peace." In his famous address at the ecumenical conference of the Life and Work Movement and of the World Alliance for Promoting International Friendship through the Churches in Fanø (Denmark), under the title "The Church and Peoples of the World," he seized upon the call for "Peace on Earth" from the Christmas story (Lk 2:14).[35] Ecumenism does not have to inquire as to "political necessities and possibilities," but "according to the commandments of God," which they proclaim amidst the world "without looking back." That is their *theological* task. All arguments presented by the churches and theologians that would seek to restrict this "binding commandment" shirk from this challenge, such as determining that humans are unalterably evil, the inevitability of war in a fallen world, the attempts at creating security through weapons arsenals as well as the difficult issues of self-defense and the protection of the neighbour from enemies. Still in present ecumenical debates these have remained the main arguments put forward by the churches in the debate over nonviolence and the necessary use of force, in order to claim that the military's use of force, even if not legitimate, was at least inevitable. Bonhoeffer radically disagreed: "Anyone who *questions* the *commandment of God* before obeying has already denied God."[36] In this sense Bonhoeffer is understood as a pacifist. For example Huber and Reuter assess Bonhoeffer

as one who wishes to participate in overcoming war and the establishment of an international peace. But he is a spokesman for the conviction that pacifism must take a deeper approach than it could in the organizational pacifism in the era of World War I.[37]

Konrad Raiser has shown how Bonhoeffer's subsequent lectures on ecumenism clarify (in Ciernohorské Kúpele and Gland)[38] that he

passionately sought to clarify the theological and ecclesiological self-understanding of the ecumenical movement, so that they could proclaim the commandment of peace with God's authority in a world, which had lost the sense of a viable order.[39]

He merges two decisive arguments that have been known since the early ecumenical conferences. On the one hand he cited the Christological prerequisite for peace: "There shall be peace because of the Church of Christ, for the sake of which the world exists."[40] On the other hand he stressed the ecclesiological argument, namely, that the ecumenical Church transcends not only all borders of a "national, political, social, racial type" but binds the members of the Church to each other in such a manner, as not to nullify other bonds (of "history, blood, classes and languages"), but to make them relational.[41] Bonhoeffer had already recognized through ecumenical meetings in Rome, but then especially during a study period in the United States,

> that the Church of Jesus Christ, because of its deep commitment to the one, common Reconciler can never be a national church, but we must always give preference to the ecumenical solidarity of all the member churches in the one world Christianity.[42]

And that is why these members of the Church cannot wage war against each other, "because they know in this way they are aiming the weapons at Christ himself."[43]

Bonhoeffer recognizes the potential influence of the churches for world peace in the self-evident solidarity among Christians across all divisive boundaries. But for that, the Church must really be Christ's Church, whereby it witnesses to Christ's actual commandment of peace, and by acting as the *una sancta* it actually embraces the other. Bonhoeffer's call to peace was made not as a moral appeal to governments or international institutions, but is intended as a theological self-assurance for the Church. He has the other religions in view at least insofar as he sees the credibility of the Christian confession being jeopardized, when the churches relativize the witness for peace: "Must we be put to shame by the heathens in the East?"[44]

Of course the difficult question remains, *how* can there be peace? Again Bonhoeffer challenges what are in fact the prevailing notions in the churches to the present, that peace could be achieved for example by political treaties, by creating economic dependencies[45] or by increasing armaments. His counterargument is as simple as it is impressive, namely, that in conventional thinking the fatal confusion of peace and security becomes manifest. To the contrary, he argues: "There is no way to peace along the way of safety."[46] Security or safety requires suspicion, a search for self-protection, which inevitably must lead to war. Peace, however, is simply a gamble that could also end on the cross for those who trust the command of God more than weapons. But this path remains at the mercy of destructive violence, precisely when following this ethic is solely left to individuals, or even individual churches. And that is why Bonhoeffer calls for "the one Great Ecumenical Council of the Holy Church of Christ." Through the strength of this ecumenical unity, real peace could be proclaimed such that when "the world hears, it is compelled to listen to it." And the people would be happy about it, "because the Church of Christ in the name of Christ has taken the weapons from the hands of their sons, forbidden war, and proclaimed the peace of Christ against a raging world."[47]

Bonhoeffer argued on the one hand against the widely-held Anglo-Saxon view that the Kingdom of God is something of an ideal state, actualized through the implementation of the Sermon on the Mount.[48] The Social Gospel movement that developed in North America at the end of the nineteenth century effectively represented this position, particularly as a counterpoint to an individualized interpretation of Christian faith, while at the same time being in danger of identifying the Kingdom of God with a specific economic and social system.[49]

On the other hand, Bonhoeffer also rejected the dominant position in continental European churches who insisted upon a creation-based theological argument in which a certain political order could bring God's will to fruition and, consequently, that this order was to be defended – if necessary even by means of war – since it was recognized as the created order, and such an action was seen as legitimate or even a Christian duty. Bonhoeffer replied that no order of the fallen world could be construed as an order of creation. For out of this position of "natural law" one derives the ability to defend this order through war. Bonhoeffer wants the state to recognize the most extreme case as an "order of preservation" which could only claim legitimacy so long as they keep themselves open to the revelation of Christ. Recognizing the realities of struggle and conflict in a broken world should not lead to the justification of war, even if the law should be defended. War does not belong to God's orders of creation.

Certainly Bonhoeffer cannot be reproached for not recognizing the realities of struggle and conflict in a broken world. Especially through his personal involvement in political conflicts, law and truth seemed to him the two basic requirements and challenges for any peace-building prospect. The political realities themselves would therefore in no way justify wars, since war can never lead to a real enforcement of law and truth, and to a peaceful community based on the forgiveness of sins,[50] instead there would be mutually assured self-destruction of both combatants.[51]

Only a radical "no" to the impending war finally opened up for Bonhoeffer the freedom for a political resistance that was appropriate for Christians.[52] The will of God for all people at all times is disclosed in the biblical witnesses. The task of the Church in the light of the current context of God's "binding commandment" is to proclaim "something concrete" for the present situation.[53] As Konrad Raiser rightly interpreted:

With this understanding of the concrete commandment Bonhoeffer could uncover the identification of peace with security as misleading and insist that the struggle for peace must never be done at the expense of justice and truth.[54]

Such a "no" does not at all imply the renunciation of the ecumenical community, nor should it be construed as a violation of the unity of the Church, but precisely that which aims at unity, as Karl Barth clearly pointed out:

It is obviously by the No that the clarification of an obscure situation is accomplished in a confession, the completed decision being charac-terised as decision by a mention and rejection of the counter-decision. ... And it is not the case that this No can and will disturb and destroy an existing unity and has therefore to be condemned as a sin against love. It is rather the case that this No makes clear once more that unity of the Church which had been obscured, that it can and will restore that threatened unity, and that it has therefore to be regarded as a particular work of love.[55]

Bonhoeffer's ideas were too radical for the prevailing positions in the churches of the ecumenical movement. And the fledgling ecumenical movement did not find the strength required for the "great ecumenical council." Representatives from all the churches who rejected war based upon Christian faith, including the historic peace churches, could be given more weight in international ecumenical discussions only after the disastrous experience of the Second World War. With its basic theological and ethical arguments and its stimulation for an ecumenical council of peace Bonhoeffer provided the decisive impetus for all other generations of the ecumenical movement and had thus served to orient, especially for many of the young churches of Africa, Latin America and Asia, those who had to endure serious conflicts amid the political struggles of liberation movements since the mid-twentieth century.

These conflicts have always challenged the ecumenical community as a whole, usually in association with the earnest question concerning alternatives to the legitimate use of force and the commandment of nonviolence. There are always questions about the unity of the Church, though there are different parts of the Church on different sides of political actions. The controversies about the *Belhar* Confession in South Africa present a notable example,[56] within the process of reception of the Barmen Theological Declaration of 1934.[57]

d. The Formation of the World Council of Churches: Lessons from Two World Wars

The creation of the WCC through merging the Life and Work Movement and the Commission on Faith and Order was delayed by the onset of World War II, which wreaked a previously unimaginable amount of violence and destruction. Again, many churches had not shown the will for a decisive call for peace, staying on the side of their respective nations and legitimizing military violence in this way, thereby contradicting the ecumenical vision of the universal Church, the worldwide community which transcended national boundaries. Parallel to this there was a strong, ecumenically-minded group that had been trained in almost all churches that recognized the challenge to a common witness of the churches. This "prophetic function" of the Church, which can be seen as quite pertinent in the midst of a violent situation, from that time forward was no longer to be repressed; it remained present. The will to overcome military violence was one of the strongest motivations for founding the World Council of Churches, which could finally happen in 1948, after the end of World War II.[58] The Christians who gathered from all over the world for the inaugural meeting in Amsterdam found words of repentance and confession of guilt, but also clear and hopeful words to "all who are in Christ, and all who are willing to hear."[59]

> We have to ask God to teach us together to say No and to say Yes in truth. No to all that flouts the love of Christ, to every system, every programme and every person that treats any man as though he were an irresponsible thing or a means of profit, to the defenders of injustice in the name of order, to those who sow the seeds of war or urge war as inevitable; Yes to all that conforms to the love of Christ, to all who seek for justice, to the peacemakers, to all who hope, fight and suffer for the cause of man, to all who – even without knowing it – look for new heavens and a new earth wherein dwelleth righteousness.[60]

In this statement one hears the clear echoes of the earlier formulations by Dietrich Bonhoeffer and Karl Barth. "War is not according to God's will"[61] – the much-quoted lesson learned by global ecumenism after the bitter experience of two world wars. War was now seen as "a sin against God and a degradation of humanity."[62] Those who objected to military service saw themselves being more than confirmed in their radical Christian pacifist position. The different positions of Oxford

(1937) were not thereby repealed, but they were further modified for the current situation, given the presence and indiscriminate destructiveness of nuclear weapons. People were united in asking the inevitable question: "Can war still be an act of justice?"[63] Many who had supported the notion of one's Christian duty to warfare, now moved to a position which was later referred to as "nuclear pacifism": "a modern war with its mass destruction [can] never be an act of justice."[64] Of course, many maintained the "last resort" argument, namely that warfare is categorically indispensable as a last resort.

The three different positions[65] represent arguments which, according to the typology of Oxford, in my opinion, basically represent only two basic types, with further sub-types:[66]

(1) The Christian Pacifist Position: It explicitly formulates its rejection of any military service and is convinced God requires that one take an unconditional position against war and in favour of peace. In this view the Church should speak as a whole in the same sense.

(2) The position of just war does not fundamentally reject war; Christians could go to war under certain circumstances.

(2a) The "nuclear pacifists" declared that the mass destruction of modern warfare means it could never be an act of justice.

(2b) Moral legitimacy (the right to protect in all circumstances): The representatives of this position state that the right also to defend with military force as the last resort was not only legitimate in view of the recent absence of impartial supranational instances, but even as the duty of every "citizen."

For everyone there was then the hope of the enforceability of international law. It is striking also that in 1948, the argument of "Christian duty" was no longer in the foreground, as it was ten years prior in Oxford. The Christian-bellicose position is no longer presented.

e. The Beginning of the "Cold War" and the Witness of the Historic Peace Churches

In 1949, then General Secretary of the WCC, Willem A. Visser 't Hooft, in pursuance of the first assembly, called for the historic peace churches (Mennonites, Church of the Brethren and Quakers) and the International Fellowship of Reconciliation, to explain the argument for a pacifist position to the worldwide community of churches. The answer came in two statements: "War is Contrary to the Will of God" (1951), and "Peace is the Will of God" (1953).[67] The historic peace churches expressed their complete agreement with the theological arguments given at Oxford and Amsterdam: the Christocentric commitment and the transcendent function of the fellowship of the Church in regard to any secular variable and allegiance were the decisive bases of the consistent rejection of any participation in wars and their search for alternative forms of peace service. They doubted whether their position could generally be considered as bearing no guilt whatever, but stressed the fundamental willingness to suffer in following Christ[68] against the argument in favour of a "lesser evil," according to the doctrine of just war. The responsibility of the Church in the world is precisely to embody the Kingdom of God "here and now," and thus to live as examples of "messianic ethics."[69]

A committee of representatives of the peace churches and the International Fellowship of Reconciliation, as well as representatives of the mainline churches was continuously active from that point onward in the so-called "Puidoux conferences" (1955-1973, named after the place of the first meeting). They form a rich treasury of discussions on theological-ethical issues and related ecclesiological problems in which the debate about the appropriate attitude to war and peace (or closely related themes such as conscientious objection) were at the forefront.[70] These conferences had far-reaching influence on the ecumenical, theological and ethical discourse within the WCC, particularly in the German and North American context of the postwar period. Also begun in the same year was the WCC study on "the Church and the nuclear threat," largely determined by contributions from the peace church traditions and the International Fellowship of Reconciliation.[71] One of the most visible results of this continuous work over several years was the launch of the "anti-militarism" program at the Fifth Assembly of the WCC in 1975 in Nairobi (the Program for Disarmament and against Militarism and the Arms Race).[72]

In parallel to this ran the politically important conversations, founded in 1958 in the Christian Peace Conference (CPC) in Prague, which placed the East-West divide at the center of their deliberations to overcome the cold war and sought a ban on nuclear weapons.[73] One of the leading theologians and initiators was the Czech theologian, Josef L. Hromádka[74] (1889-1969), who also created awareness of the relationship between Christian faith and Marxism through his "friendly" debate with Karl Barth.[75] Jan Milič Lochman[76] and Martin Niemöller were also among the founding figures.[77] This important forum for meetings between representatives of the churches from the socialist countries of the Soviet bloc and representatives from churches and Christian peace groups from the West in itself formed a significant ecumenical bridge because it created one of the few – and in those times crucial – opportunities for personal encounter.[78] However, the subsequent interpretations diverged considerably from the historical classification, and also from the role of the WCC.[79]

f. The Legitimacy of "Revolutionary Violence" and the (Re)Discovery of the Ethos of Nonviolence

Aside from that, the peace ethics discussion on the dominant global political situation of the East-West confrontation and the resulting nuclear threat, an additional field developed since the 1960s for the ultimate testing of the various peace theology and ethics positions within the *oikoumene*. They sought to examine whether Christians in the developing world might legitimately use force as a last resort in their inevitable struggle for justice and liberation from dictatorial and oppressive structures, or at least to consider it as a legitimate means of defense. The perspective presented was entirely different at that point. It was not simply a question of a governing state's use of violence in a conflict between states, involving discussions about the criteria for a "just war" in defense of the law, or a matter of conscientious objection. It was the perspective of oppressed peoples whose lives were characterized by direct, state-sanctioned violence, constantly worsening due to the underlying "structural violence."[80] The sole appeal to valid law and the enforcement of law seemed to alleviate nothing if the law itself was not designed to deliver justice. Liberation movements and a theology of revolution emerged, which inquired as to a new approach according to God's action in history. "Struggle" and "violence" appeared to many of the politically oppressed as a legitimate means to bring about justice and peace.[81] The WCC World Conference on Church and Society in Geneva in 1966 was ground-breaking in many ways, undertaking an extensive study of the question of "revolutionary violence" and assessing the notion of "the lesser evil." Nonviolence was not considered as the only legitimate position of the Church:

> The question often emerges today whether the violence which sheds blood in planned revolution may be a lesser evil than the violence which, though bloodless, condemns whole populations to perennial despair.... It cannot be said that the only possible position for the Christian is one of absolute nonviolence. There are situations where Christians may become involved in violence.[82]

Again, reference is made here to the well-known criteria of the doctrine of just war (*causa iusta, ultima ratio, recta intentio, debitus modus*), whose effectiveness had been increasingly called into question in the parallel discussions of nuclear warfare. The debate came to a head when the WCC "Programme to Combat Racism" was initiated because, in this context some of these liberation movements were supported by the WCC (also financially), and of course were always restricted by limited humanitarian aid.[83] However, this prevented some – especially those church leaders from the north, who were not otherwise on the side of the pacifists – to defame the WCC as supporting violence and communism-friendly organizations, which inflicted severe long-term damage on the reputation of the fellowship of churches. In the south the WCC earned considerable credibility through its steadfast solidarity with the weak and oppressed, precisely because it now strongly opposed the increasing "structural violence," in which the rich churches of the North and West were intertwined. The WCC and, at the height of his tenure, the General Secretary Philip Potter were no longer afraid to face this inevitable conflict.[84]

In these discussions, the struggle for human rights and the possibilities for active but nonviolent resistance were sharpened increasingly. Mohandas K. Gandhi[85] and Martin Luther King Jr.[86] were among the main protagonists of this attitude that decisively influenced ecumenical discussions. At the Fourth Assembly of the WCC in Uppsala in 1968, for which King was intended as a keynote speaker, shortly before he was assassinated, a "Martin Luther King Resolution" was adopted on nonviolent methods and the fight for social justice.[87] A few years later the text appeared, *Violence, Nonviolence and the Struggle for Social Justice* (1973).[88] Ten years later it was followed by the so-called *Corrymeela Consultation: Violence, Nonviolence and Civil Conflict.*[89] The rise of secular peace and conflict studies in the field of political science further showed the churches how persistently much their previous peace discussions on ethical issues remained in the traditional patterns of argumentation of the respective denominations. An important clarification process needed to be established, which no longer restricted the question of peace to the legitimacy or illegitimacy of violence (military or revolutionary).

g. The Expansion of Ecumenical Peace Ethics through the "Conciliar Process for Justice, Peace and Integrity of Creation"

The Sixth Assembly of the WCC in Vancouver in 1983 was the start of the "Conciliar Process of Mutual Commitment (Covenant) to Justice, Peace, and the Integrity of Creation."[90] This reached a climax at discussions in the "World Convocation on Justice, Peace, and the Integrity of Creation" in Seoul in 1990. In its notable "Declaration on

Peace and Justice" the Sixth Assembly summarized the discussion that took place following the experience of liberation struggles and also that of the growing economic dependencies in which the common issues of peace and justice are brought together; the declaration thus stressed that there could be no peace without justice. Konrad Raiser evaluates this report as "still the best summary of the ecumenical convictions on the questions of war and peace."[91] The declaration states:

> Peace is not just the absence of war. Peace cannot be built on foundations of injustice. Peace requires a new international order based on justice for and within all the nations, and respect for the God-given humanity and dignity of every person. Peace is, as the prophet Isaiah has taught us, the effect of righteousness.[92]

The delegates from the former East Germany had asked in their application to the WCC in Vancouver to check whether, as Dietrich Bonhoeffer urged 50 years prior, that the time was ripe for a general Christian Peace Council.[93] Another call for such a peace council came from the physicist and philosopher Carl Friedrich von Weizsäcker, who was of the opinion that there is a human crisis in the three areas of justice, peace and nature and that there exists an ethical consensus and politically-realizable demands for behaviour in these areas, even beyond the boundaries of religion. He called for a global, politically effective legal system and therefore turned to the churches in the ecumenical movement: "We ask the churches of the world appoint a council of peace. Peace is today the condition for the survival of humanity. It is not assured."[94] Again, the churches should make a statement "which humankind cannot fail to hear."[95] According to Raiser this was the resumption of Bonhoeffer's instigation half a century later; Bonhoeffer had discovered an approach to dealing with issues of war and peace that moves beyond positions that stand in tension with each other and is still as relevant now as then.[96]

To the present there has been no such council, but there has been a more powerful "conciliar process." The task of the conciliar process was "a response, in terms of justice and Christian faith, to the crisis brought on by the exploitation of humankind and of nature and, with members of other religions and world views, to cast this response in practical terms."[97] For the first time the churches wanted to materialize their hope in this systematically-applied dimension. They did this through analysis (identifying threats, establishing internal relationships), through contemporary confession (developing theological convictions about justice, peace, the integrity of creation), and through practical obligations (assumption of common obligations to overcome the threat). As an ecclesiological model the concept of "covenant" served the "World Convocation on Justice, Peace and the Integrity of Creation." The covenant is God's making. In faithfulness to God's covenant, the people responded by joining together in the struggle for justice, peace and creation. The binding character of the unconditional commitment to peace and justice should result from this covenant community.

> To give an adequate response to the global threats of today, the churches need to discover new ways of giving expression to their universal calling. They need to live and to act as one body, transcending the boundaries of nations and at the same time breaking down the barriers of injustice by which Christ's body is dismembered today.[98]

During the World Assembly in Seoul it was clear, however, that a well-founded hope for a common witness in a further process could only be given if the questions of ethics would be seen together with those of ecclesiology. It was recognized that the question of the Church's witness is always asked concerning its nature (*esse*): Even if one could not unanimously support general conscientious objection, the World Assembly enjoyed a broad consensus regarding the various dimensions of the ethics of peace, in the form of voluntary commitments. While reaffirming the peace of God in its full meaning the churches committed here first of all, to exhaust all possibilities to create justice and peace and to resolve conflict through active nonviolence, and secondly, to resist any understanding of security which accommodates the use of weapons of mass destruction, as well as a concept of national security, which has the goal of dominating or suppressing peoples in order to defend the privileges of a few. Military invasions, interventions and occupations are in general rejected here. War is no longer to be considered as a legal means of resolving conflicts, but the governments are asked to create an international legal system that actually serves the realization of peace. Finally, delegates undertook a third commitment, to also liberate personal relationships from violence.

The "Ten Affirmations" of Seoul may well be represented as a social-ethical confession of the ecumenical movement:

> In this world marked by injustice, violence and the degradation of the environment we want to reaffirm God's covenant which is open to all and holds the promise of life in wholeness and right relationships. Responding to God's covenant we profess our faith in the Triune God who is the very source of communion. [...] We make these affirmations as Christian people aware that many people of living faiths and ideologies share these concerns with us and are guided by their understanding of justice, peace and the integrity of creation. We therefore seek dialogue and co-operation with them, guided by a vision of the new future which is necessary for the survival for our planet. We can make these affirmations only as we acknowledge our shortcomings and failures and commit ourselves anew to the reality of God's reign. This means to resist in thought, word and action the powers of separation and destruction and to live in active solidarity with the suffering people.[99]

> 1. We affirm that all exercise of power is accountable to God
>   [...]
> 2. We affirm God's option for the poor [...]
> 3. We affirm the equal value of all races and peoples [...]
> 4. We affirm that male and female are created in the image of
>   God [...]

5. We affirm that truth is at the foundation of a community of free people [...]
6. We affirm the peace of Jesus Christ [...]
7. We affirm the creation as beloved of God [...]
8. We affirm that the earth is the Lord's [...]
9. We affirm the dignity and commitment of the younger generation [...]
10. We affirm that human rights are given by God [...][100]

Four areas were selected for this covenant, which should serve as examples for how urgently we must act jointly. They contain concrete commitments for a just economic order and for the liberation from the burden of foreign debt, and for a "real" security of all states and peoples and for a "culture of nonviolence," for a careful and protective approach to all living things, for preservation of the earth's atmosphere, and the elimination of racism and discrimination on a national and international level in the interests of all people.

For as comprehensive and as unambiguously formulated as these positions on justice, peace and the integrity of nature may seem, it must be noted that these texts were not adopted by a constituent Assembly of the WCC (the highest decision-making body of the WCC) but by a "World Convocation" convened on the topic. Although these official delegates were in fact sent by the member churches and equipped with the appropriate authority, it would be inaccurate to evaluate the formulated basic theological beliefs, creeds and obligations as an obligatory position of the entire WCC. The subsequent discussions demonstrate that this is not possible.

h. The Need to Clarify the Relationship between Ecclesiology and Ethics

It was especially the lack of clarity about the binding nature of the statements of Seoul in 1990 that led to an important, clarifying study process in the 1990s, *Ecclesiology and Ethics*.[101] This process was supposed to help clarify the necessary consequences of the conciliar process and the enduring ecclesiological question of the ecumenical community's self-understanding.

Two basic beliefs formed the framework for discussion:
(1) Ecumenical reflections on ethics and action are "intrinsic" to the essence and life of the Church.[102] A strict separation of ecclesiology and ethics is thus excluded.

The second conviction further clarifies this close interrelationship:
(2) Ecclesiology and Christian ethics must be in close dialogue, mutually respecting and learning from each other.[103]

In this way ethical behaviour is to be seen as a direct expression of ecclesiological convictions and one must "study" the development of an ecclesiology necessarily from the experience of ethical conduct. From the ecclesiological perspective this means, above all, that the understanding of koinonia, memory and hope, Eucharist and baptism, are to be developed further in view of their ethical implications. From the perspective of ethics, these core beliefs mainly include an understanding for the Church to develop, which was referred to in the course of the study process with (controversial) terms such as "moral community" and "moral formation."[104]

The study process documents include other valuable thoughts for important clarifications of the relationship of ecclesiology and ethics, and here the ecclesiological self-understandings were clearly relevant. There is still a need for further clarification, if coherent ecumenical ethics can be developed, effectively corresponding to the ecclesiologies of the WCC member churches.

PART II

FROM OVERCOMING VIOLENCE TO PILGRIMAGE AND COMPANIONSHIP

CHAPTER 6

DEVELOPING THE "DECADE TO OVERCOME VIOLENCE": 1994-1999

Do not be overcome by evil, but overcome evil with good.

— ROMANS 12:21 (NRSV)

THE SUCCESSFUL COHABITATION of humans in which each person's development can benefit, ultimately only happen in relationships that renounce acts of aggression or violence. Instead they can strive to be mutually-supportive through the collective efforts of a "culture of peace."[1] This conviction is not only derived from the message of the Judeo-Christian traditions, but its centrality for ecumenism is undisputed.[2]

As obvious as that is, societies today seem to radically contradict it. Not only personal relationships, but also large communities, even whole societies can be characterized by violence. This violence is not restricted to interpersonal relations, but also manifests itself in objects and to a large extent in the environment. Despite questioning these fundamental issues, it seems that for many, violent behavioral patterns are still considered effective, because even in the churches they are said to be legitimated by the claim that they are "realistic." The position of explicitly renouncing force is called into question in part as a denial of the seriousness of the reality of (individual and collective) evil. Martin Luther King jr. had already struggled earlier against this charge and was looking for a "realistic pacifism." King especially opposed Reinhold Niebuhr, who urged that the "reality of sin" and the "reality of collective evil" need to be taken seriously. Niebuhr criticized pacifism because of its allegedly unrealistic anthropology, which tended to promote perfectionism, instead of taking the Protestant doctrine of justification seriously.[3]

However, in almost all traditions there are examples of successful conflict resolution merely through the conscious renunciation of the use of violence.[4] This contradiction and the suppression of examples of successful nonviolent conflict management motivated the community of churches during the Eighth Assembly of the WCC in Harare, Zimbabwe in 1998 to proclaim the "Decade to Overcome Violence: Churches Seeking Reconciliation and Peace, 2001-2010," parallel to a similarly-oriented United Nations Decade.[5] The stated goals of the WCC's Decade were

> to move peace-building from the periphery to the centre of the life and witness of the church and to build stronger alliances and understanding among churches, networks, and movements which are working toward a culture of peace.[6]

This reflects the profound conviction that this issue is central to the self-understanding and mission of the church, and the plans to seek a realization together with all "people of good will." The Ecumenical Decade was so broadly conceived in terms of content and method that it could be brought to life in many different ways.

In this way the ecumenical community of churches has become involved in a subject, whose complexity is probably hard to surpass. Again one faces the ambivalences of minefields, which are full of doubts and temptations. Those answers that were believed to be invulnerable appear now to be more fragile, as the contextual situations are always different and more complicated than one would initially think in peace ethics. Beliefs that were conceived in one moment are in the next moment threatened once again to be drawn into question.

Violence is obviously an existential part of our lives and the renunciation of violence is necessary for our survival. There will always be violence in this world, but that is still not an argument for its legitimation. Since people die from violence, then should their lives not also be protected through violence? Violence often produces chaos, but does it not maintain order precisely through a monopolization of violence (*Gewaltmonopol*), preserving us from anarchism? Violence violates the dignity of people, often irreparably, but does the dignity of humans not need to be defended by force? And, since violence fascinates us, can nonviolence not be just as exciting?[7]

a. What is Violence? Further Attempts at Definition

The Decade is not a "decade of violence," or even a "decade of nonviolence" but one of *overcoming* violence. This is important to emphasize because in many discussions the very definitions of violence are repeatedly contested and the debates seem to have already exhausted this task. As important as this is for a critical reflection among theological traditions and for the analysis of the respective contexts of violence, as well as for the questions about the appropriate witness of the Church and ecumenism, the task of definition cannot be more than a first step in the real challenge of *overcoming* violence.

The importance of the diverse meanings of the German term "*Gewalt*" is not only justified for its own sake, but also for linguistic reasons. "Luther's translation of Romans 1:13 shapes the decisive paradigm for the ambivalent use of *Gewalt* to the present day," according to Wolfgang Lienemann.[8] "*Gewalt*" is intended here to refer to lawful domination, but in other contexts it can just mean the opposite of what is legal or just. The equivalent terms of "force" and "violence" in modern English or French differ slightly from *Gewalt* in that they indicate wrongful acts in a narrower sense and mean "to threaten, injure or destroy a human (or animal) life, liberty, property, or social position."[9] Power, however, is initially a neutral term that can also refer to lawful and good "governmental power." In German, concepts such as power, domination, government, and coercion are overlapping. The roots of this lack of specificity are found in the Greek and Latin languages. There, the range of meanings moves between the poles of *potestas* and *violentia*. *Potestas* means the official authority founded on *auctoritas*, legally established competence; *violentia* however, means violation.

The insufficient differentiation in German should not be resolved prematurely, because it clearly illustrates the ambivalence of the matter and prohibits a naive isolation of the interdependent elements of this range of meanings. But it will be helpful to clarify in each case, exactly what is meant. The Decade is named in English more precisely than in German: "Decade to Overcome Violence, 2001-2010: Churches Seeking Reconciliation and Peace."[10]

In his research into violence as *violentia*, Johan Galtung decisively expanded the understanding of violence by distinguishing between direct, indirect and cultural violence.[11] *Direct violence* means people hurting or killing other people, and *indirect violence* is when people are restricted such that they cannot develop as they potentially could, for example, due to unequal power relations or withholding of life opportunities (also known as "structural violence"). "Violence is present when people are influenced, such that their actual somatic and mental effectiveness is less than its potential effectiveness."[12] *Cultural violence* is any aspect of a culture that may legitimize direct or indirect violence, for example, a right-wing extremist or gender-based discrimination.

Similarly comprehensive is the widely accepted definition of Robert McAfee Brown, which suggests a supplement to Galtung's definitions, because it highlights in particular the psychological dimension:

> Whatever 'violates' another, in the sense of infringing upon or disregarding or abusing or denying that other, whether physical harm is done or not, can be understood as an act of violence (...) While such denial or violation can involve the physical destruction of personhood in ways that are obvious, personhood can also be violated or denied in

subtle ways that are not obvious at all, except to the victim. There can be violation of personhood quite apart from the doing of physical harm.[13]

These definitions make it clear that violence must be considered much more comprehensively than the sense of *violentia*, namely, as superficial or specious forms of physical injury or death. Wolfgang Lienemann has, however, strongly argued for a narrower concept of violence in order to describe the matter with greater precision: *Violentia* "always relates to physical force against the will of an originally free person or any other legally-protected living being (*violentia contra vitam, libertatem et voluntatem personae*)."[14]

Throughout the Decade the WCC has repeated the official definition of the World Health Organization (WHO), considered as a publicly-consented definition. Violence is therefore:

> the intentional use of physical force or power, threatened or actual, against oneself, another person, or against a group or community, that either results in or has a high likelihood of resulting in injury, death, psychological harm, maldevelopment or deprivation.[15]

Even though in a more conspicuous manner, violence against oneself has recently been added, violence can already be recognized, and first and foremost understood as a relational concept, if by violence one means all actions, structures and beliefs through which the unilateral exercise of power can destroy or prevent other just relationships (it is assumed that this can also imply self-inflicted violence). Here there is already an initial, important consideration of what it means to overcome violence: a precondition for a successful life that is free of violence, allowing for the construction, maintenance and the security of living in right relationships.

b. Overcoming Violence – An Unrealistic Goal?

But is it not an unrealistic goal to try to overcome violence when violence is still being described as an anthropological constant? This question arises in the face of all such broad movements of the churches. Two possible responses should suffice here:

(1) If the question relates primarily to the non-specific nature of *violence*, then one can pose the counter-question concerning alternatives: Do the witnesses in the New Testament recommend that we try to overcome only certain types of violence? Or should the differentiation concern in each case *who* is subjected to the use of force, or for what *purpose* it is used? By simply applying some of their classic teachings the church would ultimately, once again, theologically legitimize violence. The fact that this attempt at legitimation has not broken the spirals of violence in church history, but at many points has enabled it, is unquestioned. If violence is not only to be opposed in extreme cases such as martyrdom, but if we also ask, above all, whether violence is justified, then of course one may ask how this right to curb violence is to be established. That this cannot be done entirely without *coercion* is evident. The difference lies in a fundamentally distinctive motivation and goal orientation, namely, achieving the democratically-controlled monopoly of violence by the state. This seeks to ensure a reduction of violence through the regulation of relationships as to protect those who cannot protect themselves, and facilitates the actual overcoming of violence in the end.

That alone will not change the real, existing "culture of violence." But by simultaneously undertaking a serious search for nonviolent alternatives to conflict resolution, the churches could play a decisive role if they are ready to fulfill their duty of being a "guardian" in society, especially for the sake of protecting the weak. This always includes uncovering what motivates the use of violence in order to liberate the victims and the perpetrators from it. The difficult question of whether violence is to be considered legitimate in situations of dire need, such as the protection of those who are immediately threatened, represents one extreme case, which may not consume all the energy in answering this one question, because there would still be no practical change in developing everyday ethics. The primary attention should be mainly in the search for models of action that are alternatives to violence.

(2) Apart from that, there is the dubious question of *overcoming*, which generally presents a very serious challenge for the Christian faith. Here it is clearly stated *who* is committed to this Decade:

> a fellowship of churches which confess the Lord Jesus Christ as God and Saviour according to the scriptures and therefore seek to fulfil together their common calling to the glory of the one God, Father, Son and Holy Spirit.[16]

It expresses the hope that God will lead his people at the end of this history to a good end. It is not for the churches to establish the Kingdom of God on earth with their more or less courageous efforts. But just when the eschatological dimension of faith is anticipated, then this vision will be transformed into the present. Only with this understanding, Paul can state: "Do not be overcome by evil, but overcome evil with good." (Rom 12:21) To accuse Paul of being out of touch with reality would probably be interpreted as a lack of understanding of the eschatological reality and as a refusal by the churches to always be ready to "make your defense to anyone who demands from you an accounting for the hope that is in you." (1 Pet 3:15)

The churches are now more incisively than ever recognizing and identifying their own entanglement in circles of violence. They committed themselves to holding a Decade to Overcome Violence, to self-critically raise this as the ecumenical agenda above their own particular limitations, beyond the topic of the complexity of violence to make it a "cross-sectional task" of the churches. This initiative is not simply about the age-old debate between Christian pacifism or bellicosity. It is quite comprehensive, striving for nothing less than the serious inquiry into a "right life amid the wrong one."[17] It concerns a serious reflection upon well-known, key passages in the Gospel in the hopes of new discoveries: that "turning the other cheek" can be understood as an act of nonviolent civil courage, that even "from anyone who takes away your coat do not withhold even your shirt" (Luke 6:29) can constitute a provocation that disarms the perpetrator, and that the willingness to walk a second mile, if one is forced to walk one (Cf. Matt 5:41) opens up the possibility for a dialogue between different value systems.[18]

It is clear that the phenomenon of violence describes a subject area that, on the one hand, represents a permanent challenge for all Christians and all religious traditions in all contexts and secondly, reveals in rather complex ways the need for a more accurate analysis, without wanting to separate one topic from others and completely isolate it. On the *general* challenge of violence the conciliar Process for Justice, Peace and the Integrity of Creation had attempted to reply in a similarly extensive manner, by emphasizing the interdependencies between justice, peace and nature.[19]

The development of this Decade is presented in the following sections, and its key theological ideas will be dealt with, namely those that motivated the ecumenical movement toward this goal. The permanent ethical and ecclesiological challenges are also discussed. Ecumenism will have to prove itself precisely concerning the existential question of the possibility of overcoming violence.

c. Stations on the Way to the Decade to Overcome Violence

(1) The Outset: 1973

In 1973, the WCC had noted:

> The problem of Christian responsibility in a world of force and violence is as old as the church itself and has appeared in ever-changing forms through the centuries. In all these forms the agonizing question remains the same: how can Christians live and work in a world where the use of force and violence appears to be unavoidable?
> [20]

The fellowship of churches in the WCC saw itself once again being drawn into question. The end of the Cold War and the confrontation of violence shifted the focus of ecumenical debate. The time of the more or less clear political and ideological fronts had given way to the new reality of domestic conflicts and localized ethnic disputes.[21] One now saw challenges in the disintegration of states as becoming a new form of threat to peace, giving rise in some cases to such a power and legal vacuum, that there were completely uncontrolled excesses of violence, and even genocide, in which hardly any ideological positions are visible – also known as the "new wars"[22] or "asymmetrical conflicts."[23]

At the end of the twentieth century, the churches again found themselves in a previously unknown state of plurality, in a subsequent search for identity. And at the same time the advance of globalization raised awareness higher than had ever been previously possible in the ecumenical movement of our living in *one* world. The concurrent marginalization again taking place in many parts of the *oikoumene* through a structuralization of this globalizing trend can further increase the potential for conflict through relationships of economic dependency. The relationships between military conflicts and refugee crises, unemployment and crime, environmental degradation and hunger are emerging clearer than ever, and the protection of human rights is by no means adequately guaranteed. At no time was access to information about these conflicts provided so extensively and securely and yet the world community is not yet in a position to stop the newly erupting melee of violence.

(2) Johannesburg 1994: The "Programme to Overcome Violence"

In 1994, the Central Committee of the WCC gathered for the first time after the end of apartheid in the "new South Africa." The recognition for the WCC's role in having defeated apartheid through the "Programme to Combat Racism" has been given wide coverage. The effect of this ecumenical commitment was recognized by many including Desmond Tutu and Nelson Mandela. The testimonies of the

South African churches revealed clearly how grateful they were for the effort of the WCC; yet it also revealed how much they now saw themselves as challenged by the tremendous violence in the country. The South African Methodist Bishop Stanley Mogoba therefore proposed in a sermon a new "programme to combat against violence." First the ensuing discussion in WCC Unit III (Justice, Peace and Creation) produced an official request to the Central Committee in this regard, initiated by a representative of the historic peace churches, Don Miller (Church of the Brethren) and supported by the Chair of Unit III, Margot Käßmann (EKD).[24] In the context of these discussions, finally the decision was taken that in light of this, and all the other violent experiences of churches in other countries, the WCC should not remain silent. Thus the "Programme to Overcome Violence" (according to the Pauline formulation in Romans 12:21) was initiated. The text of the decision reflects the discussions:[25]

...that the WCC establishes a Programme to Overcome Violence, with the purpose of challenging and transforming the global culture of violence in the direction of a culture of just peace...

...that two initiatives already underway, i.e. (1) a consultation to be held in Corrymeela, Northern Ireland, June 1994, entitled "Building a Culture of Peace: the Churches' Contribution" and (2) a database of church-related peace groups, be among the first steps towards this programme;

...that, in the context of current discussions on *koinonia*, Units I and III engage in a joint study on the ecclesial dimensions of the pursuit of a culture of non-violence and just peace in order to address the ecclesiological and constitutional issues [...]

...that a study be initiated to assess the role of sanctions, their effectiveness and conditions of their applicability as an important means towards peaceful resolution and transformation of conflict [...]

...that, in view of the need to confront and overcome the "spirit, logic and practice of war" and to develop new theological approaches, consonant with the teachings of Christ, which start not with war and move to peace, but with the need for justice, this may be a time when the churches together, should face the challenge to give up any theological or other justification of the use of military power and to become a *koinonia* dedicated to the pursuit of a just peace.

...that the Central Committee request member churches, in cooperation with non-member churches and NGOs, to share with the WCC their positions on peace with justice, the development of a just peace culture as an alternative to one governed by the spirit, logic and practice of violence, and on education for peace [...]

(3) Boston 1998: The Question of Theological and Ecclesiological Implications

According to the conclusions at Johannesburg in 1994, to respond to the new challenges with a "Programme to Overcome Violence," the WCC commissioned what were then called the program units "Faith and Order" (Unit I) and "Justice, Peace and the Integrity of Creation" (Unit III) to jointly design a study process. Taking into account the current ecclesiological discussions around the central concept of *koinonia*[26] in particular, this study was to investigate the theological and ecclesiological implications of such a programme. Which resources are being made available to the community of churches in the effort to shape a culture of non-violence? Which resources of Christian faith can be drawn upon in creating a "just peace"?

A small consultation with experts from the fields of theology, ethics and sociology that took place in 1998 (Boston, USA), took up the task of designing such a study process.[27] The following results were identified as focal issues:

(1) a growing awareness of the need for a new paradigm in ecumenical dialogue, transcending the polarized debate over "pacifism vs. just war." The question must now be posed from the perspective of Christian responsibility as to how *active* nonviolent alternatives could be developed to resolve conflicts;

(2) the ecumenical movement looks back upon a rich tradition of ministries to communities who suffered from poverty and violent

conflict, yet new approaches are now needed in order for churches to confront the global swelling of violence in its various forms; (3) Christian peace initiatives have already become networked all over the world, but the relationship between churches and non-church peace groups is largely unclear. Here ecclesiological issues become explicitly present.

According to the consultation, a joint study process should result in the following:

... Power must be reflected upon differently in all its dimensions: at the local level, in the societies, in international relations and in the life of the churches. (Further studies that now exist on nationalism, ethnicity and religion should be brought into the discussion).[28] What are the consequences of the violence between nations and between different ethnic groups within a state in view of the fellowship of churches or the dividedness of the body of Christ?

... The role of religious institutions should be critically analyzed, especially regarding the churches. Where are they fostering a legitimization of violence, and which counter efforts to overcome violence can be identified?

... Inspired by the two-year campaign "Peace to the City" (see below), new and creative approaches to living in various local contexts should be assessed using these case studies. Christian minorities in non-Christian societies face special challenges, which once again raise the question of a methodology to enable contextual theology to communicate across cultures.

... Reflections on the relationship between ecclesiology and ethics should be deepened to include the study process, "Ecclesiology and Ethics: Ecumenical Ethical Engagement, Moral Formation and the Nature of the Church."[29]

... Baptism and Eucharist bind Christians together. They could be the primary sources for the formation of unity between churches which are themselves disrupted by violence and conflict. In Baptism and Eucharist there is potential for ethical formation.

... Churches should be encouraged to develop a "culture of peace" as a prophetic sign of reconciled humanity and new creation. Further exegetical clarifications are needed.

... There should be an investigation into the relationship between a culture of violence and the alienation of victims of violence in the life of the churches. From the realization that violent offenders were often previously victims of violence themselves, psychological and theological issues also arise.

Previous studies by the WCC had a different focus and these should be used as valuable resources. They include studies of the conflict between the pacifist position and representatives of the just war, the questions of revolution, liberation struggles and racism (in the 1960s and 70s), structural and economic "violence" (in the 1970s and 80s), and violence against nature (1980s and 90s). The "Programme to Overcome Violence" did not want to repeat the same questions. Rather, the hope was that this could now become a programme such, "that there would be an impulse from the [WCC] General Assembly in Harare for the worldwide ecumenical movement, both at the local and international level." To be freed from violence is not an impossibility, but "it is a part of the witness of Christians in the midst of a world that is replete with violence,"[30] as the conference stated.

(4) The "Peace to the City" Campaign: Concretely Overcoming Violence and Impulse for Theological Reflection

One of the impulses which encouraged the delegates in Harare to renew this commitment was the "Peace to the City" campaign started in the mid-1990s as part of the Programme to Overcome Violence.[31] Seven cities on the different continents were selected to uncover the various forms in which violence appears: drug-related criminality among youth gangs in Boston, USA; the militarized violence between the groups in Colombo, Sri Lanka; the terrorist developments between Protestants and Catholics who are blinded by fundamentalism in Belfast, Northern Ireland; the violence between those who were similarly "lost" to society in Durban, South Africa; the hatred between the representatives of different ethnicities and religions in Suva, Fiji; or the gruesomeness of organized criminality in Rio de Janeiro, Brazil.[32]

These cities are both the focus and microcosm of societies today. As such the polarities are presented in cumulative and concentrated forms: rich and poor, success and failure, life and death, intelligence and illiteracy, innovation and antiquation, hope and disappointment; everything coalesces in a radicalized form. In the near future the majority of people will be living in oversized mega-cities.

Consideration of these creative and successful initiatives for reconciliation in these cities prompted a re-examination of the contexts of violence and mechanisms for overcoming it and, on this basis, fresh theological reflection has also begun on old, familiar themes. Hopefully, this will not congeal into conceptual ethical absolutes detached from real-life stories but will enable us to jointly explore the real causes of violence and the possibilities for overcoming it, starting from the center of the Christian faith. An in-depth study of this kind obviously has to be organized along interdisciplinary lines, drawing on the knowledge available in history and political science, sociology and economics, behavioral research, psychology and law. In this sense, too, the Decade called for an "ecumenical" approach. In the light of experiences from the seven cities we shall try first to understand the dynamics and complexity of cycles of violence and peace networks, before going on to look – in a very tentative and provisional way – at suggestions for further theological work.

Analysis: Contextual Experiences as a Starting Point: The Self-Perpetuating Complexity of Cycles of Violence

The experiences in the seven cities show that the cycle of violence is a self-perpetuating phenomenon, constantly generating new violence from within itself. This understanding and experience is as old as human communal life itself (for example, as it developed in the narratives of the Old Testament).[33] It is true also of violence that is used with the most honourable intentions. Nor does it make any difference whether we are talking about direct-personal, indirect-structural or even cultural violence; in fact, there is a far greater practical connection between these different forms of violence than the theoretical distinction might suggest. The picture becomes even more complicated and difficult to understand when other levels are taken into account: the inter-relatedness of the personal, collective, national and global levels.[34] Examples from countless places of conflict around the world confirm the thesis that the cycle of violence is self-perpetuating. The motor that keeps these cycles in motion is the injustice (social, economic, political and other), which is reinforced and perpetuated by violence, such that it becomes entrenched. In what follows we concentrate on the experiences of injustice from four of the seven selected cities, namely: Rio de Janeiro, Brazil; Belfast, Northern Ireland; Colombo, Sri Lanka; Boston, USA.

Rio de Janeiro is one of the places in the world where injustice is most visible to the naked eye. Anyone who has visited this city with its idyllic setting is bound to have been struck by the wealth and poverty existing there side by side. Perhaps the visitor may even have been the victim of crime, because anyone who can afford to travel to Rio is likely to have more money than most of the local population. The wealthy protect themselves behind barbed-wire fences and walls, aided by private, armed "security forces" which do not, however, create a sense of security. The social inequality and the unfair distribution of wealth have turned the city into a hotbed of crime. Young people growing up in the *favelas* basically have no chance of ever crossing the divide and being able to a lead a normal family and working life as those affected know all too well. They feel marginalized, and see no point in education when all that awaits them at the end is unemployment. Young people can earn more through drug-dealing and theft than by any other effort they might make. So the two "sides" are armed and ready, scraping by from day to day, and the city lives in a general climate of mutual distrust. State agencies, above all the police, have at best given up, but in most cases have actually become part of the cycle of violence and try to make whatever money they can from it. A city in which the state no longer has a "monopoly on violence," cannot be rescued through legislative enactments; and for good reason there is no trust in the executive political branch. No laws are going to rescue a city where the authorities are no longer in control of violence and where all confidence in the executive has disappeared – and rightly so. It is bound to end in chaos, for injustice fosters violence and vice-versa, and so it continues.

In Belfast the motivations for violence are different. Here the equation of religious or denominational affiliation and national identity (Unionist-Protestant – Republican-Catholic) unleashed a spiral of hatred. The population was trapped for decades in "sectarian violence" backed by old traditions and symbols. Mutual ignorance and physical separation made it almost impossible for prejudices to ever be called into question. On the contrary, the flames of intolerance, mistrust and discrimination are constantly rekindled. The ironically-named "peace walls" physically mark these divisions and have even helped to reinforce them. The emotional state of the people who live in this situation is reflected in their sense of frustration at the hopelessness of the conflict, in their depression or, again, in a resurgence of anger at the injustice of it all. Many people suffer from recurring nightmares, problems in concentrating and insomnia as a result of the violence they have experienced. Others suffer breakdowns because of the permanent feeling of danger and being at the mercy of others as well as the inability to cope with their desire for revenge and their own aggressiveness. In more than a few cases these constant tensions lead to domestic violence. In some families the situation is compounded by the harsh reality of three generations of unemployment. Against this background, young people in particular are naturally drawn towards paramilitary groups which give them a sense of belonging and being needed. In 1994, the government spent 436 million pounds on social security benefits but just 1 million on the work of developing community relations.[35] Nobody seems able to break the cycle.

A third city – Colombo, the capital of Sri Lanka – illustrates how the reasons for violence can vary, though the structures remain the same. Civil war has been raging there for over two decades, fueled by a mixture of ethnic, religious and political interests. Some of the tensions stem from the events of the colonial era: first came the

Portuguese bringing Catholicism, then the Dutch bringing Protestantism, followed by the British bringing Anglicanism and Methodism. Although Sri Lanka is actually a multi-faith, multi-ethnic and multi-cultural country, the proportions speak for themselves: 74 percent Singhalese (Buddhist), 18 percent Tamils (Hindus, migrants from India brought there by the British to work on the tea plantations), 7 percent Muslims (who arrived later as traders), 1 percent Burghers (descendants of the former colonial rulers). Around 7.5 percent of the population are Christians and the Christian religion is the only one which is not directly linked with a particular ethnic group. The different ethnic groups have also retained their own languages.

The struggle for power in the country began very soon after independence in 1948, when the Singhalese denied the Tamils citizenship. A colonial situation developed within the country and the tensions mounted. The Tamils demanded the right to self-determination and the right to call Sri Lanka their home. The government allowed the Muslim and Singhalese to arm "home guards." In 1987, the Indian army tried to settle the conflict by military intervention but left the country two years later without succeeding. On the contrary, violations of human rights had increased, divisions were entrenched, prejudices, hatred and the desire for revenge had redoubled. Now society has become heavily militarized, and women, children and young people are recruited as a matter of course. Young people are particularly sought after because they are ready to be trained for the much-feared suicide commandos, the "Baby Tigers." Here too, the police are guilty of abuse and discrimination. Economically and socially, the tensions are a disaster for the whole country, causing unemployment, poverty and displacement, as the "Cost of War" report testifies.[36] All communication between the opposing sides broke down long ago. Religious fundamentalism also plays a part in these conflicts, especially among the Buddhist monks who do not want to lose their position of privilege and, in many cases, it is the clergy who rekindle the torch of violence. There are of course others who urge that Buddhism should return to its roots, i.e. "the practice of non-violence, peace-building, respect for life and the belief that all people are equal, rejecting caste and racial superiority."[37]

Despite the diversity of these contexts – Rio de Janeiro, Belfast and Colombo – common features can be noted. Cycles of violence are *circuli vitiosi* (vicious circles), in the truest sense of the word, as the examples from these cities show. The cycles are not only perpetuated by injustice within the city itself, but are reinforced by injustice from outside, be it the unfair global market economy which further marginalizes the countries of the South and gives only an elite a share of the profits;[38] or by the international arms trade, which profits from military conflicts. Cycles of violence are also perpetuated in societies with high levels of criminality, where people are prepared to invest huge amounts in private weaponry, or where there is political refusal to develop international law to allow human-rights violations to be prosecuted across national boundaries. The global is reflected in the local and vice-versa.

Whenever one begins to probe the causes of violence, one inevitably comes up against the injustices which lead to unhealthy relations, or the refusal of any relations. One also encounters relations which are wholly concerned with the exercise of power and dependence, where one side is always intent on fulfilling its own needs at the cost of others, where fear of losing power leads it to oppress others. Traditions and religions are sometimes used for this purpose, but sometimes they are themselves part of a pattern of behaviour based on the principle of seeking personal gain at the expense of others. In such situations fears are not unfounded, for the oppressors' awareness of their own ruthlessness makes them deeply distrustful of those they hold in subjection. This leads them to cultivate stereotyped enemy images which can then be used to defend their own misdeeds – which are to some extent acknowledged as such – and ultimately to justify a "war against evil."[39] The mere fact of difference is then in itself sufficient reason to argue for separation and isolation. This does not, however, bring security, because any relaxation of the pressure on the other is seized upon as a sign of weakness, therefore retaliation can be expected. These are simply observations reflecting the real-life experience of people directly affected, and are not intended as a comprehensive theory. However, these concrete examples served the WCC at the outset of the Decade to Overcome Violence, with reference to developing an approach that corresponds to the theologies of the global South.

Summary: Community-Building and Presence as Means of Overcoming Violence

None of the seven cities started with a clear strategy for overcoming violence, but rather they began with the problems affecting them. Thus it was clear from the outset that the important element is concrete human needs, and that human beings themselves are the actors. In each case the development began by building on these experiences and the wisdom gained from them, which led to visible, tangible changes. Only in retrospect could common, recurring patterns be identified. This emerged from the cities' networking among themselves. Again we will look at some examples of ecumenical projects aimed at community-building and supporting presence, in hopes of deriving more general lessons in the search for effective means of overcoming violence.

In all the cities the projects began with individuals getting together with others and before long someone's house would become the centre, serving as an open, hospitable space for building community.[40] Sometimes the media would take notice and give their support to the attempts to find alternatives to counter the culture of violence. Many volunteers were needed and were mostly given basic training on the ground as part of the programme, so that they were drawn into the movement.[41] Contacts were sought in other organizations and government offices, specialists or people exercising specific functions in society. Gradually a trend was established in a local community and a change of attitude would begin.[42] Things which once seemed impossible began to seem possible and mentalities changed. In this way a culture of nonviolence develops. In cities, opportunities for participation and community-building seem to be a key factor, as people do not by nature want to be "urban nomads." All those involved confirmed, however, that these are long and difficult processes, which are fragile and dependent upon the initiative and commitment of individuals. They say it can only be done with others in a community offering mutual encouragement and reassurance and division of labour, where individuals can sometimes be weak because others are there with them.

The Mediation Network in Belfast, founded in 1991, is a good example of this.[43] Churches, public agencies and politicians, groups working for justice, peace and reconciliation, neighbourhood groups and local communities have found points of contact because they are all affected by the violence. They draw strength from working together and building relations and their effectiveness is increased. This collective work itself becomes a touchstone of their capacity for overcoming violence, for there is always the danger that people may try to stake out territory for fear of losing power and becoming dependent. The willingness to invest in a measure of mutual trust is the basis for a common undertaking, sustained by the understanding that ultimately it benefits all sides. In Belfast the aim of education is to establish identity, tolerance and acceptance of political and cultural differences. Neighbours cannot remain strangers; using this as a principle, areas of encounter can then develop. Differences then cease to be considered first and foremost as dangers and are seen instead as an opportunity. Security is no longer based on establishing boundaries but on the resilience of the community. The goal is always the well-being of others as well as oneself, because now the idea has taken root that one's own well-being depends upon that of others.

The declared aim of the National Peace Council founded in Colombo in 1995 was to break the cycle of violence. The initiative brought together people from all religious groups, and representatives of a dozen organizations, all working for the common good.

They chose three guiding principles:

(1) to accept only a negotiated settlement of the conflict;
(2) to seek dialogue among *all* the parties involved, and

(3) to consider the hopes of all the people living in Sri Lanka.

For the conflict in Sri Lanka has made it clear that:

(a) it cannot be left only to the governing parties to find a solution to a conflict of this kind;
(b) the population must be the guarantor of a lasting peace, and everyone's democratic rights must be institutionally guaranteed;
(c) genuine peace work must be independent of all political forces and must guarantee the basic rights of the oppressed.

Each religion and culture has its own inherent conventions for satisfactorily structuring and regulating community life and for containing or overcoming violence: "We decided to begin the task by focusing actions on the long tradition of good relations that had existed before the conflict."[44] The first step was to encourage mutual hospitality, which helps to develop respect for the other's dignity. In Colombo and in many villages, workshops would reenact old traditions, and revive ancient myths through popular dramas and plays, offering the opportunity for people to participate and express their own feelings. Inter-religious dialogues were organized where the very fact that clergy are present has in itself an enormous symbolic and exemplary force ("religious leaders must be the first to be educated for peace").[45] Political decision-makers are also drawn in. For the churches in the cities the most important thing was to make their presence felt, not to barricade themselves behind stout church walls, but to be present in the places where violent conflicts are actually being conducted. This was not without repercussions in the life of local congregations.

d. The Motivation for Theological Reflection from Contextual Experiences

As we take into account the context-specific challenges and the corresponding methods that were designed according to local initiatives and needs, plus the development of activities and varying forms of organization, certain comparable mechanisms to overcoming violence become apparent. For the sake of theological reflection we will consider here the motivations for discussion, which can carry a degree of the dynamism and creativity of the concrete projects into theoretical reflection and in this way further fertilize the praxis. One might inquire here as to what degree peace activity is something that is testing the Church in general and ecumenism in particular, and how this affects the center of its faith when one of the declared goals of the Decade is "to bring peace-building from the margins to the center of the life and witness of the Church."[46]

(1) Community Formation – Trinitarian Considerations

Violence always means the destruction of relationships, the prevention of right relationships and thus the prevention of community. Therefore, an essential feature of all overcoming violence is networking, the development of right relationships, with the goal of community-building. A central aspect is reconciliation. Community thrives on the diversity of its participants and renounces attempts at uniformity. Ecumenical theology is precisely where important efforts have been taken on this topic. Not least due to the influence of the Orthodox traditions: "*koinonia*," the concept that had long been forgotten in the West, has been re-introduced and become ecumenically fruitful. The basis of this common understanding is given in the Trinitarian confession.

Meanwhile, the many fine individual contributions from different traditions no longer depend on this trinitarianism. Whether the relationship is now presented perichoretically or in a participatory manner, the conceptual step that moves from divine community to human community was exclusively interpreted economically or derived analogically. For present considerations it should be noted that this concept cannot only pertain to the ontological description of community (the Church and the churches). The task will be to base these key statements of faith and theology upon the description of the way of life and the witness of the Church and the community of churches, in view of community-building, namely, over and above the boundaries of the Church. If it is a priority to describe the nature of God using the concepts of community, and if this becomes the basis of the very nature of the Church, then the efforts of community-building are central to the activity of the Church; for the task of overcoming violence belongs to the center of the faith and life of the Church and the ecumenical community. This may be the strongest possible theological opposition to violence.

(2) Presence – Christological Considerations

The initial spark of the program for overcoming violence in the city of Boston (the "Ten-Point Coalition") was the experience of one congregation. They experienced that nothing in church life ultimately had any effect on the circles of violence surrounding them if the congregation is not really present *in* the reality of life. So members of the congregation left the secure space of their church and began specifically to meet the people on the street. Thus a movement began that has actually reduced violence, and is actually saving human lives.

God's decisive movement within creation is visibly expressed in the Christian belief about the Incarnation. God becomes human, not removed in an abstract and impersonal way, but God incarnates, even assumes human form, becomes part of the "sinful world" to sanctify it, to save it and finally to make it complete. Reflecting on this "initial spark," the renewed consideration of the performative movement of the Incarnation can be a powerful impetus for shaping church life.

Here again, there are countless contributions to the discussion, especially in the field of mission studies regarding the necessity of "inculturation" of the Gospel in different cultures. For the ecumenical movement and the WCC in particular, this common basis of speaking of God's presence in Christ is absolutely the central axiom. In view of the churches' movements beyond their previous borders and confines, what possibilities can be uncovered in their respective contexts to "incarnate" and the presence and purposes of nonviolence?

(3) Opening Spaces – Pneumatological Considerations

Experiences in the seven cities made it clear that the opening of spaces is needed for the purpose of eliminating circles of violence. This is initially to be understood quite specifically as the creation of protected places in which community-building can occur without the risk of renewed decline into patterns of violent behavior. How can churches be such "places of holiness"? In addition, however, these spaces are also to be developed in a metaphorical sense, namely, that in order to overcome violence, the creation of a protected place is needed, where issues may be brought to light in the truth, without fear of inflicting harm again; in such a space, past injustices can then come to light.

Without such spaces there can be no reprocessing, no steps on the path of reconciliation. Truth commissions have clearly demonstrated this, although such processes can certainly be regarded only as a first step in a longer journey of reconciliation. The Decade has been primarily described in some discussions as one such "ecumenical space." This metaphor clarifies the description of this project insofar as its character is one of *process*, one which at any time offers the various participants the freedom to be able to shape and to unfold it. However, on the other hand it is admitted that this does not occur arbitrarily. It is an ecumenical space that offers security, *because* it is founded on a community that is intended to be permanent – a space of habitation.

But what provides a center for this community? Even in the ecumenical debates on ecclesiology different versions are available for consideration. Related to this context pneumatological considerations appear, because this is where the metaphor of space is properly situated theologically. Jürgen Moltmann has already referred to the complementary "formative metaphors" (energy, space, shape) to describe the experiences of the Spirit:

> The divine Spirit is experienced as the Lord who sets free, and the free
> space in which 'there is no more cramping'... and people who have this

experience know that they are kept safe and set free in the broad place of the Spirit in which they can breathe deeply and unfurl their potentialities.[47]

The simultaneity of security and opportunity for development is the prerequisite for a culture of nonviolence. In the metaphorical language, the experience of the Spirit opens up a way to the possibility of expressing this in the language of faith and to be certain that this space is provided by the Spirit of life.

(4) The Other Perspective – Eschatological Considerations

What is genuine is first and foremost a viable vision of what can be introduced through the churches' engagement with existing secular social networks. People who are involved in these networks are often tired from their daily confrontation with violence and the sometimes frantic quest to interrupt power circles. One can easily lose sight of hope and the goal on this arduous journey.

The Christian articulation and vision of the Kingdom of God offer a chance to reflect anew upon overcoming violence. The Kingdom of God that is believed to already have dawned in Christ is waiting for its completion. The vision of a world of justice and peace is articulated for Christians in the language of the Kingdom of God. In the eschatological expectation of the completion and re-creation of the world there lies the profound hope in the fact that violence can indeed be overcome, as this is part of that reality that came with the Incarnation of God in Christ into the world of violence. This changes the view of the present world. This newly changed perspective is what motivates the search for how to overcome violence, which only legitimizes discussions of "overcoming" and opens up new interpretations of their own experiences. The awareness of the gift of participating in this Kingdom of God can be both a comfort and strength to persevere in an effort to break through circles of violence and construct communities of peace.

e. At the Beginning of the Decade to Overcome Violence

(1) Harare 1998: The Decision for a Decade – A Genuinely Ecumenical *Counter*-Movement

Above all else it is the *violentia* at the end of the twentieth century, which challenges the churches and the community of churches. In the Eighth Assembly of the WCC in Harare, Zimbabwe, this was continuously recognizable in various topics, if only implicitly. Such examples included the discussions and the resulting declarations to mark the 50th Anniversary of the Declaration of Human Rights, in the plenary sessions on Africa and the discussions on globalization, in the evaluation of the Decade project on "Churches in Solidarity with Women." In that case there is the crucial sentence: "Violence against women is a sin!" In the message of the General Assembly ("Together, Under the Cross in Africa") this decisive statement did not surface. But otherwise it clearly identified the following:

> We have heard from women, children,
> refugees and displaced persons
> whose lives have been ravaged by violence.
> We have been challenged to express our solidarity with them, and
>   to commit ourselves to overcome violence and to promote the
>   full human dignity of all.
> By going to those at the periphery God causes commotion,
>   making this periphery the centre [...]
> We trust in the liberating power of forgiveness,
> transforming enmity into friendship
> and breaking the spiral of violence.
> We are challenged by the vision of a church
> that will reach out to everyone,
> sharing, caring, proclaiming the good news of God's redemption,
> a sign of the kingdom and a servant of the world.
> We are challenged by the vision of a church,

the people of God on the way together,
confronting all divisions of race, gender, age or culture,
striving to realize justice and peace,
upholding the integrity of creation.[48]

In the report of the Programme Guidelines Committee, the current reference becomes more apparent and the programmatic orientation more concrete:

Violence arising from various forms of human rights violations, discrimination and structural injustice represents a growing concern at all levels of an increasingly plural society. Racism combines with and aggravates other causes of exclusion and marginalization. Conflicts are becoming increasingly complex, located more often within nations than between nations. [...] The Council should work strategically with the churches on these issues to create a culture of non-violence, linking and interacting with other international partners and organizations, and examining and developing appropriate approaches to conflict transformation and just peace-making in the new globalized context.[49]

To this declaration the following sentence was added by request and taken as a decision in the plenary session: "Therefore, the WCC proclaims the period 2000-2010 as an Ecumenical Decade to Overcome Violence."[50]

The request for this Decade came directly from the floor, because the program committee of the General Assembly had not been able to raise it themselves. For many delegates the decision to launch the Decade was only revealed organically through the discussion in the hearings and workshops (in Harare they were called *Padare*). The approval of the overwhelming majority of the delegates should be taken as a clear sign of the desire for a just and peaceful coexistence in the different parts of the world, but on the other hand also for the recognition of the presence of violence in all these societies. The experience of violence reaches into the smallest units of the society:

villages, schools, families, marriages. The common concern about the prevailing violence in all walks of life, and the apparent impotence of the churches – even including their own collusion in this "culture of violence" – motivated the decision to overcome violence and the development of a culture of reconciliation and peace through nonviolence, placing this on the common, international ecumenical agenda.

If culture is understood as the totality of the forms of human expression and language, and of the orders and institutions of human communities, their behavioral norms in ethics and morality, as well as their interpretation of reality and knowledge, it is clear how it seems justified to speak of a "culture of violence." And in the same way it is evident how a comprehensive undertaking of a culture of peace and reconciliation can be targeted by a Decade to Overcome Violence. What potential for a counterculture of overcoming violence does the Christian message already hold? And what creativity will be released when the path of nonviolence is not only attempted sporadically here and there by way of example, but is taken up by the global community of churches?

This decision can also be seen as an indication of the willingness as the community of churches to not shirk from the challenge of reviewing either their own theological convictions and traditions concerning the promotion of violence, or for their potential to overcome violence. The challenge is posed for all traditions which morally and theologically justify war; which according to their ethics may still see violence as legitimate and unavoidable means of resolving conflicts; which themselves have developed structures and liturgies; which obviously allow or support, rather than reduce it; which operate counselling practices that do not uncover violence, but rather silence the victims of violence, or cause them to leave their church, and have no alternatives to deal with offenders generally, other than turning them over to legal judgement and punishment.

Certainly the consciously general wording of the request's formulation enabled its broad support. But that was precisely because it corresponded to the new structural specifications of the WCC for the General Assembly, which should be limited to more comprehensive, larger issues, rather than getting lost in too many small programs that are no longer being received by the churches. The ecumenical Decade to Overcome Violence laid open a programmatic framework in which many different steps could be taken to develop a "culture of peace."

When the delegates decided to begin the new century with the Decade to Overcome Violence, they certainly did not yet have the subsequent global political scenario in mind, namely, a globally-organized terrorist force, cruelly manifested in the attacks of September 11, 2001, in North America and elsewhere. It is a global political community that does not know any recourse other than resorting once again to war in order to overthrow such regimes, which not only protected terrorists, but even encouraged them. Lawful states now found themselves prepared to commit elementary human rights violations in the hope of greater safety, even deeming a so-called preventive war to be legitimate (at least morally), contrary to existing international law, which already condemned such wars.

Through the Decade it was decided clearly that these questions had not been answered conclusively. Now it was important not simply to repeat the earlier discussions, but to use them as a basis for theological knowledge, because only then could one avoid those blind alleys in which ecumenical discussions sometimes got stuck. If one inquires as to the churches' role – and that of the ecumenical community – in overcoming violence at the beginning of the twenty-first century, then a predetermined Christological and ecclesiological "trench warfare" should be avoided. Jesus is the ethical teacher for some, while Christ is *Cosmokrator* for others; for some the Church is understood as an almost sectarian example that illustrates a better world here and now, for others the Church supports the state and sustains its "Constantinian" structures, etc.

The delegates in Harare had recognized that the existing cycles of violence ensnare people – moreover, all creation – and make the fullness of life impossible, or even destroy it. Yet on the other hand these cycles have always broken with initiatives, using powers both in and outside the Church, which can prove that these are not simply powerless actors, resigned to their fates in the face of violence, but that cycles can also be resisted nonviolently and this enables them to be overcome. In the Decade it was no longer simply a matter of the established polarities of passive pacifism on one side versus active responsibility to society that legitimizes violence as a last resort. The different positions were to be appreciated in their distinctness, the respective orientation of each statement, their intentions and where possible to be conducted in a constructive and mutually enriching dialogue.

(2) Geneva 1999: Formulation of Objectives for the Decade

The first meeting of the newly elected Central Committee after the Eighth Assembly faced the task of defining in more detail a conceptual framework as well as the goals of the Decade.[51] By bringing peace-building from the periphery to the center, it would foster a "culture of peace" by

> addressing holistically the wide varieties of violence, both direct and structural, in homes, communities, and in international arenas and learning from the local and regional analyses of violence and ways to overcome violence.[52]

The Decade saw itself as an invitation to the churches,

> to overcome the spirit, logic, and practice of violence; to relinquish any theological justification of violence; and to affirm anew the spirituality of reconciliation and active nonviolence."[53]

Thus a new understanding of security could be achieved, more in the sense of cooperation and community, rather than striving for security through "domination and competition." In this movement the churches also wanted to learn from the "spirituality and resources for peace-building of other faiths" by working with other religious communities. In particular, the abuse of religious and ethnic identities in pluralistic societies was to be taken into account. Ultimately the Decade was also to be understood as a protest to "the growing militarization of our world, especially the proliferation of small arms and light weapons."[54] In order to achieve the objectives, the churches strived for stronger alliances with ecumenical networks and also with secular movements.

For the first time a broad platform was initiated in the WCC and the wider ecumenical movement for comprehensively overcoming violence, which also sought cooperation with other religions. Here one could also recognize the added element of the instrumentalization of religion in recent conflicts. Here one sees an ambitious aim being defined, whose formulations were already known, partly from the conciliar process (see above). But now these should be included as programmatic objectives in the overall work of the WCC. If the spirit, logic and practice of violence are to be overcome, alongside dispensing of any theological justification of violence, then at their core the churches of the WCC will completely dispose of the classical doctrine of just war. The search for an alternative understanding of security is being raised again on the ecumenical agenda (i.e., Bonhoeffer). In any case the explicit consideration of the dimension of spirituality was a new element in ecumenical peace discussions.[55]

Within this Decade many contextual and theme-specific issues arose that have been dealt with separately over the course of ten years. The WCC did not even manage to represent in summary form all the local and regional initiatives, conferences and activities of the churches. In that sense the Decade was designed too broadly as a "movement" and would be described as an "ecumenical space." Correspondingly there ensued a pluriform manner in which these impulses were taken up by existing movements and emerging levels of initiatives and reflection among the churches.

f. Overcoming Violence and Concepts of God: Central Topics at the Beginning of the Decade

Margot Käßmann asked at the beginning of the Decade:

Is the question whether we really need to designate violence as the ethos of our epoch, as a spirituality of the modern world? Or is there a new perception in our world, that we need a *counter-movement*, new courage to overcome violence, to make room for life as God willed it? 56

The theological term for such a counter-movement, in my view, falls under what is called the Kingdom of God. The different under-standings of this term should not be pitted against each other, but here their respective directional statements and their intentions will be assessed and brought together. Examinations of this "divine counter-proposal"[57] may again and again produce new ecumenical movements, in search of what is ultimately a new understanding of *koinonia* itself, for God is not to be understood entirely as the "man-ager" in the sense of engaging in human affairs directly. As such one is always thrown back to the ultimately unsolvable and often blasphe-mously-answered problem of theodicy.[58] Rather, God must be thought of as acting through the faithful, to whom it was said, "what is good" is "to do justice, and to love kindness, and to walk humbly with your God" (Mic 6:8). Out of Harare there came, along with the Decade, an encouraging motivation for the churches in the ecumenical arena for this counter-movement.

In order to assess the image of God in regard to violence and the possibility of overcoming violence, the guiding question can be formu-lated as follows: To what extent does the image of God in the Judeo-Christian traditions provide a structure for just relationships? It is assumed that the respective image of God is formative and orienting for the design of a corresponding ethic. In my view however, it is too easy to evaluate monotheism as generally promoting violence against polytheistic religions, such as Jan Assmann has tried to demonstrate.[59] This requires a much more nuanced reflection. Undeniably in the Judeo-Christian traditions one can find elements of God's image, which, in their historical setting were not aiming toward nonviolence. But at the same time it can be observed again and again that it is precisely the image of God in these traditions that unleashed the impetus to overcome violence and to establish just relationships. Due to this ambivalence, it would be as naive to try to derive a unilinear ethics of nonviolence directly from the image of God of the Judeo-Christian tradition, as it would be equally simplistic to deduce from monotheism a greater propensity toward violence.

The relationship between the image of God and *overcoming* violence will be examined below using the four selected key topics that were set out at the beginning of the Decade by the WCC:[60]

(1) understanding the spirit and logic of violence,
(2) the abuse and use of power,
(3) human justice,
(4) identity.

(1) Spirit and Logic of Violence – Breaking through Vicious Cycles to Facilitate Reconciliation

People continually get caught in violence, because the common response to violence is to use violence. Those who have been violated want revenge, longing for satisfaction or recompense. The pain is so great and the injustice so blatant that the violence must not go unpunished. Aggression is discharged into ever new forms of violence. This also means that in most cases there cannot always be a clear-cut distinction between victims and perpetrators, as in an actual conflict in which both sides usually experience being victims (e.g., the Israeli-Palestinian conflict). This may be one reason why moral appeals are also generally ineffective for the various factions. Reconciliation – the breaking of the vicious circles of violence in favor of right relationships – obviously requires an event that allows for both sides to consider their need for retaliation.

In the Christian tradition Jesus' death is interpreted as the reconciliation event par excellence. Interpretations are already abundant in the New Testament and cannot be discussed here in detail.[61] But the answer to the question of how this death can be interpreted as act of reconciliation, on the one hand includes a statement about the image

of God contained in it, and on the other, a statement about the understanding of how such reconciliation came about.[62] Two interpretations
are taken as representative: Firstly, there is the classical doctrine of
satisfaction formulated by Anselm of Canterbury in which God
demands the death of Jesus as a necessary sacrifice for his own satisfaction, because sin cannot go unpunished.[63] Such a sacrifice that
would restore the relationship between God and humanity however,
can only be provided by God, or a God-human. Although this line of
thought surely contains the idea of a gracious God's care for God's
own creation, the logic remains imprisoned, such that for the sake of
maintaining order sin cannot be allowed to go unpunished. A victim
therefore, is imperative to restore God's honour — according to this
logic.

However, an entirely different logic of reconciliation follows from
the interpretation of the crucifixion of Jesus as an *appeasement* for a
violent death for God's sake, a unilateral suffering from violence,
precisely to facilitate reconciliation through this renunciation of power
and revenge. This is the cross as God's act of nonviolence (such as
articulated by the Mennonite theologian, John Howard Yoder).[64] The
relationship between God and humanity is then presented less as a
legal action than as a revelatory, sacrificing act of love whereby a "new
creature" is made possible, a new quality of relationship. This represents a victory over all principalities and powers, even over death,
because in the resurrection of Christ their limited power stands
convicted. One could ask pointedly: Is the death of Christ therefore a
necessary divine sacrifice both *before* and *for* God, or a voluntary divine
sacrifice *before* and *for* humanity? The answer to this question may not
only result in a shift in the image of God, but also the view of reconciliation processes in general, if they are motivated by the Christological
confession.[65] Indeed one might observe in such broad considerations
that Jesus' readiness to be sacrificed on the cross has often been
imitated in a devastating manner in church history, by encouraging
people to be "victims" (e.g. women, indigenous peoples, slaves) and in
this way victimizing them, rather than encouraging a process of
genuine liberation and reconciliation. If the Church sees itself as

"ambassadors for Christ" and holds "the ministry of reconciliation" (2 Cor 5), then it must obviously look for a "third way," as Walter Wink put it: neither a passive sacrifice, nor an active use of violence, but a third alternative, which is active *and* nonviolent, freeing victims and perpetrators alike from their roles – in this way, an existing order breaks through.

(2) Abuse and Good Use of Power – God's Omnipotence and the Power of the Weak

Power is always present. It is a "natural" condition, because it is the consequence of the different gifts (cf. Rom 12, 1 Cor 12). Power is therefore not yet in itself something negative or that which is to be avoided, but it must be rejected where it is abused in the form of violence, as in the abuse of power by the stronger over the weaker, thus preventing just relationships. Any power is subject to the temptation of abuse, even in the churches: men against women, rich churches against poor ones, majorities against minorities.

"Powers" are described in the New Testament as those which seek to separate themselves from the love of God (cf. Rom 8:38), to control the lives of those who are far from the love of God (cf. Eph 2:2), to keep people in bondage to their laws (cf. Col 2:20), to subject the people to their control or tutelage (cf. Gal 4:3). Structures and orders are supposed to serve a person, rather than have a controlling effect. It is not the person who controls these systems as instruments for achieving successful cohabitation, but the powers which exercise control over that person.[66]

Concerning the image of God we might consider here how God's omnipotence is presented. This is what has tempted some to exploit religion in order to strengthen their own power. To say "God is with us" was always a means of emboldening oneself, but also a dangerous attempt to pursue one's own goals, to enforce one's own power, claiming and thus instrumentalizing or exploiting God's power. The seduction of power has been no stranger to the Church due to the omnipotence of faith. How should the omnipotence of God be regarded if it were not abused, but protected precisely against such an abuse of power?

The foremost story related to the use of power in the New Testament is the temptation in Luke 4. The devil offered Jesus dominion over the whole earth, if he would only worship him. The significance of Luke 4 lies in the rejection of a power that would amount to the simultaneous acceptance of *its* omnipotence. In the non-acceptance of the conditions of these powers, thus in the renunciation of power the almightiness of Jesus is first demonstrated. He resists the temptation to recognize existing powers as final. The real power of God becomes visible in the denial or renunciation of power. Thus, the primary declaration does not remain isolated in God's omnipotence, but in its relativizing function over all other powers. For believers this also produces a freedom to not see themselves as completely confronted by "what is given." Based on this understanding of God's omnipotence, the perspective of faith has the ability to identify these powers in any situation of coexistence and thereby also to relativize them for the sake of building just relationships.[67]

The primary calling of the Church then lies in its freedom: it should be the Church, not one of several powers in society. Only in the freedom of renouncing power can one understand the statement: "power is made perfect in weakness." (2 Cor 12:9) That is the strength that believers gain when they recognize themselves as weak before God, as those that do not really dominate in this world or in parts of it. "God is with us" would be an expression of this recognized weakness, not the power of the Church. This weakness allows for reliance on the gifts of all, and thus promotes the building and maintaining of equitable relationships in which power-sharing is practiced.

(3) Human Justice – and God's Judgment

With regard to the distributive dimension of justice,[68] it can be stated without question that many people currently live in degrading economic conditions, while a much smaller proportion enjoys prosperity. This disparity may also be referred to as "structural violence" because equitable relationships are hereby negated, by preventing a free development of life for all. "No peace without justice" was a doctrine echoed by the Conciliar Process for Justice, Peace and Integrity of Creation.[69] But it is equally valid to say: violence does not produce justice. If peace is only possible when all justice has been served, then this peace will remain an illusion. Therefore a further consideration of the idea of justice is needed.

Concerning commutative justice, since its inception the WCC has supported and accompanied the development of international law, because violence can be avoided by ensuring adherence to law. The fact that today crimes against humanity, genocide, war crimes, and wars of aggression can be brought before international tribunals and even before the International Criminal Court is to be regarded as enormous progress.[70] Those responsible are made accountable, at least representatively. This then legal means becomes a more powerful, symbolic force, such that the international community takes responsibility when injustice is committed anywhere in the world. This contributes to overcoming violence, as victims do not remain alone with their sense of needing revenge, which would be unleashed again at the next opportunity for violence.[71]

Of course for the victims this does not yet mean reparation. The legal means conform to the motif of punishment as a deterrent and expiation.[72] Healing and reconciliation are not necessarily initiated in this way. In order to encourage, for example, traumatized populations in the direction of a culture of nonviolence, a "restorative" form of justice is required that is focused on the restoration of right relationships, rather than being limited to isolating individuals.[73]

From the perspective of faith, righteousness is not first of all an Aristotelian virtue or a general principle of equal treatment with regard to commutative or distributive justice, but justice is above all what God allows for humanity. The biblical idea of God's justice always includes the aspect of mercy. Therefore God's justice is to be understood as "saving justice," which is not punishable simply by issuing a penalty or rewarded according to merit, but speaks justly – out of love – and so establishes a new relationship between humanity and God.[74] God justifies the sinner, and thus establishes something that is just, that now allows for community. This understanding ultimately establishes the institution of the Church as a means for justice. Wherever the Church stands up for law and justice, it is primarily aimed at promoting a new community. This is referred to as a renewing "transformative justice." Victims and offenders are released from their roles, "transformed" by a process of reconciliation into a new, equitable relationship.[75] This can break the vicious cycle of violence.

For the establishment of right relationships a "healing of memories" is also necessary. The naming of an offense and ascertaining the truth(s) and the process of joint clarification are essential elements. An attempt to translate this insight into practice can be noted in the various truth commissions (South Africa, Sierra Leone, Guatemala, etc.).[76] Only in this way can a new beginning in relations be possible, though not always guaranteed. In some areas of the world church communities have recognized and accepted this "ministry" of healing. This is only possible where churches have not previously gambled away their credibility as a foundation for peace through the legitimation of violence. However, this credibility is a necessary condition for the possibility of healing.

Discussion about the judgment of God may be leading the way here, because it aims in its promise at the necessary disclosure of all issues that have broken a relationship, ultimately, such that all can be forgiven. The saving, justifying righteousness of God, which can only be granted and not earned, leads to reintegration in the community for the restoration of relations, and thus has a healing function. This eschatological promise acts as something anticipatory in the shaping of reconciliation processes in the present.[77]

(4) Identity as a Condition for Living in Relationship – and the Trinitarian Image of God

If one's identity is in danger, or is doubtful or suppressed by force, then this contributes to a culture of violence. This phenomenon could be studied in the violent conflicts in the Balkans and Chechnya. In other parts of the world very different population groups can live peacefully with each other, share common interests and common pursuits, despite great differences. The prerequisite seems to be the reassurance of the identity and a clear rejection of all attempts to impose an alien identity on another human being. Perhaps here is where the central motives for the broad support for terrorism are hidden among some segments of the population, namely, decades of humiliation due to an unacknowledged or self-chosen identity.

But how is an identity to be affirmed? The Judeo-Christian concept of God is shaped above all by several convictions: a God who is relational, the election of the Jewish people, above all else, the divine revelation in God's Son, Jesus Christ, as well as in the ongoing presence of the Holy Spirit for the completion of God's self-revelation.

In ecumenical discussions the Trinitarian image of God has become predominant. With the relationship being presented perichoretically, that is, the mutual penetration and indwelling of the Trinitarian persons of Father, Son, and Spirit; in this way the personhood of the individual members in the Holy Trinity can only be safeguarded by constituting God's internal relationality. And at the same time the community is constituted by God's permanent personhood.

A person is unthinkable without relationality, but there are also no relations without persons. Person and relation behave complementarily toward each other. Thus one can declare the fact of God's sociality and this prevents a hierarchical presentation of any domination or subordination. Personhood and sociality, autonomy and relationship, boundaries and openness, identity and communication can only be fully grasped in their complementarity.[78] Through this Trinitarian form of language, the principle of the election also ensures that the motif of the incarnation and the event of Pentecost are held together.

Through *participation* in the reality of God (made possible because God is placed in human relationality) humanity itself is constituted as a community-shaping creature in its personhood and only thus is capable of community. Herein lies the dignity of the individual and at the same time its necessary communal-relationality.[79] This constitutes the *koinonia* of humans, who are mutually persons through their relationality. This allows the community of churches in their distinct contextual and traditional expressions to be described as a unity, because, while it both ensures unity amid all plurality, it also preserves the plurality from tendencies to uniformity. Without its own reassurance of each person's identity every relationship is fragile. Just relationships are based on the strengthening of the respective identities, not their relativization.

From the perspective of faith, God cannot be considered non-relational, but the One who is relationship within Godself, who is at once also in relationship with his creation. From this state of being placed in relation, the believer gains an identity as one adopted by God, as God's beloved and thus makes one capable of relationality.

As powerful agents of formation religions can enable us to affirm identities and establish just relationships and community beyond their borders, that is, if they are not to remain self-sufficient, but rather to point beyond themselves. Wherever religion becomes motivated to use violence, this relational capacity is negated. A different identity-forming moment of God's attentiveness is pushed into the foreground. Then exclusivist groups, ethnicities, or clans primarily determine the identity. The image of God then degenerates into an idol and totally contradicts the monotheistic idea of the one and only God of all.

Summary: Ethical Implications of Language about God

We have seen how the reflection of the image of God decisively influenced the various themes of the Decade to Overcome Violence. If God is believed to be the One who reconciles, relativizes all other powers, reassures healing and identity through his justice, while being a relationship-creator and relation-enabler, then we may derive important insights for developing an ethic of nonviolence. It is therefore necessary to explicate their ethical implications based on their reflection of God's image and to verify them on the basis of the biblical traditions.

Of course, the image of God cannot simply be a projection of what was previously deemed as ethically just. But the reflection of ethical implications of God's image may serve to make language about God responsive as such. If the image of God itself is conceived as containing violence and thus at least implicitly includes violence-legitimizing elements, then critical inquiry is imperative for such language about God as to whether and how this is actually in accordance with the gospel of God who became relational through the reconciliation events in Jesus Christ as the *koinonia*-enabling event. These critical theological elements provide corrections for our language about God.

It is hoped that the international movement of the Decade to Overcome Violence will continue to contribute to this relationship between theological reflection and to clearly illustrate the development of a Christian ethic of nonviolence, in order to more self-consciously align ecclesial activity with the building of just relationships. In this way the Church will be able to make a significant and credible contribution to a culture of nonviolence and give testimony to "the hope that is in you" (1 Pet 3:15) in the midst of a culture of violence.

CHAPTER 7
THE "DECADE TO OVERCOME VIOLENCE": 2001-2011

POTSDAM TO KINGSTON AND THE
INTERNATIONAL ECUMENICAL
PEACE CONVOCATION

Public Peace, Justice, and Order in Ecumenical Conversation

AS THE ISSUES in the discussion concerning the ethos of non-violence in the context of ecumenical peace ethics were of a general nature, the present inquiry concerns the specific, more limited question of the legitimacy of military approaches to protecting those people immediately threatened by violence beginning with the period leading up to the Decade.

In 1999, the Central Committee (CC) of the WCC adopted a "Memorandum and Recommendations on International Security and Response to Armed Conflict," calling for new approaches to international peace and security in the post-Cold War world.[1] The document highlights dilemmas surrounding "humanitarian intervention," particularly as they became evident in Kosovo and in the failure of the international community to prevent genocide in Rwanda. The UN Secretary-General Kofi Annan approached the WCC with a request to contribute to international debates on the issue of intervention for humanitarian purposes from theological and ethical perspectives. Delegates from the peace churches supported this Memorandum, mainly because it inquired as to "new approaches."

The memo led to a study process, with initial findings received by the Central Committee in Potsdam at the same meeting in 2001 that launched the international Decade to Overcome Violence (DOV) at the Brandenburg gate in Berlin, just eight months prior to the terrorist attacks on 9/11 in New York and Washington.

Potsdam 2001: The Start of an Ecumenical Debate on Limited Intervention

The Commission of the Churches on International Affairs presented those initial findings in a document entitled "The Protection of Endangered Populations in Situations of Armed Violence."[2] Its promising subtitle reads: "An Ecumenical Ethical Approach," but basically it offered nothing but a new formulation of the just war theory in modern terms, without even reflecting upon its complexity. It included a list of criteria guiding UN reforms, which was to serve in the interim "whenever armed intervention for humanitarian purposes is undertaken." (§1.11)

The original goal had been to clarify issues and to develop guidelines for assisting the churches. That objective was not achieved. The document formulates the issue correctly: "The moral obligation of the international community to protect lives of civilian populations that are at risk in situations where their government is unable or unwilling to act is widely accepted." The WCC Eighth Assembly in Harare had already declared:

> We affirm the emphasis of the gospel on the value of all human beings in the sight of God, on the atoning and redeeming work of Christ that has given every person true dignity, on love as the motive for action, and on love for one's neighbour as the practical expression of active faith in Christ. We are members one of another, and when one suffers all are hurt. This is the responsibility Christians bear to ensure the human rights of every person.[3]

The Potsdam document also includes some valuable phrases for giving direction to discussions, such as these. Fundamental to conflict-prevention efforts is the task of building cultures of peace, reconciliation, and *metanoia*, which make conflict transformation a preferred option to violence. Peace education, election monitoring, civic education, inter-faith dialogue, and raising awareness on human rights are all activities which can successfully prevent escalation of conflicts in some areas. These are long-term measures in which the churches can and must play a particularly active role. The document also speaks about the responsibility of the churches in post-conflict situations and the pastoral responsibility for processes of reconciliation and forgiveness. Finally, it ends with a realistic analysis: "In practice the international community has seldom been capable of such [ethical] consistency." Therefore, many thought that the document already assumed the international community not only has the right but even the duty to use armed force to expedite assistance to people at risk and to protect them.

This triggered extensive debate, especially due to the vehement opposition of representatives from the peace churches. For the first time in history the WCC was going to adopt a document listing criteria for the use of military intervention; by doing so it would implicitly confirm just war theory as a consensus within the ecumenical family. It became obvious that the WCC could not adopt a document that so clearly conflicted with the ecclesiological identity of one of its member churches.[4]

Debates such as these are important events for ecumenism, since they indicate the wide range of experiences in contexts which make visible the divergent theological and ethical convictions of the traditions, thus challenging each other. Even if there is no agreement in the end, nor any consensus reached, arguments are sharpened when the delegates remain committed to engaging one another. They grow together into a deeper community which itself becomes a witness of peace. The following discussion process illustrates this witness.

In the end, the Potsdam document was altered considerably. The committee replaced the euphemistic term "humanitarian intervention" with another: "The protection of endangered populations in situations of armed violence." The revised document lists fundamentally different opinions, such as those at Oxford in 1937. The proposed set of criteria for military intervention was separated from the document. Above all, the Central Committee did not adopt the document but merely *received* it as a study paper for further reflection, and invited member churches to react.[5] This must surely be considered as a compromise, but the decision realistically reflects the diversity within Christian churches on this very matter.

Geneva 2003: An Interim Report on Remaining Differences and New Perspectives

At its meeting in 2003 the WCC's Central Committee received an update on the study process.[6] By now the events of 9/11 had taken place, and wars in Afghanistan and Iraq had begun. These events added new dimensions to the debate: On the one hand, globalized terrorism had sharpened awareness of the urgent question of human security in the northern hemisphere; on the other hand the United States was waging a unilateral "preemptive" war against another sovereign state in defiance of international law and the will of the UN Security Council. These developments called for discussion and showed clearly that the power of the nation-state, which seemed to be fading in the postmodern era and during the process of economic globalization, had returned. The WCC spoke unanimously against the war in Iraq and also utterly condemned the terrorist attacks.[7] The interim report from 2003 deals with the responses available at that time from the member churches.

The Position of the Lutheran Church in Norway

In the 2003 report to the Central Committee, the responses to its 2001 study document included one from the Lutheran Church of Norway, called "Vulnerability and Security."[8] The Norwegian response stresses the deep interrelationship between vulnerability and security. It also focuses on the question of humanitarian intervention, defining it as "the international use of force on the territory of other states and without their consent with the aim of (re-)establishing elementary human security when it has been grossly and persistently violated."[9] It then revisits criteria for a "just war," insisting that while discussions continue on the validity of the criteria, they nonetheless represent an important ethical framework. The most important criteria, which continue to be applied, include:

(a) just cause,
(b) right intention,
(c) legitimate authority,
(d) application of current military law,
(e) last resort,
(f) proportionality of means.

The document insists that listing criteria does not in itself endorse a general ethical legitimization of military intervention. Meanwhile, a more fundamental consideration of the relationship between human vulnerability and security, combined with a broad approach to the security problem, opened the way for a broader perspective.

The Norwegian statement points to two specific contributions that churches can make in the context of forming security policy: high-lighting the perspective of victims and offering the service of reconcili-ation. The victim's perspective (Matt 25:35) reinforces the concept of human security. And since reconciliation is at the very core of the Christian message (2 Cor 5:18), the churches must be the first to insist on peaceful solutions to confrontation and conflict. Reconcilia-tion processes require respect for truth and justice, remorse, forgive-ness, and a new beginning. Thus, the position taken had already superseded the Potsdam document in its ethical reasoning.

The Position of the Evangelische Kirche in Deutschland (EKD)

The EKD, known in English as the Protestant Church in Germany, also responded officially in a letter in ways that echoed reflections it had previously made in a document entitled, "Steps on the Way to Peace: Points of Reference on Ethics and Peace Policy."[10] It is striking that the EKD's response also insisted on relating the issue of how to protect innocent populations to a broader perspective on security. According to this perspective a reliable structure of peace and security will require the rule of international law, ensure the protection of freedom and economic justice, strengthen international organizations, and establish a culture of social behavior, as well as respect for minorities. Hence it includes conflict prevention, conflict resolution, and post-conflict reconciliation.

Here the concept of "just peace" (instead of just war) conveys the basic idea of Christian peace ethics. It calls for the strengthening of the international peace system as intended and articulated in the Charter of the United Nations. The universal acceptance and implementation of human rights is an important factor for strengthening international peace as a legal system. The EKD document continues to allow for the use of military force but insists that it remains a marginal issue. The use of military force as "last resort" has been vehemently criticized within the church's internal discussion; thus the document calls for further careful analysis. The document ends by recognizing that the fundamental ethical debate over whether to use violence or to maintain a radically pacifist position, will not and probably cannot be resolved. The EKD does not believe it can ever entirely exclude a defensive war. But the prime task is that of promoting peace, which requires strategies and policies that promote democracy and economic justice.[11]

The Position of the Historic Peace Churches (HPC)

The third response the WCC study process received between 2001 and 2003 was the statement by historic peace church leaders who met at the Bienenberg, Switzerland.[12] Representatives of all three denominations of the historic peace churches (including theologians and lay members) gathered together soon after the meeting of the Central Committee in Geneva in 1999 for a conference at the Bienenberg. It was the first meeting of this kind within the context of the new Decade to Overcome Violence. The event aimed to jointly discuss their peace theologies and highlight their views on the ecumenical situation as a contribution to the Decade.[13] It was not simply the standard peace theologies that were reformulated here, but the occasion also gave space for their joint response which was also formulated in the invitation sent to the member churches of the WCC study document.[14] This contribution of the HPCs begins with a confession of guilt for their own involvement in violence:

> We have often failed to live up to our commitment to the Spirit of Jesus Christ. We have often been silent and failed to act on behalf of those who are suffering the scourge of injustice and violence. We do not always know exactly what constitutes justice—or peace—in a given situation; we lack wisdom in addressing the complex issues of our time. In particular we share with the wider church and the larger world the perplexities of addressing the complex issues raised by conflicts such as those in Rwanda, Iraq, the Middles East, Somalia, Southern Sudan, Kosovo, Colombia, South Africa, and many other places.[15]

In five paragraphs, the paper explains that they, along with the other churches, see themselves as affected by these situations; concerning the question of the responsibility to protect, they nevertheless do not see how the WCC study document could provide a useful guide on this issue:

1. A biblically and theologically grounded pacifism regards seeking God's justice as central and integral to a nonviolent philosophy of life. To state the issue as if we have to choose between nonviolence and justice is a false dichotomy. [...]
2. We can identify a number of normative practices for seeking justice within principled pacifism: [...]
3. Nonviolent forms of defense and social transformation [...]

4. Citizen corps of observers/interveners/advocates as a "presence" in situations of conflict [...]

5. Acknowledging responsibility for violence and injustice and seeking repentance and forgiveness [...]

6. Training persons in the use of cooperative conflict methods and strategies [...]

7. The church's witness and advocacy on behalf of the marginalized and those whose lives are threatened by injustice [...]

8. The use of violent force as a "last resort" to secure justice creates conditions that inhibit the achievement of justice. Too often we work under the false assumption that, if we cannot find a nonviolent solution to a conflict, the use of violent force will take care of the problem. [...]

9. We call on the churches to emphasize the distinctive witness to the world that flows from our commitment to the Spirit of Jesus Christ and our identity as the body of Christ in the world. [...]

10. Both pacifists and those who reason with "just war" principles should make more modest claims about their ability to guarantee success. Though both traditions seek justice, neither tradition can guarantee that justice will be accomplished. [...] The pacifist commitment to nonviolence is ultimately grounded in an eschatology of trust in the victory over evil of God revealed in Jesus' life, teachings, death and resurrection [...][16]

To the signatories it was clear that with this reaction, no conclusive answer would be formulated on all aspects of the issue under discussion. The declaration is formulated in a modest spirit, which does not conceal the limitations of their own insights. But above all, it reveals weaknesses in the WCC study document and takes a position in which the traditional arguments are once again challenged, thus reopening the peace ethics debate anew.

Throughout these debates a draft document was created that was presented in 2006 for approval at the Ninth Assembly in Porto Alegre, Brazil. The interim report examined these different positions in 2006, accounting for the remaining differences over the use of force for humanitarian purposes. Concerning the categorization of position it read as follows:[17]

(1) *The Christian-pacifist position*: only supports "intervention by creative, non-violent means."

(2) *The position of the unconditional protection of human rights*: represents the idea that "the resort to force must not be avoided when it can alleviate or stop large-scale human rights violations." (But this position expressly does not want this to be understood in the sense of the traditional doctrine of just war).[18]

(3) *The position of the doctrine of just war*: it gives a "very high priority to territorial integrity and sovereignty."

On the one hand the positions here are recognizable once again as those which had been known for decades, yet their far-reaching differences can be seen in the various approaches and a growing understanding of each other. This would also be reflected in the ensuing follow-up WCC consultations.[19]

Freising 2005: Just Peace – Life in a Vulnerable Future

The Ecumenical Consultation in Freising at the midpoint of the Decade[20] was on one hand an opportunity to gather results and experiences in Germany from the first half of the Decade and to look ahead to jointly determine which priorities in Germany appeared reasonable and necessary for the second half. As a comprehensive and representative forum for churches and church groups, grassroots groups and initiatives in Germany, the consultation was in itself an important contribution to the Decade, because until then such an event had not been held anywhere else.

Various reports showcased the wealth of activities, publications, events and campaigns, most of them seeing themselves as continuing expressions of the Conciliar Process for Justice, Peace and the Integrity of Creation. And yet, the parties realized that they do not comprehensively describe only what was being undertaken in Germany. This encounter also produced the "ecumenical space" for necessary, constructive criticism, as well as an intensification of networking efforts, which should ultimately contribute to mutual reinforcement in overcoming personal, structural and cultural violence. In this respect, this event was an important contribution to the overall objective of the Decade, namely, to bring peace efforts from the margins to the center of the life and the confession of the churches.

Nonviolence as a Value of Christian Existence

In contemporary, pluralist societies for many years there has been an urgent search for reorientation. In this quest religion is and will remain a strong, orientating force because it touches all aspects of individual and community life. Since the terrorist attacks on 11 September 2001 and the subsequent military reactions, religion has dramatically re-emerged in social consciousness, even among those who predicted its gradual decay in post-modern, secular societies. Jürgen Habermas admits that religion has "a consciousness of what is missing in society," that it possesses "the sensitivity for a misguided life and the deformation of living contexts that have become distorted." Given the "derailment of modernity," religion can offer meaning and moral guidance in a post-secular age.[21]

Given this situation, in the wake of the Decade it still needs to become much clearer how efforts to overcome violence and the use of violence actually constitute basic Christian values, because these issues are rooted in the Gospel itself, namely, values of living as a Christian, which is defined by "following Jesus." Advocating for nonviolent approaches to peace and reconciliation, and seeking nonviolent conflict resolution strategies to develop a spirituality of nonviolence are both at the heart of the message and the mission of the Church. The decisive advocacy and defence of human rights is an integral part of it, which for Christians is not fundamentally based in a humanistic idea or natural law, but foremost in the Godlikeness of every human (Gen 1).[22]

Therefore, the Decade is not first and foremost to be understood as a protest movement against war, violence and terror, but as a promotional movement for the values of a life that gets its orientation to nonviolence from the confession of Jesus Christ. This approach, it is hoped, will make it possible to shepherd new and different arguments on totally different levels, to engage the following realms:

(i) With Christians from the evangelical and charismatic traditions: in the future, relations with these communities will need to be measured by the ecumenical capacity of the "historic churches" much more than by their compatibility for institutionalized ecumenism.[23]

(ii) As a member of civil society, in political processes, particularly within the structure of globalization: in the dialogue processes organized by the WCC in recent years with leading professionals from industry sectors, it became clear that in the erosion of values they recognize a great danger for the peaceful coexistence of peoples and nations. Therefore, knowing that they cannot themselves create the foundations of a free, democratic fundamental order, they expect the churches to provide a much clearer value-orientation.

(iii) In dialogue among religions, which has become increasingly important: the introduction of clear and binding values is crucial in order to be understood and to be able to confront the political instrumentalization of religion.[24]

Nonviolence must not be misunderstood as an ideology to be defended fundamentalistically, rather, the reverse is true: nonviolence is a basic Christian value-orientation that contains an appeal to ideology critique, precisely *against* every form of fundamentalism for the protection of personal dignity, freedom of the person and building of just relationships.

The Search for Coherent Theological Proposals

The preconditions for the persuasiveness of this basic Christian orientation are: coherent, theological proposals that have the integrative power to affirm nonviolence and overcoming violence as "regulative principles."[25] A Christian anthropology should keep person and relation alike in perspective and make their dialectical relationship visible to one another. Violence is always a physical or mental act of negation, injury or destruction of someone's personhood and of just relationships between people.

From the perspective of Christian theology it must be added here that the unconditional protection of human dignity is not based solely on the belief of the Godlikeness of humanity, but is also strongly established by the New Testament understanding of justification by grace through faith. No one can be reduced to one's actions alone. The promotion of just relationships is ultimately based on the understanding that through Jesus Christ, God has been placed in a new way in relation to his creation: this is a law-creating, justice-making relationship. It is the condition for the possibility of a just coexistence between humans, and between humans and nature.

A "Kingdom of God theology" could coherently hold together such thoughts, because it begins with "God's counter-proposal" presented to a prevailing culture of violence.[26] This theology has a rich tradition in the history of the modern ecumenical movement and was strongly represented in the early days of the churches of the Anglo-Saxon regions. The promise of the Kingdom of God becomes foundational for identity and thus an orientating framework. When Christians now already live in the anticipation of this Kingdom of God, this then implies "messianic ethics," a life according to the freedoms (even from violence) of the Kingdom of God. This allows the world to be recognized as the "one household of God" and liberated for a life of compassion,[27] empathy and advocacy, for others and also for creation.

On the other hand, it is important to include the Old Testament notions of law and justice in the efforts to overcome violence and make it fruitful. The entire Torah can be understood as God's appeal for the prevention of, and ultimately, the overcoming of, violence.[28] In view of the vulnerability of life, there is a protective function of law for widows, orphans, strangers, and all who would otherwise be defense-less. The confession of the God of Abraham and Sarah, the experience of this God who leads his people out of bondage, initiated a new rela-tionship that creates law. Such understandings also acknowledge the urgent need for the development of international law for overcoming violence. Yet law cannot then be restricted to its protective, preventive and punitive function, but also must always aim at healing relation-ships, if the idea of justice is to be aligned with the Old Testament witnesses. In the discussions of the WCC, therefore, the approach of a "restorative" or even "transformative" function of justice has been discussed for some time as part of the Decade.[29] This is imperative if the subtitle of the Decade "for reconciliation" is not to fall into oblivion.

Nonviolent Alternatives to Conflict Resolution and an Alternative Definition of Security

Each theological reflection in the ecumenical community earns its credibility and persuasiveness in the lived witness of believers. During the Freising consultation in 2005 there was repeated attention given to the orientating three-step method of liberation theology: See – Judge – Act.

In my view there is no actual deficit of *seeing* or analysis in many areas of the use of force. The same can be found in many parts concerning *judging*; in many contexts, the understanding has repeat-edly been formulated that violence cannot be overcome by force. The use of force cannot claim to be a Christ-worthy witness. And experi-ence has taught that the churches gamble their credibility at the moment when they think they may legitimize violence, mostly through political expediency rather than justified by theological ethics.

It is joint *action* that the churches are lacking. Yet it is not the will that is lacking, but the knowledge and experience in the application of non-violent alternatives to conflict resolution.[30] Therefore, the power of nonviolence is still given too little credit. If this observation is correct, then it is not that moral persuasion is currently insufficient, but all the power and energy must be focused on the development of non-violent alternatives and on making them visible: from victim-offender mediation,[31] to formation in children (project "Faustlos" i.e., fist-less)[32] and students ("Schritte gegen Tritte" i.e., steps against kicking),[33] to peace civil services[34] and trauma healing centres.[35]

This also means developing an alternative concept of security, if in fact, Dietrich Bonhoeffer is right, that there will be no peace on the path of safety. Prevention, conflict transformation and reconciliation processes must remain connected to the ethos, the central value of nonviolence, in order to fully inculcate a culture of peace. At a meeting of the historic peace churches in Nairobi, Kenya in 2004, it became clear just how dangerous life as a Peace Church on this continent can be and in many cases it actually leads to fatalities. At the same time it was also clear how creative and courageous Christians have become, as well as members of other religions, being witnesses of reconciliation, with practices ranging from minor, local dispute resolution to establishing and participating in national reconciliation commissions.[36]

The Decade as "Ecumenical Space"

In the second half of the Decade an even stronger notion of "ecumenical space" was necessary. This became clear during the consultation at the midterm in the Decade. Konrad Raiser was responsible for the initiation of both the "Programme to Overcome Violence" and the subsequent decision to launch the Decade as WCC general secretary.[37] He is among those who called time and again for such a space, making a decisive contribution to its success. The sharing and division of the wealth of wisdom and experience within the global ecumenical community with a view to overcoming violence was an enduring asset that had been thus far only discovered in its infancy and now it became further developed for the benefit of all involved. Usually the concrete and local efforts are both time-consuming and energy-draining, such that one loses the sight of the global ecumenical horizon.

But ecumenism is not primarily an additional task, an added function of the Church; it is first of all a self-understanding as a worldwide Church of Jesus Christ that can emerge from strength and encouragement. The networking of communities that are actively and nonviolently engaged and the efforts to make these manifestations visible are comforting, contagious and invigorating, such as the experiences within the campaign "Peace to the City" clearly demonstrated (see above).

Such networking may also have protected against efforts to make the Decade into a single topic or claim, above all other priorities. In past programs of the WCC there have been similar "hegemonic claims." The concept of violence is not to be broadened such that the concreteness and precision of the content suffer, nor can it be an overly narrow concept such that the ways each participant is impacted and the complexities and interdependencies cannot be adequately accommodated. Both of these would be counterproductive because hegemonic claims can easily lead to inflated statements, rather than jointly making a clear commitment to expressing that "word" which "the world cannot ignore" (D. Bonhoeffer).

How can such meetings be organized, and how can this wealth of experience be communicated? In the WCC, an annual geographic and thematic focus was selected for this purpose during the Decade: in 2002, it concerned Israel and Palestine, "to end the illegal occupation." The "Ecumenical Accompaniment Programme in Palestine and Israel" (EAPPI)[38] has continued so that the people from all parts of the ecumenical movement invite teams of civilian peace volunteers to contribute to non-violent conflict resolution, by being present on site and working with Palestinian and Israeli peace communities.

In 2003, the focus was on Sudan: "healing and reconciliation." The peace agreement between the North and South came not least through the long-standing efforts of the WCC and represented a major breakthrough in the country where a civil war was drawn out over decades.[39]

In 2004, the United States was selected: "The Power and Promise of Peace." In particular, the traditional civil rights movement, and with it many African-American churches, have discovered the Decade as "their" space. In many cases, one finds a greater rapprochement with the ecumenical movement.

In 2005, the churches in Asia chose the theme "Building Communities of Peace for All." Interreligious dialogue is experienced in many churches of Asia as a witness to experiential nonviolence.

In 2006, the focus was on Latin America and as the ecumenical community continues to engage the contemporary world, it allows the ecumenical space to be shaped accordingly.

The Need for Critical Self-Reflection: A Messianic Community

The ecumenical community itself can be described as an "alternative community" next to other forms of community in a globalized world, if the Church is understood as the "body of Christ," or as *mysterium*[40] or *creatura verbi divini*.[41] This description cannot remain without having an effect on the shape of the Church itself. If there is no discernible coherence between the message and the form of the Church, then how credible can the Church be as an ecumenical community? The Church not only *has* a distinct social ethics; the church always *is* in itself a social ethic: a "reconciled" community, or even a "messianic community."[42]

This idea also follows from the slogan of the World Missionary Conference in 2005 that was inspired by the Decade: "Called in Christ to be Reconciling and Healing Communities."[43] The ecumenical community proclaims not only the hope that is in it, but it is itself a community of hope. But it also follows that the Church in its "earthly-historical form of existence"[44] is invited to constant self-examination, as *ecclesia semper reformanda*. Church history and theological history themselves need to be critically revised to understand when, how and where the Church itself has been enmeshed in structures of violence and its legitimization. This task is required of all ecclesial traditions, including the historic peace churches.[45] What elements in liturgies, creeds, and in the life of the Church obscure our view of the calling to be a healing and reconciling community?

On the other hand it is necessary to point out the many possibili-

ties to overcome violence in the church traditions. In all denominations the awareness of the life and witness of nonviolence has been
preserved, though not given a central place. The impact of the Decade
can also contribute to making these discoveries jointly in the
ecumenical community. To be the "salt of the earth," "light of the
world" (Matt 5) are commitments and claims that the Church has
made since its inception. In relation to overcoming violence through
the Decade it was then possible to clearly ascertain that Christians are
people who have chosen to commit themselves freely to a life of
nonviolent action. Ecumenical community is actually recognizable as a
messianic community, because it already looks toward implementing
symbolically what they are promised in the Gospel, namely, becoming
reconciled.

Porto Alegre 2006: Convergences in the Responsibility to Protect (R2P)

The Ninth WCC Assembly in Porto Alegre, Brazil, marked the halfway
point of the Decade. Similar to the World Mission Conference in
Athens, held in 2005 ("Called in Christ to be Reconciling and Healing
Communities") the motto focused on overcoming violence as seen in
over 80 individual events during the Decade, as well as being the
central theme in one of the plenary sessions. The delegates jointly
declared and reaffirmed the goals of the Decade: "together with the
ecumenical community of churches we commit ourselves to work for a
culture of non-violence and to overcome the violence we encounter in
our lives."[46] It was clear that the Decade had already been a great
encouragement for people in situations of violence, because of the
solidarity and advocacy that can be experienced within the ecumenical
community.

In addition to the valuable process of exchanging contextual experiences of violence and encouraging practical examples for overcoming
it, within the framework of the Decade, Christian communities
around the world were discussing common, global challenges, often
together with representatives of other religions.

• • •

Terrorism and the "War on Terror"

There was unequivocal condemnation of terrorism: "The violence of terrorism – in all its many forms – is abhorrent to all who believe human life is a gift of God and therefore infinitely precious."[47] However, the response to terrorism must not be made "in kind" because this would lead to more violence and terror because "a concerted effort of all nations is needed to remove any possible justification for such acts."[48]

The General Assembly reaffirmed the statement sent by the General Secretary to the United Nations after September 11. However, "in recent times, acts of terror and some aspects of the so-called 'war on terror' have introduced new dimensions of violence."[49] Terror in the form of random acts of violence against unarmed civilians for political or religious purposes could never be justified legally, theologically or ethically. Rather, terrorist acts are crimes and should be punished at the national and international level through the instruments of the rule of law.

Through the so-called "war on terror," war itself has been redefined and international law and human rights law have been relativized. This is being clearly and decisively questioned by the churches. They call for cooperation and for strengthening of the International Criminal Court, rather than reliance on military combat. Religion is a source of peace and reconciliation. Therefore, all "religious communities and religious leaders" should work together to promote the rule of law and respect for human dignity. Interfaith initiatives have to restart violence prevention.[50]

The Proliferation of Nuclear Weapons

For decades, the WCC has consistently and persistently stood for the abolition of nuclear weapons. Already the first General Assembly in 1948 declared nuclear weapons a "sin against God." The churches are pointing out and urging nuclear powers to honor the commitment they made in 2000, to abolish all nuclear weapons under the Nuclear Non-Proliferation Treaty (NPT).[51] In a time when the international community faces the urgent task to "wisely overcome the violence of terrorism" there is a growing risk that these weapons could fall into the hands of non-state actors.[52] It was a mistake of the nuclear doctrine to maintain weapons of mass destruction as a guarantor for stability:[53]

> In the nuclear age, God who is slow to anger and abounding in mercy has granted humanity many days of grace. Through the troubled years of the cold war and into the present time, it has become clear that, in this as in other ways, God has saved us from ourselves. Although many were and are deceived, God is not mocked (Gal 6:7). If vengeance in daily life is for God (Rom 12:19), surely the vengeance of nuclear holocaust is not for human hands. Our place is to labour for life with God.[54]

The Responsibility to Protect Vulnerable Populations

The statement on "Vulnerable Populations – Declaration on the Responsibility to Protect" (R2P) deserves special attention here. In some ways it is a milestone in the peace-ethics discussions within the WCC, although by no means its conclusion. Although the churches were basically always in agreement since the founding of the WCC in 1948 that according to God's will there should be no war, differing positions continued unabated. Despite the broadening of the concept of violence and the focus on non-violent ways of overcoming violence during the Decade, there remained the ethical challenge of answering the question of violent interventions for the interruption of conflict, especially in view of the "new wars" and genocides to which the global community was exposed. This important discussion process on peace ethics will be discussed separately in a subsequent section below.

The statement on vulnerable populations at Porto Alegre requested that the WCC Central Committee, among other things, consider a study process engaging all member churches and ecumenical organizations in order to develop an extensive ecumenical declaration on peace, firmly rooted in an articulated theology. This should deal with topics such as just peace, the Responsibility to Protect, the role and the legal status of non-state combatants, the conflict of values (for example: territorial integrity and human life). It should be adopted at the conclusion of the Decade to Overcome Violence in 2010.[55]

The churches actually saw this as an urgent task as shown in the General Assembly's decision to immediately initiate the task of such a declaration. Too many questions still remained unanswered and these concerns provided orientation for theological and ethical reflection by the ecumenical fellowship of churches.[56]

a. Groundbreaking Decisions on the Decade's Methodology

In this sense, the request that was granted by consensus (unopposed) for an Ecumenical Peace Convocation at the end of the Decade is to be valued.[57] Preparations were immediately set in motion by the General Assembly. The findings prepared in numerous expert consultations were to lead to this goal.[58] That this process should more deliberately and broadly integrate participation is also reflected in the decision for organized, mutual, international, ecumenical visits, so-called "Living Letters" among the churches.[59] The Ecumenical Decade opened the space for this, and the churches seemed to be ready to fill it with content. Whether they themselves – as part of the world – are also ready to actually receive the grace of transformation remains to be seen.

By consensus the Ninth WCC General Assembly in 2006 adopted a jointly developed declaration, which was further modified during the meeting and expanded under the heading: "Vulnerable Populations at Risk – the Responsibility to Protect."[60] It can be shown clearly that perspectives shifted decisively through the discussion process up to the 2006 General Assembly, beginning with the Central Committee in Potsdam in 2001 and significant progress can be seen throughout.

Here the churches of the WCC achieved a far-reaching, joint peace-ethics position on one of the most difficult questions, although by no means were all differences resolved. Yet awareness of the *joint* responsibility as a global fellowship of churches is clearly documented in these proceedings. Open questions have remained which still need to be directed toward an ongoing dialogue for further clarification. These issues are explained below, following the convergence statements.

Argument from the Perspective of the Church

The WCC document begins with a Christological confession. This stage prepared an argument for what is authentically a *Christian* ethic. "In the New Testament, Jesus calls us to go beyond loving the neighbour to loving the enemy as well.... The prohibition against killing is at the heart of Christian ethics (Matt 5:21-22)."[61] Having considered this common ground the following wide-ranging common beliefs resulted. These had not been formulated in advance but developed out of the joint deliberations. Here one can see the actual progress in the ecumenical debate in general concerning peace ethics, in this case concerning the use of state force or violence.

The theological considerations are first examined jointly and then the challenge is formulated jointly with much greater precision:

> In the New Testament, Jesus calls us to go beyond loving the neighbour to loving the enemy as well. This is based on the loving character of God, revealed supremely in the death of Jesus Christ for all, absorbing their hostility, and exercising mercy rather than retribution (Rom 5:10; Luke 6:36). The prohibition against killing is at the heart of Christian ethics (Matt 5: 21-22). But the biblical witness also informs us about an anthropology that takes the human capacity to do evil in the light of the fallen nature of humankind (Gen. 4). The challenge for Christians is to pursue peace in the midst of violence.[62]

For the churches it was then crucial to introduce their respective self-understandings into these arguments since their ecclesiological contexts played a decisive role in determining their respective ethical positions. For the peace churches, the Church is first of all a social entity in the world, which bears witness to the truth of God's reconciliatory work in Jesus Christ. The Church structures its life in accordance with these convictions. If the Church does not "live" its mission then its *esse* (essence) as the Church is not at the disposal of society. Unaffected by this, of course, is the conviction that the Church is a community of those who always see themselves as *justus et peccator*.

Argumentation within the Context of Ecumenism

In an ecumenically-oriented theology the world is first conceived as the "one household of God." For Christians, this is the reason for the mutual responsibility toward all, which cannot be limited to one's own denomination, faith, nation or ethnicity. The responsibility to protect the most vulnerable extends accordingly over national and religious boundaries; it is an ecumenical responsibility.

If the churches could share this common ecumenical conviction then one may inquire as to the concrete consequences of the same. What is the relationship between the (given) unity of the Church and its transcendence, which constantly points beyond itself? The Roman Catholic position conceives the unity of the Church as a fundamental aspect of peacemaking.[63] This idea has not yet sufficiently borne fruit within the fellowship of churches of the WCC for the development of comprehensive, ecumenical, peace ethics.

Clearly, the WCC member churches confess the primacy of non-violence and justify it with the confession that every human being is created in the image of God and this human nature connects each of us to the incarnate Christ. Therefore the burden of proof lies primarily with those who still see the application of military force as legitimate (in extreme exceptional cases), not with those who deem it inappropriate in principle.

The document demonstrates high respect for the position of Christian "pacifism." The expression of its assumption of responsibility is the constant, preventive commitment and the willingness to take risks for a non-violent intervention in violent situations, which also includes the acceptance of risking one's own life. Any intervention may fail, but both of these positions should be respected as expressions of Christian responsibility, according to the document. [64]

The "primary option for nonviolence" of course does not exclude the use of force, but explicitly includes it as a possible option. Here peace churches will ask the question whether in this way the churches in principle simply remain in "the spirit, logic and practice of violence," and therefore contradict the objectives of the Decade to Overcome Violence.[65] How can the churches clearly and convincingly demonstrate that recourse to violence in extremely exceptional situations actually represents crossing an ethical boundary? This question has never been clarified, for example, in the positions of the EKD: on the one hand it clearly moves away from the doctrine of just war and advocates a concept of "just peace"; on the other hand it holds onto a criterion of last resort.[66] This is a key point of discussion for the broader ecumenical debates.

Shift of Perspectives

The perspectives are changing significantly, moving away from national sovereignty toward human security, and from the interveners toward those people in need of intervention.

The primary responsibility of national states is the welfare and security of its citizens. If a government is unable or unwilling, the international community has "the responsibility" to intervene in extreme situations. "States can no longer hide behind the pretext of sovereignty to perpetrate human rights violations against their citizens and live in total impunity."[67] The sovereignty of a state is no longer primarily described as the right to absolute power, but above all as the obligation to guarantee rights and the security of the civilian population. The debate is thus shifting from "national security" to "human security."[68] Security is no longer primarily defined militarily. This change in perspective has also afforded decisive progress to ecumenical discussions. Security results from economic development (meeting basic needs), universal education, respect for human rights, good governance, political inclusion and power-sharing, fair trade, control over the instruments of violence (small arms in particular), the rule of law through law-biding and accountable security institutions, and promoting confidence in public institutions.[69]

The concept of the responsibility to protect results from a perspectival shift; the center of all considerations is now no longer the intervening party, but the victims of violence. This opens up a new, shared vision, which derives *inter alia* from the Matthean understanding that Christ and this is something visible, especially in the most vulnerable (see Matt 25:40). The needs and rights of the civilian population are in the foreground and everyone has the right to be protected by others. Thus, the debate has shifted from intervention toward protection.

The question remains here, whether taking the perspective of the victims and determining their primary need in a potential conflict, according to their own interests, can actually succeed. How can the change of perspective from intervention to protection become more than a verbal shift? And who represents the "international community," which should potentially intervene in a given case? The United Nations is so far the international political forum which comprehensively represents the international community, yet the flaws in its political structure, in particular the supremacy of the Security Council, are well known. Previously the political enforceability of international law was also lacking, including against individual, powerful states.[70]

Furthermore it is necessary to inquire again in a nuanced way as to the concept of security. The question of Erhard Eppler from the Cold War era remains relevant:

Where is it written that Christians should first aim at perfect security? Doesn't security, such *relative* security as is owed to everyone, 'happen' to them while they are pursuing other, more important matters?[71]

Eppler believes that an

indissoluble remainder of uncertainty is part of the *conditio humana,* the
conditions of human life. If anyone wants to deny this remainder or
even wipe it out, this does not secure our lives but destroys them.[72]

The churches must offer their own theologically-reflective concept
of security, concerning the fundamental vulnerability of humanity and
of creation, precisely because of their creatureliness and in earnest,
without detracting in any way from the responsibility to protect. Dietrich Bonhoeffer's dictum of 1934 must be taken more seriously:

There is no way to peace along the way of safety. [...] Peace means
giving oneself completely to God's commandment, wanting no security, but in faith and obedience laying the destiny of the nations in the
hand of Almighty God, not trying to direct it for selfish purposes.[73]

The question remains, from the perspective of the churches, to
what extent these considerations must take into account the concept
of human security.

Prevention as the Primary Task

The churches agree "on the essential role of preventive efforts to
avoid and, if possible, tackle the crisis before it reaches serious stages.
.... Prevention is the only reliable means of protection."[74] The statement refers to studies of the WCC, which prove that the churches are
in agreement on this issue, despite all the differences in their attitudes
towards the use of force. Therefore, the churches call upon the
international community and individual states to strengthen their
capacity in view of preventive strategies and their capacities for
reducing the need for intervention through cooperation with the institutions of civil society.[75] "Churches are called to offer their moral
authority for mediation between differently powerful actors."[76]
National dialogues, including dialogue with non-state actors, should

be initiated when threats begin, so that problems can be recognized and admitted as such from an early stage and so that the population is involved in the search for solutions. To act before the crisis requires a special sensitivity to the situation and the needs of the population. Therefore, the active involvement of faith communities is necessary, those which are rooted in the daily spiritual and material reality of the people. Faith communities can play a key role in processes of building trust and truth.

As much as this preventative approach is to be welcomed, it still remains unrealistic so long as the international community is investing far more resources in developing and equipping their military resources than in targeted prevention measures.[77] The question is whether the focus on conflict prevention would be taken more seriously (at least by the churches and other world religions) if military intervention would no longer be legitimized under any circumstances, not even as a last resort.

b. Realistically Assessing Evil: When Prevention Fails

The document captures the realistic assessment of violence and evil in the Bible. An anthropology becomes apparent, which "takes the human capacity to do evil in the light of the fallen nature of humankind. (Gen. 4) The challenge for Christians is to pursue peace in the midst of violence."[78] When all the ways of prevention have been attempted and if these have failed, only then does the question concerning intervention arise. The prerequisite for this is, first, that this failure is acknowledged. A realistic assessment of "evil" in the world would also need to include a constant reflection upon the evil in our own selves and to take this seriously, just as we make such an assessment of political institutions.

Who is accountable for the actual motivations for intervention? There is a real danger of being gradually corrupted by acquiescing to the use of military force, to the point that "collateral damages" become considered acceptable. Even during a conflict the interests of intervening governments often tend toward those of their own economy and national defense and thus can end up succumbing to the temptation of unjustly exercising their power interests, allegedly for the common good. This temptation potentially also arises for churches. Which effective safeguards or correctives could be developed for this purpose?

Intervention: The Ethical Dilemma of Using Violence

The churches value the effective witness of many people who fulfilled their responsibility to protect by nonviolent means of intervention and sometimes have even paid for it with their lives. Churches should be involved especially where there is the capacity for local people to be strengthened so that they themselves can stand in a position to intervene. Churches are called to provide their moral authority to mediate between several powerful actors.

Thus the WCC formulated the statement extremely carefully:

> In calling on the international community to come to the aid of vulnerable people in extraordinary suffering and peril, the fellowship of churches is not prepared to say that it is never appropriate or never necessary to resort to the use of force for the protection of the vulnerable.[79]

In this negative formulation the statement was a consensus, but the document explicitly states that some in the churches refuse violence in all circumstances. Both positions agree that their approach may fail. And the churches respect *both* positions "as expressions of Christian responsibility."

Though the churches do not exclude the use of force in principle, this is not based on the naive belief that such conflicts could actually be resolved by the use of force. Rather, the attitude of the Churches is based on the certainty that the welfare of those people must be assisted in particular, "in situations of extreme vulnerability and who are utterly abandoned to the whims and prerogatives of their tormentors." It was a "tragic fact" that among the civilian population women and children are the first victims we mourn when extreme insecurity and war prevail.

In the history of the WCC the churches were previously unable to dignify such joint formulations with regard to ecumenical progress. But what is the real ethical dilemma *for the churches* which one could now examine? Is this only the case if violence is to be accepted as a last resort? The social support of the military and the toleration of the arms industry and trade is already an ethical dilemma for some churches as a whole and for some individuals within the churches. There is no further discussion of the victims of violent intervention, who are harmed or killed by the "helping nations" coming mostly from the civilian population. These questions are not addressed here, as the inquiry was rather narrowly-focused rather than comprehensive, in terms of the potentialities and responsibilities in interventions. Perhaps the context of this debate was generally far too narrow.

Reinterpretation of Predetermined Criteria

The possible use of force to protect the endangered is explicitly limited. Here one resorts to the traditional criteria of the doctrine of just war (both in the sense of *ius ad bellum* as the *ius in bello*) all the while legitimizing as the highest criterion the precondition of violent intervention as the last resort: "to be controlled by international law in accordance to the UN Charter and [intervention] can only be taken into consideration by those who themselves follow international law strictly."[80] This is even classified as an "imperative condition [...] The breach of law cannot be accepted even when this, at times, seems to lead – under military aspects – to a disadvantage or to hamper the efficiency of the intervention in the short term."[81] The call for protective assistance will always be addressed to the international community and "pre-suppose a discerning and decision-making process in compliance with the international community, strictly bound to international law." (*legitima potestas*) In this regard the "Statement on Reforming the United Nations,"[82] which was adopted at the same time at the WCC Assembly, is to be considered as a supplemental statement, as it calls

for a reminder of the necessary advancements for the effective capacity
of the United Nations. With the explicit restriction of the use of force
to the function of immediate protection (*causa iusta*), the churches
clearly demonstrate that long-term solutions for the restoration of
conditions in which the population is more exposed to the risk of
injury or death, cannot be brought about by force. Rather, a minimum
level of economic, social and medical services shall ensure respect for
the fundamental rights and freedoms, to put instruments of violence
under control and to emphasize the dignity of all people. Social and
political problems can never be solved by military means.

> The use of force for humanitarian purposes must therefore be carried
> out in the context of a broad spectrum of economic, social, political,
> and diplomatic efforts to address the direct and long-term conditions
> that underlie the crisis. (*debitus modus*)[83]

Based on the understanding of the limited effectiveness of violent
interventions, an additional, new criterion arises, namely, that such
use of armed force may be used strictly "in order to reinstate civil
means." (*recta intentio*)[84]

Concerning the realistic possibility of a further development of
international law, the further question that remains is to clarify the
enforceability of these criteria. The argumentation basically remains
trapped within the logic of just war such that it is critical to determine
more detailed distinctions of the criteria: Which means are "proportional"? What "collateral damages" are acceptable? Is it "proportion-
ate" and justifiable from the perspective of Christian faith to kill a
human, because it potentially saves other human lives? These well-
known issues from previous ecumenical peace ethics discussions[85] on
the rejection of the doctrine of just war had indeed been carried out
extensively, but have not yet been resolved to date.

c. The Concept of "Just Policing"

Just as individuals or communities in stable societies can call upon the protection of the police in the face of immediate threats, all people should have the right to obtain protection. The use of force as described here, therefore, correlates the activities of a law-abiding police force with military intervention. Therefore, the notion tries to differentiate between force that is actually used for humanitarian purposes from military force, which follows the methodology and aims of warfare. Such military intervention which aims to defeat a state is unequivocally illegitimate. The proposal is that for the protection of threatened peoples "international police forces should be educated and trained for this particular task, bound to international law."[86] Otherwise all other interventions of humanitarian assistance are supposed to be accompanied by the military. Any intervention would require a willingness to provide the necessary means to restore the foundations of order and public security. The necessary capacity to build a lasting peace would need to be demonstrably present in that region.

In these debates the concept of "Just Policing" is inserted here in short, without developing it further. This approach is being developed mainly by a selection of Roman Catholic and Mennonite scholars.[87] The distinction between military violence (*violentia*) on the one hand, and police coercion (*coactus*) on the other, indeed only makes sense if those police are strictly accountable to a public, are democratically legitimate and are under scrutiny of the law and thus can be understood as an expression of a monopoly on force (*Gewaltmonopol*). In exercising this coercion, human rights must be respected in full, personal dignity must be protected and all actions shall be directed toward minimizing violence and its prevention. The strict requirement remains that such a concept would not lead to uncertainty or even confusion between the military and police forces.[88] That distinction must be recognizable to the protected population of the country in which an act of intervention is deemed necessary.

The Impossibility of Avoiding Guilt and the Need to Confess

The churches of the ecumenical community confess their guilt for the collective failure to live justly and to work for justice. If cases should occur in which the churches actually deem violent coercion to be legitimate, then each of these requires an admission of guilt, because there was no success achieved in preventing the crisis. The ecumenical community has to the present been unable to reach a joint position on this issue.

Of course, the theological justification of such a step should have been inevitable, yet such is absent in the WCC document. If in extreme cases there is a need to assume conscious, individual guilt, because there is no possibility of avoiding liability, then from the perspective of Christian faith this is only possible in the "Christ-reality"; because only in Christ, is there hope for the forgiveness of such guilt ("costly grace" as in the oft-quoted phrase by Dietrich Bonhoeffer). This entails constantly overcoming a boundary, one which is given by the commandments, but in no way means displacing this boundary.[89]

The statement on humanitarian intervention ultimately recommends further work on the difficult issues concerning the responsibility to protect. This reflects the awareness that this statement does not answer the very specific question of peace ethics. But there is no mistaking there has been progress in ecumenical discussions on peace ethics. The member churches now recognize jointly that the

> Lordship of Christ is higher than any other loyalty .... Critical solidarity with the victims of violence and advocacy against all the oppressive forces must also inform our theological endeavours towards being a more faithful church.[90]

The churches recognize in their "ministry of reconciliation and healing" the task of building confidence.

In the ecumenical declaration on just peace, which was designed in preparation for the International Ecumenical Peace Convocation in Jamaica in 2011, one sees a further step of joint progress toward the development of ecumenical peace ethics. In this context, the debate about intervention to protect vulnerable peoples directly may certainly be regarded as the most difficult testing ground for the community of churches.

Kingston 2011: The International Ecumenical Peace Convocation

The mission statement for the International Ecumenical Peace Convocation in 2011 (IEPC) in Kingston, Jamaica, read as follows:

> The IEPC aims at witnessing to the Peace of God as a gift and respon-
> sibility of the *oikoumene*. It seeks to assess and strengthen the church's
> position on peace, provide opportunities for networking and deepen
> our common commitment to processes of reconciliation and peace.[91]

If such a broad approach is taken, then naturally it will be difficult to clearly describe individual topics and testing grounds for the church in its service for just peace. Yet it is not impossible as such an approach offers the opportunity to capture both its complexity and contextuality within a large ecumenical process of reflection and discussion. Just as the Decade was created in a nuanced manner, the IEPC cannot be artificially reduced to a single issue. Rather, it is to be understood as a forum in which the various facets of just peace are to be discussed, thus imbuing all of them with a common, activist orientation.

That approach does not need to implicitly lead to mere generalities, but should enable a balancing of all emphases, such that one does not predominate over others. That would weaken the overall movement and disown the respective contextual needs such as the rich theological insights and convictions of the respective denominations. The whole undertaking must ultimately be shaped by a conciliar process, moving towards a coherent ecumenical theology of just peace, based on a common identity as *una sancta*, jointly aiming toward concrete action, while being responsible toward each other and engaging the world.

In this way, the preparatory committee for the IEPC arrived at the following rough outline of topics:

I Peace in the Community,
II Peace with the Earth,
III Peace in the Marketplace,
IV Peace among Peoples.

The familiar themes of the *Conciliar Process for Justice, Peace and the Integrity of Creation* remain ostensibly present, but they were augmented by the concrete reality of life experiences among smaller communities. The presentation of the interdependence of individual issues is crucial so that concrete, contextual concerns may be brought for discussion, including overarching, global interdependencies.

The Ecumenical Declaration on Just Peace that resulted from the preparatory meetings for the IEPC was a concise, affirmative text submitted to the central committee at its meeting in February 2011, in the hope that this explanation – after careful deliberation and possible adaptations – would officially be accepted as a preparatory document for the 10th WCC Assembly in 2013. The declaration was to be supplemented by another longer document, outlining the contexts of justification on which the Declaration was based. There was also the expectation that this document would set out proposals and examples of successful peace actions (called "good practices"), based on the experiences during the Decade, as well as the reactions received on the first draft of the Declaration. A preliminary version of this document was drawn up by the second editorial team for the Ecumenical Declaration on Just Peace, and was brought to the participants of the IEPC as a preparatory document. The seminars, workshops and Bible studies held during the IEPC continued to develop an ecumenical theology of just peace.

Beyond the event at Kingston in 2011, the 10th WCC Assembly in Busan, South Korea in 2013, became a broader horizon in which to consider the IEPC. After the conclusion of the Decade to Overcome Violence, the chief goal became the drafting of an ecumenical theology of justice and peace. It remains to be seen whether the fellowship of churches in the WCC has the power to move beyond the Convocation, to clarify the coherence of what is now such a broad movement, and not to do so for its own sake, but so that the churches "fulfil together their common calling to the glory of the one God, Father, Son and Holy Spirit."[92] One might ask, was the IEPC 2011 therefore the "Council," which Bonhoeffer (and later von Weizsäcker and others) had requested? To answer this it is necessary first to take account of the changing context and the associated shifts in the issues at hand; secondly, the current self-understanding of ecumenism; and thirdly, the enduring plausibility of the theological arguments.

The Changed Context

At the Assembly in Porto Alegre a document was presented at the midpoint of the Decade, which made an initial evaluation and recommendations for how to proceed further.[93] Two keynote themes have developed through the Decade: "overcoming the spirit, logic and praxis of violence" and strengthening a "spirituality of reconciliation and active nonviolence." To use Bonhoeffer's words, we might call this taking seriously the "binding law" of Christ. The issues of security and the threat of militarization remain relevant, but what has become much more obvious is the necessity of working toward possibilities of reconciliation with communities of other faiths. Today, all of our theological reflection and our practical work to overcome violence take place in pluralistic contexts.

On the one hand there is the threat of international terrorism, which itself is often justified by religious fanaticism; yet on the other hand, there is an increased willingness among states to consider even preventative wars once again (!) as legitimate means of political negotiations. Both of these threats pose new challenges for the churches. In addition, there is the new problem of failing states where there is no longer a monopoly on force and political control, so that the weakest and most vulnerable are no longer protected by anyone. Furthermore, today there is a rising availability and even pervasiveness of small arms both in civil wars and among the criminal elements of large cities, and this leads to more victims – especially younger ones – than in the major wars that draw the attention of the mass media. In addition, all of these problems need to be seen within the context of a progressive economy-based globalization of all branches of our international community, a monetization of life that has become a near-universal doctrine throughout our planet. In all of these questions, we ask – with Bonhoeffer – what is to be our "concrete law"?

In some churches there are now focused efforts being placed on researching and testing out various means of nonviolent conflict prevention and transformation, various forms of civil conflict management, training for civil peace services and healing processes as a response to violence.[94] Gradually, the churches are becoming conscious of their role as "ministers of reconciliation" (2 Cor 5) and with it, their responsibility to provide nonviolent alternatives, if their call to overcome violence is to be considered credible. It is not enough to merely demand that the world community should guarantee the right of law and the protection of universal human rights at national and international levels (which should be obvious enough for the churches). Rather, a comprehensive vision of "just peace" must also include a coherent elaboration and practical explication of what that looks like in the context of our faith and confession.

The Protestant Church in Germany (EKD),[95] the Roman Catholic Bishops' Conference,[96] as well as the smaller churches, such as the Methodists[97] or the Mennonites,[98] have put forward their more recent peace memoranda which included advanced theological and ethical considerations. According to the recent peace memorandum of the EKD:

> The practice of just peace, which can be regarded as a feature of the global fellowship of Christians, will not however, be shared in its spiritual depth by all people and cannot replace practical peace policy. Yet it converges with a multidimensional concept of peace, which can be introduced as a socially ethical model in the mission of political peace.[99]

As noted above, in the biblical understanding, peace (*shalom*) denotes a broad notion which encompasses more than the mere absence of war. Peace-building and the commitment to peace and justice mutually condition each other, being reciprocal. Therefore, peace-building processes are distinguished by the fact "that they are aimed at preventing violence, promoting freedom, promoting cultural diversity and reducing poverty."[100] And through the reconciliation enacted by God in Jesus Christ, the churches are able to live with each other in a relationship of reconciliation.

The Changed Understanding of Unity

Over the last few decades the World Council of Churches has developed an entirely different understanding of its unity than the one it had earlier, for example in 1928 (Stockholm), 1937 (Oxford), 1948 (Amsterdam) or 1983 (Vancouver), 1950 (the Toronto Statement) or 1961 (Assembly in New Delhi). This development has never become clearer than during the multi-year process within the WCC in the 1990s that led toward the development of the fundamental declaration "Towards a Common Understanding and Vision of the World Council of Churches."[101] This altered understanding of our unity needed to be taken into consideration during the Peace Convocation in 2011. Bonhoeffer's ecclesiological argument that the Church of Christ transcends all other boundaries and divisions is as true now as it was then. But today the *oikoumene* needs to work through these challenges differently, both in light of its ecclesiological self-understanding and in light of the respective ecclesiologies of the member churches: as the mutual partaking, participating and contribution of the entirety of God's people, in reconciled diversity.

Today we know this presupposes that all of the various contributors to the ecumenical movement, with their very different experiences and challenges, must be given a voice, first of all within the ecumenical community of churches, and then in the broader public sphere. Some initial contributions toward the broader spectrum of an ecumenical theology of just peace have become visible within the various contexts of the DOV.[102] It is important that we share these with one another in the ecumenical community, so that "life in all its fullness" will be possible for all. That singular "word" or confession that was given voice at the Peace Convocation in Jamaica needs to be spoken by the various "witnesses": by individuals, congregations and churches. And in this manner it was possible for the announcement of the "concrete law" to take place at the Ecumenical Peace Convocation.

The Changed Foundational Axiom of Ecumenism

As noted earlier, the Christological argument, the topic of Bonhoeffer's lecture in 1934, is today being expanded into a Trinitarian understanding of God. Konrad Raiser has elucidated this "paradigm shift" from Christocentric universalism to the sociality of God; it was the Trinity who founded the "one household of life."[103] The development of an "Ecumenical Peace Declaration on Just Peace" on the way to the Peace Convocation was supposed to help bring together the theological-ethical and ecclesiological reflections of the contemporary ecumenical movement in order to formulate unambiguous statements by the churches for peace. The Declaration starts from the doxological commitment then proceeds to the triune God, who is in self-relationship (*ad intra*) and then posits himself relationally (*ad extra*) as the condition for the possibility of successful, life-enhancing relationships between individuals, men and women, young and old; within the smallest of communities, among states and in the international community; among the churches of different traditions and their relationship with believers of other religions; in relation to the created world as a loan-gift from God to be treated with responsible stewardship. The Trinitarian approach enables the coherent conceptualization of creation, reconciliation (redemption) and consummation, refusing to isolate one from another. It reveals that the God of Abraham and Sarah, the God of Israel who liberated his people from the house of bondage, the God who became human in Jesus Christ, and who then fully and spiritually inhabited this violent world (*shekhina*) in order to liberate it from violence and thus to bring it to fulfillment – not only

Christians, but also the sister religions; and not only people, but creation as a whole.[104]

This liberation from violence then results in a dynamic image of God as opposed to a static one. This image is dominated by the extensive movement *ad extra* of the communality of Divine Love. The decisive factor is not that a model of community is constructed, which is intended to reflect the Church. Rather, it becomes expressed through the common, foundational confession of faith, namely, that all Christians of the *oikoumene* – in Christ – *participate* in this communion with God. This also characterized the decisive advancement in recognition within ecumenical discussions between the peace churches and the former state churches in the 1950s and 1960s of the last century.[105] And although it is clear that neither the discussion about ethics nor actions taken toward just peace by the churches can bring forth the Kingdom of God, nonetheless, by witnessing and acting in a way that is concomitant with participation in the Kingdom of God, nonviolence becomes a condition for this possibility.

With this understanding as the basis, the self-understanding of the Church (as *oikoumene*) and the appropriate perspective concerning the realities of violence in this world result along with both the needs and opportunities for their redemption and reconciliation. All that must continue to be developed in more detail in an ecumenical theology of just peace. The Church – in the sense of the ecumenical community – is then the very *capacity of being able* to live free from violence. It is a welcoming community, which, through its nature and essence already changes realities, not in spite of but because its members see themselves as *simul justus et peccator* – at once as sinners and justified.

The chosen motto for the Peace Convocation in 2011 "Glory to God – and Peace on Earth" picks up precisely that challenge. In Fanø Bonhoeffer had cited only the second part of this calling as the "binding law" given by Christ himself. If the ecumenical community can jointly confess this truth of the divine, reconciling relationship that the Gospel purports, then they should also be able to "proclaim" the "concrete law" in their respective contexts of violence and to actually live out a non-violent alternative in "the frenzied world" as *una sancta,* both locally and globally. This assumes the churches are aware of the "wager" (Bonhoeffer) that is involved, and accept the fact that such may also end ultimately "on the cross." Then the world will not be able to "ignore" this, because through this witness the world cannot remain unchanged. In a *joint* contribution to the Decade two such different churches as a Peace Church (Mennonites) and the Roman Catholic Church, cited Pope John Paul II in this spirit:

> It is by uniting his own sufferings for the sake of truth and freedom to
> the sufferings of Christ on the Cross that man is able to accomplish
> the miracle of peace and is in a position to discern the often narrow
> path between the cowardice which gives in to evil and the violence
> which, under the illusion of fighting evil, only makes it worse.[106]

Given that the Christian faith takes the possibility of overcoming violence to be an eschatological reality, tolerating violence must be regarded as unrealistic and lacking the perspective of this very faith. Yet the ecumenical community must work together to develop such creativity, for which it will be necessary to tread the "narrow path" of nonviolence. In Christ, the Church is already a "new creation," called to this ministry of reconciliation (2 Cor 5).

CHAPTER 8

PILGRIMAGE: WALKING GENTLY WITH YOUR GOD

THE ECUMENICAL PILGRIMAGE OF JUSTICE AND PEACE – A NEW DIRECTION FOR THE ECUMENICAL MOVEMENT

> *You have been told, O humankind,*
> *what is good and what God looks for in you.*
> *Nothing other than to practise justice,*
> *to love kindness and to walk attentively with your God.[1]*
>
> *He has told you, O mortal, what is good,*
> *   and what does the Lord require of you*
> *but to do justice and to love kindness*
> *   and to walk humbly with your God?*
>
> — MICAH 6:8 (NRSV)

THE TENTH ASSEMBLY OF THE WORLD COUNCIL OF CHURCHES will certainly go down in the annals of the ecumenical movement as the one that took the decision to blaze a new trail: the ecumenical 'Pilgrimage of Justice and Peace'. In so doing it has chosen a new comprehensive programmatic approach, which, especially for the WCC brings together into one coherent relationship the many different activities and dimensions of the ecumenical movement. That gives them a common direction, which will strengthen the unity of the churches and will also open the door for new relationships, above all with other religions.[2] During the Assembly the metaphor of pilgrimage was, however, being used in such a many-faceted way that already at that time some cautionary voices were being raised. If in fact it were merely to be a new name for what was basically going to be continued in exactly the same way, and if that metaphor continued to be used in a random way, then nothing would be gained. The effectiveness of this new ecumenical approach will first need to be demonstrated. That will be dependent on whether it in fact succeeds in enabling the churches of the *oikoumene*:

(1) to arrive at a common interpretation, and
(2) to move forward on this pilgrimage to a changed and changing ecumenical praxis.

Neither will be possible without serious and wide-ranging theological reflection, which does not necessarily have to precede the new path to be followed, but must at least be in parallel with it. Yet the determination and will to do this does seem to be there.[3]

It is important to review the process leading to that Assembly's decision, so as to show which ecumenical processes in the recent past have led up to it and in what respect this new orientation undertaken by that decision might find a new alignment, significance or at least a greater emphasis. Secondly, I shall then develop a proposal that demonstrates the various dimensions of such an ecumenical pilgrimage of justice and peace, with the aim of producing an initial common interpretation of what it would contain.

a. Steps to the Ecumenical Pilgrimage – Earlier Model of 'Just Peace'

It was the Sixth WCC Assembly in Vancouver, Canada, that launched a 'Conciliar Process for Justice, Peace and the Integrity of Creation', and thereby influenced all subsequent ecumenical processes. First, the emphasis was placed on the central witness of the Church and the churches for justice, peace, and the protection of the natural world, and on how these issues are dependent on one another in terms of their content. Secondly, it also presupposed that the method to be used would be that the ecumenical movement – according to the understanding of the member churches and the self-understanding of the WCC itself – would have a conciliar nature, whereby wisdom would be sought by taking counsel together in mutual responsibility. That can only take place in the form of processes. The idea of the new ecumenical pilgrimage draws explicitly on that understanding and extends it.

(1) 'Just Peace' as a New Paradigm in Ecumenical Theology and Social Ethics

A decisive stage in the ongoing conciliar process immediately prior to the Busan Assembly was the Decade to Overcome Violence initiated by the Eighth WCC Assembly in Harare, Zimbabwe, in 1998, culminating in the Ecumenical Peace Convocation (IEPC) in Kingston, Jamaica, in 2011.[4] For its method, this Decade was able to draw on the previous Decade of Churches in Solidarity with Women, but it also attempted to follow a comprehensive programmatic approach that was to contribute to bring coherence to all WCC programmes and ultimately to give them, and thereby the WCC as a whole, a more distinct profile. The fact that this only partially succeeded need not be explained in detail here. It should, however, not be forgotten that the determination to achieve such coherence has meanwhile taken many forms, as the decision for the new Pilgrimage paradigm shows.

Yet more important is the task of aligning the results of the Decade to Overcome Violence with the new paradigm. At its conclusion there emerged an even clearer, more comprehensive consensus on 'just peace' as a helpful conceptual framework, because such an approach seems to be able not only to hold together the three key concerns of the conciliar process, but also to be in accord with its contents. That can be seen in exemplary fashion in 'An Ecumenical Call to Just

Peace.'[5] That call was issued in response to a WCC Assembly recommendation at Porto Alegre, Brazil, 2006, and it was built on insights gained in the course of the Decade.[6] As a key document of the IEPC it was then further enriched by an international team of experts in the form of an accompanying document.[7] That contributed in its turn to the future preparations for the 10th Assembly, giving it a decisive orientation, not least in the choice of the theme for Busan: "God of life, lead us to justice and peace."

'Just Peace' is defined as:

> a collective and dynamic yet grounded process of freeing human beings from fear and want, of overcoming enmity, discrimination and oppression, and of establishing conditions for just relationships that privilege the experience of the most vulnerable and respect the integrity of creation.[8]

That explicitly indicates that 'just peace' is not to be understood simply as a reversal or the opposite of the concept of 'just war', but goes much further: "In addition to silencing weapons it embraces social justice, the rule of law, respect for human rights and shared human security."[9] The scriptures of the Old and New Testaments make "justice the inseparable companion of peace (Isaiah 32:17; James 3:18). Both point to right and sustainable relationships in human society, the vitality of our connections with the earth, the 'well-being' and integrity of creation."[10]

In the *Just Peace Companion*, this notion is given further detailed and concrete shape. In fact this is made clear by abandoning the traditional style of a purely moral appeal. 'Just peace' is itself embedded as a new model in ecumenical theology, and biblical and theological (and especially ecclesiological) foundations are laid down, so as to set out the various areas in which it can be lived out: just peace in small communities, just peace between peoples and within nations, just peace in economical relationships, just peace with nature. (In discussions following the IEPC it was constantly recalled that the important dimension of just peace that is 'peace with oneself', the intrapersonal dimension, is to be added.) All further reflection on the contents of an ecumenical pilgrimage of justice and peace will follow meaningfully to these testing grounds.

The expression 'Pilgrimage of Just Peace' was not adopted and that was due to the vehement questioning of a small group of critics, who – in my opinion rightly – pointed out how the concept was misused in political circles and who unanimously asked what, and whose law and justice were being applied. They further saw the danger that justice could be reduced to the status of a weak adjective qualifying peace. During the official Ecumenical Conversations on just peace in Busan, the various interpretations were noted. In the event, however, as I saw it, such distinctions between concepts and expressions made little difference for the conversations.

(2) The Pilgrimage Metaphor – Against the Reduction of a Just Peace to a Socio-Political Aim

Within the Ecumenical Call to Just Peace, the meaning of the pilgrimage metaphor emerges in several ways, but no explicit explanation of it is given. The Preamble reads: "Inspired by the example of Jesus of Nazareth, it invites Christians to commit themselves to the Way of Just Peace."[11] This discipleship theme is then later expanded – one could say 'interpreted' – by the relevant further theological framework of God's loving purpose for creation that makes such discipleship possible: "Just Peace is a journey into God's purpose for humanity and all creation, trusting that God will 'guide our feet into the way of peace' (Luke 1:79)."[12]

The concept of 'Pilgrimage' itself then appears:

The Christian pilgrimage toward peace presents many opportunities to build visible and viable communities for peace. A church that prays for peace, serves its community, uses money ethically, cares for the environment and cultivates good relations with others can become an instrument for peace.[13]

However, even here there is some ambivalence. Are we here being invited to go on a pilgrimage *towards* just peace, or, rather, are we to go on a pilgrimage *of* just peace? In the first case, just peace would be the *goal* of the pilgrimage, which is too often reduced to a socio-political goal, or – in extreme cases – merely eschatologically 'transfigured'; in the second case, just peace would in fact be understood also as a matter of practice, the way in which we live. Already at this point all these elements appear and remain important if the richness of this metaphor is to be made fruitful. However, there is at least some element of verbal inexactitude. Now it has become sharply necessary to provide some deeper theological explanation of how these different elements relate to one another. There is certainly a great ecumenical possibility to provide clarification.

(3) The Pilgrimage *of* Justice and *of* Peace – a Journey *of* the Churches

During the meeting of the WCC Central Committee in 2012 in Crete, one year after the IEPC and one year before the Busan Assembly – some decisive proposals had to be dealt with. In the Programme Committee (a sub-committee of the Central Committee), *inter alia*, a letter from the delegates of the churches in Germany (the Evangelical Church in Germany and the Mennonite Church in Germany) was to be discussed, containing the following proposal:

> We should very much like to discuss with you how our community of churches in the WCC and our common commitment for a just peace on earth could be strengthened by a conciliar process with the theme 'Turn to life: Justice and Peace in light of Climate Change' that would continue until the Eleventh Assembly.[14]

The letter explained in detail that climate change *also* represents a spiritual crisis, as the IEPC had already stated:

The environmental crisis is profoundly an ethical and spiritual crisis of humanity. Recognizing the damage human activity has done to the Earth, we reaffirm our commitment to the integrity of creation and the daily lifestyle it demands.[15]

This proposal focussing on 'climate justice' did, however, find no consensus in the Programme Committee, since the challenge of climate change is, by far, not seen in all parts of the *oikoumene* as *the* decisive challenge facing the churches. The discussion thus ended in the following decisions:

(1) It seemed appropriate to create a comprehensive programmatic thrust to continue the concerns of the earlier Decade to Overcome Violence (and thus the link with a just peace);
(2) the *spiritual* challenge of the present crises should be presented in the form of a pilgrimage; and
(3) in so doing, it was decisive that the churches and the WCC should *themselves* make this journey if they wished to become credible in their concerns for a just peace.

Thus the proposed pilgrimage of the churches would itself have to be characterized by justice and peace. (The decisive push for that came from a delegate from Tanzania.) Finally, the Central Committee made the following recommendation indicating the way forward:

That the World Council of Churches launch a pilgrimage **of** justice and peace... at the Assembly in Busan (until the 11th Assembly) **for** and **of** the churches to focus on faith commitments to economic justice (poverty and wealth), ecological justice (climate change, etc.) and peace building.

That the World Council of Churches initiate a broad theological study process of the issues related to the pilgrimage of justice and peace in order to connect to the theological work on ecclesiology (undertaken by Faith and Order), unity, mission (CWME) and others within the member churches.[16]

The Busan Assembly adopted this comprehensive proposal and included it word for word in its Programme Guidelines.[17] At least three reasons may have been decisive for reaching this broad ecumenical consensus:

1) The key concerns of the 'just peace' continue to be an urgent challenge to the churches in their differing contexts, and also as a world ecumenical community. While the emphasis in particular contexts may be different (economic justice, environmental justice, climate justice, non-violent peace-building, and restorative justice), these mutually interdependent dimensions are seen by all in this globalized world as urgent questions for the unity, theology, and witness/mission of the Church and the churches. It would thus seem that only a comprehensive approach such as this is equal to the task in view of the complexity of the challenges.

2) The multiple repetitiveness and largely unproductive polarization in many ecumenical discussions in the past (which go right back to the beginnings of the modern ecumenical movement, in the Faith and Order movement on the one hand, and the Life and Work movement on the other) between, on the one hand, an ecumenism largely concerned with dialogue on doctrinal matters, and, on the other, an ecumenism dealing mainly with action on social and ethical questions, could finally be overcome by such an integrated theological study process. Such a study process could bring together the expertise to be found in the individual commissions and working areas (Unity, Mission, Dialogue, Public Witness, and Ecumenical Formation) in such a way that a common clear position could result, *inasmuch as* current social crises and political and violent conflicts pose *theological* questions to the churches of the oikoumene and their self-understanding. All too often these issues have been dealt with separately as a task for efficient, politically oriented advocacy work, which has increasingly given rise to the concern – and not only for representatives of the Orthodox churches – that it is no longer recognizable to what extent action is in fact being taken by the churches of the oikoumene (as opposed, for example, to any Non-Governmental Organization).

3) If there is now going to be a greater concern to establish more

securely the spiritual roots that do not only motivate the socio-political activity of the Church and the churches, but also demand it and strengthen it, then above this will address all those traditions that have the liturgy at the center of their church life and activity. Moreover, many others are more and more feeling a need for deep spiritual renewal, as they increasingly recognize that the Church's action in matters of just peace, if limited to political campaigning alone, falls short and is ultimately doomed to remain powerless and ineffective. The IEPC had already, *inter alia*, described just peace as "a pattern of life that reflects human participation in God's love for the world."[18] The dynamic character of just peace as gift and calling of the Church and churches was in that decision conceived as a pilgrimage to be undertaken together.

The Message of the Busan Assembly combines all this in one single challenge to 'all people of good will' to join in this pilgrimage.[19]

b. The Oikoumene *in via* – Transformative Spirituality and the theologically Trinitarian foundation of Just Peace

An initial attempt will now be made to describe more exactly the Ecumenical Pilgrimage of Justice and Peace in light of the most recent discussions within the WCC.

First, in the IEPC evaluation, which had significant influence on the preparations for the Busan Assembly (*inter alia*, in the Assembly document 'Statement on the Way of Just Peace'); second, in the new mission and evangelism statement presented at Busan ('Together towards Life: Mission and Evangelism in Changing Landscapes'); and third, in recent debates in the newly elected Central Committee ('An Invitation to the Pilgrimage of Justice and Peace,' 2014).

In the *Just Peace Companion* which accompanies the Ecumenical Call to Just Peace, helpful reflections are to be found which make it clear how the pilgrimage undertaken by those who wish to join it will itself be marked by justice and peace. Just peace:

...is not simply assenting to a set of ideas about God's design for the world. To be agents of God's peace requires putting on the mind that was in Christ Jesus (cf. Phil. 2:5)... In order to have that mind of Christ, peace-building requires entering regularly and deeply into communion with the Triune God, along the ways that Christ has set out for us. It is that presence in God that makes it possible for us to come to discern God's working in our world.[20]

That belief can keep Christian hope (as distinguished from optimism) alive:

Hope... is something that comes from God, who is the author of peace and reconciliation. Hope is something that we discover, drawing us forward into the mystery of peace.[21]

It is clear that this growing awareness of "participating in God's Mission of justice and peace (*missio Dei*)" enables the churches to have fresh confidence to be able themselves to become "communities of justice and peace."[22] That opens up decisive trains of thought for further discussion on ecclesiology in the WCC.

The *Just Peace Companion* had already made an attempt in broad outline to give just peace a Trinitarian theological basis:

In its own finite way, spirituality mirrors the loving relationships between the persons of the triune God who sustains, transforms and sanctifies a broken world.[23]

The Central Committee gave further thought to this in 2014 in its Statement on the Way of Just Peace: "The movement of love which is essential to the Triune God manifests itself in the promise of justice and peace."[24] These reflections become even more clear if they are linked with the three different dimensions, which in the Pilgrimage of Justice and Peace are in a dynamic mutual relationship with one another, as the Central Committee has now taken up. This followed from the fundamental differentiations made by Dorothee Sölle with her trifold "mystical paths," i.e. *the positive, negative and transformative.*[25]

(1) The *via positiva* – Celebrating the Blessing of Creation

In the form of articles of belief the Assembly stated:

> Together we believe in God, the Creator of all life. Therefore we acknowledge that every human being is made in the image and likeness of God... In wondrously creating a world with more than enough natural riches to support countless generations of human beings and other living things, God makes manifest a vision for all people to live in the fullness of life and with dignity, regardless of class, gender, religion, race or ethnicity.[26]

The ecumenical community begins its Pilgrimage of Justice and Peace not as seekers, but as those who have been found.[27] To begin with there is amazement at the goodness of creation, and the awareness that we are part of it – which means nothing other than that we know that we are *in relationship,* with God, with our fellow creatures and with one another, long before we ourselves form these relationships: we are created in God's image, we are formed according to the community within the Godhead. God's dealings with creation do not begin with original sin, but with original blessing. This sense of amazement leads us immediately to praising God and to celebrating together, as a natural reaction to "God's great gift of life, the beauty of creation and the unity of a reconciled diversity."[28] That holds before us a vision of the possibility of a life in just, non-violently liberated relationships – and not only in the relationships of humans with one another. This amazement at the miracle of life can produce in us the strength to seek to maintain these vital relationships by our careful stewardship. How else could an appropriate theology of creation be described?

(2) The *via negativa* – Being Freed from Power and Violence

Together we believe in Jesus Christ, the Prince of Peace. Therefore we acknowledge that humankind is reconciled with God, by grace, and we strive to live reconciled with one another. The life and teachings, the death and resurrection of Jesus Christ, point toward the peaceable Kingdom of God. Despite persecution and suffering, Jesus remains steadfast in his way of humility and active non-violence, even unto death. His life of commitment to justice leads to the cross, an instrument of torture and execution. With the resurrection of Jesus, God confirms that such steadfast love, such obedience, such trust, leads to life. By God's grace we too are enabled to take the way of the cross, be disciples and bear the costs.[29]

However, just because the Pilgrimage to Justice and Peace begins with being found and not with condemnation – in the ontological and not the chronological sense – (in the words of Dorothee Sölle)

> is what makes the horror about the destruction of wonder so radical... Mystical spirituality of creation will very likely move deeper and deeper into the dark night of being delivered into the hands of the principalities and powers that dominate us.[30]

For the WCC:

> the pilgrimage will lead us to the locations of ugly violence and injustices. We intend to look for God's incarnated presence in the midst of suffering, exclusion and discrimination.[31]

The painful element in the Pilgrimage is seeking the divine incarnation precisely in the places apparently abandoned by God where violence and injustice harm life or even destroy it. A pilgrimage *of* justice and *of* peace, if it is to become a path followed by the churches in discipleship to Jesus and sharing in his sufferings, cannot be a 'dream journey' which passes by horrors and the distress of the helpless. "Following Jesus means meeting him wherever people suffer injustice, violence, and war."[32] That is exactly in accord with the line taken by the new WCC Mission and Evangelism Statement when it speaks of 'Mission from the Margins.'[33] Indeed, wherever possible, those 'on the margins' must themselves become the decisive guides pointing the way to the churches in all their decisions, because the dimension of pilgrimage that is changing the *oikoumene* does not allow us to pass them by, but rather involves 'kneeling down and learning to walk upright'.[34] For only here, by actually encountering suffering in the places of our own powerlessness our "relation to the basic realities of ownership, violence, and the self is changing."[35] That can lead the Church to "repentance and – in a movement of purification – liberate us from obsession with power, possessions, ego, and violence, so that we become ever more Christ-like."[36] The *Just Peace Companion* asserts: "Putting on the mind of Christ, being formed in Christ, involves spiritual practices and disciplines that embody peace in our own bodies."[37]

This results in the following actions:

- communal acts of worship in order to be nourished by God's Word and by the Eucharist;
- making prayers of intercession as part of our mindfulness of being formed in Christ;
- seeking and extending forgiveness, so as to create truthfulness in ourselves and to forge the space for others who need to seek repentance;
- washing one another's feet, so as to learn the ways of service;
- engaging in times of fasting, to review our patterns of consumption and relationships to one another and to the earth;
- consistent and sustained acts of caring for others, especially those most in need of healing, liberation, and reconciliation;
- consistent and sustained acts of caring for the earth.

In that way the pilgrimage is also described as a learning curve as we "learn to give up looking for justifications of what we have done and train ourselves in the practice of justice."[38] The Pilgrimage will only become credible if it is a journey of repentance. It may be that this becomes the greatest challenge for the *oikoumene* – for how else could a Christology of just peace be described?

(3) The *via transformativa* – Resistance

> Together we believe in the Holy Spirit, the Giver and Sustainer of all life. Therefore we acknowledge the sanctifying presence of God in all of life, strive to protect life and to heal broken lives... We can state that: the Holy Spirit assures us that the Triune God will perfect and consummate all of creation at the end of time. In this we recognize justice and peace as both promise and present – hope for the future and a gift here and now.[39]

It is only in our becoming one with Christ – which is not to be misunderstood as self-realization – that Sölle sees that we gain strength to resist injustice and violence. Pilgrims can thus become healed healers. "Salvation means that humans live in compassion and justice co-creatively; in being healed (saved) they experience also that they can heal (save)."[40] That is the third dimension of the Pilgrimage. In their own self-transformation can the courage and strength grow (in the churches) "to resist evil – injustice and violence."[41] Therefore this Pilgrimage is much more than fresh programmes of action or fresh advocacy strategies – all of which are meaningful and necessary – and its first aim is a life in God and a transformation into a "gentle relationship with creation and a morality of enough,"[42] in order to resist the immense economic and ecological injustices. This transformative spirituality is seen as a gift of the Holy Spirit that guides us into all truth (John 16:13). How else could a pneumatology of just peace be described?

A realized eschatology, which is already anticipating in the present time the salvation of the world in all its brokenness and is seen as participation in the great *mission Dei,* can provide the theological framework to hold together the spiritual, ethical and theological dimensions of the Pilgrimage of Justice and Peace in its trifold aspects of *via positiva*, *via negativa* and *via transformitiva*. The self-understanding of the *oikoumene*, and also of the churches themselves, and their mission and service in the world, could not as such remain unaffected. How else could an ecclesiology of just peace be described?

Concluding Remarks

Many young people also participated in the Busan Assembly, as delegates of their churches, as stewards, and in the programme of the Global Ecumenical Theological Institute (GETI) – a very successful study programme accompanying the Assembly. In conversations with these participants, one complaint particularly emerged: the perceived gap between the claims of the *oikoumene* and what it is in reality. Their theoretical knowledge of the history and theology of the ecumenical movement as well as the many valuable unforgettable encounters at the margins of the Assembly stood in sharp contrast to the institutionalized *oikoumene* that they observed during the Assembly. The extent to which the 'business' of the *oikoumene* and the churches is marked by power, influence, money and sometimes injustice seemed in parts to these young participants shocking and unattractive.

One can respond to that criticism by pointing out the inevitable tension between an ecumenical movement 'at the margins' and 'at the grassroots' on the one hand, and on the other hand the ecumenical institutions 'at the centre' with their concerns for continuity and mutual accountability. It would be futile to play these off against one another. It does, however, remain important to hold the dynamism of these two opposites together to avoid the situation where the movements get nowhere because they are individual initiatives and the ecclesiastical institutions rigidify in static state of mere officialdom, structures and procedures. It is to be hoped that the ongoing Pilgrimage of Justice and Peace can make a decisive contribution in this way – that is, unless it becomes relativized into nothing more than a new ecumenical metaphor. Rather, it is hoped that its real,

concrete content is then actually lived out, not as a burdensome obligation but as a way of living in constant development, for individuals
and for whole communities. We do not necessarily have to look to the
ecumenical 'centres' for decisive initiatives here. The Pilgrimage will
simply happen when people are walking it as forgiven disciples of
Jesus Christ. May the ecumenical and church institutions be caught up
in this movement and 'walk gently.'

CHAPTER 9

ON THE PATH TO AN ECUMENICAL THEOLOGY OF COMPANIONSHIP

CHRIST AS COMPANIERO

Were not our hearts burning within us...?

— LUKE 24:32 (NRSV)

SINCE THE PILGRIMAGE of Justice and Peace (PJP) was launched at the 10th Assembly of the World Council of Churches (WCC) in Busan, South Korea in 2013, it became the new programmatic horizon for the life of the worldwide ecumenical fellowship. Conceived as a transformative journey in eschatological anticipation of God's kingdom, this Pilgrimage seeks to delve deeper into the spiritual dimensions of participation in God's righteous peace.[1] In the meantime, the worldwide ecumenical community has been able to gather different experiences on its Pilgrimage in the different contexts, so that one might explore impulses for the future of the ecumenical movement.[2]

The following draws on the learning experiences of two bodies: Within the WCC, an International Reference Group was appointed from the outset to give shape to the PJP, and a Theological Study Group to focus on the theological implications of the Pilgrimage – as recommended by the General Assembly.[3] In these two advisory bodies there are people from a wide variety of faith traditions including one each from Buddhism, Hinduism, Judaism and Islam, who are diverse in terms of gender, age, ethnic and cultural backgrounds in order to learn from the most diverse perspectives.[4]

Methodologically, both groups draw inspiration from the metaphor of pilgrimage: Pilgrim Team Visits have been taking place in different regions and communities around the world, each year with a different thematic focus,[5] following Rowan Williams' insight: "place works on the pilgrim!" The encounters at these "pilgrim stations" are each characterized by a rich spiritual life; and joys, but also sorrows and wounds are shared with the host communities in order to ultimately explore the possibilities of local and global transformations together. This procedure follows the system of the three dimensions of a spiritual path, as previously formulated by the WCC, based on the writing of Dorothee Sölle:[6] *via positiva* ("celebrating the gifts"), *via negativa* ("touching wounds") and *via transformativa* ("transforming injustices").[7] Experience shows that wisdom also lies in the inversion of Williams' phrase: the pilgrims work on the place, because the visit of the ecumenical pilgrims (of justice and peace!) does not occur without there being impact on the local contexts, according to reports from the host communities.[8] The self-understanding of the community of pilgrims and host communities that emerges from this dynamic can be appropriately described as "giving witness to God's pilgrimage of just peace."[9] Eventually, challenges are raised for the ecumenical agenda, arising from, but not limited to, the experience of actual communities in their respective contexts.

Four Themes of a Christologically-Grounded *Theology of Companionship*

During the Pilgrimage, four common issues have emerged that are relevant in all contexts, each in different ways, and are equally urgent:

(1) truth and trauma,

(2) land and displacement,

(3) gender justice,

(4) racism.

These themes serve as concrete illustrations of globally shared issues, such as the prevailing economic and/or ecological violence and injustice. Therefore, the ecumenical community is now faced with the challenge of starting from these contextually experienced injustices in order to move into joint theological reflection.

A broadening of the perspective is crucial here in which we first move away from what is commonplace in ecumenism, namely, advocacy and accompaniment, as these are sometimes experienced as one-sided or biased and even paternalistic. Then we can embrace a new way of fostering relationships inspired by the pilgrimage metaphor, which is called: companionship ("*com–pan–iero/as*," i.e. those who share the bread with each other on the way).

To illustrate the potentially transformative impact of this approach, the four themes mentioned are considered here in a Christologically-based conceptual framework of a theology of companionship. The primary goal here is not to create a systematic "coherence" as is inherent in Western theological thinking, but to focus more closely on the narratives of the peace-building ecumenical movement in general, which is gradually becoming aware of the need for its own decolonization.[10]

1. Truth and Trauma: God's Memory

Traumatized people have disturbed memories. As a result, their stories are often disregarded and their validity even denied. Their way of remembering is complex, as the power of condemnation, shame, or guilt can make one's own situation seem unresolvable.[11] Trauma is also a moral injury, "when the fabric that holds moral agency and the self together is torn asunder."[12] As a result, traumatized people are often silenced, with silence sometimes being explicitly imposed upon individuals and entire communities. And it is precisely this silence that allows injuries suffered (both mental and physical) to coagulate or freeze further into trauma. Acknowledging the truth can have a liberating, restorative power for victims, survivors, perpetrators, bystanders, and relationships within the community concerned. When truth is uncovered following the infliction of a severe injury, then repentance becomes possible for some, and forgiveness for others. In the process of mutual recognition of a truth, justice comes into view. But in order to unleash this power, truth must not be claimed solely by one perspective, nor can truth-telling be reduced to mere statements of fact.

In Colombia, many people have been traumatized by decades of civil war. One result of the peace agreement signed in 2016 between the Colombian government and the FARC guerrillas was the establishment of the Truth and Reconciliation Commission (TRC). Father Francisco de Roux, the chair of this commission, explained that the TRC does not seek to develop a definitive account of past horrific events, but rather to bring different – sometimes conflicting – narratives into dialogue with each other. Truth can only be interpreted as a joint process in which the wounds (Greek: *trauma*) have to be discussed.[13] The aim is to create space for the truth of others in one's own story.

Truth, understood as a relational concept, can be related to Christ's biblical self-description: "I am the way, the truth and the life" (John 14:6). In Christ the "Truth," as the fragility and limitations of all powers and privileges, is revealed and the wrongs done to the marginalized and traumatized are recognized. In this way, believing in this truth can free oneself to become an actor in healing processes again, because all striving for self-redemption is given up. However, Phillis Isabella Sheppard warns:

> Trauma demands that our theology and commitments begin on the ground, in the blood, sweat, and tears, and the pain-induced lesions that are carved into our bodies and psyches, and in the intersubjective realm … If our theology is not of those who live with trauma and … subject to their reflection, it is dangerous to talk about theology, and its danger lies in its power in theological discourse and theological practices to reproduce trauma.[14]

Individuals and communities need to draw from their own spiritual roots and traditions in order to embark on a (pilgrim) path of trauma healing. In fact, contextually-shaped spiritual practices open up possibilities for creative, individual and collective truth-finding processes as part of collective trauma healing.[15] Symbolism and ritual play a key role in these processes of "right remembrance."[16] For example, sharing the sacrament – remembering that 'truth' who was tortured, killed, and yet resurrected – can help recognize the bruised bodies and battered souls in a community. In the celebration of the Lord's Supper, that *companiero* is remembered, who himself went through death and who testifies in the power of the Holy Spirit that death itself – and all deaths – do not have the last word over life.

Willie J. Jennings aptly interprets this as "God's remembering" that releases the dynamic of *communio*:

> Jesus is the innocent who has been killed in conflict. Yet, he has risen not in vengeance or condemnation, but in new life... He offers forgiveness from the site of his body marked by violent death. Jesus returns to the scene of violence and betrayal, that is, to a world stamped with the memories of his murder, and he remembers with and for us, drawing our past into his future and shaping our present in his presence. In Jesus, we learn that God remembers. This is not a declaration of the divine capacities for memory, but for the communion dynamic in God's memory.[17]

In light of an emerging theology of companionship, these discoveries on the Pilgrimage of Justice and Peace demonstrate the importance of creating safe spaces in which painful wounds can be remembered and lamented along with others. Sometimes the traumatized person's trust can be placed in the companiero/as rather than in God. For some, the reality of Good Friday will be too dominant; they are reluctant to place their trust in the liberating resurrection of Christ, that "Truth." They are stuck, so to speak, in the uncertainty of Holy Saturday. Then the *companiero/as* will have to carry hope for those who are "broken in heart" and "whose spirit is crushed" (Ps 34:18). It is then up to the *companiero/as* to embody the Jesus story by re-envisioning this 'truth' (cf. Matt 25). Thus, a community of *com-pan-iero/as* might prove strong enough to 'hold' the brokenness of bodies and 'embrace' the traumas inflicted. Healing narratives can be formed in ways that rejuvenate identity and belonging. The work of remembering a faith community always takes place in the believed and known presence of God, who remembers himself and, through the power of his healing Spirit, moves people to tell a story together.[18]

2. Land and Dislocation: New Creations

In Fiji entire village communities have been "relocated" to higher ground. Man-made global warming has already caused sea levels to rise to such an extent that shorelines have moved hundreds of meters inland in some places. They feel strange in the new environment. In Torogu, seawater is increasingly covering roads, penetrating houses and ruining agricultural land with salt deposits. Leaving the ancestral graveyard behind is impossible for John Dunn. Along with a few others, he refuses to leave what is left of their home village.[19]

One of the common experiences at the various "pilgrimage stations" is the disruption in the relationship between people and the country/environment. Other illustrations of this disruption include landless peasants, and forced displacement due to armed conflicts over the concentrations of land in the hands of a few large landowners and/or international corporations. Local, rural communities often attest to land or water as their "mother," expressing a relationship that has been one of mutual caring and identity building for centuries. *Campesino* ("farmer") is not just a job title.[20] Today we clearly see that this disrupted human-land relationship was brought about by the "colonial project" which continues to this day: the claiming of a "new territory" and its inhabitants, including their bodies, as property to be exploited. Thus land has become an object to be conquered, controlled and "cultivated."[21] It no longer creates the identity of its original inhabitants, but people now define the country.[22] In this colonial logic, which often becomes theologically extended, "whiteness" replaces land/water as a force that creates identity, because only this "distortion" made it possible to divide people into "races" and separate them from each other. It leads to the exploitation and displacement of indigenous peoples and ultimately to the brutality of slavery. To this day, this colonial project continues to find new mutations.

Traditional white theologies have not only reflected but also legitimized the colonial project. Jennings ultimately blames a distorted view of creation that reduced theological anthropology to commodified bodies:

> Europeans enacted racial agency as a theologically articulated way of understanding their bodies in relation to new spaces and people... [It was done by] an inverted, distorted vision of creation that reduced theological anthropology to commodified bodies.[23]

This "distorted vision" assumes that the supposedly original chaos first had to be ordered by God's creation. Human beings – especially Europeans – became the actors who fulfilled this calling to "cultivate" by "protecting" the God-given order of nature, and for this purpose they took possession of land and people. To this day, stigmatization and "exoticism" are common (neo)colonial approaches towards indigenous peoples and their cosmologies.

A self-critical acknowledgment of one's own involvement in this (structural) sin is a prerequisite for a possible joint pilgrimage with the "others." A theological reorientation can only take place in dialogue with those communities that have at least partially preserved or are rediscovering the identity-creating bond with "Mother Nature" – also because they are usually the first to experience the effects of the violent exploitation of nature and humans. Those pushed to the 'margins' know very well that the causes for this lie mainly in the far away "centres."

God's ongoing care for land and water can be seen, among other things, in the way Jesus speaks of the Kingdom of God. The close relationship between God and creation, between people and land, takes place through images and analogies of a rural society.[24] Jesus' language corresponds to an agrarian society in which he includes himself and to which he addresses his message. When the NT describes the Kingdom of God using this conceptual field, God's will to reconcile broken relationships on land/water also becomes clear. The movement of the incarnation of God in Christ reveals an alternative understanding: the pre-existent Logos becomes "flesh" and "reveals a broad paradigm for the intimate, ontological entanglement between divinity and all materiality."[25] The interpretation of the incarnation as a material embodiment shows that God's reconciliation cannot be reduced to the salvation of the individual human being, but aims at the entire network of creation and transforms everything into a "new creation." God's purpose for the world is reconciliation and communion of the entire cosmos (cf. 1 Col 1:19; Eph 1:10). When this implication of incarnation comes into play, there grows a consciousness of being creations among other creatures of a created web of life.

William Cavanaugh proposes that a pilgrim church – as opposed to a touristic one – finds its identity in solidarity with the migrants who travel out of necessity, rather than out of a desire to transcend all need.[26] Even in a globalized world, migrants are no longer defined by the land/water they come from, but by "borders":

> The purpose of the border is not simply to exclude immigrants but to define them, to give them an identity. That identity is a liminal identity, an identity that straddles the border and defines the person as being neither fully here nor fully there. The instability and mobility of identity in a globalized world thus depends upon the borders that supposedly fix identities against the whirlwind of globalization.[27]

It is this place of a liminal existence that the pilgrim church itself must embrace in order to serve as a sanctuary for all displaced persons in search of union with God, believing in the possibility of reconciliation of all broken relationships with the world around them. The prerequisite for this is the humble service "on site" in order to be able to become *companieros/as* for one another:

To welcome and revere migrants as Christ, to feed them, pray with them, and wash their feet, is to turn migrants into pilgrims, and thus to turn fate into destiny.[28]

3. Gender-Justice: God's Word Becomes 'Body'

Selina Ahmed, Director of the Acid Survivors Foundation, and Farida Yasmin, Police Officer in the Women's Support and Investigation Division in Bangladesh work with traumatized women on a daily basis. They emphasize that women's lives will not change until patriarchal structures are overcome.[29]

Discrimination, exclusion and violence based on gender or sexual orientation are widespread realities, also within the ecumenical community: the denial of women's participation in leadership positions, sexual violence against women and children, at home and in public spaces, but also discrimination based on the sexual orientation. The silence of the victims and the silence of the communities about these forms of violence in many contexts are simply not audible. At the same time, women's groups, initiatives, organizations and LGBTQ+ networks can be found almost everywhere, resisting and trying to overcome these cultures of silence and gender-based violence, inspired by the power of a transformative spirituality.

Kwok Pui-lan reflects on the perspective of the victims of gender injustice in Christological terms and poses some basic questions in the context of the colonial project:

> How is it possible for the formerly colonized, oppressed, subjugated to transform the symbol of Christ—a symbol that has been used to justify colonization and domination—into a symbol that affirms life, dignity and freedom? Can the subaltern speak about Christ, and if so, under what conditions? What language shall we borrow?[30]

Again, the movement of the incarnation of God in Christ brings out two elements: embodiment and hybridity. The incarnation is an expression of God's will to fellowship with creation and heal broken relationships. According to John 1, this is possible because God's Word has become "body" and "dwells among us." Focusing on the physical aspect of incarnation draws attention to all bodies rather than ignoring them. As God Himself becomes "flesh," the body, which traditional theologies have often associated with impurity and sin, is elevated. The incarnation points to the body and the physical as a way of knowing God and connecting with the divine.[31]

Pui-lan interprets the incarnation as a "hybrid symbol": Jesus is neither only divine nor only human, but divine *and* human.

> The most hybridized concept in the Christian tradition is that of Jesus/Christ. The space between Jesus and Christ is unsettling and fluid, resisting easy categorization and closure. It is the 'contact zone' or the 'borderland' between the human and the divine, the one and the many, the historical and the cosmological... the prophetic and the sacramental, the God of the conquerors and the God of the meek and the lowly.[32]

By acknowledging incarnation as embodiment and emphasizing the divine-human mystery of hybridity, the ignored and silenced bodily experiences come to the fore in Christological reflection. According to Pui-lan, Jesus' question, "Who do you say I am?" (Matt 16:15) is an invitation to every faith community to fill this contact zone with new interpretations, insights and possibilities.[33]

This re-interpretation of the incarnation suggests paying special attention to Jesus' way of the cross in the context of gender-based violence. On the cross, his body was subjected to various forms of violence. Before that he was stripped naked – an act of sexual violence (as interpreted by chaplains working with victims of sexual abuse).[34] Perceiving these physical injuries of Jesus can become an opportunity for victims of gender and sexual violence to identify with the suffering of Jesus. Their wounds, like Jesus' wounds, also expose the structures that oppress and marginalize them. The mystery of Jesus' hybridity opens up new possibilities for those forced into "precarious positions."[35]

Finally, the body of the risen Christ visibly bears the scars that still reveal the cruelty of violence and yet promise the possibility of healing. The risen Christ invites us to touch his wounds (Greek: *traumata*; John 20) to understand that even those wounds caused by sexual and gender-based violence are in fact Christ's wounds.

For an emerging theology of companionship, it is first crucial to recognize the futility of suffering, the depth of the wounds, and the impact that gender-based violence has on individuals and communities. Above all, the Psalms and the Book of Lamentations offer a language of faith to express the pain, to express the experience of being forsaken by God. The quote of Jesus on the cross, "My God, why have you forsaken me?" (Ps 22, Mark 15:34) becomes a placeholder for such cries of faith. Possibly the truest expression of companionship may be to expose oneself to and join in the laments of others.

Second, the structural roots of this violence must be identified. While vulnerability is part of the human condition, a "precarious position" is brought about by people and human institutions. The challenge is not limited to taking a critical look at society as a whole, but to critically examining the life and practices of the churches and communities themselves, including theologies and traditions.

Finally, a theology of companionship must start from the wounds of the victims of sexual and gender-based violence and discrimination. Those hitherto silent and discriminated against must be empowered to take a leading role in the development of this theology by regaining the agency of their own bodies. The confrontation with the structural dimension is a parallel path that the *companiero/as* walk together, celebrating the beauty of the diverse, sacred bodies.

4. Racism: One in Christ?

When substandard work is mainly done by Afro-Brazilians in Brazil or when people in Jamaica resort to chemical products to lighten their skin, it becomes clear how deeply racism is internalized. When white police officers in the United States shoot at people of color because they are seen as a *de facto* potential threat, we witness how racism actually kills.

Racism is the combination of discrimination based on the constructed category of "race" and a disproportionate distribution of power that protects the privilege of one group and denies the thriving of another, so that injustices are reproduced across generations. WCC churches, together with Vatican officials, redefined race in 2018 as "...a social construct that claims to explain and justify division between human groups by advancing physical, social, cultural and religious criteria."[36] The consequences are devastating:

> ...the systemic and systematic impact of actions taken against groups of people based on the colour of their skin. It separates people from each other in the name of a false notion of the purity and superiority of a specific community. It is an ideological stance expressed through marginalization, discrimination and exclusion against certain persons, minorities, ethnic groups or communities.[37]

Marc MacDonald, an indigenous archbishop in Canada shows how complex the phenomenon of systemic racism functions:

> [systemic racism] is deadly in that it makes grossly unacceptable evil mimic morality. It not only makes evil acceptable; it makes evil desirable. It makes evil look good, and it is this capacity for deception that makes confronting systemic evil so urgent.[38]

Racism shaped by the "colonial project" is characterized by the construction of ubiquitous hierarchical orders, originally conceived by white "discoverers" and further established as "scientific" and "theological knowledge" in which different people have different values of superiority and inferiority, of culture and nature. This organizing principle is deeply connected to greed, access to resources of territories and to objectified persons. Whiteness and white supremacy are based upon it.[39] The constructed "others" are alienated through the deportation of their bodies from their homelands and communities; their original cultures and beliefs destroyed.

According to Robert McAfee Brown, one of the great errors of Christianity is that it divides life into two realms, two spheres, two divisions.[40] At times the *imago Dei* – the most fundamental argument for recognizing the dignity of all human beings – has been abused by separating spirituality from socio-economic realities. But if the spiritual life is reduced to the goal of individual salvation, then the corporate sin of systemic racism remains unaffected. If, on the other hand, one looks at the life of Jesus, the combination of spirituality and social action is decisive for every liberation and healing from earthly burdens and constraints (cf. Lk 4:18).

In the history of Christianity, there are institutional and structural, biblical and theological legitimations and justifications for racism on the one hand, and carelessness and ignorance, including white fragility,[41] on the other. It is not simply a narrow reading of biblical texts based on privileged racial interests that one must scrutinize, but the development of a Christian imagination that enables and fosters racism. Jennings here again identifies that "distorted vision" of creation and its anthropology.[42] Concepts such as being chosen and supersessionist theories, or the creation account itself were used by white theologians (sic.) as justifications for racism.[43] The Doctrine of Discovery provided the appropriate framework for thought.[44]

Like every human being, Jesus was born into a specific context, linked to a specific social construction of identity: a Jewish man from Galilee. In his life and ministry he identified with the marginalized (those constructed as "other") and opposed their discrimination. In this body, God identifies with a community living under an imperial system that constructed some people as pure and superior, others as impure and inferior — human and inhuman. During his resistance, Jesus exposed the systemic evil that was being cleverly "packaged" by the Roman Empire by working with the local religious elites and hierarchies. But on the cross, Christ "disarmed the rulers and authorities and made a public example of them, triumphing over them in it." (Col 2:15, *NRSV*). He saw through hierarchical and oppressive definitions of humanity, including those systemic, religious, and political powers that uphold it and are being upheld by it.

Following Irenaeus and Athanasius, Jennings points to the importance of trusting human flesh as the bearer of divine life.

> Only when trust has been established can we realize that we have been joined together as one humanity in Christ...we become convinced by the one saving human being, Jesus, we are also convinced that there is only one real flesh that binds all humanity together with the one creation, this same Jesus.[45]

Because of the One who sets us free, who is none other than the One who made the world, people are able to find hope for their bodies. The fear of the fragility of concepts, of the inadequacy of all social constructions and categories can be overcome in this way.

Racism is the denial of the possibility of companionship. In order to become each other's *companiero/as*, resistance to any form of racism is a *conditio sine qua non*. A pilgrimage of justice and peace requires pilgrims to resist any attribution by finding their deeper identity as *companiero/as* of Christ. The term "pilgrim," derived from the Latin *peregrinus*, includes the meanings: "stranger," "wanderer," "exile," "traveller," "newcomer." It recalls the ancient Israelite tradition in which hospitality was motivated by the memory of an identity once freed from slavery and wandering in the wilderness (cf. Deut 10:19-20; 24:18).

At the institutional level, an ecumenical theology of companionship must lead to a self-critical examination of how the practices, orders, compositions and structures of the church(es) have "perpetuated" discrimination, xenophobia and racism that counteract unity in Christ. The challenge for the pilgrim ecumenical community, then, is to de-center itself, especially in relation to its prevailing privileges. This could lead to a self-realization and an exercise in purification from the sin of racism. Pilgrims find their authenticity not in opposition to constructed others, but through welcoming and visiting others, a mutual gift that allows for very different identities precisely because they are one in Christ.

Continuation: Pilgrimage as Kenotic Movement

At the beginning of the Pilgrimage of Justice and Peace, the Central Committee of the WCC stated:

> Pilgrims on their way are moving – lightly as they learn that only the essential and necessary counts. They are open for surprises and ready to be transformed by encounters and challenges on the way. Everyone who will walk with us with an open heart and mind will be a welcome com-pan-ion ("the ones we share our bread with") on the way. The Pilgrimage promises to be a transformative journey, discovering ourselves anew in new relationships of justice and peace.[46]

What initially was simply a metaphor for many, has actually materialized into physically transformational experiences for some. A wide diversity of "pilgrim stations" have nevertheless allowed common challenges to crystallize, to which the WCC and the respective individual churches should now pay special attention, vis-a-vis a new self-understanding as a "pilgrim church."

New practices are also (re)discovered on the Pilgrimage thus far. A primary motif of medieval pilgrimages was the transformation of the self through the forgiveness of sin. Cavanaugh recalls that this "transformation of the self was not self-transformation, as such, because it responded to a discipline that had its source outside the self: God."[47] The virtue of humility was key. Therefore, pilgrimage can also be interpreted as "a kenotic movement, a stripping away of the external sources of stability in one's life."[48] In this regard, our Pilgrimage of Justice and Peace could become what Jesus announced to his disciples: "If any want to become my followers, let them deny themselves and take up their cross and follow me." (Mark 8:34, NRSV).

This kenotic movement of pilgrimage leads to an acknowledgment of the need to walk with others, even those who are completely other. Pilgrims welcome other pilgrims because the presence of pilgrims sanctifies a place. In this way, ecumenism could actually become a 'holy place' where fellowship with God can be experienced.

> The pilgrim ... sees all potential others as brothers and sisters on a common journey to God. The pilgrim preserves otherness ... by moving toward a common center to which an infinite variety of itineraries is possible. If God, the Wholly Other, is at the center, and not the great Western Ego, then there can be room for genuine otherness among human beings. The pilgrim church is therefore able simultaneously to announce and dramatize the full universality of communion with God, a truly global vision of reconciliation of all people [and all of creation, FE], without thereby evacuating difference.[49]

Finally, understanding pilgrimage as a kenotic movement also prevents a misunderstanding of this valuable metaphor, because in certain contexts pilgrims (in the "new world") saw themselves as part of the colonial project.[50] Only by acknowledging the need to let go of the self in connection with the search for the "completely other" – and thereby being able to actually walk with others as companiero/a – does the Pilgrimage become a transformative process for the ecumenical movement. The development of an ecumenical theology of companionship could help give expression to, and provide direction for, the ethos, the responsibility and the mission, of those who make pilgrimages in each other's lives.

"Were our hearts not burning within us...?" the disciples ask on the way to Emmaus (Lk 24:32, NRSV), realizing that it is the risen Christ, who became a *companiero*, who is going along with them and sharing the bread on the way.

NOTES

Introduction

1. See Brian Stanley, *The World Missionary Conference, Edinburgh 1910* (Grand Rapids/MI: Eerdmans, 2009).
2. See Grigorius Larentzakis, *Die orthodoxe Kirche: Ihr Leben und ihr Glauben* (Graz: Styria, 2001).
3. See Otto Hermann Pesch, *Das Zweite Vatikanische Konzil (1962–1965). Vorgeschichte, Verlauf, Ergebnisse, Nachgeschichte* (Würzburg: Echter Verlag, 1993).
4. See J. Robert Wright , ed. *Quadrilateral at One Hundred* (Cincinnati, OH: Forward Movement, 1988).
5. See Wilhelm Hüffmeier, ed. *Being Protestant in Europe: 30 years of the Leuenberg Church Fellowship* (Frankfurt am Main: Lembeck, 2003).
6. Since the late nineteenth century the following world conferences of various churches were established: World Methodist Council (1881, which began the Methodist Ecumenical Conference), Baptist World Alliance (1905), Mennonite World Conference (1925), Lutheran World Federation (1947), World Communion of Reformed Churches (2010, resulting from the merger of the Reformed Ecumenical Council and the World Alliance of Reformed Churches, which was the result of a 1970 merger of the Reformed-Presbyterian World Alliance of 1875 and the International Congregational Council founded in 1891), etc.
7. See Peter Neuner, *Ökumenische Theologie. Die Suche nach der Einheit der christlichen Kirche* (Darmstadt: Wissenschaftliche Buchgesellschaft, 1997), 1–17.
8. The local associations found in all provinces throughout Germany are called the *Arbeitsgemeinschaft Christlicher Kirchen* (ACK). http://www.oekumene-ack.de
9. See Eileen King, "World Day of Prayer," in *Dictionary of the Ecumenical Movement*, eds. Nicholas Lossky et al. (Geneva: World Council of Churches, 2002), 1242–1243.
10. See e.g., liberation theology in Latin America, Black theology in southern Africa and North America or the Minjung theology of South Korea. Cf. Giancarlo Collet, ed. *Theologien der Dritten Welt. EATWOT als Herausforderung westlicher Theologie und Kirche* (Immensee: Neue Zeitschrift für Missionswissenschaft, 1990); Pui-lan Kwok, *Hope Abundant: Third World and Indigenous Women's Theology* (Maryknoll, NY: Orbis, 2010).
11. The seven early Ecumenical Councils include: Nicaea I 325, Constantinople I 381, Ephesus 431, Chalcedon 451, Constantinople II 553, Constantinople III 680, and Nicaea II 787. See Carl Andresen and Adolf Martin Ritter, eds. *Handbuch der Dogmen- und Theologiegeschichte, Vol. 1: Die Lehrentwicklung im Rahmen der Katholizität* (Göttingen: Vandenhoeck & Ruprecht, 1999).
12. See the short introduction in Reinhard Frieling, *Der Weg des ökumenischen Gedankens: Eine Ökumenekunde* (Göttingen: Vandenhoeck & Ruprecht, 1992), 17–33.
13. See Friedericke Nüssel and Dorothea Sattler, *Einführung in die ökumenische Theologie* (Darmstadt: WBG, 2008).

14. See the approach taken in Risto Saarinen, *God and the Gift: An Ecumenical Theology of Giving* (Collegeville, MN: Liturgical Press, 2005).

15. See the important studies on ecumenism from various denominational perspectives on different themes in Michael Welker and Miroslav Volf, eds. *Der lebendige Gott als Trinität: Festschrift für Jürgen Moltmann zum 80. Geburtstag* (Gütersloh: Gütersloher, 2006).

16. See the four-volume series, *Growth in Agreement*, Jeffrey Gros, Harding Meyer, William G. Rusch, eds. (Grand Rapids, MI: Eerdmans, 2000); *Growth in Agreement II: Reports and Agreed Statements of Ecumenical Conversations on a World Level, 1982-1998*, Jeffrey Gros, Harding Meyer, William G. Rusch, eds. (Grand Rapids, MI: Eerdmans, 2000); *Growth in Agreement III: International Dialogue, Texts and Agreed Statements, 1998-2005*, Jeffrey Gros, Thomas F. Best, Lorelei F. Fuchs , eds. (Grand Rapids, MI: Eerdmans, 2008); Thomas F. Best, John Gibaut, Despina Prassas, eds. *Growth in Agreement IV: International Dialogue Texts and Agreed Statements, 2005-2013* (Geneva: WCC, 2016).

17. Fernando Enns and Jonathan Seiling, eds. *Mennonites in Dialogue:* Official Reports from International and National Ecumenical Encounters, 1975–2012 (Eugene: Pickwick, 2015), 19-114.

18. *Baptism, Eucharist & Ministry, 1982-1990: Report on the Process and Responses* (Geneva: WCC Publications, 1990).

19. Philip A. Potter and Jacques Matthey, "Mission," in *Dictionary of the Ecumenical Movement*, 783–790; also the essay in Karl Müller and Theo Sundermeier, eds. *Lexikon missionstheologischer Grundbegriffe* (Berlin: Dietrich Reimer Verlag, 1987). See especially Dietrich Ritschl, "Ökumene," 340–346 and Martin Lehmann-Habeck, "Ökumenischer Rat der Kirchen," 346–351.

20. Christine Lienemann-Perrin, *Mission und interreligiöser Dialog, Bensheimer Hefte* 93 (Ökumenische Studienhefte 11), (Göttingen: Vandenhoeck & Ruprecht, 1999).

21. "The Creed of Nicaea" in Jaroslav Pelikan and Valerie Hotchkiss, eds. *Creeds & Confessions of Faith in the Christian Tradition*, vol. 1 (New Haven: Yale University Press, 2003), 158-159.

22. See Fernando Enns, *The Peace Church and the Ecumenical Community: Ecclesiology and the Ethics of Nonviolence*, Helmut Harder, trans. (Kitchener: Pandora Press, 2008), 1-17 et passim.

23. On the concept of "missionary ecumenism" see "Evangelisches Missionswerk in Deutschland," in *Missionarische Ökumene. Im Kontext religiöser Orientierungssuche*, ed. Klaus Peter Voß (Hamburg: EMW, 2007).

24. Wolfram Weiße, *Praktisches Christentum und Reich Gottes. Die Ökumenische Bewegung Life and Work 1919–1937*, Kirche und Konfession 31 (Göttingen: Vandenhoeck & Ruprecht, 1991).

25. See Neuner, *Ökumenische Theologie*, 1–5.

26. Cf. Heino Falcke, *Wo bleibt die Freiheit? Christ sein in Zeiten der Wende* (Freiburg: Kreuz-Verlag, 2009); Marianne Subklew-Jeutner, *Der Pankower Friedenskreis. Geschichte einer Ost-Berliner Gruppe innerhalb der Evangelischen Kirchen in der DDR* (Osnabrück: Der Andere Verlag, 2003).

27. Ulrich Körtner, "In der Lehre getrennt, im Handeln geeint? Chancen und Grenzen ökumenischer Sozialethik," in Friederike Nüssel, ed. *Theologische Ethik der Gegenwart: Ein Überblick über zentrale Ansätze und Themen* (Tübingen: Mohr Siebeck, 2009), 271–294.

28. See the Constitution of the WCC: "The World Council of Churches is a fellowship of churches which confess the Lord Jesus Christ as God and Saviour according to the scriptures and therefore seek to fulfil together their common calling to the glory of the one God, Father, Son and Holy Spirit." See App. VI, 'Constitution and Rules of the World Council of Churches' (as amended by the 9th Assembly..., 2006) in Luis N. Rivera-Pagán, ed. *God, in your Grace: Official Report of the Ninth Assembly of the World Council of Churches* (Geneva: WCC Publications, 2007), 448.

29. For a discussion of these differences see, Joint Working Group between the Roman Catholic Church and the World Council of Churches, "The Ecumenical *Dialogue* on Moral Issues: Potential Sources of Common Witness or of Divisions (Geneva: World Council of Churches, 1995).

30. Cf. Christoph Schwöbel, "Trinitätslehre als Rahmentheorie des christlichen Glaubens. Vier Thesen zur Bedeutung der Trinität in der christlichen Dogmatik," in Wilfried Härle, Reiner Preul, eds. *Trinität, Marburger Jahrbuch Theologie* vol. X, (Marburg: N.G.Elwert, 1999), 129–154.

31. Klaus A. Baier, *Ökumenisches Lernen als Projekt: Eine Studie zum Lernbegriff in Dokumenten der ökumenischen Weltkonferenzen (1910–1998)*, Hamburger theologische Studien 19 (Hamburg et al.: Lit, 2001).

32. Cf. Martin Robra, *Ökumenische Sozialethik* (Gütersloh: Gütersloher, 1994) and Walter Schöpsdau, *Wie der Glaube zum Tun kommt: Wege ethischer Argumentation im evangelisch-katholischen Dialog und in der Zusammenarbeit der Kirchen*, Bensheimer Hefte 102 (Göttingen: Vandenhoeck & Ruprecht, 2004).

1. Ecumenical Theory

1. Adolf Deißmann, *Die Stockholmer Weltkirchenkonferenz: Vorgeschichte, Dienst und Arbeit der Weltkonferenz für Praktisches Christentum, 19.–30. August 1925, Amtlicher deutscher Bericht* (Berlin: Furche-Verlag, 1926).

2. Jürgen Moltmann, "Welche Einheit? Der Dialog zwischen den Traditionen des Ostens und des Westens," *Ökumenische Rundschau* 3/1977, 287–296. This article is a speech given by Moltmann in Lausanne at the celebration of the fiftieth anniversary of the Faith and Order Commission in 1977.

3. Cf. Günther Gassmann, *Konzeptionen der Einheit in der Bewegung für Glauben und Kirchenverfassung 1910–1937*, Forschungen zur systematischen und ökumenischen Theologie 39 (Göttingen: Vandenhoeck & Ruprecht, 1979); Idem, ed. *Documentary History of Faith and Order 1963–1993* (Geneva: World Council of Churches, 1993); Matthias Haudel, *Die Bibel und die Einheit der Kirchen. Eine Untersuchung der Studien von Glauben und Kirchenverfassung* (Göttingen: Vandenhoeck & Ruprecht, 1993).

4. Wolfram Weiße, *Praktisches Christentum und Reich Gottes. Die Ökumenische Bewegung Life and Work 1919–1937*, Kirche und Konfession 31 (Göttingen: Vandenhoeck & Ruprecht, 1991).

5. The many bi- and multi-lateral dialogues demonstrate this strand of ecumenism. See Jeffrey Gros et al., *Growth in Agreement I-III*.

6. The best example is the study "Ecclesiology and Ethics" in Thomas Best and Martin Robra, eds. *Ecclesiology and Ethics. Ecumenical Ethical Engagement, Moral Formation and the Nature of the Church* (Geneva: WCC, 1997). For discussion see Fernando Enns,

Friedenskirche in der Ökumene. Mennonitische Wurzeln einer Ethik der Gewaltfreiheit, Kirche – Konfession – Religion 46 (Göttingen: Vandenhoeck & Ruprecht, 2003), 64–81.

7. Dietrich Ritschl and Werner Ustorf, *Ökumenische Theologie – Missionswissenschaft*, Grundkurs Theologie, Georg Strecker, ed. vol. 10,2 (Stuttgart: Kohlhammer, 1994), 7.

8. *Ibid.*

9. For a helpful introduction to ecumenical theory development see: Friederike Nüssel and Dorothea Sattler, *Einführung in die ökumenische Theologie* (Darmstadt: Wissenschaftliche Buchgesellschaft, 2008). The many-sided ecumenical debates from the beginning of the modern ecumenical movement up to the 1990s are summarized in Reinhard Frieling, *Der Weg des ökumenischen Gedankens: Eine Ökumenekunde* (Göttingen: Vandenhoeck & Ruprecht, 1992). See also in general, Peter Neuner, *Ökumenische Theologie: Die Suche nach der Einheit der christlichen Kirchen* (Darmstadt: WBG, 1997).

10. Immediately following the formation of the WCC the ecclesiological question gave rise to the so-called "Toronto Statement," which was adopted during the meeting of the WCC Central Committee in 1950 in Toronto (Canada): "Die Kirche, die Kirchen und der Ökumenische Rat der Kirchen. Die ekklesiologische Bedeutung des Ökumenischen Rates der Kirchen" in Hans-Ludwig Althaus, *ed. Ökumenische Dokumente. Quellenstücke über die Einheit der Kirche* (Göttingen: Vandenhoeck & Ruprecht, 1962), 104–113. See also, Vitaly Borovoy, "Die kirchliche Bedeutung des ÖRK. Vermächtnis und Verheißung von Toronto," in Ökumenischer Rat der Kirchen, ed. *Es begann in Amsterdam. Vierzig Jahre Ökumenischer Rat der Kirchen*, Beiheft zur ÖR 59 (Frankfurt aM: Lembeck, 1989), 151–168; Hugh Gerard Gibson Herklots, *Amsterdam 1948: An Account of the First Assembly of the World Council of Churches* (London: SCM Press, 1948).

11. This refers generally to historical situations, political and sociological contexts, and cultural features, which have played a significant role in the separation into different traditions.

12. Cf. Anton Houtepen, "Einheit der Kirche im Bunde Gottes. Prolegomena zu einer jeden künftigen Ekklesiologie, die als eine ökumenische Ekklesiologie wird auftreten können," in Hans-Georg Link and Geiko Müller-Fahrenholz, eds. *Hoffnungswege: Wegweisende Impulse des Ökumenischen Rates der Kirchen aus sechs Jahrzehnten* (Franfurt aM: Lembeck, 2008), 197–223.

13. The conceptual distinction between *ecclesia visibilis* and *ecclesia invisibilis* can be attributed to Huldreich Zwingli (*Exposito Christianae fidei*, 1531), which harkens back to Augustine. See Albrecht Ritschl, "Über die Begriffe: sichtbare und unsichtbare Kirche (1859)" in *Gesammelte Aufsätze* (Freiburg i.Br./Leipzig: Mohr, 1893), 68f. It arises later in Johannes Calvin, *Institutio Religionis Christianae* 1559, IV,1,2–7, in *Calvini Opera quae supersunt omnia*, Johann Wilhelm Baum, Eduard Cunitz, Eduard Reuss, eds. (Braunschweig/Berlin: Schwetschke, 1863–1900). Martin Luther distinguishes between the visible and the "hidden" Church (*ecclesia abscondita*) in *D. Martin Luthers Werke. Kritische Gesamtausgabe* (cited as *WA*) vol. 18 (Weimar: Hermann Böhlau Verlag, 1883–2005) (here: 1908), 652, 23. Luther suggests the basis and the outer structure of the Church relate to each other using the image of how the soul and body relate (cf. *WA* 6, 296f.).

14. As stated in the encyclical *Mystici Corporis* by Pope Pius XII. (29 June 1943), on the Mystical Body of Jesus Christ and our union with Christ: Claudia Carlen, ed. *The Papal Encyclicals, 1939-1958* (Raleigh, NC: McGrath Publishing Co., 1981), 37-63.

For the ecumenical community the idea that the mystical body is identified with the Roman Catholic Church is especially problematic. This was not modified until the Second Vatican Council: "Haec Ecclesia in hoc mundo ut societas constituta et ordinata, subsistit in Ecclesia catholica," *Lumen Gentium*, 8, in http://www.vatican.va/archive/hist_councils/ii_vatican_council/documents/vat-ii_const_19641121_lumen-gentium_en.html.The non-Catholic Churches are seen there as "Ecclesiae vel communitates ecclesiasticae, ecclesiales [Churches or ecclesiastical communities]" (cf. *Lumen Gentium*, 15 and *Unitate Redintegratio*, 3, 19, 22). However, discussions on the appropriate interpretation of these statements also continue today within the Roman Catholic Church. See the Congregation for the Doctrine of the Faith: Responses to some Questions Regarding Certain Aspects of the Doctrine of the Church. Rome, 29 June 2007. http://www.vatican.va/roman_curia/congregations/cfaith/documents/rc_con_cfaith_doc_20070629_responsa-quaestiones_en.html (November 22, 2013), question #5.

15. Dietrich Ritschl, *Zur Logik der Theologie. Kurze Darstellung der Zusammenhänge theologischer Grundgedanken* (Munich: Kaiser, 1988), 172f.

16. Wolfgang Huber, *Kirche* (Munich: Kaiser, 1988), 32–44.

17. Wilfried Härle, "Kirche," VII. Dogmatisch, in *TRE* vol. 18, 281.

18. In general see Lukas Vischer, Ulrich Luz, and Christian Link, *Ökumene im Neuen Testament und heute* (Göttingen: Vandenhoeck & Ruprecht, 2009), esp. Lukas Vischer, "Schwierigkeiten bei der Befragung des Neuen Testaments, Schrift und Tradition," 22-27.

19. Cf. Ulrich Luz, "Unterwegs zur Einheit: Gemeinschaft der Kirche im Neuen Testament," in *Ökumene im Neuen Testament*, Vischer, Luz, and Link, 53-130. See also Jürgen Roloff, *Die Kirche im Neuen Testament* (Göttingen: Vandenhoeck & Ruprecht, 1993).

20. Ernst Käsemann, "Begründet der neutestamentliche Kanon die Einheit der Kirche?," in *Exegetische Versuche und Besinnungen*, Käsemann, 6th ed. (Göttingen: Vandenhoeck & Ruprecht, 1970), 1:214.

21. "The Church was before the Bible was." See James Barr, *Escaping from Fundamentalism* (London: SCM, 1984).

22. Nüssel and Sattler, *Einführung in die ökumenische Theologie*, 45.

23. The Deutsche Ökumenische Studienausschuss (DÖSTA) undertook this with its interpretation of John 17: Deutscher Ökumenischer Studienausschuss, *Einheit als Gabe und Verpflichtung. Eine Studie des DÖSTA zu Johannes 17 Vers 21*, ed. Wolfgang Bienert (Frankfurt: Lembeck, 2002).

24. Cf. Harding Meyer, *Ökumenische Zielvorstellungen*, Bensheimer Hefte 78 (Göttingen: Vandenhoeck & Ruprecht, 1996). This book offers another, extremely useful overview to theory formation in the ecumenical movement.

25. Cf. *Growth in Agreement*.

26. "Symbolum Nicaenum," in *Die Bekenntnisschriften der evangelisch-lutherischen Kirche* (hereafter: *BSLK*), 12th ed. (Göttingen: Vandenhoeck & Ruprecht, 1998), 26f. Cf. the ecumenical interpretation: World Council of Churches, *Confessing the One Faith. An Ecumenical Explication of the Apostolic Faith as it is Confessed in the Nicene-Constantinopolitan Creed (381)*, Faith and Order Paper 153 (Geneva: WCC Publications, 1991).

27. Luis Rivera Pagan, ed. *God, in your grace… Official Report of the Ninth Assembly of the World Council of Churches, (in Porto Alegre, Brazil from 14-23 February 2006)* (Geneva: WCC Publication, 2007), 448.

28. Cf. Leonard Swidler, *The Ecumenical Vanguard: The History of the Una Sancta Movement* (Pittsburgh, PA: Duquesne University Press, 1966); Jörg Ernesti, *Kleine Geschichte der Ökumene* (Freiburg: Herder, 2007).

29. Cf. the discussions before, during and after the fifth world conference on Faith and Order: Santiago de Compostela 1993.

30. "The Unity of the Church as Koinonia: Gift and Calling," in Michael Kinnamon, ed. *Signs of the Spirit: Official Report of the Seventh Assembly, Canberra, Australia, 7-20 February 1991* (Geneva: WCC, 1991), 173.

31. Cf. on this debate the profound reflection by Tobias Brandner, *Einheit, gegeben – verloren – erstrebt: Denkbewegungen von Glauben und Kirchenverfassung* (Göttingen: Vandenhoeck & Ruprecht, 1996).

32. Cf. World Council of Churches, ed. *Die Beziehungen zwischen dem ÖRK und den weltweiten Konfessionsfamilien: Konsultationsbericht*, vol. 9 (Geneva: WCC, 1978).

33. Cf. Neuner, *Ökumenische Theologie*, 285. Cf. the United Church of Canada (1925) or the Church of South India (1947).

34. See Heinrich Fries and Karl Rahner, *Einigung der Kirchen – reale Möglichkeit*, Quaestiones disputatae 100 (Freiburg i.B.: Herder, 1983).

35. Eilert Herms, *Einheit der Christen in der Gemeinschaft der Kirchen: die ökumenische Bewegung der römischen Kirche im Lichte der reformatorischen Theologie: Antwort auf den Rahner-Fries-Plan*, Kirche und Konfession 24 (Göttingen: Vandenhoeck & Ruprecht, 1984).

36. Cf. Oskar Cullmann, *Einheit durch Vielfalt: Grundlegung und Beitrag zur Diskussion über die Möglichkeiten ihrer Verwirklichung* (Tübingen: Mohr, 1986).

37. Cf. Peter Lengsfeld, ed. *Ökumenische Theologie: ein Arbeitsbuch*, (Stuttgart: Kohlhammer, 1980).

38. Cf. also the overview in "Kap. III.1 Einheitsvorstellungen," in *Einführung in die ökumenische Theologie*, Nüssel and Sattler, 120-131. Here the Roman Catholic and Reformation models are further differentiated.

39. Cf. e.g. the Leuenberger Kirchengemeinschaft (1973), since 2003 bears the designation of "Community of Protestant Churches in Europe" (CPCE) ["Gemeinschaft Evangelischer Kirchen in Europa" (GEKE)]. See Nüssel and Sattler, *Einführung in die ökumenische Theologie*, 126.

40. Cf. Neuner, *Ökumenische Theologie*, 289.

41. Neuner, *Ökumenische Theologie*, 291.

42. Cf. for the contemporary discussion Ulrich H. J. Körtner, *Wohin steuert die Ökumene? Vom Konsens- zum Differenzmodell* (Göttingen: Vandenhoeck & Ruprecht, 2005); see also Wolfgang Huber, *Im Geist der Freiheit. Für eine Ökumene der Profile* (Freiburg i.B.: Herder, 2007).

43. Cf. the model "Ökumene in Gegensätzen," in *Wohin steuert die Ökumene?*, Körtner.

44. Lutheran World Federation, ed. *Die gemeinsame Erklärung zur Rechtfertigungslehre, alle offiziellen Dokumente von Lutherischem Weltbund und Vatikan*, Texte aus der VELKD 87 (Hannover: Luth. Kirchenamt der VELKD, 1999). This collection contains all official documents between the Lutheran World Federation and the Vatican. On this discussion see the further study by the Deutscher Ökumenischer Studienausschuss, *Von Gott angenommen – in Christus verwandelt: Die Rechtfertigungslehre im multilateralen ökumenischen Dialog: Eine Studie des DÖSTA*, Beiheft zur ÖR 78, ed. Uwe Swarat, Johannes Oeldemann and Dagmar Heller (Frankfurt am Main: Lembeck, 2006).

45. "Towards a Common Understanding of the Church" in *Growth in Agreement II: Reports and Agreed Statements of Ecumenical Conversations on a World Level, 1982-1998*,

Jeffery Gros, Harding Meyer, William G. Rusch, eds. (Geneva: WCC, 2000), 795.

46. Ökumenischer Arbeitskreis Evangelischer und Katholischer Theologen, *Lehrverurteilungen – kirchentrennend?*, ed. Karl Lehmann and Wolfhart Pannenberg (Freiburg i.B.: Herder and Göttingen: Vandenhoeck & Ruprecht, 1986-1994): vol. 1: *Rechtfertigung, Sakramente und Amt im Zeitalter der Reformation und heute*, 3rd ed. (1988); vol. 2: *Materialien zu den Lehrverurteilungen und zur Theologie der Rechtfertigung* (1989); vol. 3: *Materialien zur Lehre von den Sakramenten und vom kirchlichen Amt* (1990); vol. 4: *Antworten auf kirchliche Stellungnahmen* (1994).

47. Cf. József Fuisz, *Konsens, Kompromiss, Konvergenz in der ökumenischen Diskussion. Eine strukturanalytische Untersuchung der Logik ökumenischer Entscheidungsprozesse* (Münster: Lit, 2001).

48. "Ecumenical dialogue" Joint Working Group between RCC and WCC, 1967, http://www.oikoumene.org/en/resources/documents/wcc-programmes/ecumenical-movement-in-the-21st-century/member-churches/special-commission-on-participation-of-orthodox-churches/sub-committee-ii-style-ethos-of-our-life-together/ecumenical-dialogue. (15 December 2014)

49. On Dietrich Ritschl see: Fernando Enns, Martin Hailer, and Ulrike Link-Wieczorek, eds. *Profilierte Ökumene: Bleibend Wichtiges und jetzt Dringliches. Festschrift für Dietrich Ritschl zum 80. Geburtstag*, Beiheft zur ÖR 84 (Frankfurt: Lembeck, 2009), 7-10.

50. Cf. summary in Dietrich Ritschl, s.v. "Lehre," in *TRE*, vol. XX, 608-621, with an expanded version in Ritschl, *Theorie und Konkretion in der Ökumenischen Theologie. Kann es eine Hermeneutik des Vertrauens inmitten differierender semiotischer Systeme geben?* (Münster: Lit, 2003) and "Kap. II: Strukturen hinter Texten," in *Bildsprache und Argumente. Theologische Aufsätze*, Ritschl (Neukirchen-Vluyn: Neukirchener, 2008), 77-172.

51. For a discussion of this approach cf. contributions in Wolfgang Huber, Ernst Petzold and Theo Sundermeier, eds. *Implizite Axiome: Tiefenstrukturen des Denkens und Handelns* (Munich: Kaiser, 1990).

52. Michael Welker, "Implizite Axiome, Zu einem Grundkonzept von Dietrich Ritschls ,Logik der Theologie'," in *Implizite Axiome*, Huber, Petzold and Sundermeier, 38. "Auch über die Logizität der Theologie ist nur insoweit nachgedacht, als die Theologie sich mit anderen kognitiven und normativen versprachlichten Interaktionsformen vergleichen lässt."

53. Wolfhart Pannenberg may be named as a convinced representative. Cf. Pannenberg, *Systematische Theologie*, vols. 1-3 (Göttingen: Vandenhoeck & Ruprecht, 1988-1993). Cf. Pannenberg, *Kirche und Ökumene*, Beiträge zur Systematischen Theologie, vol. 3 (Göttingen: Vandenhoeck & Ruprecht, 2000).

54. Cf. George A. Lindbeck, *Christliche Lehre als Grammatik des Glaubens: Religion und Theologie im postliberalen Zeitalter*, Theologische Bücherei Bd. 90 (Munich: Kaiser, 1994).

55. Lindbeck, *Grammatik des Glaubens*, 37.

56. Lindbeck, *Grammatik des Glaubens*, introduction, 17.

57. Thomas Wabel, "Sprachspiel und Wirklichkeit. Zum Gegenstandsbezug der Rede von Gott und seinen ökumenischen Konsequenzen," in *Profilierte Ökumene*, Enns, Hailer, and Link-Wieczorek, 94.

58. Thomas S. Kuhn, *Die Struktur wissenschaftlicher Revolutionen*, 4th ed. (Frankfurt: Suhrkamp, 1979). Cf. also: Welker, *Implizite Axiome*, 30f.

59. Cf. Hans Küng and David Tracy, eds. *Theologie – Wohin? Auf dem Weg zu einem neuen Paradigma*, Ökumenische Theologie, vol. 11 (Zürich: Benziger Verlag, 1984).

60. Cf. Konrad Raiser, *Ökumene im Übergang. Paradigmenwechsel in der ökumenischen Bewegung* (Munich: Kaiser, 1990).

61. *Faith and Order: Our Oneness in Christ and our Disunity as Churches: A Report from the Second Assembly of the WCC, Evanston, Ill., USA, August 15-31, 1954* (Geneva: WCC, 1955).

62. *The New Delhi report* (New York: Association Press, 1962); *Evanston to New Delhi, 1954-1961: Report to the Third Assembly of the World Council of Churches* (Geneva: WCC, 1962).

63. *New Delhi to Uppsala, 1961-1968: Report* (Geneva: WCC, 1968).

64. *Breaking Barriers: Nairobi 1975,* David M. Paton, ed. (London: SPCK, 1976).

65. David Gill, ed. *Gathered for Life, Official report Sixth Assembly of the WCC, Vancouver, Canada,* (Geneva: WCC, 1983). On the general process see: Ulrich Schmitthenner, *Der konziliare Prozeß: Gemeinsam für Gerechtigkeit, Frieden und Bewahrung der Schöpfung: Ein Kompendium* (Idstein: Meinhardt Text und Design, 1998); *Idem,* Textsammlung zum konziliaren Prozess (bilingual), CD-Rom 1999.

66. Cf. esp. Edmund Schlink, *Ökumenische Dogmatik: Grundzüge,* ed. Michael Plathow, 3rd ed., Schriften zu Ökumene und Bekenntnis, vol.2 (Göttingen: Vandenhoeck & Ruprecht, 2005).

67. Cf. Wolfhart Pannenberg, "Die Hoffnung der Christen und die Einheit der Kirche. Bericht über die Sitzung der Kommission für Glauben und Kirchenverfassung vom 15. bis 30. August 1978 in Bangalore/Indien," *Ökumenische Rundschau* 27 (1978): 473-483; M. M. Thomas, "Christlicher Ökumenismus und Säkularökumenismus," *Ökumenische Rundschau* 28 (1979): 172-178; and Wolfhart Pannenberg, "Die 'westliche' Christenheit in der Ökumene. Eine Antwort an M. M. Thomas," *Ökumenische Rundschau* 28 (1979): 306-316.

68. Cf. *Together on the Way: Official Report of the Eighth Assembly of the World Council of Churches,* ed. Diane Kessler (Geneva: WCC 1999).

69. Cf. "In deiner Gnade, Gott, verwandle die Welt," in Wilkens, *Gemeinsam auf dem Weg.*

70. Cf. "Im Zeichen des heiligen Geistes," in Wilkens, *Gemeinsam auf dem Weg.*

71. See Konrad Raiser, "Ökumene im Übergang," in Wilkens, *Gemeinsam auf dem Weg.*

72. Cf. Christoph Schwöbel, "The Renaissance of Trinitarian Theology: Reasons, Problems and Tasks," in *Trinitarian Theology Today: Essays in Divine Being and Act,* ed. Christoph Schwöbel (Edinburgh: T&T Clark, 1995), 1-30. See also: John D. Zizioulas, *Being as Communion: Studies in Personhood and the Church,* 2nd ed. (Crestwood: St. Vladimir´s Seminary Press, 1993); John D. Zizioulas, "Die Kirche als Gemeinschaft," in Gassmann and Heller, *Fünfte Weltkonferenz für Glauben und Kirchenverfassung,* 95-104; John D. Zizioulas, "The Doctrine of the Holy Trinity: The Significance of the Cappadocian Contribution," in Schwöbel, *Trinitarian Theology Today,* 44-60. See also: Jürgen Moltmann, *Trinität und Reich Gottes. Zur Gotteslehre,* 3rd ed. (Munich: Kaiser, 1994). On the present discussion of the doctrine of the Trinity cf. Michael Welker and Miroslav Volf, eds. *Der lebendige Gott als Trinität. Jürgen Moltmann zum 80. Geburtstag* (Gütersloh: Gütersloher Verlagshaus, 2006).

73. Cf. Miroslav Volf, *Trinität und Gemeinschaft. Eine ökumenische Ekklesiologie* (Neukirchen-Vluyn: Neukirchener Verlag, 1996). See also: Enns, *Friedenskirche in der Ökumene.*

74. Cf. Michael Weinrich, *Ökumene am Ende? Plädoyer für einen neuen Realismus* (Neukirchen-Vluyn: Neukirchener Verlag, 1995).

75. Cf. Eberhard Busch, *Karl Barths Lebenslauf. Nach seinen Briefen und autobiographischen Texten* (Munich: Kaiser, 1975), 373. See Barth's doctrine of election in Karl Barth, *Die Kirchliche Dogmatik I/1-IV/4*, 13 vols. (Zurich: EVZ-Verlag, 1957-1967), 215ff (II/2). See also: Peter Scherle, *Fragliche Kirche. Ökumenik und Liturgik – Karl Barths ungehörte Anfrage an eine ökumenische Kirchentheorie* (Münster: Lit, 1998).

76. Cf. the theological approach of Friedrich-Wilhelm Marquardt, *Das christliche Bekenntnis zu Jesus, dem Juden. Eine Christologie*, 2 vols. (Munich: Kaiser, 1990-91). Friedrich-Wilhelm Marquardt, *Was dürfen wir hoffen, wenn wir hoffen dürften? Eine Eschatologie*, 3 vols. (Gütersloh: Kaiser, 1993-96).

77. Cf. e.g. the "Zwei-Wege-Modell" ("Two-ways-model") of Paul van Buren, or the "Stimmgabel-Modell" ("Tuning fork-model") of Dietrich Ritschl. See *The Theology of the Churches and the Jewish People: Statements by the World Council of Churches and its Member Churches. With a commentary by Allan Brockway, Paul van Buren, Rolf Rendtorff, Simon Schoon* (Geneva: WCC, 1988).

78. Cf. World Missionary Conference 1910 Edinburgh, *The History and Records of the Conference together with Addresses delivered at the Evening Meetings* (Edinburgh: Published for the World Missionary Conference by Oliphant, Anderson & Ferrier, and New York: Fleming H. Revell, 1910). August W. Schreiber, ed. *Die Edinburgher Welt-Missions-Konferenz* (Basel: Verlag der Basler Missionsbuchhandlung, 1910). See also Brain Stanley, *The World Missionary Conference Edinburgh 1910* (Grand Rapids, Mich.: Eerdmans, 2009).

79. Cf. Hans-Martin Barth, *Dogmatik. Evangelischer Glaube im Kontext der Weltreligionen*, 3rd ed. (Gütersloh: Gütersloher Verlagshaus, 2008).

80. Theo Sundermeier, *"Konvivenz als Grundstruktur ökumenischer Existenz heute,"* in *Ökumenische Existenz heute*, Wolfgang Huber, Dietrich Ritschl, and Theo Sundermeier, vol. 1 (Munich: Kaiser, 1986), 49-100.

81. Cf. Wolfram Weiße, *"Dialog zwischen den Religionen: Jugendliche in Europa zu religiöser Homogenität und zum Religionsunterricht. Das europäische Forschungsprojekt REDco,"* in *Profilierte Ökumene*, Enns, Hailer, and Link-Wieczorek, 279-294.

82. Hans Küng, *Projekt Weltethos*, 10th ed. (Munich: Piper, 2006). Expanded in Hans Küng, ed. *Dokumentation zum Weltethos* (Munich: Piper, 2002); Hans Küng, ed. *Erklärung zum Weltethos, Parliament of the World's Religions, Chicago 1993* (Munich: Piper, 1993); Hans Küng, *Weltethos für Weltpolitik und Weltwirtschaft* (Munich: Piper, 1997).

83. In this way ecumenical theology as a discipline of systematic theology is evident in some Protestant theological faculties in Germany (University of Heidelberg), in other it is connected with studies in mission, religion and ecumenism in one institute (University of Hamburg).

84. *DÖSTA*, Deutsche Ökumenische Studienausschuss

85. Johannes Brosseder, Laurentius Klein and Konrad Raiser, *"Theologie der Ökumene – Ökumenische Theoriebildung. Eine fragende und anfragende Problemstellung,"* ed. Deutscher Ökumenischer Studienausschuss, *Ökumenische Rundschau* 37 (1988), 205-221.

2. Dialogical Ecumenism

1. On Mennonites in general see the general introduction by Diether G. Lichdi, *Die Mennoniten in Geschichte und Gegenwart: Von der Täuferbewegung zur weltweiten Freikirche* (Weisenheim am Berg: Agape, 2004); C. Arnold Snyder, *Anabaptist History and Theology: An Introduction* (Kitchener, ON: Pandora Press, 1995); *Mennonite Encyclopedia*, eds. Harold S. Bender and C. Henry Smith, 5 vols. (Hillsboro, KS: Mennonite Brethren Publishing House, 1955-1990), vol. 5 ed. by Cornelius J. Dyck and Dennis D. Martin (Scottdale, PA: Herald Press). Updated and expanded edition online: www.gameo.org

2. On the concept of free-churches and the distinct denominations in this movement see, Erich Geldbach, *Freikirchen – Erbe, Gestalt und Wirkung*, Bensheimer Hefte 70 (Göttingen: Vandenhoeck & Ruprecht, 1989).

3. Cf. Fernando Enns, "Annäherungen an die 'Historische Friedenskirche' in konfessioneller Näherbestimmung," chap. II in *Friedenskirche in der Ökumene. Mennonitische Wurzeln einer Ethik der Gewaltfreiheit* (Göttingen: Vandenhoeck & Ruprecht, 2003), 99-154.

4. All the bilateral dialogues up to 2012 in which Mennonites have participated are documented in Fernando Enns and Jonathan Seiling, eds. *Mennonites in Dialogue: Official Reports from International and National Ecumenical Encounters, 1975-2012* (Eugene: Pickwick, 2015). Cited subsequently as *Mennonites in Dialogue*.

5. Thus Mennonites are considered "non-creedal churches." Although they develop confessional statements, they refrain from creeds in the sense of established doctrine. On the difference between creedal and non-creedal see, Donald F. Durnbaugh, *The Believers' Church. The History and Character of the Radical Protestantism*, 2nd ed. (Scottdale, PA: Herald Press, 1985), 5ff. On the development of the confessional tradition among Mennonites see Karl Koop, *Anabaptist-Mennonite Confessions of Faith: The Development of a Tradition* (Kitchener, ON: Pandora, 2003).

6. On the suggestions for a method of dialogue from a free-church perspective see John Howard Yoder, "The Free Church Ecumenical Style (1968)," in *The Royal Priesthood, Essays Ecclesiological and Ecumenical*, ed. Michael G. Cartwright (Grand Rapids, MI: Eerdmans 1994), 232-241.

7. Cf. the articles in Johannes Brosseder and Markus Wriedt, eds. *Kein Anlass zur Verwerfung, Studien zur Hermeneutik des ökumenischen Gesprächs, Festschrift for Otto Hermann Pesch* (Frankfurt am Main:Lembeck, 2007). Stephen Lakkis, Stefan Höschele, and Stefanie Schardien, eds. *Ökumene der Zukunft. Hermeneutische Perspektiven und die Suche nach Identität*, Beiheft zur ÖR 81 (Frankfurt am Main: Lembeck, 2008).

8. Cf. Fernando Enns, "Mennoniten: plurale Minderheitskirche im Pluralismus," *Kirchliche Zeitgeschichte* 13, no. 2 (2000), 359-375.

9. On "reconciled diversity" see Harding Meyer, *Versöhnte Verschiedenheit: Aufsätze zur ökumenischen Theologie*, 3 vols. (Frankfurt am Main: Lembeck, 1998-2009).

10. See the position statement on Mennonite members in the WCC: Vereinigung der Deutschen Mennonitengemeinden, "Stellungnahme zu den Konvergenzerklärungen über Taufe, Eucharistie und Amt der Kommission für Glauben und Kirchenverfassung des Ökumenischen Rates der Kirchen, Lima 1982," *Brücke* 2 (1986), ed. Arbeitsgemeinschaft Mennonitischer Gemeinden. And the response of the General Mennonite Society, Netherlands (*Allgemene Doopsgezinde Societeit*) in Max Thurian,

ed. *Respond to BEM. Official Responses to the "Baptism, Eucharist and Ministry" Text*, Faith and Order Paper 135, vol. III (Geneva: WCC Publications, 1987), 289-296.

11. "Consultation on the Apostolic Faith and the Church's Peace Witness: A Summary Statement," in *The Church's Peace Witness*, Marlin E. Miller and Barbara Nelson Gingrich, eds. (Grand Rapids, MI: Eerdmans, 1994), 208-215.

12. Deutscher Ökumenischer Studienausschuss, *Von Gott angenommen – in Christus verwandelt. Die Rechtfertigungslehre im multilateralen ökumenischen Dialog. Eine Studie des DÖSTA*, Beiheft zur ÖR 78, Uwe Swarat, Johannes Oeldemann, and Dagmar Heller, eds. (Frankfurt am Main: Lembeck, 2006).

13. See the documentation of those dialogues in *Mennonites in Dialogue*, 435-470.

14. See *Mennonites in Dialogue*, 439; Enns, *Heilung der Erinnerungen*, 293.

15. On the concept "Radical Reformation" see George H. Williams, *The Radical Reformation*, 3rd ed. (Kirksville: Sixteenth Century Journal Publishers, 1992); Donald F. Durnbaugh, *The Believers' Church*.

16. Milan Opočenský and Páraic Réamonn, eds. *Justification and Sanctification in the Traditions of the Reformation. Prague V, the Fifth Consultation on the First and Second Reformations, Geneva, 13-17 February 1998*, Studies from the World Alliance of Reformed Churches (cit. WARC) 42 (Geneva: WARC, 1999).

17. *Mennonites in Dialogue*, 463-70; Walter Sawatsky, ed. *The Prague Consultations: Prophetic and Renewal Movements: Proceedings of the Prague VI and Prague VII Multilateral Ecumenical Consultations (2000 & 2003)*, Studies from the WARC (Geneva: WARC, 2009).

18. Cf. Donald F. Durnbaugh, ed. *On Earth Peace: Discussions on War/Peace Issues between Friends, Mennonites, Brethren and European Churches 1935-1975* (Elgin, IL: The Brethren Press, 1978). See also description and interpretation in Enns, *Friedenskirche in der Ökumene*, 223-235.

19. Cf. the common messages of the Historical Peace Churches in Fernando Enns, Scott Holland, and Ann Riggs, eds. *Seeking Cultures of Peace: A Peace Church Conversation* (Telford, PA: Cascadia, 2004). Donald E. Miller et al., eds. *Seeking Peace in Africa. Stories from African Peacemakers* (Geneva: World Council of Churches, 2007). Donald E. Miller, Gerard Guiton, and Paulus Widjaja, eds. *Overcoming Violence in Asia: The Role of the Church in Seeking Cultures of Peace* (Telford, PA.: Cascadia, 2011).

20. Köhler, Walther and Dennis D. Martin. "Roman Catholic Church." *Global Anabaptist Mennonite Encyclopedia Online*, 1990, (4.02. 2016). http://gameo.org/index.php?title=Roman_Catholic_Church&oldid=121294. English originally published in *Mennonite Encyclopedia*, Vol. 1, pp. 532-535. Original German article by Walter Köhler (1958) in *Mennonitisches Lexikon*, vol. 2, Christian Hege and Christian Neff, eds. (Frankfurt am Main and Weierhof, 1937), 472-474.

21. Cf. Ivan J. Kauffman, "Mennonite-Catholic Conversations in North America: History, Convergences, Opportunities," *One in Christ* 34 (1998), 220-246.

22. Cf. on this Earl Zimmermann, "Renewing the Conversation: Mennonite Responses to the Second Vatican Council," *Mennonite Quarterly Review* (cit. *MQR*) 73 (1999), 61-73.

23. Cf. Hans-Jürgen Goertz, *Antiklerikalismus und Reformation: Sozialgeschichtliche Untersuchungen* (Göttingen: Vandenhoeck & Ruprecht, 1995).

24. *Mennonites in Dialogue*, 19-114; Original publication in English: "Called Together to be Peacemakers: Report of the International Dialogue between the Catholic Church and the Mennonite World Conference, 1998-2003," *Information Service. The Pontifical*

Council for Promoting Christian Unity, no.113 (2003/II-III), 111-157. Throughout the references to the article in the report will be given in brackets (§).

25. For both Mennonites, as for Catholics, this was not the first bilateral dialogue in which they participated. Most of the international ecumenical dialogues can be found in the four published volumes: *Growth in Agreement: Reports and Agreed Statements of Ecumenical Conversations on a World Level*
    (volumes I–IV, 1982–2016).

26. See Hans-Jürgen Goertz, *Die Täufer: Geschichte und Deutung*, 2nd ed. (Munich: Beck, 1988). On the pacifistic heritage see also Clarence Bauman, *Gewaltlosigkeit im Täufertum: Eine Untersuchung zur theologischen Ethik des oberdeutschen Täufertums der Reformationszeit* (Leiden: Brill, 1968); James Stayer, *Anabaptists and the Sword* (Lawrence, KS: Coronado Press, 1972).

27. In German: Arbeitsgemeinschaft Christlicher Kirchen in Deutschland, "ACK"

28. See especially the diverging experiences in Latin America. While Mennonites in Colombia maintain close links with the Catholic Christians in the commitment to justice and peace, the mutual estrangement in other countries such as Paraguay still has a very limiting effect on relations.

29. On the term "peace churches" see Melvin Gingerich and Paul Peachey, "Historic Peace Churches," *Global Anabaptist Mennonite Encyclopedia Online*, 1989, (17 Nov 2015), http://gameo.org/index.php?title=Historic_Peace_Churches&oldid=88064

30. Cf. "Gaudium et spes," 42. See *Das Zweite Vatikanische Konzil. Konstitutionen, Dekrete und Erklärungen. Lat. and Ger. comm.*, vol. 3 (Freiburg i.B.: Herder, 1968).

31. See the general interpretation of history as construction in Hans-Jürgen Goertz, *Umgang mit Geschichte: eine Einführung in die Geschichtstheorie* (Reinbek bei Hamburg: Rowohlt, 1995); Hans-Jürgen Goertz, *Unsichere Geschichte: zur Theorie historischer Referentialität* (Stuttgart: Reclam, 2001); Hans-Jürgen Goertz, ed. *Geschichte: ein Grundkurs*, 3rd ed. (Reinbek bei Hamburg: Rowohlt, 2007).

32. John Howard Yoder, "The Disavowal of Constantine: An Alternative Perspective on Interfaith Dialogue," in *The Royal Priesthood: Essays Ecclesiological and Ecumenical* (Grand Rapids, MI: Eerdmans, 1994), 242-261; John Howard Yoder, "Peace Without Eschatology?," in *ibid.*, 144-167.

33. See Gerhard Ruhbach, ed. *Die Kirche angesichts der Konstantinischen Wende* (Darmstadt: WBG, 1976); Robin Lane Fox, *Pagans and Christians* (New York, London: Knopf, 1987); Jochen Bleicken, *Konstantin der Große und die Christen* (Munich: Oldenbourg, 1992); Michael Grant, *Constantine the Great. The Man and his Times* (New York: Prentice Hall 1994); Thomas George Elliott, *The Christianity of Constantine the Great* (New York: Fordham University Press, 1997).

34. Cf. Walter Klaassen, "The Anabaptist Critique of Constantinian Christendom," *MQR* 55 (1981): 218-230; John Howard Yoder, "The Otherness of the Church (1960)," in *The Royal Priesthood*, 54-64.

35. See *Dignitatis humanae*, http://www.vatican.va/archive/hist_councils/ii_vatican_-council/documents/vat-ii_decl_19651207_dignitatis-humanae_en.html; "Erklärung über das Verhältnis der Kirche zu den nichtchristlichen Religionen, Dignitatis humanae," in *Das Zweite Vatikanische Konzil*, vol. 2 and vol. 3 (Gaudium et spes).

36. Balthasar Hubmaier and Pilgram Marpeck are explicitly named here in § 61. Cf. Tainer Wohlfeil and Hans-Jürgen Goertz, *Gewissensfreiheit als Bedingung der Neuzeit: Fragen an die Speyerer Protestation von 1529* (Göttingen: Vandenhoeck & Ruprecht, 1980); Wayne H. Pipkin and John H. Yoder, eds. *Balthasar Hubmaier: Theologian of*

Anabaptism (Scottdale, PA: Herald Press, 1989); Pilgram Marpeck, *The Writings of Pilgram Marpeck*, William Klassen and Walter Klaassen, eds. (Kitchener, ON: Herald Press 1978).

37. See Snyder, *Anabaptist History and Theology*.
38. See Thomas Brady Jr., Heiko A. Oberman, and James D. Tracy, eds. *Handbook of European History 1400 - 1600: Late Middle Ages, Renaissance and Reformation* (Leiden: Brill, 1995); John Bossy, *Christianity in the West, 1440-1700* (New York: Oxford University Press, 1985); John W. O'Malley, ed. *Catholicism in Early Modern Europe* (St. Louis: Center for Reformation Research, 1988); Robert Bireley, *The Refashioning of Catholicism, 1450-1700: A Reassessment of the Counter Reformation* (New York: Macmillan, 1999).
39. See the concept developed by Bernd Möller, "Frömmigkeit in Deutschland um 1500," *Archiv für Reformationsgeschichte* 56 (1965), 5-30; and Eamon Duffy, *The Stripping of the Altars: Traditional Religion in England, 1400-1580* (New Haven: Yale University Press, 1992). Cf. also Alister E. McGrath, *Reformation Thought*, 3rd ed. (Oxford: Blackwell, 1999), 26-27: "Older studies of the background to the Reformation tended to portray the later Middle Ages as a period in which religion was in decline. (...) Modern studies, using more reliable criteria, have indicated that precisely the reverse is true. (...) And it is this popular interest in religion, which led to the criticism of the institutional church where it was thought to be falling short of its obligations. This criticism – treated by older studies as evidence of religious decline – thus actually points to religious growth."
40. See Regnerus R. Post, *The Modern Devotion* (Leyden: Brill, 1968), Georgette Epinay-Burgard, *Gérard Grote (1340-1384) et les débuts de la dévotion moderne* (Wiesbaden: Steiner, 1970), and John van Engen, *Devotio Moderna: Basic Writings* (New York: Paulist Press, 1988).
41. See interpretation in Christopher M. Bellitto, *Renewing Christianity: A History of Church Reform from Day One to Vatican II* (New York: Paulist Press, 2001); Cf. Ronald G. Musto, *The Catholic Peace Tradition* (Maryknoll, NY: Orbis, 1986).
42. See Kenneth Ronald Davis, *Anabaptism and Asceticism: A Study in Intellectual Origins* (Eugene: Wipf and Stock, 1998); C. Arnold Snyder, "The Monastic Origins of Swiss Anabaptist Sectarianism," *MQR* 57 (1983), 5-26; Russel Snyder-Penner, "The Ten Commandments, the Lord's Prayer and the Apostles' Creed as Early Anabaptist Texts," in *MQR* 68 (1994), 318-335; Dennis D. Martin, "Monks, Mendicants and Anabaptists: Michael Sattler and the Benedictines reconsidered," in *MQR* 60 (1986), 139-164; Dennis D. Martin, "Catholic Spirituality and Anabaptist and Mennonite Discipleship," in *MQR* 62 (1988), 5-25.
43. See Volker Leppin, *Das Zeitalter der Reformation: eine Welt im Übergang* (Darmstadt: WBG, 2009); Gottfried Seebaß, *Spätmittelalter – Reformation – Konfessionalisierung*, Theologische Wissenschaft, vol. 7 (Stuttgart: Kohlhammer 2006).
44. See the collection of quotes from Anabaptists on this theme in Walter Klaassen, "Government," in *Anabaptism in Outline. Selected Primary Sources*, ed. Klaassen (Kitchener, ON: Herald Press, 1981), 244-264; cf. Hans-Jürgen Goertz, "Gemeinde, Obrigkeit und Neues Reich," in *Die Täufer*, Goertz, 95-120.
45. Cf. "Baptism," in *Anabaptism in Outline*, Klaassen, 162-189; "Taufe als öffentliches Bekenntnis," in *Die Täufer*, Goertz, 76-94.
46. On restitutionism see John H. Yoder, "Anabaptism and History: 'Restitution' and the Possibility of Renewal," in *Umstrittenes Täufertum 1525-1975*, Hans-Jürgen

Goertz, ed. 2nd ed. (Göttingen: Vandenhoeck & Ruprecht, 1977), 244-258.

47. See "Die kritische Funktion der Apostolizität," in *Friedenskirche in der Ökumene*, Enns, 253ff.

48. Leading researchers include Hans-Jürgen Goertz, Klaus Depperman, Werner Packull, James Stayer, C. Arnold Snyder.

49. *"Damnant Anabaptistas, qui improbant baptismum puerum ac affirmant pueros sine baptismo salvos fieri."* Article IX of the Augsburg Confession. See English translation in *The Book of Concord: The Confessions of the Evangelical Lutheran Church*, eds. Robert Kolb and Timothy J. Wengert (Minneapolis: Fortress, 2000).

50. *"...itaque damnamus errorem Anabaptistarum, qui ante fidem et rationis usum negant ad pueros pertinere baptismum."* "Schottisches Bekenntnis von 1560 nebst dem Covenant von 1581 (XXXV), Art. XXIII," in *Die Bekenntnisschriften der reformierten Kirche*, ed. Ernst Friedrich Karl Müller (Zürich: Theologische Buchhandlung, 1987), 261. *"Anabaptistarum itaque errorem detestamur, qui unico et semel suscepto baptismo contenti non sunt: ac praeterea, baptismum infantium, fidelibus parentibus natorum, damnant..."* "Confessio Belgica (1561), Art. XXXIV," in *Bekenntnisschriften der reformierten Kirche*, ed. Müller, 246; *"Damnamus Anabaptistas, qui negant baptisandos esse infantulos recens natos a fidelibus..."* "Confessio helvetica posterior (1562), Art. XX," in *Bekenntnisschriften der reformierten Kirche*, ed. Müller, 221.

51. See also Andrea Strübind, *Eifriger als Zwingli: Die frühe Täuferbewegung in der Schweiz* (Berlin: Duncker & Humbolt, 2003).

52. Goertz, *Die Täufer*, 127.; idem. *The Anabaptists*, 118.

53. Cf. Goertz, *Die Täufer*, 127f.; idem. *The Anabaptists*, 118-119.

54. Thieleman van Braght, *The Bloody Theater, or, Martyrs' Mirror, The True and the False Church, as Outlined in The Bloody Theatre* (Lancaster, PA: David Miller, 1827).

55. Cf. Martin Luther, "Der Kampf gegen Schwarm- und Rottengeister," *Ausgewählte Werke*, vol. 4, ed. Hans H. Borcherdt, 3rd ed. (Munich: Kaiser, 1964).

56. This needs to be presented in a much more nuanced manner, see e.g., Eike Wolgast, "Herrschaftsorganisation und Herrschaftskrisen im Täuferreich von Münster 1534/35," *Archiv für Reformationsgeschichte* 67 (Gütersloh: Mohn 1976); Hubertus Lutterbach, *Das Täuferreich von Münster: Ursprünge und Merkmale eines religiösen Aufbruchs* (Münster: Aschendorff, 2008).

57. Cf. "Brüderliche Vereinigung etlicher Kinder Gottes, sieben Artikel betreffend," in *Bekenntnisse der Kirche*, Hans Streubing, ed. (Wuppertal: Brockhaus, 1985), 261-268.

58. Cf. "Nonresistance," in *Anabaptism in Outline*, Klaassen, 265-281. Otherwise see the foundational work by Stayer, *Anabaptists and the Sword*.

59. Cf. James M. Stayer, "Numbers in Anabaptist Research," in *Commoners and Community: Essays in Honour of Werner O. Packull*, C. Arnold Snyder, ed. (Waterloo, ON: Herald Press, 2000), 51-73.

60. See Brad S. Gregory, *Salvation at Stake: Christian Martyrdom in Early Modern Europe* (Cambridge: Harvard UP, 1999), especially the chapters on Anabaptists (ch.6) and Catholics (ch.7).

61. Menno Simons thus expresses the connection between peace and ethics: "Christ is everywhere represented to us as humble, meek, merciful, just, holy, wise, spiritual, long-suffering, patient, peaceable, lovely, obedient, and good, as the perfection of all things; for in him there is an upright nature. Behold, this is the image of God, of Christ as to the Spirit which we have as an example until we become like it in nature and reveal it by our walk." Menno Simons, "The Spiritual Resurrection" (c.

1536), in J.C. Wenger, ed. *The Complete Writings of Menno Simons* (Scottdale: Herald Press, 1956), 55-6. Catholic teaching on peace is found in *Gaudium et spes*; 38: "Undergoing death itself for all of us sinners (cf. *Jn* 3:16; *Rom* 5:8), he taught us by example that we too must shoulder that cross which the world and the flesh inflict upon those who search after peace and justice." See also *Gaudium et spes*; 28 and 32. See *Mennonites in Dialogue*, 97fn137.

62. See John Paul II, "To Build Peace, respect Minorities," World Day of Peace Message, 1989; *Gaudium et spes*, 42. For a Mennonite perspective on international conflict, see *A Declaration on Peace: In God's People the World's Renewal Has Begun*, co-authored by Douglas Gwyn, George Hunsinger, Eugene F. Roop, John Howard Yoder (Scottdale: Herald Press, 1991).

63. "Just War (lat. Bellum iustum), goes back to Roman origins (Cicero), which was further developed by Augustine and Thomas Aquinas with a powerful effect and refined in the late scholastic theology, entering into international legal discussion and to this day is considered the standard ethical theory for principles of the normative assessment of interstate violence." Rudolf Peter, "Gerechter Krieg," in *Lexikon der Politikwissenschaft. Theorien, Methoden, Begriffe*, eds. Dieter Nohlen and Rainer-Olaf Schultze, vol. 1 (Munich: Beck, 2002), 266. See the discussion concerning criteria in Michael Haspel, *Friedensethik und humanitäre Intervention. Der Kosovo-Krieg als Herausforderung evangelischer Friedensethik* (Neukirchen-Vluyn: Neukirchener, 2002).

64. Pope John Paul II, Encyclical "Centesimus annus," http://www.vatican.va/holy_father/john_paul_ii/encyclicals/documents/hf_jp-ii_enc_01051991_centesimus-annus_en.html (9 January 2014). Johannes Paul II, *Enzyklika Centesimus annus (Verlautbarungen des Apostolischen Stuhls 101)*, ed. Sekretariat der Deutschen Bischofskonferenz, (Bonn, 1991), 25.

65. For examples of Mennonites' relationship to National Socialism in Germany see, Hans-Jürgen Goertz, "Nationale Erhebung und religiöser Niedergang: Missglückte Aneignung des täuferischen Leitbildes im Dritten Reich," in *Umstrittenes Täufertum*, Goertz, 259-289; see also Diether G. Lichdi, *Die Mennoniten im Dritten Reich. Dokumentation und Deutung* (Weierhof, Pfalz, 1977); Arbeitsgemeinschaft Mennonitischer Gemeinden in Deutschland (AMG), "50 Jahre nach Kriegsende. Erklärung der Mitgliederversammlung der AMG 1995," in *Schuld und Versagen der Freikirchen im 'Dritten Reich', Aufarbeitungsprozesse seit 1945*, Karl Heinz Voigt (Frankfurt am Main: Lembeck, 2005), 110-112.

66. Cf. Schleitheim Articles, article 4 and especially article 6. "The sword is ordained of God outside the perfection of Christ. It punishes and puts to death the wicked, and guards and protects the good. In the Law the sword was ordained for the punishment of the wicked and for their death, and the same [sword] is [now] ordained to be used by the worldly magistrates. In the perfection of Christ, however, only the ban is used for a warning and for the excommunication of the one who has sinned, without putting the flesh to death, -- simply the warning and the command to sin no more." Wenger, J. C. "The Schleitheim Confession of Faith." *Mennonite Quarterly Review* 19 (October 1945) 243-253.

67. However, such expressions are also found in contemporary writings of Mennonites: "The church's most effective witness and action against war comes on a different level and consists simply in the stand she takes in and through her members in the face of war. Unless the church, trusting the power of God in whose hand the

destinies of nations lie, is willing to 'fall into the ground and die,' to renounce war absolutely, whatever sacrifice of freedoms, advantages, or possessions this might entail, even to the point of counseling a nation not to resist foreign conquest and occupation, she can give no prophetic message for the world of nations." Gwyn et al, *A Declaration on Peace*, 74-5.

68. See bibliographic references in Glenn Stassen, ed. *Just Peacemaking: Ten Practices for Abolishing War* (Cleveland: Pilgrim Press, 1998); Duane K. Friesen, *Christian Peacemaking and International Conflict: A Realist Pacifist Perspective* (Scottdale, PA: Herald Press, 1986); Fernando Enns, Scott Holland, and Ann Riggs, eds. *Seeking Cultures of Peace. A Peace Church Conversation* (Geneva: World Council of Churches, 2004); Leo Driedger and Donald B. Kraybill, *Mennonite Peacemaking. From Quietism to Activism* (Scottdale, PA: Herald Press, 1994); Duane K. Friesen, "Toward a Theology of Culture: A Dialogue with John Howard Yoder and Gordon Kaufman," *Conrad Grebel Review* (cit. *CGR*) Spring (1998), 39-64; and Duane K. Friesen, "Toward a Theology of Culture: A Dialogue with Gordon Kaufman," in *Mennonite Theology in Face of Modernity, Essays in Honor of Gordon D. Kaufman*, ed. Allan Epp Weaver (Newton, KS: Mennonite Press, 1996), 95-114.

69. Cf. *Gerechter Friede*, Die deutschen Bischöfe, vol. 66, ed. Sekretariat der Deutschen Bischofkonferenz, 2nd ed. (Bonn, 2000).

70. See the contributions to this discussion in Horst Fischer, ed. *Krisensicherung und humanitärer Schutz. Crisis Management and Humanitarian Protection, Festschrift für Dieter Fleck*, Bochumer Schriften zur Friedenssicherung und zum Humanitären Völkerrecht 46 (Berlin: Berliner Wissenschaftlicher Verlag, 2004).

71. "Die Dekade zur Überwindung von Gewalt des Ökumenischen Rates der Kirchen. Ein mennonitischer und katholischer Beitrag," ÖR 2 (2008), 222-232.

72. See also Ivan J. Kauffman, ed. *Just Policing: Mennonite-Catholic Theological Colloquium 2002*, The Bridgefolk Series (Kitchener, ON: Pandora Press, 2004).

73. See on the attitude of Anabaptists, Snyder-Penner, "The Ten Commandments, the Lord's Prayer and the Apostles' Creed as Early Anabaptist Texts," *MQR* 68 (1994), 318-335.

74. http://www.vatican.va/archive/hist_councils/ii_vatican_council/documents/vat-ii_const_19651118_dei-verbum_en.html Sections 8 and 10. Cf. "Dogmatische Konstitution über die göttliche Offenbarung 'Dei Verbum'," in *Das Zweite Vatikanische Konzil*, vol. 1, 7-10.

75. See Johann Auer, *Die Kirche – das allgemeine Heilssakrament*, Kleine katholische Dogmatik 8, Johann Auer and Joseph Ratzinger, eds. (Regensburg: Pustet, 1983).

76. Hans Denck, "Whether God is the Cause of Evil (1526)," C. Bauman, trans. & ed. *The Spiritual Legacy of Hans Denck: Interpretation and Translation of Key Texts* (New York: Brill, 1991), 113. Hans Denck, Religiöse Schriften, Quellen zur Geschichte der Täufer, Vol. 6,2, Walter Fellmann, ed. (Gütersloh: Bertelsmann, 1956), 45, 50. Cf. John Howard Yoder, *Politics of Jesus: Vicit Agnus Noster* (Grand Rapids: Eerdmans, 1994).

77. Congregation for the Doctrine of the Faith: Responses to Some Questions Regarding Certain Aspects of the Doctrine on the Church," Fifth question. (15 Dec 2014). www.vatican.va/roman_curia/congregations/cfaith/documents/rc_con_c-faith_doc_20070629_responsa-quaestiones_en.html

78. The Roman Catholic Church is a member of the Faith and Order Commission of the World Council of Churches.

79. *Baptism, Eucharist and Ministry*, Faith & Order Paper 111 (Geneva: WCC, 1982), 42.

80. National Council of Churches of Christ in the USA, *The Fragmentation of the Church and its Unity in Peacemaking*, October 27, 1995. Shortened version in "Ecumenical Chronicle," *Ecumenical Review* (cit. *ER*) 48 (1996), 122-124.

81. Lumen Gentium, section 10. http://www.vatican.va/archive/hist_councils/ii_vatican_council/documents/vat-ii_const_19641121_lumen-gentium_en.html

82. Cf. John Howard Yoder, "Walk and Word: the Alternatives to Methodologism," in *Theology without Foundations: Religious Practice and the Future of Theological Truth*, Nancy Murphy, Mark Nation, and Stanley Hauerwas, eds. (Nashville, TN: Abingdon, 1995), 77-90; John Howard Yoder, *The Priestly Kingdom: Social Ethics as Gospel* (Notre Dame, IN: University of Notre Dame Press, 1984).

83. See discussions in Gerald W. Schlabach, ed. *On Baptism: Mennonite-Catholic Theological Colloquium 2001-2002*, The Bridgefolk Series (Kitchener, ON: Pandora Press, 2004).

84. See Fernando Enns, "Die gegenseitige Anerkennung der Taufe als bleibende ökumenische Herausforderung – Konsens, Divergenzen und Differenzen," in *Profilierte Ökumene. Bleibend Wichtiges und jetzt Dringliches. FS Dietrich Ritschl*, Beiheft zur ÖR 84, Fernando Enns, Martin Hailer, and Ulrike Link-Wieczorek, eds. (Frankfurt am Main: Lembeck, 2009), 127-158.

85. Cf. Heinrich Denzinger, "Konzil von Trient, Dekret über das Sakrament der Eucharistie," in *Kompendium der Glaubensbekenntnisse und kirchlichen Lehrentscheidungen*, Peter Hünermann, ed. 37th ed. (Freiburg i.Br.: Herder, 1991), 1651.

86. See here the nuanced position of John D. Rempel, namely that the Anabaptists "made the church as a community the agent of the breaking of bread. There is still a presider who symbolizes the community's order and authority. But it is the congregation that does the action. The Spirit is present in their action, transforming them so that they are reconstituted as the body of Christ. The life of the congregation, consecrated in its faith and love, consecrates the elements." John D. Rempel, *The Lord's Supper in Anabaptism* (Scottdale: Herald Press, 1993), 34.

87. See Gunther Wenz, "Herrenmahl und Amt. Evangelische Perspektiven," in *Amt und Eucharistiegemeinschaft. Ökumenische Perspektiven und Probleme*, eds. Silvia Hell and Lothar Lies (Innsbruck: Tyrolia, 2004), 221-239; Dorothea Sattler and Gunther Wenz, eds. *Sakramente ökumenisch feiern. Vorüberlegungen für die Erfüllung einer Hoffnung. Festschrift für Theodor Schneider* (Mainz: Matthias-Grünewald-Verlag, 2005).

88. Cf. "Dekret über den Ökumenismus 'Unitatis redintegratio'," in *Das Zweite Vatikanische Konzil*, vol. 2, 3; Wolfgang Thönissen, ed. *"Unitatis redintegratio": 40 Jahre Ökumenismusdekret – Erbe und Auftrag*, Konfessionskundliche Schriften des Johann-Adam-Möhler-Instituts 23 (Paderborn: Bonifatius, 2005).

89. See Internationale Theologische Kommission, ed. *Erinnern und Versöhnen. Die Kirche und die Verfehlungen in ihrer Vergangenheit*, 2nd ed. (Einsiedeln: Johannes Verlag, 2000), 72.

90. Pope John Paul II, Apostolic Letter,"*Tertio millenio adveniente,*" Sect. 35, https://w2.vatican.va/content/john-paul-ii/en/apost_letters/1994/documents/hf_jp-ii_apl_10111994_tertio-millennio-adveniente.html.

91. "God Calls Us to Christian Unity," a statement adopted by the executive of Mennonite World Conference, Goshen, Indiana, July, 1998.

92. In the first footnote of the dialogue report between Mennonites and Roman Catholics it notes that the term "church" is used "to reflect the self-understandings

of the participating churches." However, it is expressly stated that there is no shared ecclesiology. Cf. Enns and Seiling, *Mennonites in Dialogue*, 24.

3. Theme-Centred Ecumenism

1. See Oliver Schuegraf, *Der einen Kirche Gestalt geben. Ekklesiologie in den Dokumenten der bilateralen Konsensökumene*, Jerusalemer theologisches Forum, vol. 3 (Münster: Aschendorff, 2001).
2. Dietrich Ritschl, "Konsens ist nicht das höchste Ziel," in *Theorie und Konkretionen in der Ökumenischen Theologie*, Studien zur Systematischen Theologie und Ethik 37, Ritschl (Münster: Lit, 2003), 179-192.
3. Ritschl, "Konsens ist nicht das höchste Ziel," 179.
4. Ritschl, "Konsens ist nicht das höchste Ziel," 179f.
5. Vereinigte Evangelisch-Lutherische Kirche in Deutschland
6. Arbeitsgemeinschaft Mennonitischer Gemeinden in Deutschland
7. Cf. "Das lutherisch-mennonitische Gespräch in der Bundesrepublik Deutschland 1989-1992," in *Heilung der Erinnerungen – befreit zur gemeinsamen Zukunft. Mennoniten im Dialog. Berichte und Texte ökumenischer Gespräche auf nationaler und internationaler Ebene*, ed. Fernando Enns (Frankfurt am Main: Lembeck, 2008), 151-199; "Eucharistische Gastbereitschaft. Die Predigten von den ökumenischen Gottesdiensten der Arbeitsgemeinschaft Mennonitischer Gemeinden in Deutschland und der Vereinigten Lutherischen Kirche Deutschlands am 17. und 24. März 1996 und die gemeinsame Erklärung zur Eucharistischen Gastbereitschaft," in *Texte aus der VELKD* 67 (Hannover: Lutherisches Kirchenamt der VELKD, 1996). Cf. Fernando Enns, "Mennonitisch-Lutherischer Dialog," in *Friedenskirche in der Ökumene*, Enns (Göttingen: Vandenhoek & Ruprecht, 2003), 285-299; Rainer W. Burkart, "Eucharistische Gastfreundschaft: Versöhnung zwischen Mennoniten und Lutheranern," *Ökumenische Rundschau* 45 (1996), 324-330; Menno Smid, "Der mennonitisch-lutherische Dialog," in *Was hat die Ökumene gebracht? Fakten und Perspektiven*, ed. Hermann Brandt and Jörg Rothermundt (Gütersloh: Gütersloher Verlagshaus, 1993), 43-52.
8. Rudolf Schnackenburg, *Der Brief an die Epheser*, Evangelisch-Katholischer Kommentar zum NT (EKK), vol. X (Zurich: Benziger, 1982), 161ff. "I therefore, the prisoner in the Lord, beg you to lead a life worthy of the calling to which you have been called, with all humility and gentleness, with patience, bearing with one another in love, making every effort to maintain the unity of the Spirit in the bond of peace. There is one body and one Spirit, just as you were called to the one hope of your calling, one Lord, one faith, one baptism, one God and Father of all, who is above all and through all and in all." Ephesians 4:1-6 (NRSV).
9. See the ecumenical interpretation in World Council of Churches, *Confessing the One Faith: An Ecumenical Explication of the Apostolic Faith as it is Confessed in the Nicene-Constantinopolitan Creed (381)*, Faith and Order Paper 153 (Geneva: WCC Publications, 1991); Deutscher Ökumenischer Studienausschuss, *Wir glauben, wir bekennen, wir erwarten. Eine Einführung in das Gespräch über das Ökumenische Glaubensbekenntnis von 381*, ed. Wolfgang Bienert (Eichstätt: Franz Sales, 1997). On the general discussion see, Hans-Georg Link, *Bekennen und Bekenntnis*, Ökumenische Studienhefte 7, Bensheimer Hefte 86 (Göttingen: Vandenhoeck & Ruprecht, 1998).

10. Cf. Erich Geldbach, *Taufe*, Ökumenische Studienhefte 5, Bensheimer Hefte 79 (Göttingen: Vandenhoeck & Ruprecht 1996).

11. Cf. Martin Hailer, "Taufanerkennung bei bleibend unterschiedlicher Lehre?," in *Profilierte Ökumene*, Enns, Hailer, and Link-Wieczorek, 159-183.

12. Cf. Karl Barth, *Die Kirchliche Dogmatik*, 13 vols. (Zurich: EVZ, 1932-1967), vol. IV. Karl Barth, *Die kirchliche Lehre von der Taufe*, Theologische Studien 14, 4th ed. (Zollikon-Zürich: Evangelischer Verlag, 1953). Cf. also Markus Barth, *Die Taufe – ein Sakrament? Ein exegetischer Beitrag zum Gespräch über die kirchliche Taufe* (Zollikon-Zurich: Evangelischer Verlag, 1951).

13. Dietrich Bonhoeffer, *Nachfolge*, Dietrich Bonhoeffer Werke (DBW), vol. 4, Martin Kuske and Ilse Tödt, eds. (Munich: Kaiser, 1989), 221.

14. Dietrich Ritschl, *Theorie und Konkretion in der Ökumenischen Theologie: Kann es eine Hermeneutik des Vertrauens inmitten differierender semiotischer Systeme geben?*, Studien zur systematischen Theologie und Ethik, Vol. 37, 2 (Berlin: Lit, 2005) 69.

15. Edmund Schlink, *The Doctrine of Baptism*, translated by Herbert J. A. Bouman (St. Louis: Concordia Publishing House, 1972), 169.

16. The "Lima Text": *Baptism, Eucharist and Ministry*, Faith and Order Paper no.111 (Geneva: WCC Publications, 1982). Cf. Konfessionskundliches Institut, ed. *Kommentar zu den Lima-Erklärungen über Taufe, Eucharistie, Amt*, Bensheimer Hefte 59 (Göttingen: Vandenhoeck & Ruprecht, 1983); Thomas F. Best and Tamara Grdzelidze, eds. *BEM at 25. Critical Insights into a Continuing Legacy* (Geneva: WCC, 2007).

17. Thomas F. Best and Günther Gassman, eds. *On the Way to Fuller Koinonia: Official Report of the Fifth World Conference on Faith and Order*, Faith and Order Paper no. 166 (Geneva: WCC, 1994), 247.

18. Representative here is a more recent Heidelberg dissertation, Wolfram Kerner, *Gläubigentaufe und Säuglingstaufe. Studien zur Taufe und gegenseitiger Taufanerkennung in der neueren evangelischen Theologie* (Norderstedt: Books on Demand, 2004). In this study important ecumenical documents Baptist, Lutheran and Reformed participation and dogmatic contributions are discussed (K.Barth, O.Weber, E.Schlink, W.Pannenberg, G.R.Beasley-Murray, and others). See the dispute between Joachim Jeremias and Kurt Aland: Kurt Aland, *Die Säuglingstaufe im Neuen Testament und in der alten Kirche; eine Antwort an Joachim Jeremias*, Theologische Existenz heute NF 86, 2nd ed. (München: Kaiser, 1963). The second edition contains an endorsement of a publication by Joachim Jeremias, *Nochmals: die Anfänge der Kindertaufe. Eine Replik auf Kurt Alands Schrift: Die Säuglingstaufe im NT und in der alten Kirche*, Theologische Existenz heute NF 101 (Munich: Kaiser, 1962); Kurt Aland, *Taufe und Kindertaufe* (Gütersloh: Gerd Mohn, 1971); Joachim Jeremias, *Die Kindertaufe in den ersten vier Jahrhunderten* (Göttingen: Vandenhoeck & Ruprecht, 1958).

19. As an example of a more recently, ecumenical theology of baptism and its practice see Susan K. Wood, *One Baptism: Ecumenical Dimensions of the Doctrine of Baptism* (Collegeville, MN: Liturgical Press, 2009).

20. The signing churches are: Roman Catholic Church (the German Bishops' Conference), Catholic Diocese of the Old Catholics in Germany, Protestant Church in Germany (EKD), Evangelical Old-Reformed Church in Lower Saxony, Moravian Church, United Methodist Church, Independent Evangelical Lutheran Church (SELK), Council of Anglican and Episcopal Churches in Germany, Ethiopian

Orthodox Church in Germany, Armenian Apostolic Orthodox Church in Germany, Orthodox Churches in Germany.

21. (Magdeburg 2007:) "Die christliche Taufe," *Ökumenische Rundschau* 2 (2007), 257.

22. (EKD:) *Die Taufe, eine Orientierungshilfe zu Verständnis und Praxis der Taufe in der evangelischen Kirche,* (Gütersloh: Gütersloher, 2008), 37.

23. Cf. Konrad Raiser, *Ein Herr, ein Glaube, eine Taufe. Die ekklesiologische Bedeutung der einen Taufe,* Presentation at the 222nd membership meeting of the ACK on March 12-13, 2008 in Erfurt, http://www.oekumene-koeln.de/pdf/Die%20ekklesiologische%20Bedeutung%20der%20einen%20Taufe.pdf (01.02.2014). Cf. also Konrad Raiser, "Gegenseitige Anerkennung der Taufe als Weg zu kirchlicher Gemeinschaft," in *Schritte auf dem Weg der Ökumene,* ed. Konrad Raiser (Frankfurt am Main: Lembeck, 2005), 197-217.

24. For the assessment of Magdeburg 2007 see also Rainer W. Burkart, "Die Taufe bei Konfessionswechsel als ökumenisches Problem," *Mennonitische Geschichtsblätter* 66 (2009), 31-48.

25. *Baptism, Eucharist and Ministry,* Baptism no. 1.

26. *Baptism, Eucharist and Ministry,* 2.

27. *Baptism, Eucharist and Ministry,* Baptism no. 6.

28. *Baptism, Eucharist and Ministry,* 2.

29. On the Mennonite understanding of baptism see, Marlin Jeschke, *Believers Baptism for Children of the Church* (Scottdale, PA: Herald Press, 1983). In terms of Mennonite positionality in the ecumenical debates on the Lima convergence texts see John H. Yoder, "Adjusting to the Changing Shape of the Debate on Infant Baptism," in *Oecumennisme opstellen, Festschrift for Henk B. Kossen,* ed. Arie Lambo (Amsterdam: Algemene Doopsgezinde Sociëteit, 1989), 209ff.

30. Cf. letter of the ACK-management of November 1, 2005 to the member and guest churches of the ACK (in the archive of Fernando Enns). Cf. Klaus Peter Voß, "Täuferisch-freikirchliche Positionen und Anliegen im aktuellen Gespräch über die gegenseitige Taufanerkennung," in *Ökumene und freikirchliches Profil: Beiträge zum zwischenkirchlichen Gespräch,* ed. Klaus Peter Voß (Berlin: WDL-Verlag, 2008), 162-177.

31. Letter of the AMG executive to the ACK, February 7, 2006 (personal archive of Fernando Enns).

32. *Grußwort der Arbeitsgemeinschaft Mennonitischer Gemeinden in Deutschland als eine der Kirchen aus der täuferischen Tradition im Ökumenischen Gottesdienst am 29. April 2007 in Magdeburg zur wechselseitigen Anerkennung der Taufe einiger Kirchen der ACK,* accessed June 20, 2014, http://www.mennoniten.de/fileadmin/downloads/Grusswort_wechselseitige_Taufanerkennung_07_Magdeburg.pdf.

33. *Ibid.*

34. Raiser, *Ein Herr, ein Glaube, eine Taufe.*

35. See all bilateral dialogues on national and international levels between Mennonites and Lutherans in Enns and Seiling, *Mennonites in Dialogue,* 115-307.

36. *Konkordie reformatorischer Kirchen in Europa (Leuenberger Konkordie) = Agreement Between Reformation Churches in Europe (Leuenberger Agreement). 1973,* dreisprachige Ausgabe mit einer (zweisprachigen) Einleitung von Friedrich-Otto Scharbau, im Auftrag des Exekutivausschusses für die Leuenberger Lehrgespräche, ed. Wilhelm Hüffmeier (Frankfurt am Main: Lembeck, 1993).

37. Cited in Enns and Seiling, *Mennonites in Dialogue,* 118; "Bericht des Dialogs zwischen Lutheranern und Mennoniten in Frankreich," in *Heilung der Erinnerungen,* 135.

38. *Mennonites in Dialogue,* 146. See *"Gemeinsame Erklärung der lutherisch-mennonitischen Gesprächskommission* zum Abschluss der Gespräche zwischen Vertretern der Vereinigten Evangelisch-Lutherischen Kirche Deutschlands (VELKD) und der Arbeitsgemeinschaft Mennonitischer Gemeinden in Deutschland (AMG) von September 1989 bis Dezember 1992," in *Heilung der Erinnerungen,* 159.

39. Cf. on the meaning of the *Exklusivartikel:* Eberhard Jüngel, *Das Evangelium von der Rechtfertigung des Gottlosen als Zentrum des christlichen Glaubens. Eine theologische Studie in ökumenischer Absicht,* 5th ed. (Tübingen: Mohr Siebeck, 2006), 127ff.

40. *Mennonites in Dialogue,* 147; Cf. Enns, *Heilung der Erinnerungen,* "Gemeinsame Erklärung der lutherisch-mennonitischen Gesprächskommission," 160.

41. *Mennonites in Dialogue,* 123-124; Cf. *Heilung der Erinnerungen,* "Bericht des Dialogs zwischen Lutheranern und Mennoniten in Frankreich," 135.

42. Cf. World Council of Churches, *The Nature and Mission of the Church: A Stage on the Way to a Common Statement,* Faith & Order Paper 198 (Geneva: World Council of Churches, 2005), §75.

43. *Ibid.*

44. It is arguable whether this interpretation was implied under (d) in the Magdeburg 2007 document.

45. *Ibid.,* §77.

46. *Mennonites in Dialogue,* 83; Cf. *Heilung der Erinnerungen,* 98.

47. *Baptism, Eucharist and Ministry,* baptism no. 7.

48. *Mennonites in Dialogue,* 146.

49. "Die Augsburgische Konfession. Confessio oder Bekanntnus des Glaubens etlicher Fürsten und Städte uberantwortet Kaiserlicher Majestat zu Augsburg Anno 1530 (CA)," in *Die Bekenntnisschriften der evangelisch-lutherischen Kirche (BSLK),* 12th ed. (Göttingen: Vandenhoeck & Ruprecht, 1998), 31-137. On the particular condemnations of the Anabaptists in the CA see, "Lutherische Stellungnahme zu den gegen die "Wiedertäufer" gerichteten Verwerfungen des Augburger Bekenntnisses von 1530," in *Heilung der Erinnerungen,* ed. Enns, 169-176. For the position of Luther on the Anabaptists see, Karl-Heinz zur Mühlen, "Luthers Tauflehre und seine Stellung zu den Täufern," in *Reformatorisches Profil. Studien zum Weg Martin Luthers und der Reformation,* zur Mühlen (Göttingen: Vandenhoeck & Ruprecht, 1995), 227-258.

50. *Mennonites in Dialogue,* 158; Cf. "Gemeinsame Erklärung der lutherisch-mennonitischen Gesprächskommission," 172.

51. *Mennonites in Dialogue,* 151; Cf. "Gemeinsame Erklärung der lutherisch-mennonitischen Gesprächskommission," 164.

52. *Mennonites in Dialogue,* 154; Cf. "Gemeinsame Erklärung der lutherisch-mennonitischen Gesprächskommission," 167.

53. *Mennonites in Dialogue,* 151; Cf. "Gemeinsame Erklärung der lutherisch-mennonitischen Gesprächskommission," 165.

54. *Mennonites in Dialogue,* 133.

55. *Mennonites in Dialogue,* 154; Cf. "Gemeinsame Erklärung der lutherisch-mennonitischen Gesprächskommission," 167.

56. *Mennonites in Dialogue,* 178.

57. *Mennonites in Dialogue,* 181.

58. Cf. Fernando Enns, "Mennonitisch-Lutherischer Dialog," in *Friedenskirche in der Ökumene, Mennonitische Wurzeln einer Ethik der Gewaltfreiheit* (Göttingen: Vandenhoeck & Ruprecht, 2003), 285-299.

59. *Baptism, Eucharist and Ministry*, baptism no. 8 in *Growth in Agreement*, 472.

60. *Mennonites in Dialogue*, 124.

61. *Mennonites in Dialogue*, 176; Cf. "Bericht des Verbindungskomitees," 190.

62. *Mennonites in Dialogue*, 159; Cf. "Lutherische Stellungnahme," in *Heilung der Erinnerungen*, ed. Enns, 173.

63. *Baptism, Eucharist and Ministry*, baptism no. 9. *Growth in Agreement*, 472.

64. *Growth in Agreement*, 472. *Baptism, Eucharist and Ministry*, 11. Cf. Udo Schnelle, s.v. "Taufe. II. Neues Testament," in *TRE*, vol. XXXII, 663-674.

65. See the reference to the early baptismal liturgy of Hippolytus (ca. 215), which explicitly mentions the initiation of children, who cannot speak for themselves (XX, 4), in Joint Working Group between the Roman Catholic Church and the World Council of Churches, Eighth Report, 1999-2005 (Geneva: WCC Publications, 2005), § 47.

66. "Die Taufe ist daher nicht nur ein einmaliger liturgischer Akt, sondern muss verstanden werden als Initiation in die Gemeinschaft der Glaubenden, als ein lebenslanger Prozess des Wachsens von christlicher Identität und Erkenntnis." [Baptism is not only a unique liturgical act, but must be understood as an initiation into the community of believers, as a lifelong process of the growth of Christian identity and knowledge.] Konrad Raiser, *Ein Herr, ein Glaube, eine Taufe*; See also (WCC:) *Eine Taufe: Auf dem Weg zur wechselseitigen Anerkennung christlicher Initiation*, ÖRK-Konsultation 2001; *Faith and Order at the Crossroads, Kuala Lumpur 2004, The Plenary Commission Meeting*, Faith & Order Paper 196, ed. Thomas F. Best (Geneva: WCC, 2005).

67. Joint Working Group between the Roman Catholic Church and the World Council of Churches, *Eighth Report, 1999-2005* (Geneva: WCC Publications, 2005).

68. *Ibid.*, 48, 53, 54.

69. *Ibid.*, 49, 57.

70. *Ibid.*, 57.

71. *Ibid.*, 56.

72. *Ibid.*, 57.

73. St Augustine, *On Baptism: Against the Donatists*, trans. J.R. King and revised by Chester D. Hartranft, Nicene and Post-Nicene Fathers, First Series, Vol. 4, ed. Philip Schaff (Buffalo, NY: Christian Literature Publishing Co., 1887.)

74. Joint Working Group between the Roman Catholic Church and the World Council of Churches, *Eighth Report, 1999-2005*, 56.

75. *Ibid.*, 57.

76. *Baptism, Eucharist and Ministry*, Baptism §11.

77. Joint Working Group, *Eighth Report, 1999-2005*, 56.

78. *Ibid.*, 57.

79. *Ibid.*, 57.

80. *Mennonites in Dialogue,* 152; Cf. "Gemeinsame Erklärung der lutherisch-mennonitischen Gesprächskommission," 177.

81. CPCE was formerly the Leuenberger Community of Churches

82. (Community of Protestant Churches in Europe, CPCE:) *Dialog zwischen der Europäischen Baptistischen Föderation (EBF) und der GEKE zur Lehre und Praxis der Taufe. Dialogue between the Community of Protestant Churches in Europe (CPCE) and the European Baptist Federation (EBF) on the Doctrine and Practice of Baptism*, Leuenberg documents 9, eds. Wilhelm Hüffmeier and Tony Peck (Frankfurt am Main: Lembeck, 2005). Paul S.

Fiddes describes from a Baptist perspective the permanent differences in Hüffmeier and Peck, *Dialogue between CPCE and EBF*, 211f. On the position of the Baptists see also Paul S. Fiddes, "Baptism and the Process of Christian Initiation," *Ecumenical Review: A Quarterly* (ER) 54/1 (2002), 48-65; Kim Strübind, "Baptistische Unbotmäßigkeit als notwendiges ökumenisches Ärgernis. Ist eine Verständigung in der Tauffrage möglich?," in *Gemeinschaft der Kirchen und gesellschaftliche Verantwortung*, FS for Erich Geldbach, eds. Lena Lybaek, Konrad Raiser and Stefanie Schardien (Münster: Lit, 2004), 20-30.

83. (Leuenberg Community:) *Versöhnte Verschiedenheit – der Auftrag der evangelischen Kirchen in Europa. Texte der 5. Vollversammlung der Leuenberger Kirchengemeinschaft in Belfast, 19.-25. Juni 2001*, eds. Wilhelm Hüffmeier and Christine-Ruth Müller (Frankfurt am Main: Lembeck, 2003), 281-292. See the presentations in the bilateral dialogues with Baptists in Kerner, *Gläubigentaufe und Säuglingstaufe*, 26-42 (Baptist-Protestant dialogue 1977), 62-76 (Baptist-Lutheran dialogue 1990), 77-86 (Waldensians/Methodists and Baptists in Italy 1990). Quoted in *Dialogue between the Community of Protestant Churches in Europe (CPCE) and the European Baptist Federation (EBF) on the Doctrine and Practice of Baptism*, Wilhelm Hüffmeier and Tony Peck, eds. (Frankfurt am Main: Verlag Otto Lembeck, 2005),10.

84. *Dialogue between CPCE and EBF*, 25.

85. *Dialogue between CPCE and EBF*, 19.

86. *Dialogue between CPCE and EBF*, 28.

87. *Dialogue between CPCE and EBF*, 27.

88. Cf. *Dialogue between CPCE and EBF*, 49.

89. It is different with the Baptist James McClendon, who classifies infant baptism as something deficient, which simply requires a "repair." He also insists upon repeating baptism for those already baptized when they are changing denominational membership. See James W. McClendon, *Systematic Theology*, vol. 2, *Doctrine* (Nashville, TN: Abingdon, 1994).

90. *Dialogue between CPCE and EBF*, 28, and CA, Art. IX, (see fn. 5).

91. Cf. André Birmelé, "Die Taufe in den ökumenischen Dialogen – *Baptism in Ecumenical Dialogues*," in *Dialogue between CPCE and EBF*, 52-103, here 83.

92. "Nature and Mission of the Church" 77.

93. Cf. *ibid.*, commentaries after §47 and §77.

94. On the designation and concept of "Believers' Church" see Donald F. Durnbaugh, *The Believers' Church: The History and Character of Radical Protestantism* (New York: Macmillan, 1968), cf. 2nd ed. (Scottdale, PA: Herald Press, 1985). On the sacramental understanding of the Anabaptists see John Rempel, *The Lord's Supper in Anabaptism. A Study in the Christology of Balthasar Hubmaier, Pilgram Marpeck and Dirk Philips*, Studies in Anabaptist and Mennonite History 33 (Waterloo, ON: Herald Press, 1993).

95. See Martin Hailers discussion of the concept of sacrament in Wolfhart Pannenberg und Jürgen Moltmann in Hailer, "Taufanerkennung bei bleibend unterschiedlicher Lehre?," 176ff.

96. Aurelius Augustinus, Tractat Ioh 80, 3. "The word is added to the element, and there results the Sacrament, as if itself also a kind of visible word," in reference to John 15:3. Translated by John Gibb, *Nicene and Post-Nicene Fathers*, First Series, Vol. 7, ed. Philip Schaff (Buffalo, NY: Christian Literature Publishing Co., 1888.) It is then

cited in Luther's Large Catechism; Cf. "Großen Katechismus Luthers," in *BSLK*, 694, 709 and in the "Schmalkaldischen Artikeln," in *BSLK*, 449f.

97. *Mennonites in Dialogue*, 150; Cf. "Gemeinsame Erklärung der lutherisch-mennonitischen Gesprächskommission," 163.

98. *Ibid.*

99. *Mennonites in Dialogue*, 150.

100. Gerhard May, ed. *Das Marburger Religionsgespräch 1529*, Texte zur Kirchen- und Theologiegeschichte, vol. 13 (Gütersloh: Gütersloher und Mohn, 1970). Cf. Martin Friedrich, *Von Marburg bis Leuenberg: Der lutherisch-reformierte Gegensatz und seine Überwindung* (Waltrop: Spenner, 1999).

101. On Luther's understanding of baptism see Albrecht Peters, *Die Taufe. Das Abendmahl.*, Kommentar zu Luthers Katechismen 4 (Göttingen: Vandenhoeck & Ruprecht, 1993).

102. Cf. John H. Yoder, *Täufertum und Reformation in der Schweiz. I: Die Gespräche zwischen Täufern und Reformatoren 1523-1538*, Schriftenreihe des Mennonitischen Geschichtsvereins (MGV) 6 (Karlsruhe: H. Schneider, 1962).

103. Cf. Birmelé, "Baptism in Ecumenical Dialogues," 62; Huldrych Zwingli, *Gesammelte Werke*, vol. 3 (Zurich: Theologischer Verlag, 1959), 757f.

104. Cf. Menno Simons, "Klare Beantwortung einer Schrift des Gellius Faber," in *Die vollständigen Werke Menno Simons*, trans. from Dutch, based on the Funk-edition 1876 (Aylmer/ON: Pathway, 1982), 120.

105. Cf. Andrea M. Dalton, "A Sacramental Believers Church: Pilgram Marpeck and the (Un)mediated Presence of God" in *New Perspectives in Believers Church Ecclesiology*, eds. Abe Dueck, Helmut Harder, and Karl Koop (Winnipeg, Manitoba: Canadian Mennonite University Press, 2010), 223-236. See Hans-Jürgen Goertz, "Täufergeschichtliche Aspekte zur Taufe," *Mennonitische Geschichtsblätter* 66 (2009), 7-30.

106. "It would be fruitful to have additional discussions of the relationship between the Catholic understanding of sacraments and the Mennonite understanding of ordinances, to further ascertain where additional significant convergences and divergences may lie." "Called to be Peacemakers," §144, *Mennonites in Dialogue*, 86.

107. *Mennonites in Dialogue*, 127.

108. Cf. Birmelé, "Baptism in Ecumenical Dialogues," 65.

109. Joint Working Group between the Roman Catholic Church and the World Council of Churches, Eighth report, 58.

110. Thomas F. Best and Günther Gassman, eds. *On the Way to Fuller Koinonia: Official Report of the Fifth World Conference on Faith and Order*, Faith and Order Paper no. 166 (Geneva: WCC, 1994), 231.

111. *Mennonites in Dialogue*, 176; "Bericht des Verbindungskomitees," 190.

112. *Mennonites in Dialogue*, 123.

113. Cf. "Schleitheim Articles" and other sources in Walter Klaassen, ed. *Anabaptism in Outline: Selected Primary Sources* (Kitchener: Herald Press, 1981), 101-117.

114. Cf. Walter Klaassen, "The Rise of the Baptism of Adult Believers in Swiss Anabaptism," in *Anabaptism Revisited: Essays on Anabaptist /Mennonite Studies in Honor of C. J. Dyck*, ed. Klaassen (Scottdale, PA: Herald Press, 1992), 85-97.

115. *Mennonites in Dialogue*, 132.

116. *Mennonites in Dialogue*, 127.

117. *Mennonites in Dialogue*, 128.

118. *Mennonites in Dialogue*, 143.

119. *Mennonites in Dialogue*, 128.
120. *Mennonites in Dialogue*, 128.
121. *Mennonites in Dialogue*, 154-55.
122. *Mennonites in Dialogue*, 164.
123. *Dialogue between CPCE and EBF*, 25.
124. Cf. S. Mark Heim, "Baptismal Recognition and the Baptist Churches," in *Baptism and the Unity of the Church*, eds. Michael Root and Risto Saarinen (Grand Rapids, MI: Eerdmans, 1998), 150-163.
125. "Hier hat die Lehre nicht das letzte Wort, geschweige denn das Kirchenrecht, auch letztlich nicht Fragen des Lebensstils und der religiösen Sitten. Aber hier ist ein die Differenzen der Texte umrandender Rahmen, der in der postmodernen Philosophie keinen beschreibbaren Ort und Inhalt hat." Ritschl, *Theorie und Konkretionen in der Ökumenischen Theologie*, 57.
126. "...den sich die noch nicht zu Partnern gewordenen Gruppen und Konfessionen leisten können und müssen, weil sie letztlich darin Gott zutrauen, die intellektuell schwer oder kaum zu überbrückenden Differenzen zwischen ihnen gnädig zu umfassen." Ritschl, *Theorie und Konkretionen in der Ökumenischen Theologie*, 57.

4. Missionary Ecumenism

1. See Sekretariat der Deutschen Bischofskonferenz, "Allen Völkern Sein Heil. Die Mission der Weltkirche," 23. Sept. 2004, *Die Deutschen Bischöfe* 76 (2004).
2. See Michael Bergunder and Jörg Haustein, eds. *Migration und Identität: Pfingstlich-charismatische Migrationsgemeinden in Deutschland*, Supplement to *Zeitschrift für Mission* 8 (2006). See also Alexander F. Gemeinhardt, ed. *Die Pfingstbewegung als ökumenische Herausforderung*, Bensheimer Hefte 103 (2005).
3. Geneva is the headquarters of the World Council of Churches.
4. The evangelically aligned Lausanne movement is named after the first International Congress on World Evangelization in 1974, which was held in Lausanne. It put evangelism in the foreground and consciously distanced itself from the missionary movement within the WCC. See Lausanner Bewegung Deutschland, ed. *Die Lausanner Verpflichtung (1974)*, (Stuttgart: [5]2000). Further documents found in John Stott, ed. *Making Christ known: Historic Mission Documents from the Lausanne Movement, 1974-1989* (Grand Rapids/MI: Eerdmans, 1997).
5. Thema der Jahrestagung der Deutschen Gesellschaft für Missionswissenschaft, Bad Urach, 12-14 September 2001, bei der der vorliegende Beitrag zunächst als Vortrag gehalten wurde. The theme in the present paper was first held as a lecture at the Annual Meeting of the Deutschen Gesellschaft für Missionswissenschaft in Bad Urach, 12-14 September 2001.
6. Symbolum Nicaenum or Nicene Creed. See Jaroslav Pelikan and Valerie R. Hotchkiss, eds. *Creeds and Confessions of Faith in the Christian Tradition* (New Haven, CT: Yale University Press, 2003). Even though this commitment is not always used explicitly, as found in the traditions of non-creedal-churches, they still share the Nicene-Constantinopolitan creed expressly and have never distanced themselves from it.
7. The Augsburg Confession in *The Book of Concord: The Confessions of the Evangelical Lutheran Church*, eds. Robert Kolb and Timothy J. Wengert (Minneapolis: Fortress

Press, 2000), 43.

8. See WCC, *Gospel and Culture*, Pamphlets 1-18 (Geneva: WCC, 1994-1997).

9. "Conference Message from Salvador," *International Bulletin of Missionary Research*, Vol. 21, No.2 April 1997, 54. See in German, *Zu einer Hoffnung berufen: Das Evangelium in verschiedenen Kulturen: Elfte Konferenz für Weltmission und Evangelisation in Salvador da Bahia 1996*, ed. Klaus Schäfer (Frankfurt: Lembeck, 1999), including "Botschaft der Konferenz," 117; Musimbi R. A. Kanyoro, "Zu einer Hoffnung berufen – Das Evangelium in verschiedenen Kulturen" in *ibid.*, 205-223. On the World Mission Conference see Fernando Enns, "Vom Paukenschlag in Canberra zu den vielen Trommeln in Salvador. Der Versuch einer historischen und theologischen Einordnung der XI. Weltmissionskonferenz des ÖRK in Salvador da Bahia/Brasilien 1996" in *ibid.*, 52-61.

10. See World Council of Churches, *The Nature and Purpose of the Church: A Stage on the Way to a Common Statement*, Faith & Order Paper 181 (2000), 28-30. See also Michael Welker, *Was geht vor beim Abendmahl?* (Stuttgart: Quell, 1999).

11. See *The Nature and Purpose of the Church*, 26-28. See also Erich Geldbach, *Taufe*, Ökumenische Studienhefte 5, Bensheimer Vol. 79 (Göttingen: Vandenhoeck & Ruprecht, 1996).

12. Thomas F. Best and Günther Gassman, eds. *On the Way to Fuller Koinonia: Official Report of the Fifth World Conference on Faith and Order*, Faith and Order Paper no. 166 (Geneva: WCC, 1994), 239.

13. Christine Lienemann-Perrin, *Mission und interreligiöser Dialog*, Bensheimer Vol. 93, Ökumenische Studienhefte 11 (Göttingen: Vandenhoeck & Ruprecht, 1999) 177.

14. See the related articles in Karl Müller and Theo Sundermeier, eds. *Lexikon missionstheologischer Grundbegriffe* (Berlin: Reimer, 1987). See also Dietrich Ritschl and Werner Ustorf, *Ökumenische Theologie – Missionswissenschaft*, Grundkurs Theologie 10,2 (Stuttgart: Kohlhammer, 1994).

15. See also, Karl Müller and Theo Sundermeier, eds. *Lexikon missionstheologischer Grundbegriffe* (Berlin: Reimer, 1987); Dietrich Ritschl and Werner Ustorf, *Ökumenische Theologie – Missionswissenschaft*, Grundkurs Theologie 10,2 (Stuttgart: Kohlhammer, 1994).

16. See Dietrich Werner, „Integration von Kirche und Mission. Ökumenische Erinnerung, missionarische Verpflichtung und unerledigte Aufgaben" in ÖR 3 (1998): 306-314.

17. (Ökumenischer Rat der Kirchen) "Berufung der Kirche zu Mission und Einheit" in *Ökumenische Dokumente. Quellenstücke über die Einheit der Kirche* (Göttingen: Vandenhoeck & Ruprecht 1962), 113-120.

18. Johannes Christiaan Hoekendijk, *Die Zukunft der Kirche und die Kirche der Zukunft* (Stuttgart: Kreuz, 1965).

19. Willem A. Visser 't Hooft, ed. *Neu Delhi 1961. Dokumentarbericht über die dritte Vollversammlung des ÖRK* (Stuttgart: Ev. Missionsverlag, 1962).

20. The Basel Mission Director Karl Hartenstein introduced the term "Missio Dei" at a World Mission Conference in Willingen, 1952. See Norman Goodall, ed. *Missions Under The Cross. Addresses delivered at the Enlarged Meeting of the Committee of the International Missionary Council at Willingen, in Germany, 1952* (London: Edinburgh House Press, 1953). The concept was quickly circulated, most of all by Georg F. Vicedom, *Missio Dei: Einführung in eine Theologie der Mission* (Munich: Kaiser, 1958). However, the concept was used in very different ways. See Theo Sundermeier, "The-

ologie der Mission" in Müller and Sundermeier, eds. *Lexikon missionstheologischer Grundbegriffe*, 470-495, esp. 475. See also Evangelisches Missionswerk in Deutschland, EMW, Missio Dei heute. Zur Aktualität eines missionstheologischen Schlüsselbegriffs, Red. durch Klaus Schäfer, Hamburg: EMW (und Evangelische Kirche in Kurhessen-Waldeck) 2003.

21. (WCC:) *Breaking Barriers: Nairobi 1975*, David M. Paton, ed. (London: SPCK, 1976), 46.

22. On this distinction see, Martin Luther, WA 6, 213, 14 (*Sermon von den guten Werken*, 1520).

23. Ferdinand Hahn, *Mission in neutestamentlicher Sicht*, Missionswissenschaftliche Forschungen New Series, Vol. 8 (Erlangen: Erlanger Verlag für Mission und Ökumene, 1999) 25.

24. See Fernando Enns, "Der Ökumenische Rat in Bewegung" in *Die Orthodoxen im Ökumenischen Rat der Kirchen*, Dagmar Heller and Barbara Rudolph, eds. Supplement to ÖR 74 (2004): 134-146.

25. See Wolfgang Huber, *Kirche* (Munich: Kaiser Verlag, 1988), 32ff.

26. Lienemann-Perrin, *Mission und interreligiöser Dialog*, 51-2.

27. See World Council of Churches, Central Committee, *Minutes of the Meeting, Potsdam 2001* (Geneva: WCC, 2001).

28. See the various positions of the WCC on mission in (WCC:) *"You are the light of the world": Statements on Mission by the World Council of Churches 1980-2005* (Geneva: WCC, 2005); Joachim Wietzke, ed. *Mission erklärt. Ökumenische Dokumente von 1972-1992* (Leipzig: Ev. Verlagsanstalt, in Zusammenarbeit mit der Deutschen Ev. Missionshilfe, 1993).

29. Werner, *Integration von Kirche und Mission*, 311.

30. See Robert Schreiter, "Globalisierung, Postmoderne und die neue Katholizität" in ÖR 2(2004): 139-159. This was further developed in *idem, The New Catholicity: Theology Between the Global and the Local* (Maryknoll, NY: Orbis, 1997).

31. *Church and World: The Unity of the Church and the Renewal of Human Community*, A Faith and Order Study Document, Faith and Order Paper No. 151
    (Geneva, WCC Publications, 1998); http://www.wcc-coe.org/wcc/assembly/modrep-e.html
    Gemeinsam auf dem Weg. Offizieller Bericht der Achten Vollversammlung des ÖRK, Harare 1998, hg. von Klaus Wilkens, Frankfurt/M: Lembeck 1999, Bericht des Vorsitzenden, 85.

32. See also the analysis by Jörg Hübner, *Globalisierung mit menschlichem Antlitz. Einführung in die Grundfragen globaler Gerechtigkeit* (Neukirchen-Vluyn: Neukirchener, 2004). Also see articles in *Kirchlicher Herausgeberkreis Jahrbuch Gerechtigkeit, Reichtum – Macht – Gewalt. Sicherheit in Zeiten der Globalisierung, Jahrbuch Gerechtigkeit II.*, (Oberursel: Publik-Forum, 2006).

33. Auf dem Weg zu einem gemeinsamen Verständnis und einer gemeinsamen Vision des ÖRK; in Gemeinsam auf dem Weg, 159-190, 1.8 und 2.9. [2.9]
    [http://www.oikoumene.org/en/resources/documents/assembly/2006-porto-alegre/3-preparatory-and-background-documents/common-understanding-and-vision-of-the-wcc-cuv]

34. Recommendations of the General Assembly on globalization in Gemeinsam auf dem Weg, 353. See also Junge Kirche 2/2001 "Fair geht vor – eine andere Globalisierung." In general see H. Russel Botman, "A Cry for Life in a Global Economic

Era" in Wallace M. Allston Jr. and Michael Welker, eds. *Reformed Theology: Identity and Ecumenicity* (Grand Rapids/MI: Eerdmans, 2003) 375-384; also Milan Opočenský, "Processus Confessionis" in *ibid.*, 385-397.

35. "Das Globale Ökumenische Aktionsbündnis ist ein neues und weite Teile der Ökumene einbindendes Netz für internationale Zusammenarbeit. (...) Durch das Bündeln von Mitteln und Erfahrungen der Partner im Netz sollen die prophetische Stimme und die Effizienz des ökumenischen Zeugnisses in aktuellen sozialen, politischen und wirtschaftlichen Fragen gestärkt werden. Viele beteiligen sich bereits: der ÖRK und seine Mitgliedskirchen, regionale ökumenische Organisationen und Gemeinschaften, kirchliche Hilfswerke, spezialisierte Netzwerke im Süden, weltweite christliche Gemeinschaften, internationale ökumenische und römisch-katholische Organisationen." in http://www.e-alliance.ch [10.09.2005].

36. "A Covenant for Action," http://www.e-alliance.ch/typo3conf/ext/naw_securedl/secure.php?u=0&file=fileadmin/user_upload/docs/EAA_CovenantforAction_EN.pdf&t=1422480942&hash=6c47327bab67a58a061d8f9da172cbeb (27 January 2015).

37. See the summary of some of the results in (Ökumenischer Rat der Kirchen / Team für Gerechtigkeit, Frieden und Schöpfung:) Alternative Globalisierung im Dienst von Menschen und Erde (AGAPE – *Alternative Globalisation Addressing People and Earth*), Hintergrunddokument, Genf: ÖRK 2005.

38. See the exegetical works by Ulrich Luz, *Das Evangelium nach Matthäus (Mt 26-28)*, Evangelisch-Katholischer Kommentar zum Neuen Testament (EKK) Vol.1,4, Josef Blank, ed. (Düsseldorf/Zürich: Benziger und Neukirchen-Vluyn: Neukirchener, 2002).

39. "The Alliance identified the HIV/AIDS pandemic as one of the gravest challenges to health and also to prospects of social and economic development and global security. HIV/AIDS' impact is a symptom of systematic economic problems such as under-investment in health and unequal access to effective treatment. It is thus a particularly appropriate issue for churches; while governments and private companies need to be involved, churches need to speak out on causes, prevention, treatment and consequences." in http://www.e-alliance.ch [10.09.2005].

40. In Zimbabwe, people told me that already in some regions there were hardly more trees to be found, because all the wood had been used for the coffins of those who died of AIDS. And if you have not seen someone for a long time, then you do not ask about them because the answer would already have been clear. Companies often trained several young people at the same time for one job, because they assumed that many would soon die. More recent developments in Africa are presented and interpreted by Ezra Chitando, *Acting in Hope, African Churches and HIV/AIDS 2* (Geneva: WCC, 2007).

41. See the chapter below on the Decade to Overcome Violence.

42. According to Jacques Matthey, Coordinator of the WCC-teams for Mission and Evangelization, in *Pressemitteilung des ÖRK* (PR-01-31). Meanwhile the World Missions Conference took place in Athens, see documents in Jacques Matthey, ed. *Come Holy Spirit, Heal and Reconcile! Report of the WCC Conference on World Mission and Evangelism, Athens, Greece 2005* (Geneva: World Council of Churches, 2008).

5. Action-Oriented Ecumenism

1. Wolfgang Huber, *Überlegungen zum Stand der Ökumene. Vortrag vor der Hamburgischen Kommende des Johanniterordens*, 25 August 2007, in www.ekd.de/ausland_oekumene/070825_huber_hamburg.html (1.3.2010).

2. Ulrich Körtner, "In der Lehre getrennt, im Handeln geeint? Chancen und Grenzen ökumenischer Sozialethik," in Friederike Nüssel, ed. *Theologische Ethik der Gegenwart. Ein Überblick über zentrale Ansätze und Themen* (Tübingen: Mohr Siebeck, 2009), 271–294, here: 276.

3. Walter Dietrich and Moisés Mayordomo, eds. *Gewalt und Gewaltüberwindung in der Bibel* (Zurich: TVZ, 2005), 109.

4. *Ökumenische Versammlung für Gerechtigkeit, Frieden und Bewahrung der Schöpfung, Dresden – Magdeburg – Dresden: Eine Dokumentation* (Berlin: Aktion Sühnezeichen/Friedensdienste, 1990), 131.

5. Cf. Reinhard Frieling, *Der Weg des ökumenischen Gedankens*, Zugänge zur Kirchengeschichte 10, (Göttingen: Vandenhoeck & Ruprecht, 1992), 313; Wolfram Weiße, *Reich Gottes: Hoffnung gegen Hoffnungslosigkeit*, Ökumenische Studienhefte 6 (Göttingen: Vandehoeck & Ruprecht, 1997), 15–18.

6. Frieling, *Der Weg des ökumenischen Gedankens*, 313.

7. Weiße, *Reich Gottes*, 99.

8. See the many titles of the Central Committee of the WCC, particularly the Commission of the Churches on International Affairs (CCIA), which regularly publishes volumes, e.g. Dwain C. Epps, ed. *The Churches in International Affairs, Reports 1999–2002* (Geneva: WCC, 2005), *Reports 2003–2006* (Geneva: WCC, 2007).

9. Wolfgang Lienemann, *Frieden*, Ökumenische Studienhefte 10 (Göttingen: Vandenhoeck & Ruprecht, 2000), 156–158.

10. See Ruth Rouse and Stephen Charles Neill, eds. *A History of the Ecumenical Movement*, Vol. 1: 1517–1948 (Geneva: WCC, 2004).

11. In the tradition of the Roman Catholic Church the correlation of ecumenical and peace-ethical engagement and theological reflection is found more explicitly, as is clear in "Called Together to be Peacemakers." http://www.vatican.va/roman_curia/pontifical_councils/chrstuni/mennonite-conference-docs/rc_pc_chrstuni_-doc_20110324_mennonite_en.html (1.4.2014)

12. Frieling, *Der Weg des ökumenischen Gedankens*, 313.

13. "Ein Rahmenkonzept für die Dekade zur Überwindung von Gewalt. Vom Zentralausschuss angenommenes Arbeitsdokument (Genf 1999)," in *Ökumenische Rundschau* 4/2000, 473–478.

14. See "Schwerpunkte der zukünftigen Arbeit des Ökumenischen Rates der Kirchen – Der Bericht des Ausschusses für Programmrichtlinien," in *In deiner Gnade, Gott, verwandle die Welt: Offizieller Bericht der Neunten Vollversammlung des Ökumenischen Rates der Kirchen, Porto Alegre 2006*, Klaus Wilkens, ed. (Frankfurt am Main: Lembeck, 2007), 183–194, see 193 (§ 26). Cf. Luis N. Rivera-Pagán, ed. *God, in your Grace: Official Report of the Ninth Assembly of the World Council of Churches* (Geneva: WCC Publications, 2007).

15. The first proposal was sent to the churches for discussion and reaction: (Arbeitsgemeinschaft Christlicher Kirchen in Deutschland:) *Internationale Ökumenische*

Erklärung zum Gerechten Frieden, Erster Entwurf, Ökumenischen Centrale / ACK, ed. (Frankfurt aM, 2009). After receiving many responses, a second, completely different proposal was developed by the WCC; see below, II.6.

16. A comprehensive compilation of peace ethics positions, statements, messages and speeches of the World Council of Churches and the Roman Catholic Church from the years 1946 to 1982 is found in (WCC:) *Peace and Disarmament. Documents of the World Council of Churches, presented by the Commission of the Churches on International Affairs,* and Documents of the Roman Catholic Church, presented by The Pontifical Commission "Iustitia et Pax," (Geneva and Vatican, 1982). A further overview of the most important clarifications and documents of the WCC between 1948 and 1985 is found in Ans J. van der Bent, *Vital Ecumenical Concerns: Sixteen Documentary Surveys* (Geneva: WCC, 1986), 116–146. Van der Bent stresses that in that period almost all areas of activity of the WCC were significantly involved in addressing the issues of peace and justice (116). Reinhard Frieling provides a good overview of the progress of the peace ethics discussions until 1990 in a separate section of his book on the emergence and development of the ecumenical movement. See Frieling, *Der Weg des ökumenischen Gedankens,* 313–330.

17. *Fernando Enns,* "Ehre sei Gott – und Friede auf Erden. Der lange Weg zu einer ökumenischen Friedenskonvokation," in Dagmar Heller *et al., "Arise, shine!" Ecumenical Visions in Times of Change: Festschrift für Konrad Raiser* (Frankfurt aM: Lembeck, 2008), 322–333.

18. See the historical development in Frieling, *Der Weg des ökumenischen Gedankens,* 41–48.

19. On the origin and development see Harmjam Dam, *Der Weltbund für Freundschaftsarbeit der Kirchen, 1914-1948: Eine ökumenische Friedensorganisation* (Frankfurt am Main: Lembeck, 2001).

20. See Heinz-Elmar Tenorth et al., eds. *Friedrich Siegmund-Schultze (1885-1969): Ein Leben für Kirche, Wissenschaft und soziale Arbeit* (Stuttgart: Kohlhammer, 2008); Stefan Grotefeld, *Friedrich Siegmund-Schultze: Ein deutscher Ökumeniker und christlicher Pazifist,* Heidelberger Untersuchungen zu Widerstand, Judenverfolgung und Kirchenkampf im Dritten Reich Bd.7 (Gütersloh: Kaiser, 1995).

21. See Hans Gressel, ed. *Versöhnung und Friede: 50 Jahre Internationaler Versöhnungsbund, 3. August 1964* (Dortmund, 1964). See Friedrich Siegmund-Schultze, *Friedenskirche, Kaffeeklappe und die ökumenische Vision. Texte 1919-1969,* Wolfgang Grünberg, ed. (Munich: Kaiser, 1990); Heinrich Foth et al., *Lebendige Oekumene, Festschrift für Friedrich Siegmund-Schultze* (Witten: Luther-Verlag, 1965).

22. See Thomas Aquinas, *Summa Theologica* II/2, q 40. On the history and interpretation of the doctrine of just war see: Wolfgang Huber and Hans-Richard Reuter, *Friedensethik* (Stuttgart: Kohlhammer, 1990), 145ff. A distinction is made between *ius ad bellum* (criteria: just cause, legitimate authority, last resort, proportionality, right intention, and the reasonable prospect of success) and *ius in bello* (criteria: the appropriateness of the means, non-discrimination, limited use of weapons). Further discussion of the criteria of just war, see: Michael Haspel, *Friedensethik und humanitäre Intervention: Der Kosovo-Krieg als Herausforderung evangelischer Friedensethik* (Neukirchen-Vluyn: Neukirchener, 2002).

23. See Huber and Reuter, *Friedensethik,* 119-126.

24. See conference reports in G.K.A. Bell, ed. *The Stockholm Conference 1925: The Official Report of the Universal Christian Conference on Life and Work held in Stockholm, 19-30*

August, 1925 (New York: Oxford University Press, 1926). The following resolution on disarmament is not found within the English publication.

25. Translated here from the German text of "Resolution 1" found in "Die Kirche und die internationalen Beziehungen. Bericht des Sub-Komitees 1 der Kommission III," *Die Stockholmer Weltkirchenkonferenz. Vorgeschichte, Dienst und Arbeit der Weltkonferenz für Praktisches Christentum, 19.-30. August 1925, Amtlicher deutscher Bericht,* Adolf Deißmann, ed. (Berlin: Furche-Verlag, 1926), 77.

26. See Friedrich Siegmund-Schulze, ed. *Die Weltkirchenkonferenz von Prag: Gesamtbericht des Kongresses für Frieden und Freundschaft, gehalten vom 24. bis 30. August 1928,* (Berlin: Evangelischer Preßverband für Deutschland, 1928).

27. "Report and Resolution on the Present Problem of Disarmament Regarded from the Point of View of the Christians Churches, agree to at the World Conference at Prague, August 29th, 1928" *Minutes of the International Committee held at Prague, Czechoslovakia August 25, 28 & 30, 1928* (London: The World Alliance for Promoting International Friendship through the Churches, 1928), 68. Cf. Frieling, *Der Weg des ökumenischen Gedankens,* 67f.

28. See the social analyses in the reports from the world conferences held in Stockholm 1925 and Oxford 1937. *The Message and Decisions of Oxford on Church, Community and State,* Universal Christian Council for Life and Work, ed. (Chicago: Willett Clark & Co., 1937)

29. See the differing attitudes of the Churches in the USA., France and Germany: Gerhard Besier, *Krieg – Frieden – Abrüstung: Die Haltung der europäischen und amerikanischen Kirchen zur Frage der deutschen Kriegsschuld 1914-1933* (Göttingen: Vandenhoeck & Ruprecht, 1982).

30. *The Message and Decisions of Oxford on Church, Community and State,* 77.

31. *Ibid.,* 83.

32. *Ibid.*

33. *Ibid.*

34. *Ibid.,* 84.

35. *"The Church and Peoples of the World,"* Address at Fanø, August 28, 1934; *DBW* 13:302- 306.

36. Cited in Ferdinand Schlingensiepen, *Dietrich Bonhoeffer 1906-1945* (London: T&T Clark, 2010), 171; Cf. *DBWE* 13, 307ff.

37. Huber and Reuter, *Friedensethik,* 123. Besides the general aversion toward war in Bonhoeffer's family, at the beginning of his theological reflection Dietrich Bonhoeffer hardly dealt the question of war and peace. This only changed, along with his reflections on ecumenism, during his studies in New York. There he met the avowed pacifist Jean Lasserre, who argued for a consistent implementation of the commandment to be peacemakers in the Sermon on the Mount. Bonhoeffer was initially rather critical toward this view. During the ecumenical conference in 1934, when a Swedish delegate asked him what he would do in a time of war he answered "I would ask that God give me the power to not take up arms." [Ich bitte darum, dass Gott mir die Kraft geben wird, nicht zu den Waffen zu greifen] On the categories of militarist and pacifist he preferred not to accept such blatant distinctions, as they are not ultimately helpful in responding to the difficult questions of war peace. See Fernando Enns, "Dietrich Bonhoeffer: Saint? – Ecumenist! – Pacifist? Remembering Dietrich Bonhoeffer" in Jeremy M. Bergen, Paul G. Doerksen, Karl

Koop, eds. *Creed and Conscience: Essays in Honour of A. James Reimer* (Kitchener: Pandora, 2007), 167-180.

38. Dietrich Bonhoeffer, "Zur theologischen Begründung der Weltbundarbeit," *DBW* 11, Eberhard Amelung and Christoph Strohm, eds. 327-344; *Idem*, "Ansprache auf der Internationalen Jugendkonferenz in Gland 1932," *DBW* 11, 350-357.

39. "leidenschaftlich darum mühte, das theologische und ekklesiologische Selbstverständnis der ökumenischen Bewegung zu klären, sodass sie mit Vollmacht Gottes Gebot des Friedens in einer Welt verkündigen konnte, die den Sinn für eine lebensfähige Ordnung verloren hatte." Konrad Raiser, "Bonhoeffer und die ökumenische Bewegung: Historische Rekonstruktion und Bedeutung für heute" in *Ökumenische Rundschau* 2/2005, 205-222, 207.

40. Dietrich Bonhoeffer, *No Rusty Swords*, vol. 1 (New York: Harper & Row, 1965), 290.

41. *Ibid.*, see also Michael Welker, *Theologische Profile* (Frankfurt am Main: Hansisches Druck- und Verlagshaus, 2009), 83-102.

42. "dass die Kirche Jesu Christi wegen ihrer tiefen Bindung an den einen, gemeinsamen Versöhner niemals Nationalkirche sein kann, sondern der ökumenischen Verbundenheit aller Teilkirchen in der einen Weltchristenheit immer den Vorzug geben muss." Heinz Eduard Tödt, *Theologische Perspektiven nach Dietrich Bonhoeffer*, Ernst-Albert Scharffenorth, ed. (Gütersloh: Kaiser, 1993), 175.

43. "weil sie wissen, dass sie damit die Waffen auf Christus selbst richteten." *DBW*, 13, 299.

44. *DBW*, 13:298ff.

45. See Immanuel Kant, *Zum ewigen Frieden: Ein philosophischer Entwurf (1795/96)*; in *Werke*, Wilhelm Weischedel, ed. Vol.9 (Darmstadt: Wissenschaftliche Buchgesellschaft, 1968), 195-251. Cf. Otfried Höffe, ed. *Immanuel Kant: Zum ewigen Frieden*, Klassiker Auslegen Vol.1 (Berlin: Akademie Verlag, 2004). Kant rejected armament as a means to deterring war, just as Bonhoeffer did later.

46. "'The Church and Peoples of the World,' Address at Fanø, August 28, 1934" in *London: 1933-1935*, vol. 13, *DBWE*, ed. Keith Clements, trans. Isabel Best (New York: Fortress Press, 2007), 308.

47. *DBWE* 13:302- 306.

48. See Bonhoeffer, Zur theologischen Begründung der Weltbundarbeit, 338f.

49. Walter Rauschenbusch was one of the key influences of this movement. See Robert T. Handy, ed. *The Social Gospel in America: 1870-1920* (New York: Oxford UP, 1966); Dores Robinson Sharpe, *Walter Rauschenbusch* (New York: Macmillan, 1942).

50. See Raiser, *Bonhoeffer und die ökumenische Bewegung*, 212.

51. Bonhoeffer, Zur theologischen Begründung der Weltbundarbeit, 341. Cf. Bonhoeffer, *No Rusty Swords* (London: Fontana, 1977), 153–69.

52. See Dietrich Bonhoeffer, *Ethics*, *DBW*, Vol. 6.

53. See Bonhoeffer, Zur theologischen Begründung der Weltbundarbeit, 331-335 and Bonhoeffer, Kirche und Völkerwelt, 298f.

54. Raiser, *Bonhoeffer und die ökumenische Bewegung*, 213.

55. Karl Barth, *Church Dogmatics* 1,2, 630.

56. See Piet Naudé, "Reformed Confessions as Hermeneutical Problem: A Case Study of 'the Belhar Confession'" in Wallace M. Alston and Michael Welker, eds. *Reformed Theology, Identity and Ecumenicity, Biblical Interpretation in the Reformed Tradition* (Grand Rapids: Eerdmans, 2007), 242-260; Dirk J. Smit, "Social Transformation and Confessing the Faith? Karl Barth's View on Confession Revisited" *Scriptura*

72/2000, 76-86; Niko N. Koopman, *"Status confessionis* im Blick auf Apartheid, *processus confessionis* zu Fragen der ungerechten Weltwirtschaft: zur Rezeption der Barmer Theologischen Erklärung in Südafrika" ÖR 2/2009, 167-180.

57. Rolf Ahlers, ed. *The Barmen Theological Declaration of 1934: The Archeology of a Confessional Text* (Lewiston: Edwin Mellen, 1986).

58. See Willem A. Visser 't Hooft, *Ursprung und Entstehung des Ökumenischen Rates der Kirchen,* Beiheft zur ÖR 44 (Frankfurt/M.: Lembeck, 1983).

59. "Message: First Assembly of the WCC, Amsterdam, 1948," in Kinnamon, ed. *The Ecumenical Movement,* 21.

60. *Ibid.,* 22.

61. "Krieg soll nach Gottes Willen nicht sein." See "Die Kirche und die internationale Unordnung. Bericht der Sektion IV," in *Die Unordnung der Welt und Gottes Heilsplan,* 116-141, 117.

62. *Ibid.*

63. *Ibid.,* 118.

64. "ein moderner Krieg mit seinen allumfassenden Zerstörungen [kann] niemals ein Akt der Gerechtigkeit sein." *Ibid;* also cited in *God, in your Grace...,* 304.

65. The various positions are named in *Die Unordnung der Welt und Gottes Heilsplan,* 118.

66. See the discussion of typologization in Haspel, *Friedensethik;* Huber and Reuter, *Friedensethik;* Heinrich Bedford-Strohm, "Kirche – Ethik – Öffentlichkeit. Zur ethischen Dimension der Ekklesiologie," *Verkündigung und Forschung* 2/2006, 4-19.

67. "Peace is the Will of God: By Historic Peace Churches, International Fellowship of Reconciliation Committee, Geneva, October 1953"; in Douglas Gwyn, et al., *A Declaration on Peace: In God's People the World's Renewal Has Begun: A Contribution to Ecumenical Dialogue Sponsored by Church of the Brethren, Fellowship of Reconciliation, Mennonite Central Committee, Friends General Conference* (Waterloo: Herald Press, 1991), 53-78, Appendix A.

68. "The avoidance of suffering is no criterion of good: on the contrary, we are warned, as disciples of Jesus, to expect suffering...," in *ibid.* Cf. on the notion of being prepared to suffer as an identity marker of the Church: John H. Yoder, *Body Politics: Five Practices of the Christian Community before the Watching World* (Nashville: Discipleship Resources, 1993).

69. On the concept of "messianic ethics" see: Stanley Hauerwas, *The Peaceable Kingdom: A Primer in Christian Ethics* (Notre Dame: University of Notre Dame, 1986). Hauerwas explicitly refers to the thought of John H. Yoder.

70. See Fernando Enns, *The Peace Church and the Ecumenical Community: Ecclesiology and the Ethics of Nonviolence* (Kitchener: Pandora Press, 2007).

71. WCC: *Christians and the Prevention of War in an Atomic Age: A Theological Discussion* (Geneva: WCC, 1955). The Central Committee distanced itself later from the results of this study, which contained a pacifist exhortation. On the various ethical discussions in the General Assembly of the WCC, see: Ans J. van der Bent, *Commitment to God's World: A Concise Critical Survey of Ecumenical Social Thought* (Geneva: WCC, 1995).

72. See (WCC:) *Breaking Barriers: Nairobi 1975,* David M. Paton, ed. (London: SPCK, 1976). From this impulse the peace initiative "Ohne Rüstung Leben" [living without armaments] arose from Germany.

73. See V. D. Schneeberger, ed. *"...and on Earth Peace,"* Documents of the First All-Christian Peace Assembly, 13th-18th June 1961, Prague (Prague: Christian Peace Conference,

1961).

74. Cf. Josef Smolík, *"Josef L.Hromádka* und die ökumenische Bewegung" in *ÖR* 1980, 327-341; Josef Smolík and Heinz Kloppenburg, eds. *Von Amsterdam nach Prag, Festschrift für Josef Lukl Hromádka*, Evangelische Zeitstimmen 45/46 (Hamburg: Reich, 1969).

75. Karl Barth, Josef Lukl Hromádka, Josef B. Souček, Martin Rohkrämer, eds. *Freundschaft im Widerspruch. Der Briefwechsel zwischen Karl Barth, Josef L. Hromádka und Josef B. Souček 1935-1968* (Zurich: Theologischer Verlag, 1995); Josef Lukl Hromádka, *An der Schwelle des Dialogs zwischen Christen und Marxisten* (Frankfurt/M.: Stimme-Verlag, 1965).

76. See Jan Milič Lochman, *Wahrheitssuche und Toleranz. Lebenserinnerungen eines ökumenischen Grenzgängers*, Rudolf Bohren, trans. (Zurich: TVZ, 2002).

77. From West Germany the participants included, among others: Ernst Wolf, Friedrich-Wilhelm Marquardt and Martin Stöhr. Heinold Fast represented the Mennonites. From East Germany came Hanfried Müller, Klaus-Peter Hertzsch, among others. For a complete list see: *"...And on Earth Peace,"* 172-187.

78. On the history of the Christian Peace Conference in Prague, see Reinhard Scheerer, ed. *Gott schreibt auch auf krummen Linien gerade. Zur Geschichte der Christlichen Friedenskonferenz (CFK)* (Frankfurt/M.: Haag und Herchen Verlag, 1993).

79. See Gerhard Lindemann, "'Sauerteig im Kreis der gesamtchristlichen Ökumene': Das Verhältnis zwischen der Christlichen Friedenskonferenz und dem Ökumenischen Rat der Kirchen" in Gerhard Besier, Armin Boyens and Gerhard Lindemann, eds. *Nationaler Protestantismus und Ökumenische Bewegung. Kirchliches Handeln im Kalten Krieg (1945-1990)* (Berlin: Duncker & Humblot, 1999), 653-932. On the debates see Heinz Joachim Held, *Der Ökumenische Rat der Kirchen im Visier der Kritik. Eine kritische Lektüre der Forschungsarbeit "Ökumenischer Rat der Kirchen und Evangelische Kirche in Deutschland zwischen West und Ost"* (Frankfurt am Main: Lembeck, 2001); Katharina Kunter, *Erfüllte Hoffnungen und zerbrochene Träume. Evangelische Kirchen in Deutschland im Spannungsfeld von Demokratie und Sozialismus (1980-1993)* (Göttingen: Vandenhoeck & Ruprecht, 2006).

80. The sociologist Johan Galtung developed distinctions between various concepts of violence. See Johan Galtung, "Gewalt, Frieden und Friedensforschung" in Dieter Senghaas, ed. *Kritische Friedensforschung* (Frankfurt am Main: Suhrkamp Verlag, 1971), 55-104.

81. See Frieling, *Der Weg des ökumenischen Gedankens*, 322.

82. *Christians in the Technical and Social Revolutions of our Time: World Conference on Church and Society, Geneva, July 12-16, 1966: The Official Report*, M.M. Thomas and Paul Albrecht, ed. (Geneva: MCC, 1967), 115-116.

83. See Wolfram Weiße, *Südafrika und das Antirassismusprogramm: Kirchen im Spannungsfeld einer Rassengesellschaft*, Studien zur interkulturellen Geschichte des Christentums Bd.1 (Bern: Lang, 1975); *Die Kirchen, das südliche Afrika und der politische Kontext*, Kirchliche Zeitgeschichte (KZG) 9,2 (Göttingen: Vandenhoeck & Ruprecht, 1996).

84. See Fernando Enns and Philip A. Potter, "Was sollen wir tun? Wegbereiter einer handlungsorientierten Ökumene" in Christian Möller et al., eds. *Wegbereiter der Ökumene im 20. Jahrhundert* (Göttingen: Vandenhoeck & Ruprecht, 2005), 354-375.

85. See Michael Blume, *Satyagraha: Wahrheit und Gewaltfreiheit, Yoga und Widerstand bei M.K.Gandhi* (Gladenbach: Hinder u. Deelmann, 1987); Huber and Reuter, *Friedensethik*, 123f.

86. See Michael Haspel and Britta Waldschmidt-Nelson, *Martin Luther King: Leben, Werk und Vermächtnis* (Weimar: Wartburg-Verlag, 2008).

87. David Gill, "Violence, Non-violence and the Struggle for Justice," *Ecumenical Review* 25/4 1973, 430-446.

88. WCC: "Violence, Nonviolence and the Struggle for Social Justice: A Statement commended by the WCC Central Committee, 1973," in *Violence, Nonviolence and Civil Conflict* (Geneva: WCC, 1983), 16–32.

89. WCC: "Violence, Nonviolence and Civil Conflict: The Report of the Corrymeela Consultation," in *Violence, Nonviolence and Civil Conflict* (Geneva: WCC, 1983), 9-15.

90. David Gill, ed. *Gathered for Life, Official report Sixth Assembly of the WCC, Vancouver, Canada* (Geneva: WCC, 1983). On the general process see Ulrich Schmitthenner, *Der konziliare Prozeß: Gemeinsam für Gerechtigkeit, Frieden und Bewahrung der Schöpfung: Ein Kompendium* (Idstein: Meinhardt Text und Design, 1998); *Idem*, Textsammlung zum konziliaren Prozess (bilingual), CD-Rom 1999.

91. Raiser, *Bonhoeffer und die ökumenische Bewegung*, 211.

92. "Declaration on Peace and Justice" in *Gathered for Life*, 132.

93. See Lothar Coenen and Wolfgang Traumüller, eds. *Vancouver 83. Zeugnisse, Predigten, Ansprachen, Vorträge, Initiativen von der Sechsten Vollversammlung des Ökumenischen Rates der Kirchen in Vancouver, B.C./Kanada, 24. Juli – 10. August 1983*, Beiheft zur ÖR 48 (Frankfurt am Main: Lembeck, 1984), 203-206, 206. In the former East Germany there was a conciliar process in 1988-89 toward the Ecumenical Assemblies for Peace, Justice and Integrity of Creation. See *Ökumenische Versammlung für Gerechtigkeit, Frieden und Bewahrung der Schöpfung, Dresden – Magdeburg – Dresden. Eine Dokumentation* (Berlin: Aktion Sühnezeichen/Friedensdienste, 1990).

94. "Wir bitten die Kirchen der Welt, ein Konzil des Friedens zu berufen. Der Friede ist heute die Bedingung des Überlebens der Menschheit. Er ist nicht gesichert." Cited in Carl Friedrich von Weizsäcker, *Die Zeit drängt: Eine Weltversammlung der Christen für Gerechtigkeit, Frieden und die Bewahrung der Schöpfung* (Munich: Hanser, 1986). See also Götz Planer-Friedrich, ed. *Frieden und Gerechtigkeit: Auf dem Weg zu einer ökumenischen Friedensethik* (Munich: Kaiser, 1989); Hans-Richard Reuter, ed. *Konzil des Friedens: Beiträge zur ökumenischen Diskussion I* (Heidelberg: FEST, 1987), Huber and Reuter, *Friedensethik*, 204ff..

95. Cited in Raiser, *Ecumenism in Transition: A Paradigm Shift in the Ecumenical Movement?* (Geneva: WCC, 1991), 118.

96. See Raiser, *Bonhoeffer und die ökumenische Bewegung*, 212.

97. WCC: *Now Is the Time: Final Document and Other Texts of the World Convocation on Justice, Peace and the Integrity of Creation, Seoul 1990* (Geneva: WCC, 1990). Cited in Enns, *The Peace Church and the Ecumenical Community*, 32.

98. *Now is the Time*, 8.

99. Michael Kinnamon and Brian E. Cope, eds. *The Ecumenical Movement: An Anthology of Key Texts and Voices* (Grand Rapids: Eerdmans, 1997), 317-318.

100. Kinnamon and Cope, *The Ecumenical Movement*, 318-324.

101. All three documents of this study process (Costly Unity, Costly Commitment and Costly Obedience) are found in Thomas F. Best und Martin Robra, eds. *Ecclesiology and Ethics: Ecumenical Ethical Engagement, Moral Formation and the Nature of the Church* (Geneva: WCC, 1997). Cf. Duncan Forrester, *The True Church and Morality: Reflections on Ecclesiology and Ethics* (Geneva: WCC, 1997).

102. "Ecumenical ethical reflection and action (…) are intrinsic to the nature and life of the church" in Best and Robra, *Ecclesiology and Ethics*, ix.
103. "Ecclesiology and Christian ethics must stay in close dialogue, each honouring and learning from the distinctive language and thought-forms of the other," *ibid.*
104. See *ibid.*, 53-61 and 72-87. See also Enns, *The Peace Church and the Ecumenical Community*, 35-43.

6. Developing the "Decade to Overcome Violence": 1994-1999

1. On the concept of "culture of peace" see György Konrád, "Kultur des Friedens?" in Horst-Eberhard Richter, ed. *Kultur des Friedens* (Gießen: Psychosozial-Verlag, 2001), 39-49. "What is a culture of peace? Perhaps something that does not need to be mentioned by name. What we do everyday, without realizing it." [Was Kultur des Friedens ist? Vielleicht etwas, das nicht beim Namen genannt werden muss. Was wir täglich tun, ohne es so zur Kenntnis zu nehmen.] (49).
2. "No other issue has been discussed more widely and intensively in the ecumenical movement from its very beginning and in the World Council of Churches since 1948 than peace and disarmament." Ans van der Bent, *Commitment to God's World: A Concise Critical Survey of Ecumenical Thought* (Geneva: WCC, 1995), 107. See also various accounts of the history of the WCC, e.g. Reinhard Freiling, *Der Weg des ökumenischen Gedankens: Eine Ökumenekunde: Zugänge zur Kirchengeschichte*, vol. 10 (Göttingen: Vandenhoeck & Ruprecht, 1992), esp. vol. VI: *Friedensbewegung und Friedensethik*, 313ff.; Wolfgang Lienemann, *Frieden*, Ökumenische Studienhefte 10 (Göttingen: Vandenhoeck & Ruprecht, 1991), esp. Part B. "Ökumenische Konflikte und Klärungen"; Wolfram Weisse, *Praktisches Christentum und Reich Gottes: Die ökumenische Bewegung Life and Work, 1919-1937* (Göttingen: Vandenhoeck & Ruprecht, 1991); Gerhard Besier, *Krieg – Frieden – Abrüstung: Die Haltung der europäischen und amerikanischen Kirchen zur Frage der deutschen Kriegs-schuld 1914-1933* (Göttingen: Vandenhoeck & Ruprecht, 1982).
3. See Reinhold Niebuhr, *An Interpretation of Christian Ethics* (San Francisco: Harper & Row, 1987); *Idem*, Reinhold Niebuhr – Theologian of Public Life, ed. Larry L. Rassmussen (London: Collins, 1989).
4. See Hans-Martin Barth, ed. *Innerer Friede und die Überwindung von Gewalt. Religiöse Traditionen auf dem Prüfstand*, Internationales Rudolf-Otto-Symposion Marburg, (Schenefeld: EB-Verlag, 2007); Hagen Berndt, *Gewaltfreiheit in den Weltreligionen: Vision und Wirklichkeit*, (Gütersloh: Gütersloher, 1998). Pete Hämmerle and Thomas Roithner, eds. *Dem Rad in die Speichen fallen: Stimmen von FriedensnobelpreisträgerInnen und das Österreichische Netzwerk für eine Kultur des Friedens und der Gewaltfreiheit: Ein Arbeitsbuch*, Österreichisches Netzwerk für Frieden und Gewaltfreiheit, (Haid: Roithner, 2003).
5. "International Decade for a Culture of Peace and Non-Violence for the Children of the World 2001-2010" in http://www.un-documents.net/a56r5.htm [01.03.2016].
6. (World Council of Churches) "A Basic Framework For The Decade To Overcome Violence"
   https://www.oikoumene.org/en/resources/documents/commissions/in-

ternational-affairs/peace-and-disarmament/peace-concerns/a-basic-framework-for-the-decade-to-overcome-violence (01.06.2016)

7. See Geiko Müller-Fahrenholz, ed. *Faszination Gewalt. Aufklärungsversuche*, (Frankfurt/M.: Lembeck, 2006).

8. See Wolfgang Lienemann, "Gewalt, Gewaltlosigkeit" in *Evangelisches Kirchenlexikon*, Vol.2, 164.

9. *Ibid.* 163ff.

10. In French, *La Décennie vaincre la* violence: *les Eglises en quête de réconciliation et de paix;* Spanish: *El Decenio para Superar la Violencia: las iglesias en busca de reconciliación y de paz.*

11. See Johan Galtung, "Gewalt, Frieden und Friedensforschung" in Manfred Funke, ed. *Friedensforschung: Entscheidungshilfe gegen Gewalt* (Munich: List, 1975), 99-132.

12. Johan Galtung, "Gewalt, Frieden und Friedensforschung" in ed. Dieter Senghaas, *Kritische Friedensforschung* (Frankfurt/M.: Suhrkamp, 1971), 55-104, 57.

13. Robert McAfee Brown, *Religion and Violence* (Westminster: John Knox Press, 1987).

14. Wolfgang Lienemann, "Kritik der Gewalt" in Walter Dietrich and Wolfgang Lienemann, eds. *Gewalt wahrnehmen – von Gewalt heilen: Theologische und religionswissenschaftliche Perspektiven* (Stuttgart: Kohlhammer, 2004), 7-30, 12.

15. WHO, ed. World Report on Violence and Health. Summary, 2002, p.4. http://www.who.int/violence_injury_prevention/violence/world_report/en/summary_en.pdf (01.03.2016).

16. "Constitution and Rules of the World Council of Churches" (updated 2013) https://www.oikoumene.org/en/resources/documents/assembly/2013-busan/adopted-documents-statements/wcc-constitution-and-rules. (01.06.2016)

17. Cf. the expression by Adorno, the Frankfurter School philosopher: "There is no right life in the wrong one." Theodor W. Adorno, *Minima Moralia* (I,18).

18. See the exegesis of Matt 5:38-42 in Walter Wink, *Naming the Powers: The Language of Power in the New Testament* (Philadelphia: Fortress Press, 1984); idem, *Unmasking the Powers: The Invisible Forces that Determine Human Existence* (Philadelphia: Fortress Press, 1986), idem, *Engaging the Powers: Discernment and Resistance in a World of Domination* (Philadelphia: Fortress Press, 1992).

19. Cf. for example, D. Preman Niles, *Between the Flood and the Rainbow Interpreting the Conciliar Process of Mutual Commitment (Covenant) to Justice, Peace and the Integrity of Creation* (Geneva: WCC, 1992).

20. *Violence, Nonviolence and Civil Conflict* (Geneva: WCC, 1983), 9.

21. This insight has been clearly recognized in the discussion of the WCC especially with the disintegration of Yugoslavia and the genocide in Rwanda, namely as a new kind of challenge to the joint action of the churches.

22. See the concept in Herfried Münkler, *Die neuen Kriege* (Hamburg: Rowohlt, 2003); Frank Ettrich, "'Neue Kriege' und die Soziologie des Krieges: Anmerkungen zu drei neueren Arbeiten der soziologischen Kriegs- und Gewaltforschung" in *Gewalt – interdisziplinär* (Hamburg: Lit, 2002), 195-221; Wolfgang Schreiber, "Neue Kriege oder neue Gewaltkonflikte?" in *Idem, Söldner, Schurken, Seepiraten* (Münster: Lit, 2010), 47-60; August Pradetto, "Neue Kriege" in *Handbuch Militär und Sozialwissenschaften* (Wiesbaden: VS, 2006), 214-225; Andreas Zumach, *Die kommenden Kriege: Ressourcen, Menschenrechte, Machtgewinn – Präventivkrieg als Dauerzustand?* (Köln: Kiepenheuer & Witsch, 2005).

23. See Hans Krech, *Asymmetrische Konflikte – eine existentielle Herausforderung für die NATO: welche Lehren können aus dem Irak-Krieg (2003-2008) und dem Luftkrieg im Libanon*

2006 für die Lösung des Afghanistan-Konfliktes gezogen werden? Hamburg, Wissenschaftliches Forum für Internationale Sicherheit (Bremen: Ed. Temmen, 2008).

24. See the further description in Donald E. Miller, "The Historic Peace Churches in the Asian Context," in *idem* et al, *Overcoming Violence in Asia: The Role of the Churches in Seeking Cultures of Peace* (Telford: Cascadia, 2011), 43–47. Cf. also Margot Käßmann, *Gewalt überwinden: Eine Dekade des Ökumenischen Rates der Kirchen* (Hanover: LVH, 2000); *idem, Gewalt überwinden,* ÖR 3/1998, 329–336.

25. (WCC:) *Programme to Overcome Violence: An Introduction* (Geneva: World Council of Churches, 1995), 17.

26. See passim, Thomas F. Best and Günther Gassman, eds. *On the Way to Fuller Koinonia: Official Report of the Fifth World Conference on Faith and Order,* Faith and Order Paper no. 166 (Geneva: WCC, 1994).

27. (WCC:) *Theological Perspectives on Violence and Nonviolence: A Study Process* (Geneva: WCC, 1998).

28. See the unpublished study (WCC:) "Ethnic Identity, National Identity, and the Search for the Unity of the Church," Faith & Order with the collaboration of Justice, Peace and Creation team. This study resulted in (WCC:) Participating in God's Mission of Reconciliation. A Resource for Churches in Situations of Conflict, Faith & Order Paper 201, Geneva: World Council of Churches. See also: (WCC:) *Christian Perspectives on Theological Anthropology,* Faith & Order Paper 199, Geneva: World Council of Churches.

29. See Thomas F. Best, Martin Robra, eds. *Ecclesiology and Ethics. Ecumenical Ethical Engagement, Moral Formation and the Nature of the Church* (Geneva: WCC Publications, 1998); Lewis S. Mudge, *The Church as Moral Community: Ecclesiology and Ethics in Ecumenical Debate* (New York: Continuum, 1998).

30. Margot Kässmann, *Gewalt Überwinden: Eine Dekade des Ökumenisches Rates der Kirchen* (Hannover: LVH, 2000), 336.

31. See the development of this campaign in WCC, *Report of the Consultation on the Programme to Overcome Violence,* Rio de Janeiro, Brazil, 13-18 April 1996 (Geneva: World Council of Churches, 1996).

32. Dafne Plou, *Peace to the Cities: Creative Models of Building Community amidst Violence* (Geneva: WCC, 1998).

33. See "Die Realität der Gewalt in der Bibel" in Dietrich and Mayordomo, *Gewalt und Gewaltüberwindung in der Bibel,* 28-104.

34. See Jennifer Turpin and Lester R. Kutz, *The Web of Violence: From Interpersonal to Global* (Urbana and Chicago: University of Illinois Press, 1997).

35. Plou, *Peace to the Cities,* 26.

36. Nisha Arunatilake, Sisira Jayasuriya, Saman Kelegama, eds. *The Economic Cost of the War in Sri Lanka,* Research Studies, Macroeconomic Policy and Planning Series, 13. Colombo: *Institute of Policy Studies.*

37. Plou, *Peace to the Cities,* 56.

38. See Ulrich Duchrow and Franz J. Hinkelammert, *Property for People, not for Profit: Alternatives to the Global Tyranny of Capital* (Geneva: World Council of Churches, 2004).

39. "It is very difficult for a Tamil to understand the official discourse of a 'war to peace'. It is as if they are being told, 'We are killing you to help you'." Plou, *Peace to the Cities,* 54.

40. E.g. "Baker-House" in Dorchester, a neighbourhood of Boston.

41. For example, the *agentes de futuro* involving more than 10,000 young adult volunteers in Rio, agents of peace in Belfast, and others.

42. "The new movement decided to take the name 'Viva Rio' as a way of affirming that it was possible to create a trend among citizens to overcome violence, promoting dignity and equal opportunities for all." Plou, *Peace to the Cities*, 8.

43. "The network promotes the idea of working for peace while developing mutually respectful relations within and throughout a divided community. It is an open network, with the capacity to maintain liaisons with dozens of private and public groups and organizations." *Ibid.*, 27.

44. *Ibid.*, 51.

45. *Ibid.*, 56.

46. See *A Basic Framework For The Decade To Overcome Violence*,
    https://www.oikoumene.org/en/resources/documents/commissions/international-affairs/peace-and-disarmament/peace-concerns/a-basic-framework-for-the-decade-to-overcome-violence
    "A Basic Framework for the Decade to Overcome Violence," working document adopted by the WCC central committee, Geneva, 1999, *Minutes of the Fiftieth Meeting of the Central Committee* (Geneva: WCC, 1999).

47. Jürgen Moltmann, *The Spirit of Life: A Universal Affirmation*, trans. Margaret Kohl (London: SCM Press, 1992), 277.

48. Excerpts from the '*Together on the Way Being Together Under the Cross in Africa: The Assembly Message*' including the prayer. http://www.wcc-coe.org/wcc/assembly/fmesc-e.html
    (02.01.2016)

49. In "3.8. Report of the Programme Guidelines Committee: HEARINGS PHASE II," *ibid.* Cf. http://www.wcc-coe.org/wcc/assembly/fpgc-e.html (02.01.2016)

50. *Ibid.*

51. See *A Basic Framework For The Decade To Overcome Violence*.

52. "A Basic Framework," https://www.oikoumene.org/en/resources/documents/commissions/international-affairs/peace-and-disarmament/peace-concerns/a-basic-framework-for-the-decade-to-overcome-violence (02.01.2016)

53. *Ibid.*

54. *Ibid.*

55. See Emmanuel Clapsis, "Ambivalenz, Subjektivität und spirituelles Leben. Für eine Kultur des Friedens durch Achtung von Andersartigkeit" in ÖR 2/2006, 183-200; *Idem, ed. Violence and Christian Spirituality. An Ecumenical Conversation* (Geneva: WCC and Brookline/MA: Holy Cross Orthodox Press, 2007), especially the contributions from the Orthodox tradition in the chapter, "Contributions towards an Ecumenical Spirituality," 236ff.

56. Käßmann, *Gewalt überwinden*, 330.

57. On this concept see Dietrich Ritschl, "Gottes Gegenentwurf zur Menschlichen Weltgestaltung," in *idem, Theorie und Konkretion in der Ökumenischen Theologie: Kann es eine Hermeneutik des Vertrauens inmitten differierender semiotischer Systeme geben?*, Studien zur systematischen Theologie und Ethik, 37 (Münster: Lit, 2003), 119–142.

58. See Walter Dietrich and Christian Link, *Die dunklen Seiten Gottes*, Vol. 1: *Willkür und Gewalt*, Vol. 2: *Allmacht und Ohnmacht* (Neukirchen-Vluyn: Neukirchener, 2009).

59. See these theses in Jan Assmann, e.g. in *Moses der Ägypter: Entzifferung einer Gedächtnisspur* (Munich: Hanser, 1998); *idem, Monotheismus und die Sprache der Gewalt*, Wiener

Vorlesungen, 116 (Vienna: Picus, 2006).Cf. Alfons Fürst, ed. *Friede auf Erden? Die Weltreligionen zwischen Gewaltverzicht und Gewaltbereitschaft* (Freiburg i.Br: Herder, 2006).

60. See (WCC:) *Nurturing Peace, Overcoming Violence: In the way of Christ for the sake of the World. An invitation to a process of theological study and reflection on Peace, Justice and Reconciliation during the Decade to Overcome Violence: Churches Seeking Peace and Reconciliation 2001–2010*, Programme desk on Theological Study and Reflection on Peace, Faith & Order (Geneva: WCC, 2003).

61. See Jörg Frey and Jens Schröter, eds. *Deutungen des Todes Jesu im Neuen Testament* (Tübingen: Mohr Siebeck, 2005).

62. See Gerhard Sauter, ed. *Versöhnung als Thema des Theologie* (Gütersloh: Gütersloher Verlagshaus, 1997).

63. Anselm of Canterbury, *Cur Deus Homo?* (London: Griffith, Farran, Browne & Co., 1909).

64. This approach is further developed by J. Denny Weaver, *The Nonviolent Atonement* (Grand Rapids: Eerdmans, 2011). See also the various works by John Howard Yoder, especially *Preface to Theology: Christology and Theological Methods* (Grand Rapids: Brazos, 2002). Further discussion of Mennonite positions found in Willard Swartley, ed. *Violence Renounced: René Girard, Biblical Studies and Peacemaking*, IMS Studies in Peace and Scripture 4 (Telford, PA: Pandora, 2000).

65. On the interpretation of mimetic violence see, René Girard, *Things Hidden since the Foundation of the World: Research undertaken in collaboration with J.-M. Oughourlian and G. Lefort*, S. Bann and M. Metteer, trans. (Stanford: Stanford University Press, 1987); *idem*, *Violence and the Sacred*, P. Gregory, trans. (Baltimore: The Johns Hopkins University Press, 1977); *idem*, *The Scapegoat*, Y. Freccero, trans. (Baltimore: The Johns Hopkins University Press, 1986).

66. See Martin Hailer, *Götzen, Mächte und Gewalten*, Biblisch-theologische Schwerpunkte 33 (Göttingen: Vandenhoeck & Ruprecht, 2008).

67. "Here we have for the first time to do with someone who is not the slave of any power, of any law or custom, community or institution, value or theory…Thus it is his death that provides his victory." With reference to Phil 2:9-11. John H. Yoder, *The Politics of Jesus*, 2nd Ed., 147.

68. On the distinctions between various concepts of *Gerechtigkeit* (justice/righteousness) see: Ottfried Höffe, *Gerechtigkeit: Eine philosophische Einführung* (Munich: Beck, 2001).

69. There is a collection of German ecumenical documents on this theme in Stierle, Werner, Heider, eds. *Ethik für das Leben, 100 Jahre Ökumenische Wirtschafts- und Sozialethik, Quellenedition ökumenischer Erklärungen, Studientexte und Sektionsberichte des ÖRK von den Anfängen bis 1996* (Rothenburg o.d. Tauber: Ernst Lange-Institut, 1996).

70. According to the Rome Statue (2002), Art. 7, "crimes against humanity" are defined as follows: (a) Murder; (b) Extermination; (c) Enslavement; (d) Deportation or forcible transfer of population; (e) Imprisonment or other severe deprivation of physical liberty in violation of fundamental rules of international law; (f) Torture; (g) Rape, sexual slavery, enforced prostitution, forced pregnancy, enforced sterilization, or any other form of sexual violence of comparable gravity; (h) Persecution against any identifiable group or collectivity on political, racial, national, ethnic, cultural, religious, gender as defined in paragraph 3, or other grounds that are universally recognized as impermissible under international law, in connection

with any act referred to in this paragraph or any crime within the jurisdiction of the Court; (i) Enforced disappearance of persons; (j) The crime of apartheid; (k) Other inhumane acts of a similar character intentionally causing great suffering, or serious injury to body or to mental or physical health. http://legal.un.org/icc/statute/rome fra.htm (02.02.2016)

71. See Heinz-Gerhard Justenhoven, *Internationale Schiedsgerichtsbarkeit: Ethische Norm und Rechtswirklichkeit* (Stuttgart: Kohlhammer, 2006).

72. On the concept of "punitive" (Strafzwecke) see: Jens Kreuter, *Staatskriminalität und die Grenzen des Strafrechts: Reaktionen auf Verbrechen aus Gehorsam aus rechtsethischer Sicht*, Öffentliche Theologie Bd. 9, (Gütersloh: Kaiser, 1997).

73. See Howard Zehr, *Changing Lenses: A New Focus for Crime and Justice* (Scottdale, PA: Herald Press, 1995).

74. See Bernd Janowski, *Die rettende Gerechtigkeit*, Beiträge zur Theologie des Alten Testaments 2 (Neukirchen-Vluyn: Neukirchener, 1999).

75. On the concept of "schöpferischen Gerechtigkeit" (creative justice) see Günther Thomas, "Gottes schöpferische Gerechtigkeit," in Ruth Heß and Martin Leiner, eds. *Alles in Allem: Eschatologische Anstöße* (Neukirchen-Vluyn: Neukirchener, 2005), 109–132, 117.

76. In contrast to tribunals or court processes the Commissions have no power to bring cases before court. Audrey R. Chapman, "Truth Commissions of Forgiveness and Reconciliation" in Rodney L. Petersen and Raymond G. Helmick, eds. *Forgiveness and Reconciliation. Religion, Public Policy, and Conflict Transformation* (Philadelphia: Templeton Press, 2002), 257-277. Definition: "Truth commissions are temporary bodies mandated by governments or international agencies to investigate and make findings about acts and patterns of violence and gross human rights violations that took place during a specified period of time (…) truth commissions can go beyond a court of law and render a moral judgement about what was wrong and justifiable and in that way help to frame the events in a new national narrative of acknowledgement, accountability, and civic values," *ibid.*, 257. "In a few situations, nongovernmental organisations and church agencies have also sponsored the work of unofficial truth commissions," *ibid.*, fn 2.

77. See Heinrich Bedford-Strohm, ed. "… *und das Leben der zukünftigen Welt": Von Auferstehung und Jüngstem Gericht* (Neukirchen: Vluyn, 2007); Gregor Etzelmüller, "… *zu richten die Lebenden und die Toten": Zur Rede vom Jüngsten Gericht im Anschluss an Karl Barth* (Neukirchen-Vluyn: Neukirchener, 2001).

78. Cf. Jürgen Moltmann, *Trinität und Reich Gottes: Zur Gotteslehre* (Munich: Kaiser, 1994)

79. See Christoph Schwöbel and Colin E. Gunton, eds. *Persons, Divine and Human* (Edinburgh: T&T Clark, 1991).

7. The "Decade to Overcome Violence": 2001-2011

1. "Memorandum and Recommendations on Response to Armed Conflict and International Law. Recommendations adopted by the Central Committee and memorandum received and commended to the churches, Geneva, 26 August - 3 September 1999" in World Council of Churches, Central Committee, *Minutes and Reports of the Meeting*, (Geneva: WCC, 1999). https://www.oikoumene.org/en/resources/documents/commissions/international-affairs/commission-on-

international-affairs-policy/memorandum-and-recommendations-on-response-to-armed-conflict-and-international-law

2. "The Protection of Endangered Populations in Situations of Armed Violence" in http://www.oikoumene.org/en/resources/documents/commissions/international-affairs/commission-on-international-affairs-policy/the-protection-of-endangered-populations-in-situations-of-armed-violence-toward-an-ecumenical-ethical-approach (2.2.2016).

3. WCC, Together on the Way: *Official Report of the Eighth Assembly*, 5.8. A Statement on Human Rights, Sect. 4.4, http://wcc-coe.org/wcc/assembly/hr-e.html. (8.1.2016)

4. This argument has been constantly put forward by the Orthodox Churches. See "Final report of the Special Commission on Orthodox Participation in the WCC" 14 February 2006, https://www.oikoumene.org/en/resources/documents/assembly/2006-porto-alegre/3-preparatory-and-background-documents/final-report-of-the-special-commission-on-orthodox-participation-in-the-wcc?set_language=en (01.08.2016)

5. To read the document as received, see "The Protection of the Endangered Populations in situations of Armed Violence: Toward an Ecumenical Ethical Approach," Document No. PI 2 rev, http://www.wcc-coe.org/wcc/who/cc2001/pi2rev-e.html (01.02.2016).

6. WCC, Central Committee, Geneva, 26 August - 2 September 2003, "The Responsibility to Protect: Ethical and Theological Reflections," https://www.oikoumene.org/en/resources/documents/central-committee/2003/the-responsibility-to-protect-ethical-and-theological-reflections (01.03.2016).

7. See "Erklärung zum Nachkriegsirak," Ökumenischer Rat der Kirchen, Zentralausschuss, Geneva, 26. August - 2. September 2003, http://www2.wcc-coe.org/ccdocuments2003.nsf/index/pub-3.l-en.html (01.03.2010).

8. "Vulnerability and Security: Current Challenges in Security Policy from an Ethical and Theological Perspective," prepared by the Commission on International Affairs in Church of Norway Council on Ecumenical and International Relations; in https://kirken.no/nb-NO/church-of-norway/resources/peace-justice-and-human-rights/vulnerability-and-security/?id=1386121 (08.01.2016).

9. *Ibid.*, 29.

10. (Evangelische Kirche in Deutschland:) "Schritte auf dem Weg des Friedens. Orientierungspunkte für Friedensethik und Friedenspolitik. Ein Beitrag des Rates der EKD (1993)," ed. Kirchenamt der EKD in *EKD Texte* 48, Hannover, 2001.

11. Further on the position of EKD see Haspel, *Friedensethik und humanitäre Intervention: Der Kosovo-Krieg als Herausforderung evangelischer Friedensethik*, (Neukirchen-Vluyn: Neukirchener, 2002). See also Catholic scholars: Heinz-Gerhard Justenhoven and Gerhard Beestermöller, eds. *Gerechter Friede – Weltgemeinschaft in der Verantwortung: Zur Debatte um die Friedensschrift der deutschen Bischöfe* (Stuttgart: Kohlhammer, 2003), especially: Arnulf von Scheliha, "'Gerechter Friede' in der Auslegung der christlichen Konfessionen. Das Wort der deutschen Bischöfe im Vergleich mit den Orientierungspunkten des Rates der EKD," 104-112.

12. This position is presented in greater detail here, in order that some of the nuances, which are sometimes not grasped, can be better understood. Cf. Michael Haspel, *op cit.*, 82: "The pacifist testimony of the Historic Peace Churches – such as the Mennonites – deserves the utmost respect. ... In the perspective of 'pacifism by conviction' there is no need to develop a concept for criteria concerning the limited

application of military force in exceptional situations, because any use of military force must appear to be obsolete by its assumed normative requirements. This is an ethically respectable position, however, with regard to the resolution of international political conflicts as a comprehensive conception it can provide little regulative potential." [Das pazifistische Zeugnis der Historischen Friedenskirchen – wie der Mennoniten – verdient größten Respekt. [...] In der Perspektive des ‚Gesinnungspazifismus' besteht keine Notwendigkeit, eine Konzeption für Kriterien des begrenzten Einsatzes militärischer Gewalt in Ausnahmesituationen zu entwickeln, da von den eingenommenen normativen Voraussetzungen her jegliche militärische Gewaltanwendung obsolet erscheinen muss. Dies ist eine ethisch respektable Position, die allerdings in Hinsicht auf die Lösung internationaler politischer Konflikte als umfassende Konzeption wenig regulatives Potential zur Verfügung stellen kann.]

13. See Enns, Holland, Riggs, *Seeking Cultures of Peace.*
14. (Historic Peace Churches:) "Just Peacemaking: Toward an Ecumenical Ethical Approach from the Perspective of the Historic Peace Churches," in *ibid.*, 232-242.
15. *Ibid.*
16. *Ibid.*, 234-241.
17. "Vulnerable Populations at Risk: Statement on the Responsibility to Protect 23 February 2006,"
    https://www.oikoumene.org/en/resources/documents/assembly/2006-porto-alegre/1-statements-documents-adopted/international-affairs/report-from-the-public-issues-committee/responsibility-to-protect?set_language=en
18. See the same argumentation in the more recent peace statement by the EKD: *Aus Gottes Frieden leben – für gerechten Frieden sorgen: Eine Denkschrift des Rates der EKD* (Gütersloh: Gütersloher, 2007).
19. See Semegnish Asfaw, Guillermo Kerber, Peter Weiderud, eds. *Responsibility to Protect. Ethical and Theological Reflections* (Geneva: World Council of Churches, 2005). Cf. Konrad Raiser, "Verpflichtung zum Schutz. Völkerrechtliche und ethische Aspekte ‚Humanitärer Intervention," in *idem, Schritte auf dem Weg der Ökumene* (Frankfurt/M.: Lembeck, 2005), 292-312.
20. See *epd-Dokumentationen* 20/2005 and 30–31/2005: Thementeil I: Die Überwindung von Gewalt und das Reich Gottes (Heiko Lietz, Arbeitslosigkeit als persönliches und gesellschaftliches Problem / Persönliches Zeugnis, Franz Segbers, Dein Reich komme – Überwindung von Gewalt im Lichte des Reiches Gottes), Thementeil II: Täter und Opfer (Salomea Genin, ›Unsere Zukunft hängt davon ab, wie viel wir vergessen dürfen und an was wir uns erinnern müssen‹, Urs Eigenmann: Gottes rechtfertigendes Handeln – Befreiung aus der Opfer-TäterFixierung), Halbzeitbilanz: Auswertung der 1. Hälfte der ›Dekade zur Überwindung von Gewalt – Kirchen für Frieden und Versöhnung‹, Fernando Enns, Bericht des Beobachters der Konsultation.
21. Jürgen Habermas, "Glauben und Wissen. Die Rede des diesjährigen Friedenspreisträgers des deutschen Buchhandels" in *FAZ* Nr.239, October 14 2001, 9; *idem, Zwischen Naturalismus und Religion: Philosophische Aufsätze*, (Frankfurt/M.: Suhrkamp, 2005). The "return to religion" in philosophy should not be overlooked, e.g., contributions by Hilary Putnam, Charles Taylor, Richard Rorty, Jacques Derrida and Gianni Vattimo.

22. See Wolfgang Huber, *Gerechtigkeit und Recht: Grundlinien christlicher Rechtsethik*, 3rd ed., (Gütersloh: Gütersloher, 2006), Ch. IV, Gerechtigkeit und Menschenwürde, 265ff; Michael Durst, Hans J. Münk and Katrin Bentele, eds. *Theologie und Menschenrechte*, Theologische Berichte Vol. 31 (Freiburg/Schweiz: Paulusverlag, 2008).

23. On this thesis see the contribution by Rudolph von Sinner, "Ökumene im 21. Jahrhundert: Thesen zur Diskussion," in Fernando Enns, Martin Hailer, Ulrike Link-Wieczorek, eds. *Profilierte Ökumene: Bleibend Wichtiges und jetzt Dringliches. FS für Dietrich Ritschl* (Frankfurt am Main.: Lembeck, 2009), 76–93. See discussions in (WCC:) *Reflections on Ecumenism in the 21st Century* (Geneva: WCC, 2004); (WCC:) *Ecumenism in the 21st Century: Report of the Consultation convened by the World Council of Churches, Chavannes-de-Bogis, Switzerland, 30 November to 3 December 2004* (Geneva: WCC, 2005); (WCC:) "Reconfiguration – Neugestaltung der ökumenischen Bewegung," *ÖR* 1/2005. The works of Philip Jenkins are foundational for this discussion, e.g. Philip Jenkins, *The Next Christendom: The Coming of Global Christianity* (New York: Oxford University Press, 2007) idem, *The New Faces of Christianity: Believing the Bible in the Global South* (New York: Oxford University Press, 2006).

24. See Reinhard Hempelmann and Johannes Kandel, eds. *Religionen und Gewalt. Konflikt- und Friedenspotentiale in den Weltreligionen*, Kirche – Konfession – Religion Bd. 51 (Göttingen: V&R unipress, 2006).

25. See the concept of "regulative principles" in George A. Lindbeck, *Christliche Lehre als Grammatik des Glaubens. Religion und Theologie im postliberalen Zeitalter*, Theol. Bücherei Bd. 90 (Munich: Kaiser, 1994). See also Thomas Wabel, "Sprachspiel und Wirklichkeit. Zum Gegenstandsbezug der Rede von Gott und seinen ökumenischen Konsequenzen," in Enns, Hailer, Link-Wieczorek, *Profilierte Ökumene*, 94–123.

26. See speech at the consultation by Franz Segbers, "Dein Reich komme – Überwindung von Gewalt im Lichte des Reiches Gottes," in *epdDokumentation* 20/2005.

27. See Ingolf U. Dalferth and Andreas Hunziker, eds. *Mitleid: Konkretionen eines strittigen Konzepts*, Religion in Philosophy and Theology 28 (Tübingen: Mohr Siebeck, 2007).

28. Walter Dietrich, "Der rote Faden im Alten Testament," in *EvTheol* 3/1989, 232–250; Frank Crüsemann, *Die Tora: Theologie und Sozialgeschichte des alttestamentlichen Gesetzes* (Gütersloh: Kaiser, 2005).

29. Guillermo Kerber, "From Violence to Justice. Keynote Speech to a Seminar on "Overcoming violence: Rethinking our ministry of reconciliation" Ecumenical Institute Bossey, 8 August 2001, www.wcc-coe.org/wcc/what/international/kerber.html (01.02.2016).

30. Klara Butting, ed. *Träume einer gewaltfreien Welt: Bibel – Koran – praktische Schritte*, Glaubenszeugnisse unserer Zeit 4 (Wittingen: Erev-Rav, 2000).

31. See Dieter Dölling and Gerson Trüg, *Täter-Opfer-Ausgleich. Eine Chance für Opfer und Täter durch einen neuen Weg im Umgang mit Kriminalität; Kurzfassung des 1997 vorgelegten Gutachtens der Forschungsgruppe Täter-Opfer-Ausgleich für das Bundesministerium der Justiz*, Bundesministerium der Justiz, ed. 1st Ed. (Mönchengladbach: Forum-Verlag Godesberg, 1998); Erich Marks, ed. *Täter-Opfer-Ausgleich: Vom zwischenmenschlichen Weg zur Wiederherstellung des Rechtsfriedens* (Bonn: Forum-Verlag Godesberg, 1990).

32. Manfred Cierpka, *Faustlos: Das Buch für Eltern und Erziehende* (Freiburg i.Br.: Herder, 2005).

33. http://schrittegegentritte.hkdh.de/pub/english-information.php (2.2.2016).

34. www.ziviler-friedensdienst.org/ (2.2.2016).

35. See Judith Herman, *Die Narben der Gewalt: Traumatische Erfahrungen verstehen und über-winden* (Paderborn: Junfermann, 2006); Hannes Fricke, *Das hört nicht auf: Literatur, Trauma und Empathie* (Göttingen: Wallstein, 2004).

36. Donald E. Miller, Scott Holland, Dean Johnson, Lon Fendall, eds. *Seeking Peace in Africa: Stories from African Peacemakers* (Telford, PA: Cascadia, 2007).

37. See Konrad Raiser, "Remarks to the Bienenberg Consultation," in Enns, Holland, Riggs, eds. *Seeking Cultures of Peace,* 19–28; idem, *For a Culture of Life: Transforming Globalization and Violence* (Geneva: WCC, 2002), 75–140; idem, "Gewalt überwinden: Ökumenische Reflexionen zu einer Kultur aktiver und lebensfreundlicher Gewalt-freiheit," in Enns, *Dekade zur Überwindung von Gewalt,* 11–30; idem, "On the Eve of the Third Millenium," in *To be the Church* (Geneva: WCC, 1997), 17–37; idem, *Wir stehen noch am Anfang: Ökumene in einer veränderten Welt* (Gütersloh: Kaiser, 1994), 63–112.

38. See www.eappi.org/ (2.2.2016).

39. In the Darfur region, it is far more difficult for the WCC to play a role, since that conflict generally involves violence of Muslims against Muslims, which nevertheless does not release the churches of their responsibility.

40. See Werner Löser, "Anmerkungen zur Ekklesiologie aus römisch-katholischer Sicht," in *Deutscher Ökumenischer Studienausschuss, Kirchen in Gemeinschaft – Gemein-schaft der Kirche. Eine Studie des DÖSTA zu Fragen der Ekklesiologie,* Dietrich Ritschl and Peter Neuner, eds. Beiheft zur ÖR 66 (Frankfurt/M.: Lembeck, 1993), 117.

41. "Ecclesia enim creatura est Euangelii," in *D. Martin Luthers Werke: Kritische Gesam-tausgabe* (WA) (Weimar 1883ff., Neudruck Graz, 1964ff): WA 2, 430, 6f.

42. John Howard Yoder shaped the usage of this term, which was notably popularized in Stanley Hauerwas, *The Peaceable Kingdom: A Primer in Christian Ethics* (Notre Dame, IN: University of Notre Dame, 1986).

43. *Come Holy Spirit, Heal and Reconcile! Report of the WCC Conference on World Mission and Evangelism, Athens, Greece 2005,* ed. Jacques Matthey (Geneva: World Council of Churches, 2008). See *ibid.* Fernando Enns, "Mission and Violence – Building a Culture of Peace. Plenary and Workshop during the World Mission Conference Athens 2005," 187–189; 303–305.

44. cf. Karl Barth's famous formulation in *CD,* IV/2, 653.

45. Cf. Donald F. Durnbaugh, ed. *On Earth Peace: Discussions on War/Peace-Issues between Friends, Mennonites, Brethren and European Churches 1935-1975* (Elgin, IL: Brethren Press, 1978).

46. See text of DOV Launch in "Messengers of Peace" https://www.oik-oumene.org/en/resources/documents/wcc-programmes/unity-mission-evangelism-and-spirituality/spirituality-and-worship/messengers-of-peace-dov-launch (01.02.2016)

47. *God, in your Grace.... : Official Report of the Ninth Assembly of the World Council of Churches,* ed. Luis N. Rivera-Pagán (WCC: Geneva, 2007), 311.

48. *Ibid.*

49. *Ibid.*

50. *Ibid.,* 312.

51. In the context of the debates over the Iranian atomic weapons program this issue became highly relevant.
    See "Minute on the Elimination of Nuclear Arms" in *God, in your Grace...,* 322-324. The second WCC Assembly in 1954 in Evanston had already realized that the

only sure protection against nuclear weapons requires ban, elimination and control and called on the nations to urge their governments to ensure security without the use of massive destruction weapons.

52. *Ibid.*, 323.

53. Notably the WCC called upon India, Israel and Pakistan to sign the treaty, for North Korea to rejoin and Iran to make a fully verifiable reentry.

54. "Minute on the Elimination of Nuclear Arms" in *ibid.*, 322.

55. *Ibid*, 311.

56. See Deenabadhu Manchala, ed. *Nurturing Peace. Theological Reflections on Overcoming Violence* (Geneva: WCC, 2005).

57. *God, in your Grace*, 269.

58. Some of the many expert consultations in the second half of the Decade are documented in www.overcomingviolence.org/en/peace-convocation/expertconsultations/events.html (1.3.2010).

59. See the documentation of this international ecumenical visiting team at:
     http://www.overcomingviolence.org/en/peace-convocation/preparatory-process/expert-consultations/past-events.html (2.2.2016).

60. "Vulnerable Populations at Risk: Statement on the Responsibility to Protect" in *God, in your Grace....*, 334-344. https://www.oikoumene.org/en/resources/documents/assembly/2006-porto-alegre/1-statements-documents-adopted/international-affairs/report-from-the-public-issues-committee/responsibility-to-protect?set_language=en

61. *Ibid.*, 304.

62. *Ibid.*, 304.

63. See the advances in the Catholic-Mennonite dialogue in "Catholic Perspectives on Peace" in Enns and Seiling, eds. *Mennonites in Dialogue*, 87-93.

64. Afterwards the document distinguishes only between position (1) over against (2)/(3).

65. See "A Basic Framework for the Decade to Overcome Violence," working document adopted by the WCC central committee, Geneva, 1999 *Minutes of the Fiftieth Meeting of the Central Committee*, Geneva, WCC, 1999, 190. https://www.oikoumene.org/en/resources/documents/commissions/international-affairs/peace-and-disarmament/peace-concerns/a-basic-framework-for-the-decade-to-overcome-violence

66. See the discussion on peace ethics within the EKD: "After the war in Kosovo the argumentation of the use of military force as a last resort has been heavily criticized, especially in the intra-church discussions of peace ethics. A major criticism was that the use of violence as a "last resort" did not adequately consider the complexities of the decision on the use of military force, but sought an expiation of guilt. Thus warfare has been legitimized by the appeal to this concept. In this criticism it is not always clearly recognizable whether the use of military force is generally condemned as a valid means, or whether it only seeks a more ardent version of peace ethics criteria by which the decision for the use of military force is effectively narrowed. In the first case it is clear that the surprisingly broad consensus on peace ethics gained in 1993/94 in the Protestant church, although not being complete, became fragmentary with regard to the ethical legitimacy of the use of military force. In the second case there is agreement as far as the intention to admit restrictively the application of military force solely as an extreme possibility, which must allow itself to be measured against the credibility of preventive measures. (...) The

current debate over the use of the traditional term "last resort" generally shows that this term requires a more careful reflection, than previously thought." See German original in "Schritte auf dem Weg des Friedens," II. Unterstreichungen und Verdeutlichungen, 5. Der Einsatz militärischer Gewalt als *ultima ratio*. http://www.ekd.de/EKD-Texte/44654.html. See a critique of this position by Haspel, *Friedensethik*, 63ff.

67. "Vulnerable Populations at Risk: Statement on the Responsibility to Protect," 305.

68. The Human Development Report of the United Nations Development Programme in 1994 defined "human security" as follows: economic, food, health, environmental, personal, community, political, in (UNDP): *Human Development Report 1994* (Oxford, Oxford University Press, 1994), 24-25. On the concept of "human security" see: Stephan Neil MacFarlane and Yuen Foong Khong, *Human Security and the UN: A Critical History*, (Bloomington: Indiana University Press and Chesham: Combined Academic, 2006).

69. "Vulnerable Populations at Risk," 306.

70. See Stefan Oeter, "Menschenrechte, Demokratie und Kampf gegen Tyrannen als Probleme der Friedenssicherung? Voraussetzungen und Grenzen der Autorisierung militärischer Gewalt durch den Sicherheitsrat der Vereinten Nationen," in Bruha, Heselhaus, Marauhn, eds. *Legalität, Legitimität und Moral*, 183-209.

71. Erhard Eppler, *Die tödliche Utopie der Sicherheit* (Reinbek bei Hamburg: Rowohlt, 1983), 140. "Wo steht denn geschrieben, Christen sollten zuerst nach der perfekten Sicherheit trachten? Gehört nicht Sicherheit, das, was Menschen an – relativer – Sicherheit zukommt, zu dem, was ihnen ,zufällt', wenn sie nach Anderem, Wichtigerem trachten?"

72. Erhard Eppler, *Die tödliche Utopie der Sicherheit*, 140. "unaufhebbarer Rest an Unsicherheit gehört zur *conditio humana*, zu den Bedingungen menschlichen Lebens. Wer diesen Rest leugnen oder gar tilgen will, sichert unser Leben nicht, er zerstört es."

73. Bonhoeffer, Robertson and Bowden, eds. *No Rusty Swords: Letters, Lectures and Notes, 1928-1936*, in *The Collected Works of Dietrich Bonhoeffer*, Vol. 1 (London: Collins, 1970), 286.

74. "Vulnerable Populations at Risk," *God, in your Grace...*, 306. Sect. 7 and Resolution b.

75. Prevention includes economic development and fair trade, education, human rights, good governance, political participation and power-sharing, control of the means of violence, law and the building of trust in public institutions, the strengthening of the local population to help themselves by strengthening structures of civil society and modern public-private partnerships. See (Evangelische Kirche in Deutschland:) "Vertrauen auf die Kraft des Zivilen," *Kommentar zum 2. Bericht der Bundesregierung über die Umsetzung des Aktionsplans "Zivile Krisenprävention, Konfliktlösung und Friedenskonsolidierung," Gemeinsame Konferenz Kirche und Entwicklung*, Gertrud Casel, ed. (Berlin: GKKE, 2008).

76. "Statement on the Responsibility to Protect," §7. https://www.oikoumene.org/en/resources/documents/assembly/2006-porto-alegre/1-statements-documents-adopted/international-affairs/report-from-the-public-issues-committee/responsibility-to-protect?set_language=en

77. See the cost analysis of the war in Iraq by Joseph E. Stieglitz and Linda J. Bilmes, *Die wahren Kosten des Krieges: Wirtschaftliche und politische Folgen des Irak-Konflikts*

(München: Pantheon, 2008).

78. "Statement on the Responsibility to Protect," §3.

79. *Ibid.*, §12.

80. *Ibid.*, §13.

81. *Ibid.*, §13.

82. "Statement on UN Reform" in *God, In your Grace*, 313-320.

83. *Ibid.*, §16.

84. *Ibid.*, §13.

85. See the Puidoux-Conferences in Enns, *Friedenskirche in der Ökumene*, IV.3., 223-235; idem, *The Peace Church and the Ecumenical Community: Ecclesiology and the Ethics of Nonviolence* (Kitchener: Pandora Press and Geneva: World Council of Churches, 2007).

86. *Vulnerable Populations at Risk – the Responsibility to Protect.*

87. On this approach see: Gerald W. Schlabach, ed. *Just Policing, Not War: An Alternative Response to World Violence* (Collegeville: Liturgical Press, 2007), including *idem*, "Just Policing and the Reevaluation of War in a less Divided Church"; Glen H. Stassen, "War on Terrorism? A Realistic View at Alternatives"; Drew Christiansen, "The Wider Horizon: Peacemaking, the Use of Force, and the Communion of Charisms"; et. al. See also the joint contributions by Mennonites and Catholics: "Die Dekade zur Überwindung von Gewalt des Ökumenischen Rates der Kirchen: Ein mennonitischer und katholischer Beitrag" in *ÖR* 2/2008, 222-232.

88. This is different that the concept of "networked security" in Germany: (Bundesministerium der Verteidigung): *Weißbuch 2006 – Zur Sicherheitspolitik Deutschlands und zur Zukunft der Bundeswehr*, (Berlin, 2006). See critique by Michael Haid, "Die alte Trennung von innerer und äußerer Trennung ist von gestern"; in *Friedensforum* 1/2008, 32.

89. Dietrich Bonhoeffer: "It is true that all historically important action is constantly overstepping the limits set by these laws. But it makes all the difference whether such overstepping of the appointed limits is regarded in principle as the superseding of them, and is therefore given out to be a law of a special kind, or whether the overstepping is deliberately regarded as a fault which is perhaps unavoidable, justified only if the law and the limit are re-established and respected as soon as possible." See Bonhoeffer, *Letters and Papers from Prison*, Eberhard Bethge, trans. (New York: Macmillan, 1971), 10. On the concept of "costly grace" see Dietrich Bonhoeffer, *Works*, Vol. 4, Discipleship, eds. Geffrey B. Kelly and John D. Godsey, trans. Barbara Green and Reinhard Krauss (Minneapolis: Fortress Press, 2001).

90. "Vulnerable Populations as Risk," Resolution c).

91. http://www.overcomingviolence.org/en/peace-convocation.html (08.01.2016).

92. Constitution and Rules of the World Council of Churches, Basis, 449. https://www.oikoumene.org/en/resources/documents/assembly/2013-busan/adopted-documents-statements/wcc-constitution-and-rules

93. See "Mid-term of the Ecumenical Decade to Overcome Violence 2001-2010" https://www.oikoumene.org/en/resources/documents/assembly/2006-porto-alegre/3-preparatory-and-background-documents/mid-term-of-the-ecumenical-decade-to-overcome-violence-2001-2010?set_language=en

94. See, e.g., Markus Weingardt, *Religion Macht Frieden: Das Friedenspotential von Religionen in politischen Gewaltkonflikten* (Stuttgart: Kohlhammer, 2007). See German-language studies of the Roman Catholic Institut für Theologie und Frieden (Hamburg) and Forschungsstätte der Evangelischen Studiengemeinschaft (Heidelberg) and the

yearly surveys on peace from the above-named institutes, and the Institut für Entwicklung und Frieden (INEF), Institut für Friedensforschung und Sicherheitspolitik an der Universität Hamburg (IFSH), Hessische Stiftung Friedens- und Konfliktforschung und Bonn International Center for Conversion (BICC).

95. For a Protestant perspective see: (Evangelische Kirche in Deutschland:) *Aus Gottes Frieden leben – für gerechten Frieden sorgen: Eine Denkschrift des Rates der EKD* (Gütersloh, 2007), esp. 50-56.; Hans-Richard Reuter, "Gerechter Friede! – Gerechter Krieg? Die neue Friedensdenkschrift der EKD in der Diskussion" in *Zeitschrift für Evangelsche Ethik* 52/2008, 163-168.

96. See Sekretariat der Deutschen Bischofkonferenz, ed. "Gerechter Friede," *Die deutschen Bischöfe* 66, Bonn, 2000. Cf. Justenhoven/Beestermöller, *Gerechter Friede*. On the development of the concept of "Just Peace" by the EKD see: (Evangelische Kirche in Deutschland:) *Frieden wahren, fördern und erneuern 1981, Eine Denkschrift der EKD*, (Gütersloh, 1982); *Idem*, "Schritte auf dem Weg des Friedens. Orientierungspunkte für Friedensethik und Friedenspolitik. Ein Beitrag des Rates der EKD (1993)," in *EKD Texte* 48, Hannover 2001, 6-37; *Idem*, "Friedensethik in der Bewährung. Eine Zwischenbilanz 2001," in *EKD Texte* 48, Hannover 2001, 57-92.

97. (Evangelisch-methodistische Kirche in Deutschland:) *Frieden braucht Gerechtigkeit: Friedenswort der EmK, EmK-Forum* 29 (Stuttgart: Medienwerk der Evangelisch-methodistischen Kirche, 2005).

98. (Vereinigung der Deutschen Mennonitengemeinden, VDM:) *Richte unsere Füße auf den Weg des Friedens, Erklärung der VDM zum gerechten Frieden* (Hannover, 2009).

99. (EKD): *Aus Gottes Frieden leben – Für gerechten Frieden sorgen*, 53.

100. *Ibid*, §2.5.2 "imensionen des gerechten Friedens."

101. (WCC), *Together on the Way: Official Report of the Eighth Assembly*, 3.5. A Common Understanding and Vision: Plenary Discussion, http://wcc-coe.org/wcc/assembly/or-3e-e.html (8.1.2016).

102. See the many position statements on the first draft of the ecumenical peace declaration, partially published in (Arbeitsgemeinschaft Christlicher Kirchen in Deutschland:) *Gerechter Friede. Handreichung zum Diskussionsstand* (Frankfurt: ACK, 2010).

103. See Konrad Raiser, *Ökumene im Übergang: Paradigmenwechsel in der ökumenischen Bewegung* (München: Kaiser, 1990).

104. On cosmic eschatology see, Jürgen Moltmann, *Das Kommen Gottes: Christliche Eschatologie* (Gütersloh: Kaiser / Gütersloher, [2]2005).

105. See Fernando Enns, *The Peace Church and the Ecumenical Community: Ecclesiology and the Ethics of Nonviolence* (Kitchener/Ontario: Pandora Press and Geneva: World Council of Churches, 2007); *Idem, Friedenskirche in der Ökumene. Mennonitische Wurzeln einer Ethik der Gewaltfreiheit* (Göttingen: Vandehoeck & Ruprecht, 2003).

106. http://w2.vatican.va/content/john-paul-ii/en/encyclicals/documents/hf_jp-ii_enc_01051991_centesimus-annus.html, 25. [01.03.2016]

8. Pilgrimage: Walking Gently with Your God

1. Micah 6:8. English translation of the German translation produced for the German Protestant Kirchentag, Hamburg, 1995. Jürgen Ebach translates it as "...and walk gently with your God." *Theologische Reden* 3 (Bochum: SWB Publishers, 1995).

2. Cf. *Official Report of the 10th Assembly, Busan, South Korea* (WCC Publications: Geneva, 2014), (hereafter 'Official Report') Report of the Programme Guidelines Committee, pp.242-249.

3. *Ibid.*, paras 10-12, p.244.

4. Cf. http://www.overcomingviolence.org (15.11.2014) Cf. also Mathews George Chunakara, ed. *Building Peace on Earth. Report of the International Peace Convocation*, Geneva, WCC Publications, 2013.

5. WCC, An Ecumenical Call to Just Peace, (hereafter 'Ecumenical Call') at www.over comingviolence.org/fileadmin/dov.

6. *Ibid.*, 1.

7. WCC, *ibid.*, 1, The 'Just Peace Companion'

8. WCC, *Ecumenical Call*, op. cit., para. 11

9. *Ibid.*, para. 10

10. *Ibid.*, para 3

11. *Ibid.*, Preamble

12. *Ibid.*, para. 12

13. *Ibid.*, para. 29

14. Letter dated 28 June 2012 (author's own records)

15. WCC, "Message of the International Peace Convocation, Kingston, Jamaica, 2011 ('Glory to God and Peace on Earth')" (hereafter 'Message') at http://www.overcom ingviolence.org (15 November 2014)

16. WCC Central Committee, "Report of the Programme Committee" (Document no. GEN PRO 10) 28 August – 5 September 2012, Kolympari, Crete, Greece, para 10, b and c.

17. Cf. *Official Report*, op. cit., "Report of the Programme Guidelines Committee," p.244, paras 10-12.

18. WCC, *Message*, op.cit.

19. Cf. "Official Report," op. cit., Message of the 10th Assembly of the World Council of Churches, 'Join the Pilgrimage of Justice and Peace', 36.

20. WCC, *Ecumenical Call*, 'Just Peace Companion', ch. 2, para. 59.

21. *Ibid.*, ch. 2, para. 61

22. WCC, "An Invitation to the Pilgrimage of Justice and Peace, WCC Central Committee, 2014" (hereafter 'Invitation')

23. WCC, *Just Peace Companion*, op.cit., ch.2, para.62

24. WCC, "Invitation," op.cit., II

25. Dorothee Sölle, *The Silent Cry: Mysticism and Resistance* (Minneapolis: Fortress Press, 2001)

26. WCC, "Statement on the Way of Just Peace" (hereafter 'Statement')

27. Sölle, *Mysticism and Resistance*, op. cit.

28. WCC, "Invitation," op.cit., IV

29. WCC, "Statement," op. cit., 1

30. Sölle, *Mysticism and Resistance*, op. cit., p. 92

31. WCC, "Invitation," op. cit., IV.

32. *Ibid.*, II.

33. WCC, "Official Report," op. cit., p.121

34. Dorothee Sölle sees this as the teaching role of the poor. Cf. *Mysticism and Resistance*, 285.

35. Dorothee Sölle, *Mysticism and Resistance*, 92.

36. WCC, "Invitation," op. cit., IV
37. WCC, *Just Peace Companion*, op. cit., ch.2, para.60.
38. WCC, "Ecumenical Call," op. cit., para.13
39. WCC, "Statement," op. cit., 1
40. Sölle, *Mysticism and Resistance*, op. cit., p. 93
41. WCC, "Invitation," op.cit., IV
42. "Letter of the delegates from churches in Germany," op.cit.

9. On the Path to an Ecumenical Theology of Companionship

1. See WCC Central Committee, "An Invitation to the Pilgrimage of Justice and Peace" (July 2014, Doc GEN 05, revised), https://www.oikoumene.org/en/resources/documents/central-committee/geneva-2014/an-invitation-to-the-pilgrimage-of-justice-and-peace (23.02.2021), 2.
2. See Susan Durber and Fernando Enns, eds. *Gemeinsam unterwegs: Theologische Überlegungen zum Ökumenischen Pilgerweg der Gerechtigkeit und des Friedens* (Leipzig: Evangelische Verlagsanstalt, 2019).
3. See WCC, "Report of the Programme Guidelines Committee," in Erlinda N. Senturias and Theodore A. Gill, Jr, eds. *Encountering the God of Life: Report of the 10th Assembly of the World Council of Churches* (Geneva: WCC, 2014) 243-44. (§§7-12)
   https://www.oikoumene.org/sites/default/files/Document/10thAssemblyReport.pdf
4. Fernando Enns is co-facilitator of both groups, along with Jennifer Martin (Jamaica).
5. Starting in Europe in 2015, Israel/Palestine and Middle East in 2016, 2017 Nigeria and the Great Lakes region of Africa, 2018 Colombia and other countries in South America, 2019 Thailand and surrounding countries, 2020 Fiji in the Pacific Rim. Pilgrimages to North America were planned in a hybrid format for 2021 due to COVID-19 restrictions. The annual meetings were planned and conducted in collaboration with national and regional councils of churches and other ecumenical organizations.
6. See Dorothee Sölle, *The Silent Cry: Mysticism and Resistance* (Minneapolis: Fortress Press, 2001).
7. Vide supra, Fernando Enns, "Walking Gently with your God. The Ecumenical Pilgrimage of Justice and Peace – a New Direction for the Ecumenical Movement."
8. Personal notes, Aussagen von Yusuf Ibrahim Wushishi (Generalsekretär des Nationalen Kirchenrates in Nigeria), Kaduna 2017.
9. See WCC Pilgrim Team Visits 2018, September 5, 2018, https://www.youtube.com/watch?v=AHDat3v-7i8&feature=share (11.04.2021).
10. Catherine Keller, Michael Nausner and Mayra Rivera, eds. *Postcolonial Theologies: Divinity and Empire* (St. Louis: Chalice Press, 2004).
11. "... because it [trauma] carries the power of condemnation, shame, and guilt that can unleash a view of the self as irredeemable and un-reparable." Willie James Jennings, "War Bodies: Remembering Bodies in a Time of War," in Stephanie N.

Arel and Shelly Rambo, eds. *Post-Traumatic Public Theology* (Cham: Palgrave Macmillan, 2016), 23-25, 24.

12. *Ibid.*

13. Personal notes at the meeting, Bogotá, 2018.

14. Phillis Isabella Sheppard, "Afterword," in Stephanie N. Areland Shelly Rambo, eds. *Post-Traumatic Public Theology*, 291–300, 292.

15. See Susanna Snyder, "La Mano Zurda with a Heart in Its Palm: Mystical Activism as a Response to the Trauma of Immigration Detention," in *Post-Traumatic Public Theology*, 217-240, 217.

16. See Miroslav Volf, *The End of Memory: Remembering Rightly in a Violent World* (Cambridge: Eerdmans, 2006), 66–84.

17. Jennings, *War Bodies: Remembering Bodies in a Time of War*, 30.

18. *Ibid.*, 32.

19. Personal notes, Fiji, 2020.

20. See Andrés Pacheco Lozano, "Towards a Theology of Reconciliation: A Pilgrimage of Justice and Peace to Heal Broken Relations in Colombia," Dissertation, Vrije Universiteit, Amsterdam 2020.

21. María Castro Varela and Nikita Dhawan, *Postkoloniale Theorie: Eine kritische Einführung* (2nd ed.), (Bielefeld, 2015).

22. "[t]he deepest theological distortion [in the disruption of our understanding of land] is that the earth, the ground, spaces and places are being removed as living organizers of identity and as facilitators of identity." Willie James Jennings, *The Christian Imagination: Theology and the Origins of Race* (New Haven: Yale University Press, 2010), 39.

23. *Ibid.*, 58.

24. See Alain Marchadour and David Neuhaus, *The Land, the Bible, and History: Toward the Land That I Will Show You*, The Abrahamic Dialogues Series, Nr. 5 (New York: Fordham University Press, 2007), 63-86.

25. "...*reveals a wider paradigm for the intimate, ontological entanglement between divinity and all materiality.*" Matthew Eaton, "Enfleshed in Cosmos and Earth" in *Worldviews: Global Religions, Culture, and Ecology* 18, no. 3 (2014): 230-254, 244.

26. "...pilgrim church is to find its identity in solidarity with the migrant who travels from necessity, not from a desire to transcend all necessity." William T. Cavanaugh, "Migrant, Tourist, Pilgrim, Monk. Mobility and Identity in a Global Age," *Theological Studies* 69, no. 2 (2008), 340–56, 352.

27. *Ibid.*, 344.

28. *Ibid.*, 355.

29. Personal notes from Susan Durber, Dhaka, 2019.

30. Kwok Pui-lan, *Postcolonial Imagination and Feminist Theology* (Louisville, KY: Westminster John Knox, 2005), 168.

31. Peter-Ben Smit, "Die Auferstehung des Leibes Christi in 1 Korinther 11. Paulus als Theologe des Leibes im Gespräch mit Judith Butler," *Lectio Difficilior, European Electronic Journal for Feminist Exegesis* 2019, Nr. 1 (2019): 1-24.

32. Pui-lan, *Postcolonial Imagination and Feminist Theology*, 171.

33. "Jesus' question 'Who do you say that I am?' is an invitation for every Christian and local faith community to infuse that contact zone with new meanings, insights and possibilities." *Ibid.*, 171.

34. Elaine Heath emphasizes this connection: "In Jesus' culture... to be stripped naked in front of a watching crowd was an act of sexual violation." Elaine Heath, *We Were the Least of These. Reading the Bible with Survivors of Sexual Abuse* (Grand Rapids: Eerdmans, 2011), 123. See also Rocío Figueroa and David Tombs, "Recognising Jesus As a Victim of Sexual Abuse. Responses from Sodalicio Survivors in Peru," *Religion and Gender* 10, no. 1 (2020): 57-75.

35. By "precarious" Judith Butler means "...politically induced condition in which certain populations suffer from failing social and economic networks of support more than others, and become differentially exposed to injury, violence, and death." Judith Butler, *Notes Toward a Performative Theory of Assembly* (Cambridge: Harvard University Press, 2015), 33.

36. "...a social construct which claims to explain and justify the separation between human groups by advancing physical, social, cultural and religious criteria." WCC, Message from the conference "Xenophobia, Racism and Populist Nationalism in the Context of Global Migration," Conference organized jointly by the Vatican Dicastery for Promoting Integral Human Development and the World Council of Churches in collaboration with the Pontifical Council for Promoting Christian Unity, in Rome, 18 - 20 September 2018, §6(a), https://www.oikoumene.org/en/resources/documents/message-from-the-conference-xenophobia-racism-and-populist-nationalism-in-the-context-of-global-migration-19-september-2018 (10.01.2021).

37. *Ibid.*

38. Mark MacDonald, "Systemic Evil and Christian Discipleship," *The Ecumenical Review* 72, no. 1 (2020), 108-115, 111.

39. "...a social construct which claims to explain and justify the separation between human groups by advancing physical, social, cultural and religious criteria." WCC, "Xenophobia, Racism and Populist Nationalism," §6(a).

40. See Robert McAfee, *Spirituality and Liberation: Overcoming the Great Fallacy* (Philadelphia: Westminster Press, 1988), 25.

41. This concept is influenced by Robin DiAngelo, *Wir müssen über Rassismus sprechen: Was es bedeutet, in unserer Gesellschaft weiß zu sein* (Hamburg: Hoffmann und Campe Verlag, 2020).

42. "Europeans enacted racial agency as a theologically articulated way of understanding their bodies in relation to new spaces and new peoples and to their new power over those spaces and people. Before this agency would yield the 'idea of race,' 'the scientific concept of race,' the 'social principle of race,' or even a fully formed 'racial optic' on the world, it was a theological form—and inverted, distorted vision of creation that reduced theological anthropology to commodified bodies. In this inversion, whiteness replaced the earth as signifier of identities." Jennings, *The Christian Imagination*, 58.

43. Jennings suggests that the doctrine of *creatio ex nihilo* exemplifies this Christian doctrine, which formed the basis of the colonial project. *Ibid.*, 28.

44. E.g., Larissa Behrendt, *Discovering Indigenous Lands: The Doctrine of Discovery in the English Colonies* (New York: Oxford University Press, 2010).

45. Willie James Jennings, "He Became Truly Human. Incarnation, Emancipation, and Authentic Humanity," *Modern Theology* 12, no. 2 (1996), 239-255, 249.

46. WCC Central Committee, An Invitation to the Pilgrimage of Justice and Peace (revised), §IV,

https://www.oikoumene.org/sites/default/files/Document/GEN05rev_AP-PROVED_InvitationPilgrimageJusticePeace.pdf

47. Cavanaugh, "Migrant, Tourist, Pilgrim, Monk," 349.
48. *Ibid.*
49. *Ibid.*, 352.
50. Mark MacDonald, "Walking in Beauty: The Sacred Walk," in Susan Durber and Fernando Enns, eds. *Walking Together: Theological Reflections on the Ecumenical Pilgrimage of Justice and Peace* (Geneva: WCC, 2018), 3-7, 4-6.

ACKNOWLEDGMENTS

The translations were prepared by Jonathan Seiling and reviewed by John D. Rempel. Most of these chapters were translated during 2014-2016 when Seiling worked under the direction of Fernando Enns in Hamburg at the Institute of Peace Church Theology, University of Hamburg. Funding for this position was partially supported by the Mennonite Church of Eastern Canada and Mennonite World Conference in cooperation with Conrad Grebel University College, with subsequent financial support from de Algemene Doopsgezinde Sociëteit. Jonas Widmer and Johanna Schade also provided editorial assistance.

Lyn van Rooyen of WCC Press has been generous in supporting the process of promoting this publication, even in the busy phase of preparing for the 11th WCC Assembly.

Biblical quotations: NRSV everywhere noted *in situ*, except where a direct translation of the German biblical text was preferred, to retain the terminological consistency with the original German meaning as expressed by the author.

The nine chapters of this volume comprise revised articles previously published elsewhere in German, as indicated in the details below. As a collection in German, chapters 1-6 also appeared as the *Habilitationsschrift* (Ruprecht-Karls-Universität Heidelberg, 2010), which was later published with the title, *Okumene und Frieden: Bewahrungsfelder Okumenischer Theologie* (Göttingen: Vandenhoeck & Ruprecht, 2012), including the following sections: "Einleitung" (Ch.1), section AI-V (Ch. 2-4), and section BI-II (Ch. 5-6). The articles in *Okumene und*

Frieden, section C are not included in the present volume, but are being updated and combined with other theological essays by Fernando Enns, which is expected to appear in the near future.

The original German articles can be located in the following publications: "Ecumenism 'in the making'" (Ch.1), appeared as: "Ökumenische Theoriebildung: Was tun eigentlich Ökumeniker?" in *Leitfaden Ökumenische Theologie*, Christoph Dahling-Sander and Thomas Kratzert, eds. (Wuppertal: Foedus, 1998), 13–27.

"Dialogical Ecumenism" (Ch.2) appeared as: "Friedenskirche mit ökumenischem Profil. Einleitung" in *Heilung der Erinnerungen – befreit zur gemeinsamen Zukunft. Mennoniten im Dialog: Berichte und Texte ökumenischer Gespräche auf nationaler und internationaler Ebene* (Frankfurt/M.: Lembeck und Paderborn: Bonifatius 2008), 12–28.

"The Ecumenical Challenge of Mutual Recognition of Baptism" (Ch.3) appeared as: "Die gegenseitige Anerkennung der Taufe als bleibende ökumenische Herausforderung – Konsens, Divergenzen und Differenzen" in Fernando Enns, Martin Hailer, Ulrike Link-Wieczorek, eds. *Profilierte Ökumene: Bleibend Wichtiges und jetzt Dringliches*, Beiheft zur Ökumenischen Rundschau (ÖR) 84 (Frankfurt/M.: Lembeck 2009), 127–158.

"Missionary Ecumenism" (Ch.4) appeared as: "Kirche als Ereignis: Mission im Blick auf die Kirche weltweit" in *Zeitschrift für Mission* 3/2002 Frankfurt/M.: Lembeck, 206–220, which also appeared in a revised version as "Church as Event: Mission as an Essential Mark of the Global Church," in *Mission Focus: Annual Review* 11 (2003):136–148.

"Action-Oriented Ecumenism" (Ch.5) is a revised translation of "'Ehre sei Gott – und Friede auf Erden': Das Ringen der Gemeinschaft der Kirchen um friedensethische Positionen (gemeinsam mit Stephan von Twardowski),' in Hans-Georg Link and Geiko Müller-Fahrenholz, eds. *Hoffnungswege: Wegweisende Impulse des Ökumenischen Rates der Kirchen aus sechs Jahrzehnten* (Frankfurt/M.: Lembeck, 2008), 348–377.

Chapter 6 includes a revised translation of "Auf dem Weg zu einer Kultur des Friedens: Die ökumenischen Dekade zur Überwindung von

Gewalt," *Una Sancta* 55/2 (2000):131–143; "Dekade zur Überwindung von Gewalt: Vier Schritte und zwei Gegenfragen," *Mennonitisches Jahrbuch* (2004): 9–14; "Impuls zur Gegenbewegung: eine Ökumenische Dekade: Das ÖRK- 'Programm zur Überwindung von Gewalt' vor und nach Harare," *Ökumenische Rundschau* 2 (1999):167–175; a revision of "Breaking the Cycle of Violence: Building Community – Mechanisms for Overcoming Violence and Some Suggestions for Theological Reflection," *The Ecumenical Review* 53/2 (April 2001):180-89; "Overcoming Violence and Concepts of God" is a revision of the German original, which was published in French as "Vaincre la violence: un défi pour l'Église et pour la théologie," in *Dieu est-il violent? La violence dans les représentations de Dieu*, Matthieu Arnold and Jean-Marc Prieur, eds. (Strasbourg: Presses Universitaires de Strasbourg, 2005), 89–102; "Beobachtungen zur ACK-Konsultation in der Mitte der ökumenischen 'Dekade zur Überwindung von Gewalt. Kirchen für Frieden und Versöhnung. 2001–2010', Freising, April 2005," in (Arbeitsgemeinschaft Christlicher Kirchen in Deutschland:) Gerechter Friede – Leben in einer gefährdeten Zukunft. Ökumenischen Konsultation zur Halbzeit der 'Dekade zur Überwindung von Gewalt' (2001 bis 2010)," in epd-Dokumentation 20 (2005): 45–49; "'Lass Dich von Gott verwandeln, dann wirst Du die Welt verwandeln': Dekade zur Überwindung von Gewalt in Porto Alegre 2006," in *Ökumenische Rundschau* 4 (2006):464–475.

Chapter 7 contains materials that previously appeared as, "Lass Dich von Gott verwandeln, dann wirst Du die Welt verwandeln. Dekade zur Überwindung von Gewalt in Porto Alegre 2006," in *Ökumenische Rundschau* 4(2006):464–475, which was separately translated into English as "Public Peace, Justice, and Order in Ecumenical Conversation," in Duane K. Friesen and Gerald W. Schlabach, eds. *At Peace and Unafraid: Public Order, Security, and the Wisdom of the Cross* (Scottdale/PA: Herald Press, 2005), 241–259; "Ehre sei Gott – und Friede auf Erden: Der lange Weg zu einer ökumenischen Friedenskonvokation," in Dagmar Heller et al., eds. *"Mache Dich auf und werde Licht! Ökumenische Visionen in Zeiten des Umbruchs: FS für Konrad Raiser* (Frankfurt/M.: Lembeck, 2008), 322–333, which appeared separately as

"'Glory to God and Peace on Earth.' The Decade to Overcome Violence 2001–2010: An Ecumenical Journey Towards a Common Understanding of Just Peace. The XXXI. Paul Wattson Lecture of the Franciscan Friars of the Atonement and the Jesuit University of San Francisco, February 2010," in *Ecumenical Trends* 39, No. 6, Garymoor Ecumenical & Interreligious Institute, June 2010, 6–10, and "Die Bilanz der Dekade zur Überwindung von Gewalt – Theologische und friedensethische Einführung," in *Ökumenische Friedenskonvokation 2011. 'Ehre sei Gott und Friede auf Erden' – Herausforderungen durch die Internationale Ökumenische Friedenskonvokation. Beiträge der Ökumenischen Konsultation der ACK und des Offenen Forums zur Dekade zur Überwindung von Gewalt vom 8.–10. Februar 2010 in Freising*, epdDokumentation 16–17/2010, 22–30.

Chapter 8 is a revision of an English translation of "'Behutsam mitgehen mit deinem Gott'. Der Ökumenische Pilgerweg der Gerechtigkeit und des Friedens – als Neuausrichtung der Ökumenischen Bewegung," in *Ökumenische Rundschau* 63 (1/2015), 16-30.

Chapter 9 appeared as, "'Brannte nicht unser Herz in uns?': auf dem Weg zu einer ökumenischen 'Theology of Companionship': der Pilgerweg der Gerechtigkeit und des Friedens" *Interkulturelle Theologie* 47 (2021): 112-130.

ABOUT THE AUTHOR

Dr. Fernando Enns is Professor of Theology and Ethics at the Vrije Universiteit in Amsterdam, Netherlands, and Director of the Center of Peace Church Theology at the University of Hamburg, Germany. Since 1998, a member of the Central Committee of the World Council of Churches (WCC) and member of the German Ecumenical Study Committee (DÖSTA), Enns is also a member of the Mennonite community of Hamburg and Altona and vice chairperson of the Association of Mennonite Churches in Germany (AMG).

Enns studied Protestant theology at the University of Heidelberg and at the Anabaptist Mennonite Biblical Seminary in Indiana, United States. In 1992, he graduated from the University of Heidelberg with a Master of Theology degree with a study entitled, "One Household of God: The Crisis of the Ecumenical Movement: Theological Causes and Newer Concepts." In the same year he was ordained as pastor of the Mennonite Church in Krefeld, Germany.

From 1996 to 2005, Enns was Director of Studies at the Ecumenical Institute of Heidelberg University, where he received his doctorate in 2001. His dissertation was translated and published as *The Peace Church and the Ecumenical Community. Ecclesiology and the Ethics of Nonviolence* (2007), co-published by Pandora Press and the World Council of Churches. He has also edited several volumes on topics related to peace and ecumenism, including: *Mennonites in Dialogue: Official Reports from International and National Ecumenical Encounters, 1975-2012* (Pickwick, 2015).